W9-BIB-918

HOLOCAUST JOURNEY

BOOKS BY MARTIN GILBERT

HOLOCAUST
JOURNEY

TRAVELLING IN SEARCH OF THE PAST

Martin Gilbert

Columbia University Press
NEW YORK

First published in Great Britain in 1997
by Weidenfeld & Nicholson

First published in the United States in 1997
by Columbia University Press
Publishers Since 1893
New York   Chichester, West Sussex

Copyright © 1997 Columbia University Press
All rights reserved

Library of Congress Cataloging-in-Publication Data

Gilbert, Martin, 1936–
Holocaust journey : travelling in search of the past / Martin
Gilbert.
p.   cm.
Includes bibliographical references and index.
ISBN 0–231–10964–4
1. Holocaust, Jewish (1939–1945)—Miscellanea.   2. Holocaust
memorials.   3. Gilbert, Martin, 1936–   —Journeys—Poland.
4. College students—Travel—Poland.   I. Title.
D804.3.G54   1997
940.53'18—dc21   97–15895
r97

∞
Casebound editions of Columbia University Press books are printed on permanent
and durable acid-free paper.
Printed in the United States of America
c 10 9 8 7 6 5 4 3 2 1

This book is dedicated to my MA students at University College, London, who asked me if I would take them to some of the places we had been studying during their course on the Holocaust. Without their companionship this diary could not have been written:

Jon Boyd
Rachael Fraenkel
Caroline Harris
Herut Hoskin
Angela Jayson
Marie Lindblad
Rosalind Morris
Paul Neville
Robin O'Neil
and
Petra Wöstefeld

CONTENTS

ILLUSTRATIONS

LIST OF MAPS

INTRODUCTION

Halfway through the first year of the newly introduced Holocaust MA degree at University College, London, my students asked me if I would take them, once term was over, to some of the places we had been learning about. It was an unexpected proposal, but an intriguing one. I set about preparing an itinerary, and we made the journey in the summer of 1996. It lasted two weeks.

Our group was a mixed one. As well as the eleven graduates, there was my friend Ben Helfgott. As a boy, he lived in the Polish town of Piotrkow Trybunalski, and survived the Piotrkow ghetto and several slave labour camps. We were to visit his home town on the last day of our journey. We were also joined by Suzanne Bardgett, who had recently been put in charge of preparing a permanent Holocaust exhibition within the Imperial War Museum. A member of her team, Kathy Jones, joined us when we reached Poland.

The graduates met together for our two-hour class each week for nineteen weeks, and had begun to establish a close rapport. The often appalling nature of the subject that we were studying seemed to help create a bond of friendship. One of the graduates, Robin O'Neil, was a retired Detective Inspector who had become, in the previous few years – after twenty-five years in the police force – an expert on everything relating to Oskar Schindler. He would take us to Schindler's factory in Cracow.

The material I prepared for the journey related to the history of the places we would visit, both before and during the war. We would be in cities and towns which had experienced an important and creative Jewish past, as well as destruction. We would also be making our way to the sites of ghettos, concentration camps and death camps, where the written and oral evidence that has survived was painful to read out. The plan was for me to read aloud from letters, documents and memoirs that related to what had happened at the places we were visiting or passing through.

It took several months of preparation, working out a detailed itinerary, and finding the archival material, and memoirs, that related to each town we would visit, and to the streets we would walk along. As well as the death camps established by the Germans on Polish soil, we would be visiting Germany, and the Czech and Slovak Republics. I planned to be in cities, towns and villages where Jewish life had been prosperous, and also those where it had been poor: places where Jews had been accepted, and places where they had been persecuted; places where they had lived for generations, and places to which they had been deported after swift and cruel uprootings.

For our visit to the Lublin area in south-eastern Poland, Mike Tregenza, an Englishman living in the region, and an expert on its Nazi past, would join us. For our visit to Konin, Theo Richmond helped with suggestions as to where we should go, as well as providing an indispensable map. Throughout the journey I was also able to read out recollections that had been sent to me by those who had lived in places through which we passed: for this I am grateful to Joseph Finkelstone (recollections of Chelm), John Freund (Theresienstadt), Hana Greenfield (Kolin), Arieh Handler (Magdeburg), Solly Irving (Ryki), Charles Shane (Lancut) and Professor Felix Weinberg (Usti nad Orlici).

From my book *The Boys, Triumph Over Adversity*, I have drawn on the recollections that were sent to me by Chaim Fuchs, Jona Fuchs, Moniek Goldberg, Pinhas Gutter, Mala Helfgott, Arek Hersh, Jerzy Herszberg, Kurt Klappholz, Simon Klin, Chaim Liss, Bob Roberts and Alec Ward. From *The Holocaust, The Jewish Tragedy*, I took the wartime diary extracts of Wilhelm Cornides, Alexander Donat, Yakov Grojanowski, Zygmunt Klukowski, Dr Johann Kremer, Salmen Lewental, Tadeusz Pankiewicz and Emanuel Ringelblum; and the post-war recollections of Mojsze Bejski (Plaszow), Alexander Donat (Warsaw), Dov Freiberg (Sobibor), Kurt Gerstein (Belzec), Chaim Hirszman (Belzec), Eric Lucas (Hoengen), Gisella Perl (Birkenau), Vladka Meed (Warsaw), Moishe Shklarek (Sobibor), Franciszek Zabecki (Treblinka) and Tadeusz Zuchowicz (Warsaw).

From the published transcripts of the Nuremberg Trials (1945–6) I have taken extracts from evidence submitted by Madame Vaillant Couturier, and documentation relating both to the Wannsee Conference in 1942 and Himmler's speech at Poznan in 1943. I have also included an extract from the evidence given at the Eichmann Trial (1960–61). Further historical material to which I referred during the journey was sent to me by Dr Vojtech Blodig, Pamatnik Terezin, Muzeum Ghetta; Michael Chapman, Air Queries Librarian, Ministry of Defence; Graham Day, Air Historical Branch (RAF), Ministry of Defence, London; Jeremy Gee OBE, Director of Information and Secretariat, Commonwealth

War Graves Commission; Richard Judd, Hebrew Specialist Librarian, Bodleian Library, Oxford; Sheila Grossnass, Nicholas Lane, Janina Martinho, Mikhail Salman and Hallam Tennyson (the story of Dr Hautval).

I am grateful to the copyright holders of the poems printed here by Mordechai Gebirtig, Yitzhak Katzenelson, Dan Pagis and Zdenek Weinberger; and for the extracts from the writings of I. L. Peretz and Isaac Bashevis Singer. I have also quoted from an article by John Izbicki in the *Jewish Chronicle*, and from published works by John Bierman, Hugo Gryn and Vlasta Kladikova. I have listed all the books quoted in the bibliography, including guide books. Special thanks are due to the pioneering efforts in helping travellers of Stephen Birnbaum, Ruth Ellen Gruber and Andrzej Trzcinski.

We stopped in many places in our fourteen days, and went through many more where we did not have time to stop, but had time (in train or bus) to read and reflect. Sometimes a road sign would tell us that ten or twenty kilometres off our route was a place with a Jewish past, and we would talk about it. Each day, the events of the Holocaust determined our itinerary, but did not always dominate it; we were glimpsing at all times the history of Jewish communities, some of which dated back many hundreds of years, and in several cases more than a thousand years.

I have added to the text of the diary a few thoughts and comments – clearly indicated as such – from letters which members of the group sent me after our return, about specific moments on the journey. I have also brought together some of their reflections in the epilogue, which I compiled during our frequent reunions.

In preparing the itinerary and booking train seats, minibuses and hotel rooms, I am grateful to Nick and Sam of British Rail International, and to Laraine Abrahams of LestAir Services, for their considerable help. I am also grateful to those who, by their generous sponsorship, made the journey possible: Manfred Altman, Chairman of the Institute of Jewish Studies, Sidney Corob CBE, the Holocaust Educational Trust, the Kozlowsky-Kon Trust, and the Hebrew and Jewish Studies Department of University College, London. The Chairman of the Department, Professor John Klier, was particularly encouraging.

My son Joshua photocopied all the extracts of the books and documents that I read on the journey. Yogi Mayer and Terry Charman scrutinised several of the chapters; Kay Thomson typed them out for this book. Jennifer Ohrenstein helped me compile the index. The fifty-

three maps were expertly drawn from my rough sketches by Tim
Aspden. The final typescript was read by Celia Levett and by Elsbeth
Lindner, who also saw the book through the press. A final reading
was undertaken by my wife Susie, my constant guide and inspiration.

University College
London
9 April 1997

DAY 1

LONDON – BERLIN

'Powerless against evil people'

6 a.m.

We assemble at Waterloo Station. Two taxis that began their respective journeys an hour ago (in East Finchley and Stanmore) have collected seven of us between them. The remaining five come under their own steam. The last to arrive is Ben Helfgott; born in Poland in 1929, he was nearly ten years old on the outbreak of war. He will be our Polish speaker, having never forgotten the language of his youth.

6.55 a.m.

The train draws out of Waterloo Station. The first link with the war comes almost immediately, as we pass (on our left) a church with brick bands around its spire. It is at the corner of Westminster Bridge Road and Kennington Road. The spire is all that remains of the pre-war Christ Church. The buildings in this area were systematically destroyed during the London Blitz, but this distinctive spire remained standing. Although the church was bombed, the spire remained, defiant and alone. Travellers coming into Waterloo by rail from the South of England would see it, and could feel reassured that all was well – just about.

The journey to the coast takes us through 'Bomb Alley' in Kent, above which the German V1 flying bombs (the doodlebugs) flew towards London, and where some of them were shot down.

8.05 a.m.

We enter the Channel Tunnel. I study the Berlin guide books that I have brought with me. The Baedeker for 1912, *Berlin and Its Environs*, captures one of the eras which we will explore, before the First World War and before the Holocaust. The Wannsee, where the Endlösung (the euphemistically named 'Final Solution') of the Jewish Question, received its bureaucratic endorsement, is described in the guide book as 'a fashionable villa-colony, the handsome houses of which are grouped in a wide curve on the high banks of the picturesque Wannsee'. We should be there forty-eight hours from now.

8.30 a.m./9.30 a.m. (*French time*)
We come out on French soil. To the south, Calais is clearly visible. We are travelling through a countryside from which the Germans deported Jews to their deaths. They did so from the spring of 1942 until the summer of 1944. The Jews in the region we are going through now lived so close to the English Channel, yet they were totally vulnerable. From this moment of our journey, each town and many of the villages through which we will pass – today, and every day during the next two weeks – from northern France to eastern Poland, had Jews living in them. These were Jewish communities that often dated back five hundred years and more. Each of them was to be uprooted and destroyed in the course of those two years.

10.40 a.m.
We cross the line of the Western Front; a small British war cemetery in the corner of a field is the only visible sign of where the fighting had been. There is hardly much chance of seeing more, given the speed we are going, which is 300 kilometres per hour, as the announcer told us shortly after we emerged from the tunnel.

10.42 a.m.
The train speeds through the area of north-western France which was occupied by Germany in both world wars. I report to the group whenever there seems a point of interest from our historical perspective.

10.45 a.m.
Lille. As the train stops in the station, I stand in front of the group – who look at me from their seats on both sides of the aisle – and tell them a story involving this city. Among the 6,000,000 Jews murdered during the Holocaust was Mozes Hirschsprung. He was born in Auschwitz in 1901 when it was an Austro-Hungarian border town. His wife Helene was also born in Auschwitz, in 1909. Between the wars they emigrated to Holland, where their two children were born (in 1933 and 1938). When war came, the family fled from Amsterdam to Lille. And from Lille they were deported back to Auschwitz – their

home town – and murdered there, within two miles of where they had been born.

The Hirschsprungs were among 1,000 Jews deported from Lille to Auschwitz on a single day, 15 September 1942. Also deported that day was Fanny Yerkowski. Forty-eight years old, she had been born in London on the eve of the First World War. Having married a Frenchman before the Second World War, she went to live in Lille, and shared the fate of the Lille deportees. Adolf Eichmann's department in Berlin, which was responsible for the deportations, was not interested in nationality, but in race. Another of the Lille deportees, twenty-one-year-old Bernice Winer, had been born in Switzerland. In the eyes of the Gestapo, the neutrality of Switzerland was irrelevant to her fate.

More than seven weeks after the Normandy landings of June 1944, there was a deportation from Paris which included 300 young orphans, all of whom were gassed in Auschwitz concentration camp. Among the orphans were two brothers from Lille, Marcel and Gaston Leibovicz, aged fourteen and thirteen.

11.00 a.m.
As I follow on the map the train's rapid movement, it crosses the French border into Belgium.

11.10 a.m.
We reach Brussels, and leave the train for an hour, before our connection. We pass the time in a small station café.

Reaching the platform from which we will leave for Berlin, I speak of another of the orphans deported from Paris on 31 July 1944, and gassed in Auschwitz: the seven-year-old Alain Jurkovitch, born in Brussels. He was born in 1936, as I was. Our birthdays were only a few months apart.

A Jewish community already existed here in the mid-thirteenth century. The Jews of Brussels, like Jews throughout Europe, were massacred at the hands of the local mob at the time of the Black Death, in 1348 and 1349, when Jews were held responsible for the spread of the plague. There was a further massacre in 1370 when the Jews of Brussels were accused of 'desecrating the Host', another frequent medieval charge. To this day, the allegedly desecrated wafers – which became an object of worship here in Brussels – are commemorated in annual prayers on the third Sunday of July, and in the stained-glass windows of St Gudule Cathedral (which alas, in changing trains for Berlin, we do not have time to visit).

12.07 p.m.
Leave Brussels, on the Berlin express.

1.17 p.m.
Liège. We are travelling through a part of Belgium where many young
Jewish children were hidden by Christian families, and brought up as
Christians. This saved their lives.

The train goes through Verviers, Herbesthal and Welkenraedt. From
Welkenraedt, a branch line and a road leads three kilometres south to
Eupen, the main town of the small border region which was transferred
to Belgium after the defeat of Germany in 1918.

Ben recalls how, as a young boy in Poland, he learned about history
from the stamps that he collected before the war. One prized set was
the German stamps from the First World War overprinted 'Eupen-
Malmedy'. Germany again annexed the area on conquering Belgium
in May 1940. Ben recalled: 'When we were ordered to move into the
ghetto, a German gendarme took my stamp album. I asked him, "May
I have it back?" He gave a swipe at me and kicked me away. I never
saw my stamp collection again.'

After Germany's defeat in 1945, Eupen and Malmedy were returned
to Belgium.

Six kilometres after Welkenraedt, we cross into Germany. After
emerging from a tunnel, we see, to the north, the spires of Aachen
cathedral.

1.55 p.m.
Aachen. As we stop briefly in the station, I have time to give a short
survey, in this case courtesy of the *Encyclopaedia Judaica*, whose very
first entry Aachen is. This particular entry was written by Ernst Roth,
the Chief Rabbi of the State of Hesse, in Frankfurt-on-Main.

Jews were living here in Aachen when it was the capital of the
Carolingian Empire. Among a delegation sent by Charlemagne to the
Caliph Harun al-Rashid in Baghdad in 797 AD was a Jew, by the
name of Isaac, who later wrote an account of the journey to Baghdad
and back. Isaac was probably the delegation's interpreter or guide.
Jewish settlement was virtually continuous at Aachen for more than
a thousand years. An expulsion in 1629 was effective only for a
decade. Those expelled were not sent very far: just a mile or two out
of the city, to the village of Burtscheid, now an eastern suburb.

The modern Jewish community here in Aachen was organised in
1847 under the Prussian Jewish Community Statute. Two years earlier

it had established a Jewish elementary school. The synagogue was built in 1862. On the portal was a Hebrew inscription from Isaiah: 'For my house shall be called a house of prayer for all peoples.' The synagogue was destroyed on the night of 9–10 November 1938, Kristallnacht – the Night of Breaking Glass – when at the instigation of the Nazi leaders, synagogues throughout Germany were set on fire.

On the outbreak of war in September 1939 there were 1,700 Jews living in Aachen and 3,500 in the towns and villages around it. Seven hundred were deported at the end of 1941 and during 1942 to the eastern death camps – most of them to Belzec, which we will visit on this journey. A further 250 were deported to Theresienstadt, which we will also visit. Of those deported to Theresienstadt, twenty-five returned after the war.

In 1957 the German government paid for the building of a synagogue and a Jewish community centre here. The community today numbers about two hundred. With the exception of the war years, and the brief expulsion in the seventeenth century, there have been Jews in Aachen for at least 1,200 years.

The year 1997 will mark the 1,200th anniversary of the arrival of Jews in Aachen. Hitler's self-proclaimed 'Thousand Year Reich' lasted for twelve years.

Ben tells us of a German girl from Aachen, a non-Jew, who was working with other German women in the same hut as he in the slave labour camp at Schlieben, south of Berlin. These woman were forcibly evacuated from Aachen with thousands of other Germans just before the Allied forces took the town: 'It was a whole family from Aachen, the parents and two teenage daughters. It was from them that we learned of the Allied bombing of Aachen. The conditions for the Jews at Schlieben were atrocious, and my physical state was fast deteriorating. One day I asked the girl to let me have a ride on her bicycle. I wanted to see whether I still had some strength left in me. I hadn't ridden a bicycle for over two years. There was a boy in the Hitler Youth, he was keen on her but she detested him. As I was riding on the bike, overjoyed at the thought that my strength and confidence had not entirely gone, he suddenly appeared and ordered me to stop riding. When the next soup distribution came – it was not really soup, just putrid, lukewarm water – and I held out my rusty tin, the Hitler Youth took the ladle from the cauldron and threw the soup in my face. Luckily for me the soup was never really hot. But it was a terrible humiliation.'

1.59 p.m.
The train leaves Aachen and continues eastward.

2.02 p.m.
We pass through Burtscheid, the village – now suburb – to which the Jews of Aachen were expelled in the seventeenth century.

2.12 p.m.
Eschweiler. In the nineteenth century the Jewish community here was proud of its distinguished rabbi. Five kilometres across the fields to the north is the village of Hoengen. As in many hundreds of German villages, half a dozen Jewish families lived here before the war. In Hoengen, most of the Jews were farmers; one, Michael Lucas, was the local butcher. The Jews of Hoengen built their first synagogue in 1926. Twelve years later came Kristallnacht. What happened to the synagogue was witnessed by Michael Lucas's nephew Eric, who, a few weeks later, was sent to Britain on one of the Kindertransport trains that took ten thousand German-Jewish children to safety in those tumultuous months. Forty-five years later, Eric Lucas recalled how, at first, the Nazi Stormtroopers – the Sturm Abteilung (known as the SA) – stood on guard outside the small synagogue:

'After a while, the Stormtroopers were joined by people who were not in uniform; and suddenly, with one loud cry of, "Down with the Jews", the gathering outside produced axes and heavy sledgehammers. They advanced towards the little synagogue which stood in Michael's own meadow, opposite his house. They burst the door open, and the whole crowd, by now shouting and laughing, stormed into the little House of God.

'Michael, standing behind the tightly drawn curtains, saw how the crowd tore the Holy Ark wide open; and three men who had smashed the Ark, threw the Scrolls of the Law of Moses out. They threw them – these Scrolls, which had stood in their quiet dignity, draped in blue or wine-red velvet, with their little crowns of silver covering the tops of the shafts by which the Scroll was held during the service – to the screaming and shouting mass of people which had filled the little synagogue.

'The people caught the Scrolls as if they were amusing themselves with a ball-game – tossing them up into the air again, while other people flung them further back until they reached the street outside. Women tore away the red and blue velvet and everybody tried to snatch some of the silver adorning the Scrolls.

'Naked and open, the Scrolls lay in the muddy autumn lane; children stepped on them and others tore pieces from the fine parchment on which the Law was written – the same Law which the people who tore it apart had, in vain, tried to absorb for over a thousand years.

'When the first Scroll was thrown out of the synagogue, Michael made a dash for the door. His heart beat violently and his senses became blurred and hazy. Unknown fury built up within him, and his clenched fists pressed against his temples. Michael forgot that to take one step outside the house amongst the crowds would mean his death.

'The Stormtroopers who still stood outside the house watching with stern faces over the tumultuous crowd which obeyed their commands without really knowing it, would have shot the man, quietly, in an almost matter-of-fact way. Michael's wife, sensing the deadly danger, ran after her husband, and clung to him, imploring him and begging him not to go outside. Michael tried to fling her aside, but only her tenacious resistance brought him back to his senses.

'He stood there, in the small hall behind the front door, looking around him for a second, as if he did not know where he was. Suddenly he leaned against the wall, tears streaming from his eyes, like those of a little child.

'After a while, he heard the sound of many heavy hammers outside. With trembling legs he got up from his chair and looked outside once more. Men had climbed on to the roof of the synagogue, and were hurling the tiles down, others were cutting the cross beams as soon as they were bare of cover. It did not take long before the first heavy grey stones came tumbling down, and the children of the village amused themselves as they flung stones into the many-coloured windows.

'When the first rays of a cold and pale November sun penetrated the heavy dark clouds, the little synagogue was but a heap of stones, broken glass and smashed-up woodwork.

'Where the two well-cared-for flowerbeds had flanked both sides of the gravel path leading to the door of the synagogue, the children had lit a bonfire and the parchment of the Scrolls gave enough food for the flames to eat up the smashed-up benches and doors, and the wood, which only the day before had been the Holy Ark for the Law of Moses.'

The Germans were burying the Scrolls of their own Old Testament: the Holy Bible of more than a thousand years of German Christianity.

2.42 p.m.

Cologne. Under the enormous arched roof of the station there is a great air of bustle. The station announcer is calling out the next trains. In twelve minutes, an express leaves for Nuremberg and Munich.

We have time to leave the train, go into the cathedral square, walk down to the Rhine, and return to the train. In the shadow of the cathedral, where Paul photographs the flag of the European Union flying next to the German flag, I recount a brief history of the Jews of Cologne. Theirs was one of the oldest Jewish communities in Germany. Jews first came here in Roman times, several hundred years before Christianity. When Christianity came to Cologne, the Jews were at once affected by it. Two edicts of the Emperor Constantine, dated 321 AD and 331 AD imposed heavy taxes on the Jewish community, but exempted the community officials from some of these obligations. The first of these edicts, which survives to this day in the Biblioteca Apostolica Vaticana in Rome, is precisely dated 11 December 321 AD.

One of the first synagogues in Germany was built here, possibly as early as 1012, certainly by 1040. The synagogue in Worms dates from the same period. A Jewish chronicler described Cologne in the late eleventh century as 'a distinguished city from where life, livelihood and settled law issued for all our brethren scattered far and wide'. In 1096 the crusaders of the First Crusades murdered most of the Jews here. When the Jews were expelled in 1424, the synagogue was turned into a Christian chapel. Its ancient Jewish foundations were laid bare during a British bombing raid in 1942. By then, all 11,000 Jews who had been unable to emigrate before the war were deported either to Theresienstadt, or to the Lodz ghetto, or to the Lublin region: to perish there, or to be murdered later on, when deported to the eastern death camps and to Auschwitz.

After the war, some six hundred Cologne Jews – the remnant of the 11,000 who had been deported – returned to the city. The first synagogue to be rebuilt and reopened in Germany after the war was here. A plaque records that it was opened by Konrad Adenauer in 1959. As Chancellor of the German Federal Republic from 1949 to 1963, Adenauer negotiated with David Ben-Gurion the reparations agreement whereby Germany paid compensation to survivors, and to the State of Israel. To this day there is a medieval mikveh (ritual bath) in the centre of one of the main squares of Cologne, leading off a street that is still called Judengasse (Jewish Street).

I recall my first visit to Cologne, in 1953, and how shocked I was at the acres and acres of bombed houses; a moonscape of devastation even then. It was here in Cologne, on 30 May 1942, that the British launched their first bombing raid over Germany with 1,000 bombers (of which thirty-nine were shot down during the raid). In one of the Jewish listening posts, Geneva, the raid was a sign of hope, making it possible, as Richard Lichtheim wrote, that 'the war could be finished this year by heavy bombardment from the air'. For the Jews inside the Warsaw ghetto the news of the Cologne raid had an immediate impact on morale. This is what Emanuel Ringelblum, one of the leading Jewish historians in Poland before the war, wrote in his diary in the Warsaw ghetto (where he was later killed):

'Day in, day out, in hundreds of cities throughout Poland and Russia, thousands upon thousands of Jews are being systematically murdered according to a preconceived plan, and no one seems to take our part. The bombing of Cologne, the destruction of thousands of buildings, the thousands of civilian victims, have slaked our thirst for revenge somewhat. Cologne was an advance payment on the vengeance that must and shall be taken on Hitler's Germany for the millions of Jews they have killed. So the Jewish population of tortured Europe considered Cologne its personal act of vengeance. After the Cologne affair, I walked around in a good mood, feeling that, even if I should perish at their hands, my death is prepaid!'

3.20 p.m.
The train pulls out of Cologne station, past the equestrian statue of Wilhelm II ('Kaiser Bill' to the British in the First World War), and crosses the Rhine.

There were two transports of Jews from Cologne in the autumn of 1941. Both were sent to the Lodz ghetto in Poland. The precise German records noted that both trains arrived in Lodz on October 23, and that on them were 2,014 deportees. Three months later, most of those deportees had been deported again, to a camp near the village of Chelmno, where they were murdered. We shall be going to Lodz and Chelmno on our last day.

3.25 p.m.
Leave Cologne-Mülheim station, on the east bank of the Rhine.

3.40 p.m.
We reach Solingen. Robin O'Neil (our retired Detective Inspector) is reading a book about the Piotrkow ghetto. He is struck by the factories that employed a number of Jewish children. Ben, who was in two of

those factories – Hortensja and Bugaj – from the age of twelve to the age of fourteen, tells us: 'The pre-war owner of the glass factory where I worked in Piotrkow during the war was a German. He continued to own it once the Germans had taken over the town. He was a decent man. He was prepared to employ Jews, and he would make a case to employ them. He took on boys from the age of twelve. He didn't have to. Had he been a Jew hater, those boys would not have survived. In the woodwork factory the director was also a decent man who allowed children to work. He would never lay a hand on anybody. A higher percentage of children survived in Piotrkow than any other town – because of these two employers. We were beaten, but there were no killings, except on one occasion when the Gestapo killed thirteen slave labourers in Bugaj. We did not starve. We worked alongside the Poles. The railway ran just outside the factory, and we saw the deportation trains go by.'

3.55 p.m.
The train stops at Wuppertal. In 1935 there were 2,471 Jews living here. Those who did not emigrate before 1939 were deported to their deaths.

It was when he saw a Royal Air Force film of the bombing of Wuppertal in 1943 that Churchill turned to his guests with the words: 'Are we beasts? Are we taking this too far?'

4.10 p.m.
Hagen. Ben is reflecting on the contrast between those who suffered and those who did not. 'Millions die. In the march of history it is of no consequence. For those who suffer directly, it is a tragedy. For the rest, they say, "Tragic," but it does not affect them. It does not affect their lives or their outlook. I was in it. Had my parents left Poland for Palestine, as they might have done, I would have had some relatives somewhere – I would have had someone.'

Ben's uncle, his father's elder brother, after whom Ben is named, was one of the victims of the post-First World War influenza epidemic, in which as many as twenty million people died. 'Who now remembers it?' Ben asks. 'Who cares? Who puts it in the history books?'

4.50 p.m.
Soest. This is the region which was flooded when the British bombed the nearby Möhne dam. There was an enormous water reservoir here that supplied large numbers of factories. When the waters were

breached, the factories could not operate. In the resultant floods, several thousand German civilians were killed. The work of reconstruction was formidable. Ben reflects on the failure of the Germans to make full use of the Jewish manpower at their disposal for such tasks. 'They could have used us from the beginning. But their hatred for the Jews was greater than their self-interest – the aim to win the war. They talked themselves into the killings.'

5.25 p.m.

Paderborn. We pass Sennelager, for many years the headquarters of the British Army of Occupation on the Rhine (BAOR), and one of the largest British military camps in post-1945 West Germany. For the survivors of the Holocaust, the British soldiers came, not as conquerors but as liberators, as did the French and American armies further south, and the Russians in the east. Ben, who was liberated by the Russians at Theresienstadt in May 1945, is in philosophical mood, reflecting on how swiftly, in the timespan of this century, events unfolded: between Hitler coming to power and the Allied armies overrunning Germany was only twelve years. 'What matters is human relations,' he says. 'Families, living, looking after children, living in peace and harmony with each other, enjoying each other's company, making a life that should be decent and palatable to everyone. There is little else any of us can do. We are powerless against nature; we are powerless against evil people.'

6.10 p.m.

Bad Lippspringe. There seems to be a story for every place we go through; it was here, at the end of the Second World War, that an American officer, Captain Irving Gruber, who was then serving as a medical officer with the Ninth Army, took over, with a single enlisted man, the local hospital that had been run until then by German nuns. The patients were Russian slave labourers who had been liberated while working in the nearby salt mine. It was in this way that Dr Gruber, a Jew, learned of the cruel wartime fate of another group of Hitler's victims. We will be visiting many places where non-Jewish victims of Nazism were murdered, including a total of more than three million Soviet soldiers who were killed after they had been captured, while prisoners-of-war.

Here in Germany the train goes through rolling countryside. There are no brick and concrete pillboxes here, as in France and Britain, at the edge of rivers or at the approach to gorges; this is not surprising, as the Germans did not fear invasion.

6.12 p.m.
Bad Pyrmont. Beautiful rolling wooded hills.

6.25 p.m.
Hameln. A Jewish woman from this town, Glueckel of Hameln (1645–1724), told her fellow-Jews: 'Above all, my children, be honest in money matters with Jews and non-Jews alike. If you have money or possessions belonging to other people, take better care of them than you would if they were your own. The first question that is put to a man on entering the next world is whether or not he was faithful in his business dealings.'

This is the Pied Piper's town. Now more than twelve hours into our journey with the group, I feel something of a Pied Piper, with my regular readings as the stations pass and the countryside rolls by.

7.05 p.m.
We cross the River Leine and draw into Hanover station. The train stops for five minutes.

Jews were first recorded living here in 1292: 'Two hundred years before Columbus discovered America,' comments Ben. It was never a very large community; in 1933 there were just under five thousand Jews. But they boasted more than twenty cultural and welfare institutions. Among the Jews living here between the wars was Zyndel Grynszpan. Born in Poland in 1886, he came to Hanover in 1911. When 15,000 Polish-born Jews were taken from their homes all over Germany on 27 October 1938, he was told by a policeman: 'You are going to come back immediately; you shouldn't take anything with you. Take with you your passport.'

Zyndel Grynszpan later described what happened: 'They took us to the concert hall on the banks of the Leine and there, there were about six hundred people from all the areas. There we stayed until Friday night; about twenty-four hours; then they took us in police trucks, in prisoners' lorries, about twenty men in each truck, and they took us to the railway station. The streets were black with people shouting, "The Jews out to Palestine." After that, when we got to the train, they took us by train to Neubenschen on the German–Polish border.'

We shall be going through Neubenschen (now Zbaszynek) on the last night of our journey. Zyndel Grynszpan's account of what had happened to him in Hanover that evening so angered his son Hirsch, who was then in Paris, that he shot and killed a German diplomat stationed there; the sequel was the Kristallnacht, during which hundreds of synagogues and shops were attacked, plundered and burned throughout Germany, including Hanover.

More than half of Hanover's Jews had managed to emigrate before the outbreak of war. Those who were in the city when war broke out in September 1939 were deported to the East two years later. After the war, sixty-six survivors returned (out of 2,900 deportees). A new synagogue was opened in 1963; today it serves about five hundred Jews.

As with so many German towns, there were several slave labour camps near Hanover where Jews were forced to work. One was a stone quarry. Chaim Liss, who had been deported from the Polish city of Lodz with his father when he was thirteen years old, later recalled their time there. I read aloud from his letter to me: 'This was of course very hard labour, and the death rate among the prisoners increased drastically, and the people died like flies, due also to the meagre food rations we were getting. My father was among those who did not survive.' Unknown to Chaim Liss at the time, his mother was also dying of malnutrition at a slave labour camp elsewhere in Germany.

7.25 p.m.
Lehrte. A railway junction. Belsen is forty-three kilometres to the north of us. Here, at the end of 1944 and in the first three months of 1945, in the very last months of the war, tens of thousands of Jews from slave labour camps throughout central and eastern Germany were brought and literally dumped. More than 10,000 died of illness or starvation before the British army arrived, among them Anne Frank. Another 5,000 died after liberation, being too weak or too sick to survive.

7.30 p.m.
The countryside that rolls past our windows is pastoral and seemingly unremarkable. But it hides a terrible past. Seventy-five kilometres to the south is Nordhausen, the site of a slave labour camp that was liberated by the United States Army on 15 April 1945. On the same day, British troops (then fighting to the north of where we are travelling now) liberated Belsen. Hundreds of Jews were found there. They were, the United States Signal Corps recorded, 'almost unrecognisable as human. All were little more than skeletons: the dead lay beside the

sick and dying in the same beds; filth and human excrement covered the floors. No attempt had been made to alleviate the disease and gangrene that had spread unchecked among the prisoners.'

7.50 p.m.

Brunswick. This town – in German, Braunschweig – had a Jewish community from the twelfth century. When the Black Death came in 1348–9, and Jews all over Central Europe were blamed for it, half the Jewish community here, then numbering about one hundred and fifty, was murdered as punishment for allegedly being the harbingers of death.

In 1543 there were anti-Jewish riots here, provoked by the 'honest advice' given to pious Christians that year by Martin Luther, about how Jews should be treated. Luther had first hoped to convert the Jews to Christianity. But when he failed, he turned against them.

As the train sits in Brunswick station, I read out Luther's words: 'First, their synagogues should be set on fire, and whatever does not burn up should be covered or spread over with dirt, so that no one may ever be able to see a cinder or stone of it.' Jewish homes should likewise be 'broken down or destroyed'. All the Jews in the town should then be 'put under one roof, or in a stables, like Gypsies, in order that they may realise that they are not masters in our land'. They should be made to earn their living 'by the sweat of their noses'. And if, even then, they were too dangerous, these 'poisonous bitter worms' should be stripped of their belongings – 'which they have usuriously extorted from us' – and driven out of the country 'for all time'.

Driven out, not murdered.

Ironically, Luther's linking of Jews and Gypsies was to be repeated by the Nazis 400 years later, when Gypsies, like Jews, were murdered in the concentration camps and death camps.

In the nineteenth century German Jews flourished in Brunswick, which was a centre of Jewish Enlightenment (Haskalah). Two progressive schools were opened, the first in 1801 and the second in 1807. Reform Judaism had an important early base here. In 1928 there were 1,750 Jews in the town, but even before 1933 it was a centre of vigorous Nazi activity, and many Jews left for other towns. But there were still 683 Jews here on the outbreak of war. Almost all of them were deported to the eastern death camps, primarily Belzec, and murdered there. Less than fifty survived the war.

The factories of Brunswick, like those of Hanover, and almost every other German town, made use of Jewish slave labour. Among those

Jews sent here was Jerzy Herszberg, who had been born in the Polish town of Poznan (which we will be going through by train on the last night of our journey). I read his account of conditions in the slave labour camp:

'The commandant of the camp, a stocky, rather plump, SS man, indulged his sadistic impulses by keeping us waiting for the food (soup with a potato) and then throwing two potatoes into our midst for the dubious pleasure of seeing some of us fight for it. There was little for us to do outside the factory and the main object seemed to be to humiliate us. The commandant would address us as "FFF" ("faul, frech und fett" – lazy, insolent and fat) and we were driven to recite slogans like "Wir, Juden, haben den Krieg gewollt" (We Jews wanted the war). The bodies of those who died during the day were stacked in the lavatories.'

Jerzy Herszberg later recalled the British and American air raids on Brunswick, and, as the train draws out of the station, I read from a letter that he wrote (forty years after the war) to a British bomber pilot: 'The sound of the sirens always filled me with joy, as it did all other prisoners. The brave pilots of the Allied armies probably never realised how much hope and joy they gave us flying over Braunschweig. This letter is my first opportunity to express my appreciation.'

8.13 p.m.
Helmstedt. To my generation, this name means so much: the border crossing from West to East, the Iron Curtain with all its ugly and frightening formalities; the passage from freedom to servitude, from hope to fear. To the younger members of the group, the name means nothing.

8.45 p.m.
Magdeburg. Our first stop in what used to be East Germany. It looks run down, decrepit. Arieh Handler is from here. Today he lives in London. In the 1930s he worked to get Jews out of Germany; in the 1970s he was one of the leaders of the efforts to force the Soviet Union to allow Jews to leave from behind the Iron Curtain.

Pilsudski was imprisoned here by the Germans in the First World War. After Germany's defeat he defended the new Polish State from attack by the Russians from the east. As Poland's dictator, he was well disposed to the Jews. When he died in 1935, many Polish Jews wept.

This was one of the centres of the Ottonians. It was a Jewish refugee from Germany, Karl Leyser, who taught a whole generation of Oxford historians the story of that great imperial structure, and its fall. I never thought, as I looked out of his study window across Magdalen College deer park to the River Cherwell in the late autumn of 1957, that, almost forty years later, I would cross the Elbe, and remember him and his teaching.

As early as 965 AD, at the time of the Ottonians, Jews were living here. Otto the Great put them under the protection of the archbishop. But Otto's successor Otto IV was not so benign; in 1213 his soldiers destroyed the Jewish quarter.

Persecution followed the usual, cruel pattern, but during the Black Death riots the archbishop and the city authorities did what they could to protect the Jews from the mob. There was a flourishing Yeshiva – a Jewish religious academy – here in the fifteenth century, but in 1493 the Jews were expelled from the town, their synagogue converted into a chapel, and their cemetery, the oldest tombstone in which is dated 1268, was destroyed.

A modern community was set up early in the nineteenth century. Jewish social, charitable and cultural clubs abounded. By the mid-nineteenth century, ninety per cent of the Jews of Magdeburg were Liberal Jews. The Orthodox community was a very small one. There was no Jewish school. Arieh Handler, who is today the President of the Religious Zionist movement in Britain (the Mizrachi movement), studied, as did all his Jewish friends, in the Monastery School. 'I did nine years Latin and seven years Greek, studying every day,' he later recalled. And, as a Zionist, he wrote with pride: 'While Liberal Jews in Germany usually identified with non-, almost anti-Zionist attitudes, in Magdeburg the situation was different. Within the non-Orthodox community there were some very active Zionists long before Hitler came to power, and, of course, long before the establishment of the State of Israel. The first Zionist whom the Zionist Executive appointed to open the first Zionist Office in Jaffa, in 1908, was Arthur Ruppin, who came originally from Aschersleben near Magdeburg, and who, together with other members of the family, were the builders of the new sections of Jerusalem. It should be added that this almost first pioneer of the Zionist movement in Palestine-Israel was still not able to speak Hebrew for many years after the British Mandate was established in 1922. There were other leading Zionists in Magdeburg, which also had several Zionist youth movements and strong Zionist and Mizrachi groups (including a very active Women's Mizrachi). Some leading youth leaders (also from my family) went to Palestine and become active members of the slowly growing Jewish community there.'

There was no Jewish school in Magdeburg, Handler added, 'but a few of us managed to bring a Hebrew teacher, who, in addition to the normal Talmud Torah (religious school) established a Jewish afternoon school with the particular emphasis of learning modern Hebrew'.

In 1933 there were 2,361 Jews here in Magdeburg. The synagogue was burned down on the night of 10 November 1938. Those Jews who, unlike Arieh Handler, had not emigrated before the outbreak of war – 679 in all – were deported. But the 185 Jews who were married to non-Jews were not deported, and survived the war. Today about a hundred Jews remain in the town.

8.50 p.m.

We cross the Elbe. It is now dark. As a result of the detour east of Cologne, we are running late. It is not until well after ten o'clock that we pass through Potsdam (the scene of the last of the wartime Big Three conferences), Wannsee (where the logistics of the 'Final Solution' were planned) and Grünewald (the small suburban station, in the midst of Berlin's most charming woodland, from which the Jews of Berlin were deported to the eastern ghettos and camps, and to Theresienstadt). Ten minutes after passing through Grünewald we draw into Berlin-Zoo station.

10.30 p.m.

We take three taxis, and drive through the Brandenburg Gate – once the dividing line between East and West Berlin – along the Unter den Linden, over the River Spree, and into what was, from 1945 to 1989, East Berlin. Crossing the former divide between West and East there is a sudden change from neon lights to drab vistas, much as there was twenty or thirty years ago.

We drive down Karl-Marx-Allee, still bearing its Communist-era name, and turn into Richard Sorge Strasse. Sorge was Stalin's German Communist spy in Japan. From his vantage point in German Embassy circles in Tokyo, he was able to tell Stalin in the late autumn of 1941 that Japan had no plans to attack the Soviet Union. This enabled Stalin to transfer eastern-based troops to take part in the counter-offensive in December 1941 that saved Moscow.

We reach our hotel in the Landsberger Allee, the Hotel BCA Wilhelmsberg. At the desk, I am given the keys to distribute. Some of us then gather in the hotel lounge and talk over the events of the day. We have done nothing but sit in railway trains for the last seventeen hours, but a great swathe of Jewish history has unfolded outside the carriage windows.

DAY 2

BERLIN

'Grim eagles above the door'

7 a.m.
Breakfast in Berlin, at our hotel, recently built in former East Berlin.

8 a.m.
We gather in the lobby. We have a lot to see today, most of it on foot, and I had hoped to leave at eight o'clock sharp. At Ben's suggestion (he has been on a number of journeys with groups), before we went up to our rooms last night I gave a little speech about how important it is to start today (and every day) punctually.

8.08 a.m.
We get into three taxis to be driven across the city.

8.12 a.m.
We pass the wall of the Weissensee Jewish Cemetery (we do not have time to enter). It is the largest Jewish cemetery in Europe. The Nazis did not touch it. One section contains the graves of some of the 12,000 German Jewish soldiers who were killed in action in the First World War. There is a post-1945 memorial to the Jewish Communist student, Herbert Baum, and his fellow anti-Nazi activists, executed in 1942.

We continue through former East Berlin, through the Prenzlauer Berg working-class district, along the Greifswalder Strasse. The façades of the houses here were specially painted and kept immaculate in the Communist years because they led along the route taken by high Communist Party functionaries and foreign Communist leaders. In the side streets the houses were drab; even the sides of those houses whose fronts were done up for show were peeling and unkempt.

We drive along the main east–west axis of Berlin's East End, the

Unter den Linden, and through the Brandenburg Gate, across the former divide to the Victory Column – commemorating the Prussian victories of 1864 over Denmark, 1866 over Austria and 1871 over France – and then on to Zoo station (where we arrived last night). I had hoped to find a hotel near the station but had failed. Hence this second three-quarters-of-an-hour taxi journey back to the station.

8.55 a.m.
We walk from the front of the station and then along a path that runs alongside the side of the Zoo. Crossing the Landwehr Canal, we are at the edge of Berlin's wooded heartland, the Tiergarten. An exhibition of old street lamps, standing rather forlornly along the path, lends a quaint charm to the wooded scene. One of the lamps is from Westminster.

9.05 a.m.
Our first stop, the bank of the Landwehr Canal. The sunlight is flooding through the trees, dappling the grass. On the opposite bank is a plaque, the first of many that we will be looking at. Such plaques are often the sole reminders of historic events. Here, Rosa Luxemburg was thrown into the canal on 15 January 1919, having been murdered earlier that day, not far from here, by army officers.

The group gathers round, some standing, some sitting on the grass verge, as I, leaning against a silver birch, tell her story. Now, on what was East German soil until a few years ago, we remember her career, and her hostility to all nationalism, whether German, Polish or Russian, or (like herself) Jewish. For her, socialism and nationalism were in conflict. Her fatherland was the international working class, and her aim, world socialist revolution. Yet she is probably best remembered for her fate, here on the banks of this canal.

Rosa Luxemburg was born in Zamosc, then a city in the Tsarist Empire, which we will be visiting next week. Before 1899 she was one of the founders of the Social Democratic Party of Poland and Lithuania. After 1899 she lived mostly in Germany. But she was in Warsaw during the 1905 revolution, participated in it as a fiery orator and organiser, was arrested by the Tsarist police, and imprisoned. Escaping, she returned to Germany, where she was active in revolutionary circles. When war came, she opposed it as an 'imperialist' war, and was again imprisoned, this time by the Germans. After her release she formed, with her fellow revolutionary leader Karl Liebknecht, the Spartacus League, intended as the spearhead of revolution. But when the hour of revolution came in Germany, she opposed it as premature. She also opposed Lenin's reign of terror in the Soviet Union. In 1955 an East German stamp honoured her as the 'Leader of the German workers' movement' (Führer der Deutschen Arbeiterbewegung).

Further down the canal (we do not have time on this itinerary to go there) is the remaining side building of one of Berlin's largest synagogues, the Orthodox Linden Synagogue (at Nos. 10–16 Fraenkelufer). Built between 1913 and 1916, it was badly damaged in Kristallnacht, but survived. A Jewish kindergarten functioned there until 1942. In 1945 Allied bombers reduced it to ruins; the ruins, except for the side building, were torn down in 1958.

Standing by the canal bank opposite Rosa Luxemburg's memorial plaque, I speak of the origins of the Jewish community in Berlin. The first mention of Jews here was in a letter from the local town council, dated 28 October 1295, forbidding wool merchants to supply Jews with wool yarn. During the Black Death plague of 1348–9, the Jewish houses in Berlin were burned down by a mob, and the Jews were either murdered or driven out of the town. They were allowed back four years later.

In 1510 the Jews of Berlin were accused by the Church of desecrating the Host and stealing sacred Christian vessels from a church in a nearby village. More than a hundred Jews were arrested and interrogated. On 15 July 1510, thirty-eight were burned at the stake, together with the person who had actually stolen the vessels – a Christian. Thirty years later, as a result of the strenuous efforts by two Jews, Joseph ben Gershom and Philip Melanchthon, the accused were all declared innocent.

Until 1543, Berlin Jews were buried some miles away, in Spandau – just as, in twelfth-century Britain, London's Jews were first obliged to bury their dead fifty miles from the city, in Oxford. I could see the site of that cemetery from my first rooms as an undergraduate in 1957.

In 1571 the Jews were expelled from Berlin 'for ever'. Over the next hundred years, a few returned. In 1663, Israel Aaron, who was the official supplier to the army, was allowed to settle in Berlin. Eight years later, after the Jews had been expelled from Vienna, the Margrave of Brandenburg, the ruler of Berlin, admitted fifty wealthy Jewish families to the city. A writ of privileges was issued to the Jewish community on 10 September 1671. This is the date that is usually given for the foundation of the new Berlin Jewish community.

Frederick the Great rewarded his Jewish banker, Veitel Heine Ephraim (who died in 1775), with a palace near the Unter den Linden, which is still there today. It is one of the most beautiful buildings in Berlin.

9.30 a.m.

From the site of where Rosa Luxemburg's body was thrown into the canal we go down a path to a corner of the Neuer See. It was while fleeing along the northern shore of this small, pleasant lake that Karl Liebknecht, the founder with Rosa Luxemburg of the German Communist Party (and a former anti-militarist Reichstag deputy), was caught and shot. We were going to sit in the café by the shore and have a reading, and a drink, but the café is closed (and it is quite cold).

9.40 a.m.

We walk on to the villa district of the Tiergarten. The first building we come to is the pre-war Spanish Embassy, built in 1938. Its monumental façade is decaying but intact. It was the late Stephen Birnbaum, a guidebook writer, who drew me to this spot two years ago, through his book, when I came to Berlin with my son David. Of the building, he wrote in his *Birnbaum's 95 Berlin* (a wonderfully informal, and informative guide book):

'Its rear section is now occupied by the Spanish Consulate, but the main, abandoned section stands as a powerful symbol of fascist power – and downfall. Four massive stone columns, blackened by moisture and neglect, support a heavy portico. The unadorned geometric windows and doors – trademarks of Third Reich architecture – are sloppily bricked up. Grim eagles above the door and higher up near the roof bear the unintentionally ironic motto of Spain under the dictator Francisco Franco: "Una, grande, libre" (One, great, free).'

We speak of how Franco, unlike his fellow Slovak – and Roman Catholic – dictator, Father Tiso, refused to deport any Jews from Spain to Germany; indeed, he gave sanctuary to several thousand Jews who managed to cross the Pyrenees from France into Spain. At Wannsee (which we will visit tomorrow) all 6,000 Spanish Jews were marked out for deportation and destruction. But Franco refused to deport them to Germany, and they survived.

Following Stephen Birnbaum's directions, and my own tracks last year, we come to the former Danish Legation, built by Albert Speer, Hitler's friend and favourite architect, at the height of the Nazi era. It is now a training centre for the employees of the German telephone company. Everyone in the group is surprised by the dullness of the Nazi architecture, its uniformity, the un-grandiose columns and under-ornamented façades, and standard, upright windows. 'Clinical,' says Paul, 'it reminds me of the racial ideology.'

The same feeling is expressed a minute later when, crossing the street, we reach two more of the buildings designed by Speer for the ambassadors of friendly States: the former Norwegian and Yugoslav Legations. In 1937, Hitler gave Speer the ostentatious title of 'General Construction Inspector for the Imperial Capital Berlin'. The title is more imposing than the buildings.

The Yugoslav Embassy was built during the period when Hitler was wooing the Regent Paul. On 25 March 1941 these two Heads of State finally forged their alliance. Two days later that alliance was destroyed by a popular revolution in Belgrade. On 6 April 1941 the Germans invaded Yugoslavia. The Legation then became a Nazi guest house, for visiting Heads of State and senior diplomats. Today it is the office of the High Court for Restitution, which looks into claims for the return of property confiscated by the Nazis on racial, religious or political grounds. On its façade is a sculpted head of a woman, dating from the building's pre-war prime. The sculptor, Arno Brecker, was one of Hitler's favourites. Like the windows and the façades, the sculpture is modest. He is best known for the giant statues that he made for the Olympic Stadium in 1936; they are still there today.

We walk through a post-1945 area of apartment blocks built as part of the International Building Exhibition held in Berlin in 1987. Each building was designed by a different architect. They are more colourful, more varied and more whimsical than the Nazi-era constructions.

10.15 a.m.

We cross Hofjägerallee, with another view (looking northward) of the Victory Column. Then we come to the Tiergartenstrasse. The first building which we look at is the Krupp Villa, Nos. 30–31 Tiergartenstrasse, built in the Nazi style as Krupp's Berlin residence and guest house for industrialists. It is now a Jesuit school. The architecture is dull and bland, with the typical grey austerity and low, unexciting lines of the Nazi period.

Then we reach the former Japanese Embassy. Four houses were demolished in 1942 in order to make way for it. Two years later it was bombed so badly that it had to be vacated. Its ruins stood here for forty years, until they were pulled down in 1986. Now it has been rebuilt according to the original plan, which was itself a scaled-down version of Hitler's Chancellery. Today it is a Japanese cultural centre.

The next building along the Tiergartenstrasse, No. 1, was the Italian

Embassy in the Nazi era. It was built to honour Germany's alliance with Italy, but before it was finished that alliance was over, and Italian soldiers fighting alongside the Germans on the Eastern Front were suddenly made prisoners-of-war. We shall be visiting (just outside Chelm) the site where many Italian soldiers were murdered by the Germans in 1943.

Bullet holes from the street-fighting for Berlin in 1945 scar the ochre-painted stucco walls of the Italian Embassy building, and also remain, like spiders' webs, in the thick glass windows. Unlike the Japanese Embassy façade, which has Albert Speer-inspired square unimaginative columns, the façade of the Italian Embassy has magnificent tall rounded columns rising above the single-storeyed columned portico. Further along the street, several former embassies are still, even fifty-plus years after the war, nothing more than bombsites; now wastelands of grass and bushes.

The pre-war Greek and Estonian Legations are intact but abandoned. Both countries lost their independence, as well as their embassies, during the war. Today these buildings recall the period of diplomatic niceties, and League of Nations pacts and protocols. One of them, the Kellogg–Briand Pact, outlawed war altogether, making it seem that the independent States in Europe would be permanent features of the post-1918 landscape. Alas, they were not.

We walk along the Tiergartenstrasse, passing, on the park side of the street, a monumental statue of Wagner.

We reach the corner of the former Bendlerstrasse, now named the Stauffenbergstrasse, in honour of one of the senior army officers who were executed following their attempt to kill Hitler in 1944. The only building that survives on the righthand side of the street, though badly damaged in the Second World War and subsequently rebuilt, was the Imperial German Navy Office during the First World War, and the Armed Forces Ministry between the wars. Throughout the Second World War it was the Military High Command. Here were planned the invasions of a dozen countries.

There is a memorial in the inner courtyard to those who were executed here after the failed bomb plot. We are at the site not only of the planning of two world wars, but of a desperate attempt in July 1944 to end the suffering, and of the savage outburst of cruelty and revenge which followed the collapse of the plot.

A wreath has been placed below the plaque. Its leaves have turned russet and, as Paul notices, have left a russet stain on the wall and a sinister red patch on the ground.

For quite a long time the group is silent. Each one thinks his or her own thoughts as we drift out of the courtyard and back into the street.

11.15 a.m.

We walk back along the Stauffenbergstrasse to the Tiergartenstrasse. New buildings have replaced the old. There is no picture or pattern of what was here before the war. There is no indication of where specific numbers had been, such as No. 17 Tiergartenstrasse, the British Passport Control Office, from which many thousands of permits were granted for Berlin Jews and Jews from elsewhere in Germany to enter Britain (the Office's telegraphic address was 'Pasbrit, Berlin').

A minute later we reach the site of No. 4. Like so much of the street, including the former South African and Egyptian Legations, and Turkish Embassy, it is a bombsite. It was here that those who directed the Nazi euthanasia programme made their plans. Because of its location, their department was known as 'T4'. In the two years before any Jews were murdered by gas, 70,000 Germans – including young babies judged 'unfit for life', old people, disabled people, and the mentally ill – were put to death in a dozen institutions throughout the Reich. An estimated 10,000 German children under the age of sixteen were murdered by gas in this way. The preparations for this unbelievably horrible operation were made here.

We hesitate at first to go in. Robin, intrepid, strides forward. After a while, we follow, wandering across the unkempt grass, where some bushes have grown, and many weeds, and where the occasional brick or broken stone is a reminder that a building once stood on this site. Those who worked in T4's head office here inhabited, apparently, quite a pleasant villa, in the Wilhelmine style from before the First World War. The enormity of the crime makes us pause, almost stop in our tracks. It is hard to comment on what was decided upon here; hard, as we stand on the actual site, to react personally other than by silence and stillness. It takes a while before we are able to gather ourselves together – mentally as well as physically – and continue on our way.

We leave Tiergartenstrasse and walk to a corner of the Tiergarten itself. From that corner we see twenty or thirty tall cranes participating, like a colony of nesting birds, in the rebuilding of the devastated central area of Berlin, to the Brandenburg Gate. The first sight to halt us at the Gate are a dozen white, and somewhat flimsy, crosses on a metal fence. Each cross has on it the name of an East German who was killed by East German guards while trying to cross the wall, hoping to find sanctuary in West Berlin.

Just beyond the white crosses is the Reichstag building, now being busily restored in order to house the Parliament, which is still located in Bonn, of united Germany. We cross the Pariser Platz to the Adlon Hotel, once the pride of Wilhelmine Berlin, then reduced to a shell in the last phase of the war, and finally pulled down in the early Communist days. A year ago the restored hotel, intended as a replica of the hotel which was the pride of Berlin before the First and Second World Wars, was nothing more than an architect's design. It is now a complete building, almost ready for occupation.

We walk down the Wilhelmstrasse. It is made up today of almost all new buildings. In the fifty years before 1945 it was the hub of Imperial, Weimar and Nazi German officialdom, including both the President's Palace and the Reich Chancellery.

At the start of the walk down the street, on the righthand side, is the site of what was once No. 70 Wilhelmstrasse. Between the wars, and before the First World War, this was the British Embassy. It is now an empty lot. It reminds me of the bombsites of London which were so much a feature of my schoolboy days in the late 1940s.

We reach, on the lefthand side, the only surviving example of the street's pre-First World War magnificence, the building at Nos. 63–4, with an ornate entrance. This was the Prussian Parliament building both before and after the First World War. It was here, from May 1931 to March 1933 – until dismissed and arrested by Hitler – that Konrad Adenauer was President of the Prussian State Council. In 1925 Adenauer stood unsuccessfully as candidate for the presidency of Germany. Twenty-four years later he was to become Chancellor of the Federal Republic of Germany.

Further down the street, what was once the President's Palace (No. 73) and the Foreign Ministry (Nos. 74–6) are now entirely new buildings. Not even a plaque records their former importance, or shows what they looked like in the days of their glory and power.

Just beyond the former Foreign Ministry building was the Reich Chancellery at No. 78. and next to that Hitler's Chancellery, on the corner of the Wilhelmstrasse and Voss Strasse (his postal address was No. 1 Voss Strasse). Neither building survives. A large block of shops, offices and flats was built on the site in East German days, one of a number of six- and seven-storey, red-roofed buildings on both sides of the Wilhelmstrasse that transformed this historic street from a ruined government centre into a modern, if characterless, shopping street. One of the shops which have taken the place of Hitler's Chancellery is today the Indonesia Restaurant.

Behind the new corner building is the spot where Hitler's body was burned in 1945, with that of his mistress (whom he had just married), Eva Braun. Today it is a children's playground, fenced with bright-red railings, containing equally brightly coloured red and blue slides, and a sandpit. No plaque or memorial marks the spot: only, ironically, a dustbin. We have a discussion about whether it is right or wrong to have no memorial here, and to have a children's playground on this spot of hideous association.

We stand on 'Hitler's' corner of the Wilhelmstrasse and Voss Strasse and look across Voss Strasse. The building facing Hitler's Chancellery was the Directorate General of the German Railways. In the building that stood on this site were planned hundreds, indeed thousands, of deportations, worked out according to precise timetables that would not disrupt essential military traffic. On the opposite side of the street was the Finance Ministry, whose coffers were so enriched by the belongings, first of emigrants, and later of those who were deported.

One block further down the Wilhelmstrasse, at the corner of the Leipziger Strasse, is a building that survived the war almost intact, the massive Reich Air Force Ministry building. The building was completed in 1936, after only fifteen months' construction, and was shown off to foreigners visiting the Olympic Games that year as a symbol of the 'new' Berlin. Its austere architecture (known at the time as the Deutsche Monumentalstil) represents the height of Nazi ideals: two rows of square, plain windows above a line of three-storey windows topped with pediments, themselves above the entrance, which consists of a few low concrete steps and a row of square columns framing the doorways. There is nothing dramatic or ornamental. Everything is right-angled. We look in vain for a curve to relieve the starkness.

In this building were planned and directed the air attacks on Poland, Holland, Belgium, Britain, France, Yugoslavia and the Soviet Union. British bombers, that destroyed almost everything in this street, failed to do sufficient damage to its substantial structure for it to have to be pulled down after the war, as happened to most of the buildings in the Wilhelmstrasse and around it. It is being renovated and converted into the Finance Ministry for the new German capital.

We walk on to the corner of the former Prinz-Albrecht-Strasse, where a section of the Berlin Wall remains intact. It was in place, dividing the city and its inhabitants, from August 1961 to November 1989. Just beyond this section of the wall we come to a large empty lot. This is the former Gestapo headquarters. It was in what had earlier been an industrial art school, and in the hotel next to it (No. 102

Wilhelmstrasse), that Reinhard Heydrich had his main office – as did, after Heydrich's assassination, his successor Ernst Kaltenbrunner. Heydrich was assassinated by the Czech resistance in 1942. We will visit the site of the attack in three days' time. Kaltenbrunner was hanged at Nuremberg on 16 October 1946. His last words were, 'Germany, good luck!'

Nothing survives of these two buildings except the sinister remains of the cellars. Plaques indicate, with photographs, the location of the buildings that once stood on what remains to this day an empty lot. Although badly battered by repeated Allied bombing raids, the buildings survived the war, but were too badly damaged to be restored. They were pulled down in the 1950s.

Many of the conspirators involved in the July 1944 bomb plot against Hitler were brought to these cellars and tortured. Earlier 'enemies of the Reich' had also been executed here. Shortly after the war a passer-by found a piece of paper in the ruins here. On it one of the Red Orchestra spy ring, Harro Schulze-Boysen, executed in 1942, had written the words, which I read out:

> Die letzten Argumente
> Sind Strang und Fallbeil nicht.
> Und unsere heutigen Richter sind
> Noch nicht das Weltgericht.

('Nooses and guillotines are not the final arguments. And our judges today are not the final court of justice.')

Until 1987 this bombed-out Gestapo complex, some of it a mound of rubble, most of it levelled to the ground, was a parking lot where new drivers liked to practise. Today it is a museum site. The exhibition is called Topography of Terror, which is also the name of an active anti-Nazi organisation throughout Germany.

12.30 p.m.
We reach Checkpoint Charlie, the former crossing point between East and West Berlin. There is a café-restaurant here, the Café Adler, where we break for lunch. I study the guide books and maps for the afternoon ahead.

1.45 p.m.
We walk north from Checkpoint Charlie to the Unter den Linden. After 1938, Berlin's Jews were forbidden to walk here. We walk along the Unter den Linden to the former Prussian State Library (No. 8 Unter

den Linden), built between 1903 and 1914. On a plinth high above a door in the inner courtyard is mounted a magnificent imperial eagle, carved in stone and surmounted by a crown. In the Second World War the Library's 3,820,000 books were distributed for safety to more than thirty places throughout Germany. Today it is the German State Library, with more than six million books. Students and readers bustle about.

Across the street is the imperial palace, from the steps of which Karl Liebknecht declared the German Soviet Republic on 9 November 1918. We walk on to No. 6 Unter den Linden, the Humboldt University – formerly the Frederick William University. Albert Einstein was among those who taught here. In the square outside the university, facing the Opera House, the Nazis' burning of books took place on 10 May 1933. In a night of enthusiastic dancing around a great bonfire, the works of several hundred liberal and humane authors, among them books by many Jewish authors, were consigned to the flames. Today, on this very spot, bookstalls are set out against the university railings, for the students to browse and buy. Some are copies of the very books that were burnt here sixty-three years ago.

Robin buys the memoirs of Sir Nevile Henderson, the last British Ambassador to Berlin before the Second World War. He gave his book the title *Failure of a Mission*.

The Opera House which faces us was built in 1844. Badly damaged in a bombing raid in 1941, it was rebuilt while the war was still being fought, then burnt out in a further bombing raid in February 1945. It was rebuilt again after the war, and reopened in 1955 with a performance of Wagner's *Meistersinger*.

We walk on, to the Neue Wache (New Guardhouse), a small, neo-classical structure dating from 1818. During the Communist period it was used as a monument to the 'victims of fascism and militarism'. After the reunification of Berlin in 1989, the German government turned the guardhouse into a monument to all German war dead, military and civilian. The memorial inscription reads: 'To the victims of war and the rule of violence.' In the centre of an otherwise empty and stark space is a small sculpture by Käthe Kollwitz. It is of herself and, cradled in her arms, her son, looking up into her eyes. Her son was killed on the Somme in 1916. Not Jewish, but a pre-war socialist of passionate beliefs whose sculpture and lithographs stressed the lives of the poor, Käthe Kollwitz was denounced by the Nazis as a 'publicly injurious element' and placed under house arrest. There is now a museum of her work off the Kurfürstendamm, in former West Berlin.

We cross the Lustgarten, the former parade ground where both the Kaiser and Hitler reviewed German troops, and where a friend of mine, Yogi Mayer, then a twenty-year-old student at the Humboldt University, heard Dr Goebbels, Hitler's Minister of Propaganda, speak.

Near the Berliner Dom, the cathedral which since 1905 has dominated the eastern side of the square with its ornate ecclesiastical façade, is a small stone cube, a monument to Herbert Baum and his friends, young, mostly Jewish Communists, opponents of Nazism, who, on 18 May 1942, set fire to the wartime anti-Bolshevik exhibition, 'The Soviet Paradise', that had been erected in the Lustgarten on Goebbels' orders. The fire was quickly put out, and the conspirators were caught. They were tried on 16 July 1942. Seventeen of the conspirators, all of them Jews, were executed on August 18: they were decapitated with an axe. Twelve of them were women.

Following the attack on the exhibition (which portrayed the Jews as the evil force behind Bolshevism), Goebbels, in his capacity not as Minister of Propaganda but as Gauleiter of Berlin, ordered the immediate execution of 500 Berlin Jews. They were first taken to the SS barracks at Lichterfelde, and then to Sachsenhausen, where they were shot. The deportation of Jews from Berlin to Theresienstadt, and to the East, began soon afterwards.

We cross the River Spree. Standing on the Friedrichsbrücke and looking north, we can see – across a wide expanse of water, framed by green trees – the cupola of the recently restored and gilded Oranienburger Strasse Synagogue. Across the bridge we enter the Scheunenviertel (the Barn Quarter). As its name implies, it once – several centuries ago – lay outside the city limits. Tens of thousands of Jewish immigrants from the Russian provinces of Poland came here at the end of the nineteenth century, and in the first decade of the twentieth century, just as tens of thousands of others went to London's East End and New York's Lower East Side.

In front of us is Burg Strasse, where the Gestapo had its local headquarters, and where, in March 1943, 4,700 Jews who were married to non-Jews were rounded up for deportation and held. Walking across the main road we come to Rosen Strasse. It was in this street that an estimated 2,000 of these non-Jewish wives demonstrated – as close as they could to where their husbands were being held – and demanded their husbands' release. Their protest began on a Sunday morning. By nightfall as many as 2,000 more wives had joined them. They stayed in the street all that night, refusing to leave until their husbands were released. At midday on the Monday Dr Goebbels gave in. Suddenly the about-to-be-deported Jews became 'privileged persons'; free men who, the official announcement explained, 'are to be incorporated in the national community'. The 4,700 Jewish husbands thereby survived the war, living in Berlin. Their wives' protest is a little-known tale of courage – and of successful defiance.

From Rosen Strasse we continue north, under the S-Bahn track, to Rosenthaler Strasse, surrounded by the noisy evidence of the rebuilding of former East Berlin. At No. 39 Rosenthaler Strasse we enter a quiet, narrow, dilapidated alleyway. Otto Weidt had a factory here, making brushes. As a non-Jew, he employed several hundred blind Jews in his factory, insisting, in his discussions with the authorities, that the work the Jews did was essential for the German war economy. By employing them, he saved them from deportation. A plaque at the entrance to the alleyway records his persistence and his courage. Its last line reads: 'Many men thank him for having survived.'

We leave the alleyway and walk back down Rosenthaler Strasse, then on to the bottom of Grosse Hamburger Strasse. As we walk up the street, the first sight is a poignant one, a group of thirteen free-standing sculpted figures, less than life-size. Placed here in 1985 – the work of Will and Mark Lammers – they represent the Jews who were deported from the building that was once on this spot, the Jewish old people's home. This building, No. 26 Grosse Hamburger Strasse, was taken over by the Gestapo in 1942. To it were brought 56,000 Berlin Jews during 1942 and 1943, before they were taken by truck to Grünewald station, and then by train to Theresienstadt or Auschwitz. Many of those who were deported to Theresienstadt also ended up in Auschwitz. Very few of them survived.

In November and December 1941, a few months before the first of these deportations, several thousand Berlin Jews were deported to Riga, and executed in the nearby Rumbuli forest. Among those killed at Rumbuli was Lili Henoch, ten times German athletics champion, and the holder of two world records. She had been a teacher in a Jewish school in Berlin before the school, like all Jewish schools, was forced to close. Today, a sports hall in the city is named after her, as a memorial.

I also tell the story of a German barber, Leon Knychala, who had his barber's shop in the street parallel to Grosse Hamburger Strasse. From his rear window he could look into the garden of the old people's home. He would smuggle food into the home. Later, he hid two Jews, a widower in his sixties, Louis Link, and a man in his thirties, Salli Strien, in a cellar whose entrance was covered by a wardrobe. On one occasion Leon Knychala was taken by the Gestapo for interrogation and badly beaten up, but he revealed nothing. Unfortunately, when the two Jews decided it was safe for them to venture out, both were caught and deported: Louis Link to Theresienstadt (where he survived the war) and Salli Strien to Auschwitz, where he was killed.

As well as the small, sculpted figures on the site of the old people's home, there is a memorial plaque, on which, according to Jewish custom, many small stones have been placed, as a sign that the grave has been visited. Some of us place stones of our own. A memorial service is held here every year on February 27, the anniversary of the last large-scale deportation of Jews from Berlin in 1943, the so-called 'Factory Action' (many of the Jews were working in 'protected' jobs for various German war industries, but this could not save them in the end).

Behind the sculpted figures, and behind the site of the old people's home, is a large green enclosure, bounded on two sides by a brick wall and tall pre-war buildings. This was the site of the oldest Jewish cemetery in Berlin. It was opened in 1672 and was in use until 1827. During the war the Gestapo dug up the cemetery, threw away the bones of an estimated 12,000 people, and carted the headstones away to be used as trench supports on the battlefield. Twenty-eight headstones somehow survived, tossed aside and mostly broken. They are set today in the wall of the cemetery.

Among the graves that were desecrated here was that of the Jewish philosopher Moses Mendelssohn, who died in Berlin on 4 January 1786. On the spot where his tombstone once stood, another has been placed in recent years in his memory. Mendelssohn was a leading advocate of religious toleration. Ten years before destroying his grave, the Nazis, with their hatred of all things Jewish, had banned the music of his grandson, Felix Mendelssohn-Bartholdy, whose father had converted to Christianity.

Continuing a few yards up Grosse Hamburger Strasse, we come to No. 27, a building guarded by a German policeman. This is now, as it was many years ago, a Jewish school. Modern terrorist threats and the possibility of neo-Nazi violence mean that it has to be guarded. The school was founded by Moses Mendelssohn in 1778, to teach secular as well as traditional Jewish subjects; it came to this site in 1863, and the present building was put up in 1906. The original inscription survives above the entrance: 'Knabenschule der jüdischen Gemeinde' (Boys' School of the Jewish Community). In Communist times it was a vocational institute. After the collapse of Communism it was handed back to the Jewish community, and is now a school again, dedicated to Mendelssohn's liberal ideals. We read the plaque that has been placed here, quoting Mendelssohn:

> Nach Wahrheit forschen,
> Schönheit lieben,
> Gutes wollen,
> das Beste tun.

('Search for truth, love beauty, desire virtue, do the best.')

We walk down the street to the Sophienkirche. The land on which this church was built, in 1732, was bought from the Jewish community (its own cemetery backs on to the former Jewish cemetery). In the graveyard lies Leopold von Ranke, the historian who made it his task to write 'history as it actually was'. Were I wearing a hat, I would doff it to him. Across the street is Berlin's first Catholic hospital, St Hedwig's, built in 1844. The presence of Jewish, Protestant and Catholic institutions in the same street led to it being called Tolerance Street in the years before intolerance came to dominate the whole city. But it is said that when the synagogue was being attacked on Kristallnacht the nurses here were warned not to look out of their windows with the admonition: 'Don't make yourself a witness.'

We walk down the street and turn left into August Strasse. At Nos. 14–16 were a Jewish girls' school and a Jewish orphanage. The building, which survived the war, is in the neo-classical style. The plasterwork around the arched, ornamental entrance, also survived – 'a garland of plaster greenery' is how Stephen Birnbaum described it in his guide book.

We go into the courtyard. Facing us is a large and imposing red-brick building, with an ornamental pediment, the former Jewish hospital. It was built in 1860, designed by Edward Knoblach. Free medicine was provided for those who could not pay. For seventy years this hospital served Jews and non-Jews alike. In 1943, all the Jewish patients, doctors and nurses were all deported. A plaque near the front entrance commemorates this black moment.

From August Strasse I had wanted to go through an alleyway where, earlier this year, in one of the courtyards inside the alleyway, my son and I, led there by Stephen Birnbaum's pages, had seen a scuffed but surviving sign for Goldstein's Clothing Factory. The courtyard has been closed; renovation and rebuilding are rapidly changing this part of former East Berlin, neglected for half a century. Goldstein too, and his factory, are a thing of the past.

We turn right at the corner of August Strasse and Tucholsky Strasse (named after a Jewish novelist and poet of the pre-Nazi era), and walk to No. 40. An Orthodox Jewish congregation was established here in 1869 as a counter to the participation of Berlin's Jews at that time in the life and culture of the city. Such participation had begun more than half a century earlier, when the Jews of Prussia were granted full citizenship, under the emancipation edict of 1812. In the front part of the building was a rabbinical seminary, and the mikveh – the ritual bath. The synagogue was built in the courtyard in 1904. It was damaged during the wartime Allied bombing raids, and torn down in 1952. The original stone portal, with a carved Star of David, remains. In the 1970s, survivors of the Holocaust successfully reclaimed the property, reorganised the congregation, and built a new synagogue. At the front of the building is a kosher restaurant. The courtyard is also used as a restaurant when the weather is fine.

We walk back along Tucholsky Strasse to Oranienburger Strasse. This street leads in the direction of the village of Oranienburg, just over fifteen miles to the north of Berlin, a village which, from 1933, was notorious for its concentration camp, also known as Sachsenhausen. Almost immediately, we reach No. 31 Oranienburger Strasse. This building housed several Jewish communal institutions before the war. The pre-war Berlin Jewish Museum was located here. It was opened on 24 January 1933, six days before Hitler came to power. The building now houses a gallery for Jewish Art. Next to it, at Nos. 29–30, now fully restored, is the New Synagogue, also known as the Oranienburger Strasse Synagogue. Like the hospital, it was designed by Edward Knoblach, in the Moorish style so popular among prosperous Jewish communities at that time. The recently restored and reopened Dohany Street Synagogue in Budapest is in a similar style.

The New Synagogue was consecrated on 5 September 1866, six years after the opening of Knoblach's hospital in the parallel street. The Prussian Prime Minister – later German Chancellor – Otto von Bismarck, was present. It was a triumphal moment for him, as Prussian troops were even then on their way back to Berlin, having defeated the Austrians and paved the way for a united Germany under Prussian leadership. Berlin Jews welcomed this unification, and were as patriotic as any German in their national fervour. Their service in the Prussian army in the war against France in 1812 had led to an edict that gave them equality within the Prussian domains.

There were two unexpected sequels to the opening of the New Synagogue in Oranienburger Strasse. In 1869 the Orthodox Jewish community, in rebellion against the Reform tendencies of the New Synagogue, broke away and formed its own congregation (which was located at No. 40 Tucholsky Strasse from 1904 until it was closed down by the Gestapo in 1939, and re-established in 1989). Then, in 1888, Berlin's superintendent of buildings, Hermann Blankenstein, who had authorised a Postal Transport Office further down the street, and not wanting a State building to be overshadowed by a synagogue, authorised the construction of a lavish, imposing building for the Prussian postal authorities. We go to see it. It, too, is in an exotic, Eastern style, with tall rounded windows along the side, topped by ornamental panels, and with a Byzantine-style octagonal tower facing the street. 'It looks like a synagogue,' one of the group comments.

The Oranienburger Strasse Synagogue retained its magnificence until well after the First World War. Albert Einstein gave a violin concert here on 29 September 1930, a red-letter day for the congregation. In recent years the interior has been renovated, and the dome gilded; we saw it as we crossed the River Spree.

At the time of Kristallnacht, violent scenes took place here as the synagogue was ransacked. Peter Fritzsche and Karen Hewitt, in their constantly informative *Berlinwalks*, quote the recollections of Ruth Gross, then a young child in this district, who walked with her father along this street on the morning of 10 November 1938: 'Glass shards, Bibles, and prayer books lay in heaps on the sidewalk. I wanted to pick up one of the holy books since it is a sin to throw them in the dirt, but my father pulled me back with a frightened start. I couldn't understand this – I was seven years old then. He knew the danger that surrounded us; I only slowly came to realise it.'

An extraordinary episode took place here in Oranienburger Strasse. As the Gestapo prepared to set the synagogue on fire, the head of the local police precinct, Police Lieutenant Wilhelm Krützfeld, insisted that they stop, citing the fact (for it was a fact) that this was a protected municipal building, and had been for many years, because of its historic importance in the architecture of the city. The Gestapo went away, and there was no fire. Krützfeld was severely reprimanded. It was only during the war, at the time of the British bombing raid on Berlin of 22 November 1943, that the synagogue was set on fire as part of the general conflagration. There is a famous photograph, often reproduced (including by me, in error, in one of my books, before I knew the real story) that purports to show the Oranienburger Strasse synagogue burning during Kristallnacht. It actually shows the flames at the time of the British air raid five years later. Ten months after the Kristallnacht, in September 1939, the Jewish New Year services were held in the synagogue.

Four years later, in 1942, Lieutenant Krützfeld retired from the police force rather than enforce the deportations.

The restored Oranienburger Strasse Synagogue, with its gold-decorated dome, was re-inaugurated on 7 May 1995. One of those present at the ceremony was John Izbicki, a British journalist, who had prayed at the synagogue as a young boy, and who emigrated to Britain in December 1939 with his parents. I read from an article in the *Jewish Chronicle* which he wrote five days after the ceremony:

'We all sat outside, on the ground where two-thirds of the original building once stood. This empty space, where the main hall of the synagogue used to be, is to be left as a lasting scar of history. It is the remaining one-third that has been transformed into a museum, a place for researchers to come and study the history of German Jewry. The roof of that one-third is adorned now, as it was before, with two golden cupolas that shine like beacons across the Berlin skyline. As I listened to the speeches of eminent personalities and looked up to the windows of the restored building, I thought I saw – and certainly felt – the presence of so many others who had once prayed there.'

Next to the New Synagogue is the Café Oren, a busy and popular eating house, not only for Jews. Here, as earlier at Checkpoint Charlie, we come to rest. Then, our hour of refreshment over, we walk down Tucholsky Strasse, to No. 9, an imposing building on our right, the rabbinical seminary where Reform rabbis were trained. In 1922 Franz Kafka studied here; and in 1932 the first female rabbi was ordained here. Among the teachers between the wars was Rabbi Leo Baeck; after 1933 he was not only the Chief Rabbi of Berlin, but also the President of the Reich Representation of German Jews, responsible for the problems of the Jewish community in Germany, and its relations with the Nazi authorities. He was deported to Theresienstadt in 1943 but survived the war, to become a central figure in Reform Judaism in Britain and the United States. In London today, the Reform rabbinical seminary is named after him – the Leo Baeck College.

6.30 p.m.

We cross the River Spree and take the S-Bahn to Zoo station, where we change for Savigny Platz. From there we walk to the Kurfürstendamm, the main street of this part of Berlin, and for many years the star attraction of West Berlin. Everyone's attention in the street is focused on a fire that is being put out on the top floors of one of the buildings.

We reach the building – No. 200, now restored – where the Jewish soldiers who had fought in the First World War, the Reich League of Jewish Front Line Fighters, had their headquarters. Many of them had won the highest awards for bravery in action. These awards were no protection when it came to the deportations. Hundreds, even thousands, of German Jews would show their Iron Cross or other wartime decoration when they reached the death camps in the East, hoping that as a result of their proved patriotism and bravery they would be spared. The reverse happened; they would be treated with added savagery by the SS guards.

Other pre-war Jewish organisations that had their offices here in the Kurfürstendamm were the Hebrew Club (Bet Am Ivri) and the Hebrew World League (Bet Am Olamit), both at No. 61; the Jewish gymnasium – high school – at No. 119 (now a petrol station); the Jewish League of Peace at No. 136, and the Rachel Women's Society at No. 186. The Nazis also made use of the fine buildings on the Kurfürstendamm. At No. 115–16 was the Office for Jewish Affairs, from which Adolf Eichmann directed the emigration of Jews from Germany before 1939. At No. 140 was the Reich Security Main Office (RSHA), the department responsible for counter-measures against sabotage and political forgery, counter-intelligence, and all matters relating to treason.

We continue down the Kurfürstendamm to Meineckestrasse. Here, at No. 10, a substantial building with a courtyard, was where the Palestine Office was located. It was one of several dozen Palestine Offices throughout pre-war Europe, run by Zionist officials, that were authorised by the British government to issue Palestine certificates to would-be immigrants. These certificates guaranteed entry into Palestine. Many of them were issued to students who had places to study at the Hebrew University in Jerusalem.

A plaque on the building records that 50,000 Berlin Jews emigrated, mostly to Britain and the United States, before the bureau was closed down in 1941. Several thousand of them (about ten per cent) made their way to Palestine, where they played an important part in the establishment of the Jewish institutions, especially in the spheres of education, medicine and science.

Also in this building, around the inner courtyard into which we peer, were the headquarters of the Berlin Zionist Association, and of the publishing house of the Berlin Zionist newspapers and periodicals, the most well known of which was the *Jüdische Rundschau*, edited by Robert Weltsch. It was Weltsch who wrote an editorial on 4 April 1933 about the Yellow Star: 'They meant to dishonour us. Jews, take it upon yourselves, that Star of David, and honour it anew.' This is usually rendered, somewhat more tersely as: 'Wear it with pride, the Yellow Star.'

Another of the organisations which had its headquarters here was Maccabi, the worldwide Zionist sports organisation (of which Ben Helfgott was to be a post-war luminary in Britain).

Also established here at No. 10 Meineckestrasse, once war began, was a department of the Reich Security Main Office. This one dealt with 'political churches, sects and Jews', Catholicism, Protestantism, freemasonry – another Nazi hatred – and matters relating to newspapers, magazines and literature.

We walk back to the Kurfürstendamm. Our final street today is Fasanenstrasse. At No. 24, in a villa built in 1871, the year of German unification, is the museum of the work of Käthe Kollwitz. At No. 13, behind an apartment block and bookstore, is a 1902 neo-Renaissance building which was bought by the Jewish community in 1935 and turned into a synagogue. Not visible from the street, it was untouched during Kristallnacht, and survived the war.

We walk on to what was the main synagogue in this street, and in this part of Berlin, the Fasanenstrasse Synagogue. It was built in 1912, and in its day was a striking building with three great domes one behind the other. It was badly damaged, first in the Kristallnacht in 1938 and then by Allied bombing five years later. It was only after the war that the much-damaged building was pulled down, but a small part of the façade has been incorporated in the new building, which is now the Jewish community centre. Here, we will dine. The restaurant is called the Noah's Ark.

7.30 p.m.
Among the diners tonight is Rabbi Dick, the Chief Rabbi of Berlin. He speaks of his flock, and of the Jews of Germany today. There are sixty thousand Jews in the whole country, half of whom have come from the former Soviet Union in the last ten years. There are ten thousand Jews here in Berlin. Again, half of them are recent immigrants from Russia. 'Almost all of them came without even a smattering of Jewishness,' he says. 'Do they consider themselves Jewish? When they need something, then I, as the rabbi, have to receive them.'

As the group eats, Rabbi Dick talks about his own community here in Berlin. 'It is not a very religious community; irreligious, I would say. Living in Germany still has a stigma for religious Jews – it is a tremendous problem, the biggest scourge from the Jewish point of view. The Jewish community, the Gemeinde, is not just a synagogue or even just a community. All religious groups are a part of it, including Orthodox, Reform and Liberal, under one roof. We have a staff of four hundred to do social work, work in the old people's homes, etc. The government have been very generous with funds. The head of the community has to deal with rabbis, cantors – and, of course, complainers.'

I ask, 'How many rabbis?' to which Rabbi Dick replies: 'One. Me. I am the only active rabbi. The Reform rabbi returned home three years ago. They can't find a replacement. It's the German stigma. If anyone has any talent, he has no need to come here. But we do have a need. Three to four Germans call the rabbi every day asking to convert to Judaism. They feel a burden, a burden of guilt. They are young: thirty, forty. They have had no involvement in Nazi crimes, but they feel the burden.'

Towards midnight
We take taxis back across Berlin to our hotel. It has been a long sixteen-hour day.

Midnight
In the lounge, some of us discuss what we have seen. The imposing public buildings of Berlin with their imperial splendour, and the magnificent parks and avenues, are in grim contrast with the ugly story that unfolded here after 1933.

DAY 3

BERLIN – PRAGUE

'A short meeting, a few orders ... trains ... and camps'

7 a.m.
On waking, I look through my notes for what we hope to see and do today.

7.30 a.m.
Breakfast alone for a few minutes; then members of the group join me.

8 a.m.
We are ready to leave the hotel. I have arranged for a bus to take us this morning to various ports of call, but the bus driver tells me that he has no instructions to take us anywhere but the Lichtenberg station, where we do not want to be until three hours from now. We board the bus, but he, having telephoned to his base, refuses to take us for the morning. I see all my arrangements unravelling. We leave the bus. More phone calls, and finally the company agree to provide another bus. I have never led a tour group before, and feel uneasy at what other slips and upsets might be in store.

8.50 a.m.
Another bus arrives, to take us where we want to go. We drive past the wall of the Weissensee cemetery, but have lost the time we needed to go into it. The cemetery, which was opened in 1880, contains 115,000 graves. Just inside the entrance to the cemetery is a monument erected in 1949 to the young Jewish Communists led by Herbert Baum, who were executed in Berlin in 1942 and 1943. Baum was thirty years old when he was killed. Most of those with him were in their early twenties. More than half of them were women. Edith Fraenkel

and Marianne Joachim were both twenty-one. Lotte Rotholz was twenty. Alice Hirsch was nineteen.

The address of the Jewish cemetery used to be No. 45 Elsass Strasse (Alsace Street). The name was changed after the war to Herbert Baum Strasse.

We drive on through Berlin to the Heerstrasse, passing the entrance to the Olympic Stadium, which was built between 1934 and 1936. At the time of the Berlin Olympic Games, which opened on 1 August 1936, Gretel Bergmann, the German high-jump champion, who had been living as a refugee in England for two years, was invited back to compete as part of the German team. At the last moment, she was told that, being Jewish, she could not participate. It was not until the Atlanta Olympic Games in 1996 that – at the age of eighty-two, living in the United States – she was invited to attend the Games again, this time as the guest of honour of the German Olympic Committee. One of Germany's champion fencers in 1936, Helene Mayer, whose father was Jewish (but not her mother), did compete in the German squad, and won a silver medal for them.

During the 1936 Olympic Games all anti-Semitic posters and slogans were removed from the streets and public buildings of Berlin so as not to 'offend' the visitors from democratic or liberal countries. But even as the Games were taking place, construction was continuing, just north of Berlin, of a concentration camp at Sachsenhausen.

After 1945 the Olympic Stadium became the headquarters of the British troops in Berlin.

9.10 a.m.

We reach the British military cemetery, where the Cross of Sacrifice looks out, through a high bank of pine trees, over the Heerstrasse, a main German traffic thoroughfare. Many pilots are buried here, who were shot down during the British bombing raids over Berlin. The cemetery covers seven acres. The site was chosen in 1945 by the British occupation authorities and the Imperial – later Commonwealth – War Graves Commission. 'To this green and pleasant place,' records the Commonwealth War Graves register of those buried here, 'were moved the graves from the Berlin area and Eastern Germany. The great majority of those buried here, approximately 80 per cent of the total, were airmen who lost their lives in the air raids over Berlin and the towns of Eastern Germany. The remainder were men who died in prisoner-of-war camps in these regions, some of whom were victims of the notorious forced march into Germany of prisoners from camps in Poland, in front of the advancing Russians.'

There are 3,576 war graves here, of which 386 are of unidentified British dead. A series of seven-grave rows running up to the Stone of Remembrance, and on as far as the Cross, each contain a seven-man bomber crew, many in communal graves. As well as the crosses that mark most of the headstones are several with the Star of David on them. Among these is the grave of Sergeant Samuel Cohen, of the Royal Air Force Volunteer Reserve. He was nineteen when he was shot down and killed on 6 January 1944.

9.15 a.m.

Just around the corner from the Commonwealth War Graves cemetery is one of Berlin's Jewish cemeteries, the Heerstrasse cemetery. A few fifteenth-century Jewish gravestones from an older, abandoned cemetery have been set out here, at the entrance, in a wide expanse of grass. Beyond them are more than a hundred rectangular rose-coloured memorial stones to Berlin Jews who were deported to the East, some of them to the Lodz ghetto (from which they were taken to their deaths at Chelmno). Both Lodz and Chelmno are on our itinerary. The memorial stones are set starkly on gravel, framed by lush greenery. I read out some of the names: Rudolf Bernstein, Frieda Saphierstein, Regina Katz, Pauline Wolff, Hermann and Johanna Less ...

In front of the rose-coloured memorial stones, a granite stone with gold-engraved writing marks the spot on which, on 30 September 1984, ashes brought from the crematorium area at Auschwitz were buried. Also in the cemetery, facing the entrance, is the imposing black marble grave of Dr Heinz Galinski, who led the Jewish community in Berlin from 1945 until his death. He died on 19 July 1992, at the age of seventy-nine.

10.15 a.m.

Having driven along the wooded shore of the Havel (along the Havel Chausee) we come to the small suburban resort of Wannsee, and drive along Am Grossen Wannsee, a street lined with villas. Our destination is Nos. 56–58, the lakeside villa, built in the First World War. There, on 20 January 1942, Reinhard Heydrich, then aged thirty-seven, introduced the 'Final Solution' – which had already been decided upon – to the various ministerial bureaucrats who would have to take part in carrying it out. Heydrich's assistant at the meeting was his contemporary, Adolf Eichmann, just two years his junior.

The meeting was one which brought together the two centres of power in Nazi Germany, the RSHA (the Reich Security Main Office) represented by Heydrich and five others – plus a female secretary – and the Nazi Party and German government, represented by seven people from different ministries, among them the Ministry of Transport, which was to have such an important part in the deportations.

We reach the entrance to the villa. Seen through the gate, its elegant portal is framed by a hedge and tall dark trees. I hesitate to ring the bell, it seems a place of such enormity. We walk down to the water's edge, a peaceful, almost idyllic scene. This is Heckshorn Point, a ferry stop, around which – to our left – are a number of popular restaurants. The statue of a lion looks out over the water, a memento of the German defence of this region in medieval times. From the lion, we can look into the Wannsee villa garden. We then return to the entrance of the villa. A gardener, his wheelbarrow next to him, is bending over the flowerbeds in front of the columned entrance. He is weeding.

10.20 a.m.

Standing in the forecourt, before we enter the villa itself, I give a summary of what was said and decided here, fifty-four years ago. According to the official notes of the Conference, Heydrich began by telling the assembled senior civil servants of his appointment 'as Plenipotentiary for the Preparation of the Final Solution of the European Jewish Question'. As a result of this appointment it was his aim 'to achieve clarity in essential matters'. Reichsmarshall Goering, he explained, had asked to see 'a draft project' of organisational, factual and material 'essentials' in consideration of this 'final solution'. Such a draft would require the 'prior joint consultation' of all the ministries involved, 'in view of the need for parallel procedure'.

The fourteen people – including the female secretary – who gathered around the table here listened as Heydrich told them that the struggle waged against the Jews 'so far' had first involved the expulsion of the Jews 'from various spheres of life of the German people'. It had been followed by the expulsion of the Jews 'from the living space of the German people'. Now, as a result of what he called the 'pertinent prior approval of the Führer', the 'evacuation of the Jews to the East' had emerged 'in place of emigration' as a 'further possible solution'. But both emigration and evacuation were, he explained, to be considered 'merely as a measure of expediency'. From them, experience could be gained which would be of importance 'in view of the approaching final solution of the Jewish question'.

Heydrich then explained that this 'final solution' concerned, not only those Jews who were already under German rule, but 'some eleven million Jews' throughout Europe. He then gave the meeting; including the Gestapo chief, Heinrich Müller, a list of the numbers involved.[1]

The figures presented by Heydrich included 34,000 for Lithuania. The other 200,000 Jews of pre-war Lithuania had already been murdered – between July and November 1941. The largest number of Jews listed by Heydrich were those in the Ukraine: his figure was 2,994,684. The second largest was for the General Government (German-administered central Poland): 2,284,000. The third largest was for Germany's ally, Hungary: 742,800, a figure which included the Jews in Ruthenia, the eastern part of Czechoslovakia which had been annexed by Hungary at the beginning of the war.[2]

The fourth-highest figure was for unoccupied France: 700,000. This figure included the Sephardi Jews in France's North African possessions. Next largest in the list was White Russia, with 446,484 Jews listed, followed by the 400,000 Jews of the Bialystok region.

Estonia was listed as 'without Jews'. This was true. Of Estonia's 2,000 Jews in June 1941, half had fled to safety inside the Soviet Union. The remaining half had already been murdered in the six months since the German occupation of the Baltic.

Listening inside the Wannsee villa to this statistical survey of the numbers of Jews who were marked out for death were a dozen German civil servants. Eight of them had university doctorates. They had come to the meeting from their offices in the Ministry for the Occupied Eastern Territories, the Ministry of the Interior, the Justice Ministry, the Foreign Office, the Chancellery, the SS-Race and Resettlement Office, and – having made the journey from Cracow by train – from the General Government. Also present at Wannsee that January morning was the Plenipotentiary for the Four Year Plan, responsible for disposing of Jewish property, and representing six more ministries.

Heydrich asked all those present, and their ministries, to co-operate 'in the implementation of the solution'. He told them: 'In the course of

[1] These numbers included 330,000 Jews in as yet unconquered Britain. All the Jews in the neutral countries of Europe were also listed: 55,000 in European Turkey, 18,000 in Switzerland, 10,000 in Spain, 8,000 in Sweden, 4,000 in the Irish Republic and 3,000 in Portugal.

[2] As well as Hungary, Jews living in five other countries which were allied to Germany were also listed: 342,000 in Roumania, 88,000 in Slovakia, 58,000 in Italy (including Sardinia), 40,000 in Croatia and 2,300 in Finland. The smallest number given was the 200 Jews of Italian-occupied Albania.

the final solution, the Jews should be brought under appropriate direction in a suitable manner to the East for labour utilisation. Separated by sex, the Jews capable of work will be led into these areas in large labour columns to build roads, whereby doubtless a large part will fall away through natural reduction. The inevitable final remainder which doubtless constitutes the toughest element will have to be dealt with appropriately, since it represents a natural selection which upon liberation is to be regarded as a germ cell of a new Jewish development.

'In the course of the practical implementation of the final solution,' Heydrich said, 'Europe will be combed from West to East. If only because of the apartment shortage and other socio-political necessities, the Reich area – including the Protectorate of Bohemia and Moravia – will have to be placed ahead of the line. For the moment, the evacuated Jews will be brought bit by bit to so-called transit ghettos from where they will be transported farther to the east.'

The many extreme euphemisms in Heydrich's account were the result of several rewritings of the protocol of the meeting.

It was intended, according to the statistics presented to the Wannsee Conference, that a total of 11,000,000 European Jews should 'fall away' (in the language of the conference), including those in the neutral and unconquered countries.

There followed a discussion of what were seen as the various problems involved. 'In Slovakia and Croatia,' Heydrich told them, 'the situation is no longer all that difficult, since the essential key questions there have already been resolved.' As for Hungary, 'it will be necessary before long,' he said, 'to impose upon the Hungarian government an adviser on Jewish questions.' Roumania posed a problem, as 'even today a Jew in Roumania can buy for cash appropriate documents officially certifying him in a foreign nationality'. Speaking of the occupied and unoccupied zones of France, however, Heydrich commented that there 'the seizure of the Jews for evacuation should in all probability proceed without major difficulty'.

By far the largest number of Jews lived in the General Government (Generalgouvernement) – the main expanse of German-occupied Poland. The attitude of its administration was crucial to any 'final solution'. Dr Josef Bühler, the representative of the General Government – who was accompanied by the Commanding Officer of the Security Police in the General Government, SS Standartenführer (Lieutenant-Colonel) Dr Karl Schoegarten – stated that his administration 'would welcome the start of the final solution in its territory, since the transport problem was no overriding factor there and the course of the action would not be hindered by considerations of work utilisation'. Bühler added: 'Jews should be removed from the domain of the General Government as fast as possible, because it is precisely here that the Jew constitutes a substantial danger as carrier of epidemics and also because his continued black market activities create constant disorder in the economic structure of the country. Moreover, the majority of the two and a half million Jews involved were not capable of work.'

Dr Bühler had, he said, 'only one favour to ask', and that was 'that the Jewish question in this territory be solved as rapidly as possible'.

The meeting was drawing to its end. 'Finally,' the official notes recorded, 'there was a discussion of the various types of solution possibilities.' What these 'possibilities' were, the notes of the Conference do not record. At his trial in Jerusalem in 1960, Eichmann told the court: 'I remember that at the end of this Wannsee Conference Heydrich, Müller and my humble self settled down comfortably by the fireplace, and that then for the first time I saw Heydrich smoke a cigar or a cigarette, and I was thinking: today Heydrich is smoking, something I have not seen before. And he drinks cognac – since I had not seen Heydrich take any alcoholic drink in years. After this Wannsee Conference we were sitting together peacefully, and not in order to talk shop, but in order to relax after the long hours of strain.'

What Eichmann called the 'long hours of strain' were over. It had all taken less than a day. Heydrich was certain that the time was right for the deportation and destruction of millions of people. The technical services such as the railways, the bureaucracy and the diplomats would work in harmony, towards a single aim. Local populations would be cajoled or coerced into passivity. Many would even co-operate, and some would co-operate gladly: that had been made clear already.

10.25 a.m.

The time has come for us to enter the villa. It is now a memorial, consisting of a museum and an educational centre. It has an archive and a library, and a department which organises study days and seminars. Up to now, 210,000 visitors – groups and individuals – have found their way, like us, to its door.

We walk up the path, some hesitating, and then enter. As we walk round the villa, it quickly becomes clear that the presentation is most impressive. The story of the Holocaust is set out in the downstairs rooms, with clear explanations and excellent photographs and facsimile documents. There are fourteen rooms with exhibits, and a fifteenth room with the history of the villa before 1939 and after 1945. We walk through the rooms in their historical sequence: the National Socialist dictatorship in Germany, the pre-war period, the war against Poland (1939), the ghettos, mass executions (in German-occupied Russia after the German invasion of the Soviet Union in June 1941), the Wannsee Conference itself, deportations, the 'Hall of the Countries', death camps and transit camps, Auschwitz (a room on its own), concentration camps, the Warsaw ghetto uprising, 'The End', and liberation.

In what is believed to have been the actual room in which the Wannsee Conference took place, with its tall picture windows looking out over the patio and lawn down to the lake, there is a stillness. We walk into the room, through it, round it and then out of it, as if it must not be disturbed. It is as if the voices of those who spoke here, and the heads of those who nodded their agreement here, must not be alerted to our presence. One feels a palpable sense of the presence of evil. Despite the bright sunshine outside, and the large windows, the room seems eerily dark. Along one wall are the photographs of all those who were at the meeting, and descriptions of who they were: most of them professional civil servants of the highest degree of bureaucratic competence.

In an adjoining room are various artefacts, including a roll of yellow cloth on which innumerable yellow stars with the word 'Jude' on them have been printed, ready to be cut out and sewn on to Jewish coats and jackets. The lines for cutting around the stars have been marked on the cloth. Also on display is an original telegram, dated 30 July 1943, about the despatch of a consignment of Zyklon-B poison gas to Auschwitz.

10.29 a.m.

I go up in the lift – which was already here in those days, and very evocative it is too, with its plush furnishings – to see the founding director, Gerhard Schoenberner. His office is on the third floor (the second floor houses the library and seminar rooms), and overlooks the lake. He notes that there are three such memorials in Berlin: the one in the former Bendlerstrasse – where many of the conspirators against Hitler were killed – the one at the former Gestapo headquarters, and this. 'Three attempts to deal with a chapter of contemporary history' is how he expresses it.

Schoenberner explains that immediately after the war the villa was first used by the Red Army. Shortly afterwards it was used as a United

States Army officers' club. Then it became the Centre for Political Education of the Social Democratic Party of Berlin. They rented it from the city. 'I first came here as a schoolboy in short trousers,' says Schoenberner with a smile. 'I was a very young boy, just fifteen years old. We came here to listen to lectures on democracy. There were just ten to twelve of us. I remember one of the lectures was on the model of Scandinavian socialism. Nobody had heard of the lecturer. It was Willy Brandt.' Brandt was an anti-Nazi who had fled from Germany in 1933, living first in Norway and then in Sweden. He was German Chancellor from 1969 to 1974.

Schoenberner himself came from an anti-Nazi family. In 1957 (two years before I did the same) he went on a student exchange to Poland. He was then head of the editorial board of the West German socialist students' monthly magazine. One result of his visit was a documentary volume, *The Yellow Star*, published in English in 1960. It was one of the very first books that I read on this subject: I still have my original, now somewhat dog-eared copy.

A second result of Schoenberner's Polish visit was the preparation – 'with enormous difficulties', he recalls – of an exhibition entitled 'The Past is Warning'. It was shown in the West Berlin Congress Hall, and elsewhere in West Germany. 'I remember how I went to the United States Press Office to ask for technical assistance. But the man in charge said to me: "This is not in the interests of American policy." The main goal then was to win over Germany as a military ally against the Soviet Union. Then, in 1965 Joseph Wulf, a German Jewish historian, and a survivor of Auschwitz, who was a pioneer in documenting Nazi crimes in Germany, together with a couple of friends and colleagues of whom I was one, made a proposal to transform the villa into a museum, to give it a new function, relating to its history. We got prominent backing in Germany and abroad. The list of names signing our demands read like an excerpt from *Who's Who*. But then nobody in politics understood the necessity. Nobody was interested; the political priorities were different. It took almost a quarter of a century before the City of Berlin and the Bonn Government decided to agree, and to finance the whole undertaking.'

Schoenberner has devoted considerable energy and thought to making this museum work. 'The house opened on the fiftieth anniversary of the meeting – in January 1992. I started preparing several years before. I had to write the concept for the house, and have the building renovated, and last but not least I had to prepare the permanent exhibit. Thank Heaven I was familiar not only with the theme but with the international archives as well. In the last decade we had a children's recreation home here. Everything had to be regenerated – to make a little bit visible the historical focus of the house.'

As he began his work, Schoenberner was concerned about how to tell the story of the Holocaust in fifteen rooms, not designed for exhibitions, some of them rather small. 'I had the ambition,' he tells me, 'to avoid the typical mistakes, which had angered me so many times as a visitor to other exhibitions of that kind. I had seen so many textual explanations on exhibits, very often much too long, placed much too low. In many museum exhibits you have to be as low as a basset hound to see them. I was also concerned about the legibility of words in the textual descriptions where a word is broken into two lines. I am very interested in these aspects as well, it is so important that the exhibits should be clear and the text clear.

'I am interested in transmitting something. You have to think how to do it. This house was never built for exhibitions. I knew this building since the end of the war. It is an unbearable combination – this late bourgeois interior and the terrible story of what happened in these rooms. But once we are here, in this house, we have to show the visitor where we are, and what happened here at the beginning of 1942. I was concerned with what materials to use. The designer came with glass. I said, "My God, this is much too elegant. It might be suited to a Gold from Peru exhibit, but not for our purpose." So we decided to use frosted glass.'

Schoenberner has certainly succeeded. Suzanne Bardgett, from the Imperial War Museum, who is travelling with us, asks him about security. 'Up till now,' he says, 'nothing has happened. Not one little word sprayed on the walls. But you have to be prepared. You don't need a mass neo-Nazi movement – two fanatics are enough. Recently some skinheads came up here with the school classes. But they quickly understood that this was not the proper background for their parades, and they disappeared.'

10.50 a.m.

We leave the Wannsee villa, our visit curtailed as a result of the morning bus delay. This also means that we cannot go to the Grünewald railway station, to see the place from which Berlin Jews were deported, and to read the plaque there. It was unveiled on 3 April 1987. The first deportation took place from here on 18 October 1941, to the Lodz ghetto.

11 a.m.

We are driving into Berlin. Everyone has been deeply affected by the visit to the Wannsee. There is an animated, but at the same time subdued discussion in the bus about how the Holocaust should be studied, and about its uniqueness. 'To enter the actual house in which the Final Solution was decided on was so uncanny; it made it so real,' comments Marie.

'You come here to Wannsee, you see this beautiful place, everything is so civilised,' says Ben. 'People come here, and you have a map in front of you, how to dispose of eleven million human beings, never mind who they are, except that they are Jewish. And who are you? You are all educated people, some with doctorates, discussing how to get rid of eleven million cattle – it is as if we were cattle, we were cattle for them. When the beef crisis broke out, the British government announced they would have to kill ten million cattle. I was so sad. How can we destroy ten million cattle? I felt terrible. These people didn't feel anything at all. The fact that they were destroying children didn't bother them. They just wanted to destroy them.'

Ben is emphatic. 'Everyone who comes to Berlin should come here,' he says. 'We should make sure people don't behave like this to other people – ever.'

Like most of the group, Ben was struck by how brief the meeting at the Wannsee was, and how clinical. 'It is frightening to think that educated and sophisticated men can be so bereft of feeling towards other human beings. The exhibition is so direct. It is unencumbered. You don't get lost. You don't get bogged down. It's all depicted in a nutshell. Very comprehensive. It is a credit to the authorities that they have decided on this place – of all places – to have this mind-boggling exhibition.'

Less than two months before the Wannsee meeting, on 7 December 1941, when the Japanese had attacked the American fleet at Pearl Harbor, President Roosevelt had called it 'a day that will live in infamy'. The same could be said of the day when the German bureaucrats gathered at Wannsee and listened to the SS plans, nodded their assent, and then, their work having been completed, had lunch. Ben comments: 'They were laughing, enjoying the fresh air, having a good meal – and then they presided over the life and death of millions of people. Not only did they have this power, but they were mostly bureaucrats. The really senior people, the air marshals and the generals, and the ministerial heads of the great government departments, were fighting a different war – a war against the Allies. As for the war against us, it only required a short meeting, a few orders, and trains, and camps in remote regions.'

11.22 a.m.

We pass the Victory monument and drive once again down the Unter den Linden. As the bus continues on its way, I read out Hitler's speech of 30 January 1942, ten days after the Wannsee Conference, in which he spoke here in Berlin of his confidence of victory. He also spoke of the Jews, telling his listeners, as reported by the Allied monitoring service on the following day: 'They are our old enemy as it is, they have experienced at our hands an upsetting of their ideas, and they rightfully hate us, just as much as we hate them.' The Germans, Hitler added, were 'well aware' that the war could only end when the Jews had been 'uprooted from Europe', or when 'they disappear'.

Hitler then declared, again as recorded by the Allied monitoring service: 'The war will not end as the Jews imagine it will, namely with the uprooting of the Aryans, but the result of this war will be the complete annihilation of the Jews. Now for the first time they will not bleed other people to death, but for the first time the old Jewish law of an eye for an eye, a tooth for a tooth, will be applied. And – world Jewry may as well know this – the further these battles [of the war] spread, the more anti-Semitism will spread. It will find nourishment in every prison camp and in every family when it discovers the ultimate reason for the sacrifices it has to make. And the hour will come when the most evil universal enemy of all time will be finished, at least for a thousand years.'

Such was Hitler's message, as received in London and Washington: that the war would end with 'the complete annihilation of the Jews'. Even as Hitler spoke, the first death camp, at Chelmno, was in operation, and new death camps were being prepared. Three of the sites chosen were remote villages on the former German–Polish border, just to the west of the River Bug. We will be visiting each of them during the next week. Although remote, each site was on a railway line linking it with hundreds of towns and villages whose Jewish communities were trapped and starving by the beginning of 1942.

We have seen where the paperwork was done and the decisions made to murder millions of people; soon we will see where so many of those people were taken and killed.

11.25 a.m.

We drive through the Brandenburg Gate and back across the line of the former Berlin Wall, into former East Berlin. How easy it is now to make the crossing, compared to those decades of separation, division and, for so many, danger. Unless one is looking out of the bus window, one does not notice it. Even when one looks out of the window, it is merely a square and a gate and another square.

11.35 a.m.

We drive down Karl-Marx-Allee.

11.42 a.m.

We reach Berlin-Lichtenberg station and have an hour to rest and have a snack before our train leaves. Had we been able to spend another day in Berlin, I would have wanted to add the two main Nazi-period prisons, the Moabit and Plötzensee prisons, and also Sachsenhausen concentration camp (an hour north of the city), to our itinerary.

There is still much talk about Wannsee. Robin comments on what a short time it took to reach the decisions taken there, compared to the impact they had. 'Ninety minutes that sealed the fate of East European Jewry' are his words. His area of expertise is the killing that took place in the six months before Wannsee, during the German conquest of eastern Poland, western Russia and the Baltic States.

12.43 p.m.

Our train, the Porta Bohemica express (from Hamburg to Prague), draws out of Berlin-Lichtenberg and heads south.

1.10 p.m.

The train passes to the west of Köpenick. I speak of the time before the First World War when the Germans found themselves held up to considerable ribaldry. In October 1906 a cobbler by the name of Voigt dressed himself up in the uniform of a captain in the elite 1st Regiment of Prussian Guards, and used his military 'authority' to arrest the mayor of the town of Köpenick. He then ordered the mayor to go immediately to Berlin. The mayor did as ordered, whereupon the cobbler-captain made off with the Köpenick city cash. It was not until nine days after the crime that the bogus captain was arrested, and his true identity revealed. The episode was a perfect illustration, said many English and French observers – and many Germans – of the absurd deference accorded to military officers. It made Prussian obedience look ridiculous, and the 'Captain of Köpenick' became a figure of fun for liberals throughout the Reich. Obeying orders was to have ominous overtones in the Second World War, when the phrase, 'I was only obeying orders,' was used to justify war crimes at every level.

Ironically, opposition to Hitler was strong in Köpenick during the early years of the Nazi regime. It was savagely crushed during the Köpenick Week of Blood (Köpenicker Blutwoche), when ninety-one opponents of Nazism were killed and almost five hundred imprisoned.

1.40 p.m.

The train passes ten miles to the east of the town of Schlieben. We are sitting in the restaurant car. Mineral water, coffee and snacks.

I ask Ben to speak about his time as a slave labourer there. He recalls his first day. 'We were given a quarter of a pound of old, almost inedible bread,' he said. 'The soup smelt like excreta; it was overpowering; the taste buds wouldn't accept it. When those who had been in the camp for a while came back from work, when they heard that there was soup left uneaten, they all ran for it, they were fighting for it. One cauldron overturned. They tried to lick it up from the floor. Psychologically, we almost died at that moment. We couldn't believe what we saw. The soup didn't change, but on the following day we ate it, and were sorry we had given it away on the previous day.

'The German women with whom a number of us boys worked were very decent, they never beat us up, they never shouted at us. They even made a request to the camp commandant that we should be allowed to have a shower twice a week. The commandant agreed. The front line was getting nearer. The German women were petrified of what would happen when the Red Army arrived. They were afraid of being raped, not just once or twice, but over and over again. That was what they heard was happening further east. No doubt it happened to them too. But we had been sent out, sent southward by train towards Prague.'

In 1945, Ben's train journey from Schlieben to Theresienstadt lasted seven days. Today it would be little more than three hours.

2.05 p.m.

We pass fifteen miles west of Ruhland, one of the German synthetic oil plants that enabled the German army to fight on throughout 1944. It was massively bombed. Another of these synthetic oil plants was at

Monowitz, on the outskirts of Auschwitz. We will see Monowitz in a few days' time.

2.15 p.m.
We see the town of Meissen in the distance. Dresden is just beyond it. Ben recalls how, on the night of the bombing of Dresden in February 1945, 'We could see the orange sky. What a lovely night that was. It gave us a new lease of life.'

2.20 p.m.
We pass the first vineyards, on the outskirts of Dresden. In the outer suburbs, Roman Halter, a friend of mine in London, who came to Britain in August 1945, worked as a slave labourer in a munitions factory in the last winter of the war. When the death march began, he and some friends managed to break away and hide in the adjacent cigarette factory. Because of the omnipresent smell of tobacco, the SS dogs were unable to sniff them out.

2.29 p.m.
The train draws into Dresden-Neustadt station. Ben recalls how, as the Russian soldiers went through Dresden in 1945, they had come across the cigarette factories there. 'The factories had been destroyed. The Russian soldiers took cartons and cartons of cigarettes. When they reached Theresienstadt, they distributed the cigarettes to everyone they found. Those who had left the camp and gone out foraging for food missed the cigarettes.'

2.35 p.m.
The train draws out of Dresden-Neustadt. Outside the window we see a large mosque under construction, for the Turkish 'guest workers'. As we drew into Potsdam two nights ago, we saw a similar mosque across the lake, brightly illuminated.

2.40 p.m.
We reach Dresden-Hauptbahnhof. There is a fifteen-minute stop here. We stay in the compartment, and I speak of the bombing of Dresden in February 1945. The Russians had learned (through British signals intelligence) that the Germans were withdrawing several army divisions from the Rhine, Italy and Norway to join in the struggle on the Breslau front. They were desperate to prevent these troops arriving, and asked Britain and the United States to bomb the road and railway junctions,

and bridges, along which the reinforcements would be travelling. At that moment, Dresden was within the zone of Russian bombing activities.

The Allies agreed to the Russian request. The Russians gave up that section of the zone and transferred it to Britain and the United States, so that it could be bombed more effectively. The result was the Anglo-American raid in which tens of thousands of German civilians were killed, the largest number since the British bombing of Hamburg almost two years earlier.

2.55 p.m.
The train pulls out of Dresden-Hauptbahnhof.

3.02 p.m.
After travelling through the suburbs of Dresden, we reach the Elbe. Across the river, two miles to the north, is Oberpoyritz. Fifty years ago it was a small farming village. In March 1945, after escaping from the death march, my friend Roman Halter found refuge here with a German couple, Kurt and Hertha Fuchs. 'Liberation came in the form of a Russian soldier reaching the farm and demanding watches,' Roman told me. A few days after liberation, when Roman had already set off for his home in Poland, the Nazis in the village, having found out that the Fuchs's had hidden him and two other young Jews, went to the farm and killed Kurt Fuchs. Roman's friend Josef Szwajcer, who had stayed on the farm, was also killed.

3.05 p.m.
We go through Pirna. At the end of 1944 the Germans had an underground factory here, where slave labourers made tanks: two tanks a day were produced. To this day, the SS guards who tormented the slave labourers receive pensions. Having been registered as fighting soldiers, they are entitled to an army pension. Only those who were specifically convicted of war crimes – a very small minority indeed of those involved in tortures – receive no pension. The slave labourers who worked here, however, like slave labourers from all over Hitler's Reich, can get no compensation. Some are still fighting, today, in an uphill struggle with the German bureaucracy, for some form of compensation. Roman Halter is one of them.

3.07 p.m.
As we leave Pirna, we pass, on our right, the suburb of Sonnenstein.
Here, shortly after the outbreak of the Second World War, the Germans
established a euthanasia centre where sick Germans were brought,
and killed by injections or by gas. This was the T4 operation, the
headquarters of which (or, rather, the bombsite on which the headquarters had stood) we visited in Berlin yesterday. Jews were also
brought here and killed.

3.10 p.m.
We are travelling along the Elbe, through rural Saxony. The scenery
becomes extremely attractive: hills and vineyards, small riverside towns,
gorges and castles. No wonder the old Baedeker guide books regarded
it as one of the prettiest rail journeys in Europe.

3.15 p.m.
The train goes through the attractive village of Königstein, with the
Elbe below us on the left, and the hills to our right. Ben becomes
animated. 'It was during the journey in the cattle trucks from Schlieben.
I looked out of a little window and caught a glimpse of a man lying
on his bed, reading. I thought to myself, "My God, what a lucky
person, what a luxury – he is lying on his bed, reading." My great
love had been reading. I thought to myself – a prisoner – when will
the time come when I will be able to lie on my bed reading?'

3.20 p.m.
The train pulls in to Bad Schandau. Ben has become more animated
than I have ever seen him before, and agitated too. 'I was here. It was
just fifty years ago. Here, in a cattle train. Here, on this line. Here we
were. It comes back to me often in my memory.'
   We pass a house that could be the house into whose first-floor
window Ben looked. The first-floor windows are on the level of our
window in the train.

3.25 p.m.
We draw out of Bad Schandau and enter the Elbe gorge. We are only
thirty-four kilometres from the south-west corner of post-war Poland.

3.30 p.m.
The train is running through the gorge – the Porta Bohemica of our
train's name: the Gate of Bohemia – and approaching the border of

the Czech Republic. As we run along the Elbe, still inside Germany, we can see the Czech border and customs posts across the river. On the far side, it is already the Czech Republic.

3.34 p.m.

We reach Dolni Zleb, the Czech Republic border post on our side of the Elbe. We enter the Sudetenland, the area of inter-war Czechoslovakia which Hitler annexed in October 1938. The stunning beauty of the landscape is in contrast with the ugly memories of the time when Britain and France put pressure on Czechoslovakia to give up this large region in order to prevent the possibility of Britain and France having to go to the aid of Czechoslovakia if Hitler invaded. A friend of mine, who was made a Companion of the Order of the Bath as a reward for his part in the diplomacy of those days, was humiliated by a senior colleague who remarked that, in being awarded the CB, he had received his just deserts, as the initials stood, not for Companion of the Bath, but for Czechoslovakia Betrayed.

I was just two years old, celebrating my birthday in Britain, when this beautiful river gorge became a focal point of international tension, and the German-speaking people here, who had never before been a part of Germany (but of Austria-Hungary), found themselves under Hitler's rule. The Jews among them fled – mostly to Prague.

Ben recalls the excitement in Poland when the disintegration of Czechoslovakia in October 1938 enabled the Polish government to seize the border town of Teschen (about thirty miles from here). The town had been divided between Poland and Czechoslovakia at the end of the First World War. A stamp was issued to mark this territorial gain. 'I can still see this stamp,' says Ben, 'and the slogan: "Teschen has returned to the motherland."' Ben was then a not-quite-nine-year-old stamp collector.

3.45 p.m.

Reach Decin, our first town in the Czech Republic, and in Bohemia. Jews first settled here more than four hundred years ago, in 1537. Almost five hundred Jews were living here, and in neighbouring Podmokly, in 1930. When war came, those who had not managed to emigrate were deported to Theresienstadt.

3.52 p.m.

Leave Decin.

4.05 p.m.
Reach Usti, in German, Aussig. A small Jewish community was expelled from here in the late seventeenth century. A new community was founded after 1848, and forty years later was large enough to have its own rabbi. In 1930 there were almost a thousand Jews here. Among them was Ignaz Petschek (who died in 1934), a coal merchant who became a central figure in the region's domestic and export trade. He was the owner of the North Bohemian lignite mines; lignite, an inferior form of coal, is also known as yellow coal.

The synagogue, built in 1880, was destroyed by the Nazis after the German occupation of Bohemia and Moravia in March 1939. Most of Usti's Jews were deported to Theresienstadt. In their memory a memorial tablet was affixed in 1953 to the wall of a prayer room opened after the war (at No. 26 Moskevsa Street).

The old Jewish cemetery is now part of a park. The new cemetery, first used in 1892, remained in use for the small community that was re-established here after the war. It was closed down in 1980, and a factory built on the site.

4.15 p.m.
Across the Elbe, on a great rocky outcrop, is the gothic Strekov Castle, parts of which date from the fourteenth century. After he was liberated by the Russians in 1945, Ben came through this region. 'I haven't been here for so many years,' he says, 'but I look at the countryside, and it is as if I haven't been away.'

Rolling wooded hills, low conical peaks, stark cliffs and stone quarries.

4.20 p.m.
Vineyards.

4.30 p.m.
The train goes through Lovosice. We have left the Sudetenland and are in Bohemia, the historic heart of Czechoslovakia. Lovosice (in German, Lobositz) had an ancient Jewish cemetery dating from the seventeenth century and a synagogue built in 1762; both were destroyed by the Nazis.

4.35 p.m.
The train speeds through Bohusovice. It was here that the trains with deportees for Theresienstadt came from Berlin (as we have done), and from many other German cities, as well as from Prague, and from

where they had to walk to the camp, which is a mile or two to the north. We will come back here, by coach, the day after tomorrow.

The train runs along the River Elbe. 'Many German civilians were found in this river after liberation,' comments Ben, who was liberated at Theresienstadt. He is referring to Germans from the Sudetenland who were driven out of their homes by the Czechs soon after liberation, and some of whom were drowned.

4.40 p.m.

Roudnice. A castle on a hill. This town has a venerable Jewish history, the earliest record of Jewish settlement dating from the documentary record of a pogrom in 1541. It was never a very large Jewish community – 448 people in 1724, and only 166 in 1930 – but the tombstones that have survived, from the Renaissance, baroque and classical periods, are preserved in the Jewish cemetery, which, founded in 1613, is now a historical monument. Among the distinguished Jewish citizens of Roudnice was Albert Kohn, who in 1837 introduced the Czech language into Jewish schools.

I read from the recollections of my friend Arek Hersh, from the Polish town of Sieradz. He was sixteen years old, being deported by train, when the train reached Roudnice. 'After about ten minutes we were ordered to get off the train. I saw that on the platform were several Czechoslovakian policemen, young fellows who came over to talk to us and ask us where we had come from. They saw our starved bodies and the horror of our conditions on the train, and seemed unable to believe that such a thing could be happening. Some of them wept in front of us. We stood and watched them silently. They asked us if we would like some food, and we begged them to give us some. One of the policemen went away to get it.

'When he returned we did not snatch it from him, but just held out our hands. I saw that on the other side of the transport another policeman was giving boys some bread and meat. One of the Ukrainian SS guards also saw this, and he turned his rifle round to get hold of the barrel to hit one of the starving boys over the head. A Czech policeman saw what was happening and drew his revolver. He pointed it at the SS guard and said, "If you touch this child, I will shoot you." I saw the SS guard immediately put his rifle down and walk away. We realised that something we had never seen before was happening: an SS guard had taken orders from someone else.

'Soon after that the Czech policemen rounded up all the SS guards and took them away. It was said later that they had shot them. Our train was slowly taken into Theresienstadt.'

Says Ben: 'When a place was liberated, out came the pictures – Benes, the Czech leader, and Stalin. The Russians were greeted as liberating friends.'

4.57 p.m.

Melnik. A small town in a pastoral landscape. Jews first settled in this town in 1402. It was always a small community. There were eighty-four Jews here in 1930, a settled, hopeful time for Czech Jewry. Twelve years later they were among the approximately 75,000 Czech Jews deported to Theresienstadt. The synagogue survived the war, but was demolished in the late 1960s, during the Communist era.

5 p.m.

We reach the village of Veltrusy. Before the war there were two Jewish families living here in Veltrusy: nine people in all. We run along the River Vltava – in German, the Moldau. This is the river beloved of the composer Smetana, whose beautiful symphonic poem *Ma Vlast*, My Fatherland, contains a tune, 'Vltava', that is hauntingly similar to the Zionist (and later Israeli) anthem, 'Hatikvah', The Hope. The melody of the Jewish anthem was, however, directly inspired – as indeed Smetana might have been – by a Moldavian (Roumanian) folk song, transformed into the anthem by Samuel Cohen, an immigrant to Palestine from Moldavia in 1878.

5.08 p.m.

Kralupy. There were fifty-two Jews living here on the eve of war. The railway line is still running along the Vltava river. A small gorge. Cliffs on one side, hilltops on the other. As the track curves, we look back down the gorge. In the hills above, Reinhard Heydrich – then Acting Protector of Bohemia and Moravia, and a general in the SS – had his villa. It was while on his way by car from the villa to Prague that he was assassinated.

5.30 p.m.

The train comes to a halt on a hillside overlooking Prague, whose many church spires are cradled in the valley. On the western horizon, the Castle.

5.55 p.m.

We draw into Prague Main station. We leave the train, go down into a subterranean hall, change money, and find three taxis to take us to the hotel. South of where we are going is Belgistska Street, where Hugo Gryn and other young survivors of the concentration camps lived after liberation, before being flown from Prague to Britain at the end of 1945 and early in 1946.

Our hotel is a former student hostel at No. 1 Jenstejnska Street. There are plaques on the wall to students who lived here, and were killed in the war. My bedroom looks out over the sharply-pitched roof and ornamental bell-tower of a church.

It is Friday night, and the Sabbath has begun. We walk into the city, along the River Vltava. The service is about to begin in the Altneuschule (the Old-New Synagogue). The building we enter was built in 1338, after a fire had burned down the existing Jewish quarter. A large flag is suspended from the high vaulting. It was presented to the Jewish community nearly three hundred and fifty years ago, by King Ferdinand III, in recognition of the bravery of the Jews during the siege of Prague by the Swedes in 1648. We tease Marie, the Swedish member of our group, every time the guide books tell us, as they frequently do, of seventeenth-century Swedish military activity in the lands through which we travel; the Swedish soldiers, she tells us, in their defence, were only in search of beer.

Some of my women students are distressed that the women's gallery in the Altneuschule is cut off from the main hall by thick buttress-style windows. They leave, and take a horse and carriage ride around the town. Robin and I sit together in the main hall. I explain to him the sequence of the service as it unfolds. The synagogue is packed; many of those praying are Americans, some are tourists exploring as we are the Prague of yesterday, others with jobs in the ever-burgeoning Prague of today.

We dine in the hall near the synagogue, where several hundred kosher meals have been prepared. We sit as a group. At the adjacent tables are other groups. There are so many people dining that we have been put into what is, in normal times, a corridor, and so we cannot really hear the prayers over the wine and bread.

11.30 p.m.

A long day is coming to an end. We walk back in small groups from the synagogue past Franz Kafka's birthplace at the edge of Old Town Square, through Wenceslas Square, dominated at one end by the imposing façade of the Bohemian Museum, completed in 1890, which inspired Czech national sentiment in the Habsburg days, and towards the hotel.

As we get near to the hotel, walking along Resslova Street, Caroline, who is looking down, notices a pattern in the paving stones. There are some blue stones set like a mosaic among the white ones. She stops and makes out a date written in the blue stones: it is 1942. We look at the building nearest to the date. It is a church. There are bullet holes around a small window, a memorial plaque with a sculpted soldier and priest on either side of it, and an inscription. Caroline asks, 'What is this?' It is the church where the assassins of Heydrich were trapped and killed.

Our hotel is five minutes' walk away.

DAY 4

PRAGUE

Ghosts and golems

8 a.m.
I leave the hotel and walk down to the river. It is a bright, sunny morning, and Prague is at peace. It is hard to bring the horrors of the past to mind in such a placid setting. Some ducks float by, and some driftwood. This is where, in the months immediately after liberation, Ben and his fellow-survivors used to row each day, striving to regain their strength, to regain the power of their muscles.

8.45 a.m.
I return to the hotel for breakfast. Several of the group join me.

9.35 a.m.
We leave the hotel on foot and walk towards the centre of Prague. In the very first street running up from the river, Resslova Street, is the church which Caroline and I saw last night, where Heydrich's assassins were trapped and killed. It is the Orthodox Cathedral Church of St Cyril and St Methodius (the inventors of the Cyrillic alphabet about a thousand years ago – though the Czechs use the Latin alphabet). We have to wait a while before the church opens.

In the street opposite, looking across to the church, I speak of Heydrich's assassination. Two of the assassins, Jan Kubis and Josef Gabcik, had been trained in Britain and parachuted into Czechoslovakia on 28 December 1941. Their flight path, shown in the crypt, took them over Le Crotoy at the mouth of the River Somme, Darmstadt and Prague. After the assassination, in May 1942, they were hiding here in the church with two other parachutists, and three local members of the Czech resistance. After some weeks in hiding, they were about to slip away and try to return to Britain when they were betrayed, on

18 June 1942, by a member of the Czech resistance – who had also been trained in Britain – who was in fact working for the Germans.

We enter the crypt. The entrance is on the street below the church. There is an exhibition, provided by the Imperial War Museum in London, as well as a film. The story is tragic; the trapped men barricaded themselves in the crypt and tried to dig their way through the brickwork into the sewers. The hole they dug penetrated six feet into the brickwork, but they could get no further. The Germans pumped water into the crypt. When this failed, they pumped in smoke. Finally they burst in. The men refused to surrender and were killed in the crypt. The hole they were digging is preserved as a memorial; it is a shattering site.

The film starts. It is a dramatic reconstruction, and it is a strange sensation to be standing in the room which is being portrayed in the film. After the silence and the sombre nature of the crypt, however, the noise of guns firing is jarring. Most of us drift out before the end. There is something unreal, but also unnerving, about the reconstruction.

We walk on into Prague, along the river, and come to rest at the Café Mozart, overlooking the water. I tell of the early history of the Jews of Prague. According to ancient tradition, the first synagogue here was founded by the Jewish fugitives from Jerusalem after the destruction of the Second Temple by the Romans. Jews were recorded here 1,000 years ago, when a Jewish merchant, Ibrahim ibn Jacob, wrote: 'Russians and Slavs come here from the royal town with goods, and Muslims, Jews and Turks from the land of the Turks also come here with goods and coins.' The 'royal town' was Kiev. Prague was on a trading crossroads linking the River Dnieper with the Danube and the Rhine.

Permission for the Jews to settle in Prague was granted in the year 995, as a reward (according to a seventeenth-century Jewish chronicler) for having helped the local Christians in their fight against the pagans. A century later, in 1096, during the anti-Jewish violence generated throughout Europe by the zealots of the First Crusade, many Jews were killed here in Prague. Following these killings, the Jews left the city. On their way out, they were robbed of all their possessions. The Czech chronicler Cosmos writes: 'The prince sent his valet along with several warriors to fleece them from head to foot. They left them nothing but a grain of corn, enough to keep them alive only. Oh what a lot of money was taken from the miserable Jews that day, such wealth was not taken even from burned Troy.' That was in 1098.

From then on, expulsion and return became a pattern of Jewish life.

The first records of a Jewish cemetery here date from the thirteenth century. A decree of King Ottakar II, dated 29 March 1254, stated: 'If a Christian devastates in any way their graveyard or enters it by violence, he ought to be sentenced to death, and all his fortune will go to the royal treasury.' My own rabbi and friend, Hugo Gryn, reflected on this in 1990, in a film about the Jews of Prague: 'So the Jews had protection, and King Ottakar might have done well out of it as well.'

After refreshments – in sunshine but also a stiff breeze – we walk through the city, to the statue of Rabbi Judah Loew ben Bezalel in Marianske Square. Erected in 1910, the statue is the work of Ladislav Saloun, the sculptor of the Jan Hus statue in the Old Town Square. In his lifetime Rabbi Loew was known as the Maharal, after the Hebrew acronym for Morenu HaRav Loew – 'Our teacher, Rabbi Loew'. His tomb in the old Jewish cemetery was, and remains, a place of Jewish pilgrimage, where Jews write their wishes on a piece of paper and place it in one of the cracks on the tomb.

Rabbi Loew first came to Prague in 1573. He died here on 22 August 1609, when he was eighty-seven (or, according to another version, ninety-six). He was a biblical scholar of distinction, establishing a Yeshiva – a Talmudic academy – here. He was also a practical administrator, establishing many Jewish charitable societies in Prague, including the Burial Society. As a judge and arbitrator, he believed that the law had to be upheld without bias. He opposed the messianic speculation that was rife among the Jews of Prague in his day that redemption was imminent, and was 'fearful', as Hugo Gryn expressed it, 'that before that redemption would come, Israel's degradation would be greatest'.

It was Rabbi Loew who is said to have made a figure of clay and then breathed life into it, creating one of the 'Golems' of Jewish legend. The word 'golem', which appears only once in the Bible, in Psalm 139, has no clear translation. The Hebrew word may mean 'unformed substance', or possibly 'unmarried woman'.

It was while standing where we are standing now that Hugo Gryn told the story of the Golem. Speculations and coincidences being a feature of Jewish tradition, just as Rabbi Loew claimed descent from King David, so Hugo Gryn's family trace their descent from Rabbi Loew. Speaking of the spring of 1590, a time of persecution for the Jews of Prague, Hugo Gryn tells in the film of how Rabbi Loew went with his son-in-law, who was a Cohen, and with another of his followers, who was a Levy, to the River Vltava. There they found a clay bed, shaped a human figure from some of the clay, walked around the figure reciting cabbalistic formulae, took some mud, and fashioned a human form.

Rabbi Loew then wrote on the forehead of the clay figure the three Hebrew letters אמת (emet = truth). The form came to life, was clothed in a sexton's robe, and introduced as a dumb stranger who would henceforth be part of the rabbi's household. Thereafter the Golem did the rabbi's bidding; once, when he asked the Golem to get him some fish for the festive dinner on the eve of the Jewish New Year, the Golem did so with zeal, filling the whole house with fish. 'Many things the rabbi had that year,' comments Hugo Gryn, 'but not a sweet New Year.'

At a certain point the Golem seemed to be getting out of control. Rabbi Loew went with his two helpers up into the attic where the Golem was sleeping, and erased the letter א, the first of the three letters on its forehead, leaving מת (met = death). The Golem then collapsed on to the floor as a pile of lifeless clay. Loew ordered the room to be sealed, and it has remained sealed to this day. 'When I was a child,' Hugo Gryn relates in the film, standing in a corridor inside the synagogue building, 'I used to pray around here. I would go as high as I could. I sometimes thought I heard some movement – but it couldn't be true – could it?'

This statue in Marianske Square, erected between the wars, shows a naked young woman clinging to Rabbi Loew's side. He appears to be trying to ward her off. As we look at the statue, I read out Sadakat Kadri's comment, in his *Prague* guide book, that the sculptor intended this, in the same way as the Hus statue, to be 'no less solemn a tribute to a man who represented "everything noble which was produced from the ghetto". In fact, the hook-nosed and slovenly figure, grasping his robes with gnarled fingers, looks rather like an extra from that classic of the Nazi screen, *Jew Süss*. (The Nazis themselves didn't think so, and removed the figure during the war.) The lion to the left represents Loew's name in German; the rest of the work portrays one of the legends surrounding his demise. Death shied away from a direct confrontation with the fearsome rabbi, and pounced on the ninety-six-year-old after hiding in a rose being given to him by his granddaughter; Saloun's freestyle adaptation omitted the rose, and transformed the granddaughter into a voluptuous nude flinging herself at his cloak (which may have been what the sex-obsessed fascists objected to most).'

Ironically, there is no historical basis for ascribing the creation of a Golem to Rabbi Loew. The original sixteenth-century version of the story was first associated with Rabbi Elijah of Chelm, whose town we will visit on the journey.

Many Jewish writers have been attracted to the legend of the Golem and written about it. Elie Wiesel is one of the most recent. Another account is by the much-loved Jewish writer, I. L. Peretz – whose birthplace, Zamosc, we will also visit in a few days' time, as well as the site of his home in Warsaw. Peretz described, in one of his short stories, how, when the ghetto of Prague was being attacked, and a mob was about to 'rape the women, roast the children, and slaughter the rest', Rabbi Loew had put aside the holy book which he was studying, 'went into the street, stopped before a heap of clay in front of the teacher's house, and moulded a clay image. He blew into the nose of the Golem – and it began to stir; then he whispered the Name into its ear, and our Golem left the ghetto. The rabbi returned to the House of Prayer, and the Golem fell upon our enemies, threshing them with flails. Men fell on all sides.'

Peretz's story continues: 'Prague was filled with corpses. It lasted, so they say, through Wednesday and Thursday. Now it is already Friday, the clock strikes twelve, and the Golem is still busy at its work. "Rabbi," cries the head of the ghetto, "the Golem is slaughtering all of Prague! There will not be a Gentile left to light the Sabbath fires or take down the Sabbath lamps." Once again the rabbi left his study. He went to the altar and began singing the psalm "A song of the Sabbath".

'The Golem ceased its slaughter. It returned to the ghetto, entered the House of Prayer, and waited before the rabbi. And again the rabbi whispered into its ear. The eyes of the Golem closed, the soul that had dwelt in it flew out, and it was once more a Golem of clay. To this day the Golem lies hidden in the attic of the Prague synagogue, covered with cobwebs that extend from wall to wall. No living creature may look at it, particularly women in pregnancy. No one may touch the cobwebs, for whoever touches them dies. Even the oldest people no longer remember the Golem, though the wise man Zvi, the grandson of the great Rabbi Loew, ponders the problem: may such a Golem be included in a congregation of worshippers or not?

'The Golem, you see, had not been forgotten. It is still here! But the Name by which it could be called to life in a day of need, the Name has disappeared. And the cobwebs grow and grow, and no one may touch them. What are we to do?'

I. L. Peretz died in 1915, twenty-five years before that 'hour of need' was to return in the most savage of all its guises.

We continue our walk until we reach the former Jewish quarter. It is already bustling with visitors. We reach the Pinkas Synagogue, on Siroka Street. It was completed in 1535. Inside, on a memorial wall, are inscribed the names of the 77,297 Jews of Bohemia and Moravia who were murdered by the Nazis between 1939 and 1945.[1] There are 20,000 more names here than on the Vietnam memorial wall in Washington.

Turning from Siroka Street south into Maislova Street, we reach the Maisel Synagogue, which was completed in 1592. The tower and the clock were added in 1765. The clock has Hebrew rather than Arabic numerals, and the hands turn, like the Hebrew alphabet in which the numerals are written, from left to right, that is, anti-clockwise.

We retrace our steps down Maislova Street to No. 18, the Jewish Town Hall, which dates from the 1560s. Here, from across the street, I give a short account of Jewish Prague. The first Jewish community dates from the early ninth century. There are records of a synagogue burning down in 1142. Known as the Jewish Town, the ghetto flourished, and also suffered. There were at least six devastating fires between 1240 and 1754, and several pogroms in which the local population set upon the Jews and slaughtered them. The most destructive was in 1389. There were also three major, if temporary, expulsions: in 1543–5, 1557 and 1745–8. In the early sixteenth century Prague Jewry constituted the second-largest Jewish centre after Constantinople. By 1729 the Jewish population of Prague was 12,796.

The expulsions from Prague were on a massive scale, devastating for such a large community. Hugo Gryn, who was himself born in inter-war Czechoslovakia – in the most easterly province of Sub-Carpathian Ruthenia – told me many years ago that an eighteenth-century print of one of these expulsions, that of 1745, seemed to him to be the archetypical scene of Jewish suffering throughout the ages. He often contrasts that scene, which shows Jews leaving across a bridge carrying their bundles and belongings to a strange and often hostile town, with the actual achievements of Prague Jewry whenever they were allowed to return, and after they were finally accepted, as rabbis, teachers, scholars, writers, philosophers, musicians – every area of culture and civilisation.

Before the First World War, Albert Einstein was a professor at Prague University for two years. Franz Kafka was born in the city in 1883,

---

[1] Among the names is that of Arnost Korbel, the grandfather of Madeleine K. Albright, American Ambassador to the United Nations (1993–7) and subsequently Secretary of State.

and is buried here. Also born in Prague, in 1896, and educated here was the 1947 Nobel prizewinner for physiology and medicine, Gerta Theresa Cori, who died in the United States in 1957. The list of distinguished Jews from Prague could fill many pages.

By the time of Dr Cori's birth, there were about twenty-seven thousand Jews in Prague, and in 1930, according to the precise figures of the census, 35,463. Their story of emancipation, enlightenment and achievement contrasts strangely, uneasily – as I recount it here in the sunlight – with what was to come. Immediately after Hitler came to power in Germany, many thousands of German Jews found refuge here. In 1933 the Eighteenth Zionist Congress was held in Prague, with leading Zionists from all over the world, and from Palestine, calling on the nations of the world to take in Jewish refugees. Of course, those German – and later Austrian – Jews who found refuge here were caught up within a decade in the tragic fate of Czech Jewry.

Many Czech Jews had converted to Christianity during the early twentieth century. Under the race laws introduced by the Nazis after the German occupation in March 1939, the number subjected to those laws was 54,500. Of these, 36,500 were murdered during the war, most of them deported to Theresienstadt and dying there of starvation and disease, or deported from there to Auschwitz. Among those murdered were so many of the leading writers, scholars, teachers, musicians, painters and poets.

Two leading officials of the Prague Jewish community, H. Bonn and Emil Kafka, tried to slow down the pace of the deportations by fudging the paperwork. They were found out and sent to Mauthausen concentration camp, where they were killed.

In 1942 the Nazis brought to Prague the treasures of all the Jewish communities of Bohemia and Moravia (Slovakia had become an independent – though Fascist – country, and Ruthenia had been annexed by Hungary). Their aim was to establish a Museum of the Lost Jewish Race. An enormous number of religious and household objects were collected, also manuscripts, paintings and prints – including many prints of expulsions like the one of which Hugo Gryn had a copy. The Nazi collection survived the war, to become the main part of the State Jewish Museum, established by the Czech Communist government in 1950. It is still a museum now (though closed today, Saturday).

We walk a few yards from the Jewish Town Hall down Cervena Street to the High Synagogue, which was completed in 1568. The Altneuschule faces it, and may well date back 600 years, to the last third of the thirteenth century. It was in this synagogue that we prayed last night. We then walk across Maislova Street and along Hrbitova, along the wall of the Jewish cemetery. Among those buried in the cemetery is Marcus Mordecai ben Samuel Maisel, the builder of both the Jewish Town Hall and the High Synagogue, and one of the principal financiers of the Czech crown. He died in 1601, at the age of seventy-three, an extremely wealthy man, but as he had no children, his money was confiscated and his widow left in penury. The inscription on his tomb describes him as a man whose 'mercy knew no boundary, and who showed charity with his whole body and soul' and it goes on:

> He built a shrine, a temple on a small scale
> In honour and praise of the Lord in a magnificent robe
> Baths and hospitals, he paved the streets with stone
> In our Jewish town
> And he purchased a garden for the cemetery
> Built a house for the gathering of the wise
> And he bestowed his grace
> On tens of thousands of scholars of the Holy Writings.

The earliest tombstone in the cemetery is dated 1439. Burials continued here until 1787. The tombstones are crowded together, many of the burials having been, because of the confined area of the cemetery, one on top of the other, in some places up to twelve layers of graves. There are 12,000 tombstones here. They vary in style from the late gothic to the rococo. Among those buried here is the bibliophile Rabbi David Oppenheim, Chief Rabbi of Prague and, in his last years, of the whole of Bohemia. His collection of more than four thousand books and a further 780 manuscripts was bought (at Hamburg) by the Bodleian Library in Oxford in 1829; one of the major Hebrew collections in the world, if not the major, it is still housed in the Bodleian today. In his lifetime, wanting the books to be available to any reader who wished to consult them, Oppenheimer moved them from the restricted confines of Prague, where a censorship of all Hebrew books was in force, to Hanover (which we went through on the first day of our journey). This move was fortunate, as all Jewish libraries that were in Prague in 1714 were confiscated and burned. Oppenheimer travelled from time to time from Prague to Hanover to check and review his books, which were cared for by librarians specially hired for the purpose. He died in Prague in 1735.

We walk down Vezenska Street, to the Spanish Synagogue, which was built in 1867–8 in the Moorish style (like the Oranienburger Strasse Synagogue in Berlin). Services were held here until the outbreak of war; the building, with its interior arabesque ornamentation from the 1880s, was restored in 1958–9.

We walk on to the Tyn Church, begun in 1370 by German merchants, and into the Old Town Square. It was this square that witnessed, during the seventeenth-century wars of religion, the execution, on 21 June 1621, of twenty-seven leading Protestants, most of them Bohemian nobles. And it was here, against the backdrop of the Jan Hus statue, that some three hundred young Holocaust survivors were photographed on 14 August 1945, before being taken to Prague airport and flown to Britain. Ben Helfgott was among them.

At one side of the Old Town Square, a main centre-piece of tourist curiosity today in Prague is the Astronomical Clock, which has displayed its multiple activities on the hour every hour since 1572. It was under this clock that, twenty-five years ago, I came with a message for a Czech dissident, and waited, as so many messengers did at that time, fearful that I was being followed. The dissident arrived, he was quite an elderly man, I gave him the message, and we parted. To this day I do not know what became of him. Hopefully he lived until the revolution here in 1989, and found in it peace and strength.

We look at the clock. As the hour strikes, various windows open and the Twelve Apostles emerge, while on the outside Death rings a bell and is mocked by Vanity, the Turk and the Jew. This Jew once had a beard and horns, the medieval caricature. After 1945 both beard and horns were taken off, and he is called, not the Jew, but Greed. Comments Sadakat Kadri in his guide book: 'This post-Holocaust decision was understandable; but the paradoxical effect was to whitewash the bloody feature of Central Europe's history that had just reached its culmination.'

We go down to the Charles Bridge, and over the bridge. The sun is shining brightly over the river and Castle Hill. The bridge was begun in 1357 and has survived floods, wars and traffic (it has been traffic-free since 1950). Among the many statues on the bridge, and the one we go to first, is the oldest, a bronze Crucifixion erected here in 1657. It has Hebrew lettering around the crown of thorns. Like so much in Prague's Jewish history, several versions exist as to what it represents. Some say it was paid for by a Jew who had wandered past the crucifix absentmindedly muttering blasphemies. According to another account, it was put up, at the expense of the Jews, after a group of Jews were accused of mocking a crucifix being carried in procession. The inscription on the base of the statue says that in 1696 Judaism itself was judged by the royal court to be blasphemous, and that the fine imposed on the Jews as a result was used in part to put up the words from the synagogue liturgy, 'Kadosh, Kadosh, Kadosh' (Holy, Holy, Holy) in Hebrew letters. This was done, as Hugo Gryn comments in his film, 'above the image of this Jew from Nazareth'.

We walk a little further along the bridge, to the joint statue of two saints, Saint Vincent Ferrer and Saint Procopius, who are said, according to the inscription, to have converted 2,500 Jews to Christianity. Among the figures supporting their statue is a very downcast-looking Jew.

We walk across the bridge and up the roads towards the castle. Three-quarters of the way up, at a somewhat steep point in the climb, we stop for lunch.

Hradcany Castle is a world of its own. Here the President of the Czech Republic, Vaclav Havel, has his offices, as did the first President, Thomas Masaryk, when Czechoslovakia achieved its independence after the First World War; and also the German and the Czech Communist rulers in the bad times. We spend some time at St Vitus's Cathedral, and then walk on to St George's Basilica and Golden Lane, which boasts, among its tiny houses, one in which Franz Kafka lived from December 1916 to March 1917, writing most of the short stories that were published in his lifetime.

It was outside this house that my rabbi, Hugo Gryn, in the film on Jewish Prague, read a passage from Kafka's novel, *The Castle*, which seemed, in portraying the way in which Jews were then perceived, to foreshadow what was soon to come: 'But what are you? You are not from the castle. You are not from the village. You are – nothing at all, or rather, unfortunately, you are something – a stranger, a man who isn't wanted and is in everybody's way, a man who's always causing trouble.'

Hugo Gryn comments, in the film: 'Now, I ask myself, is it reading too much into this, but is this not how the Jews came to be perceived?'

It was Kafka's sister Ottla who had rented the house outside which we stand, and through which a steady stream of tourists is passing. Ottla later married a German non-Jew and was therefore exempted from the first round-ups and deportations in 1941. But after her two sisters and their husbands had been deported to the Lodz ghetto, she felt the need to identify fully with her fellow-Jews, and divorced her husband so as not to be protected any longer by his 'Aryan' status. She was then sent to Theresienstadt – in August 1942. While there, she volunteered with a number of doctors and nurses to go with a group of 1,260 children, recently brought from the Bialystok ghetto, who were sent to Auschwitz, where they, and she, were killed.

Prague is so full of life and tourism, it is hard to think of such terrible episodes while one is walking in the bustling, commercially-vigorous, untroubled streets. It seems – unlike parts of Berlin – so much a city of today. Even the recently vanished Communist night is difficult to imagine. The war years seem very far away indeed.

3.30 p.m.

A free afternoon, the only one in our schedule. On the Charles Bridge I meet Alexandra Finkelstein who, with her husband Eitan, was active fifteen years ago, and more, in the human rights movement in the Soviet Union. Their base was Vilna, then the capital of the Lithuanian Soviet Socialist Republic (the very name sounds antique today). Eitan was also a strong advocate of emigration to Israel. The two of them suffered considerably for their determined stance. An international campaign led to their being allowed to leave; I was at Ben-Gurion Airport on the night they finally arrived, together with their young daughter Miriam, exhausted by their journey. A Soviet official had ordered them off the train at the Soviet-Hungarian border, on a fiercely cold night, telling them that their documents were not in order. Luckily it was a cruel moment of spite rather than a real setback. Alexandra now works for television news here in Prague. Eitan works for Radio Free Europe.

Walking along the riverbank with Alexandra, in the bright light of the late afternoon, reminds me of just how dramatic have been the changes in the last ten years. In a strange way, the fall of Communism puts another historical era between today and the Holocaust, pushing the Holocaust further into the past. When my youngest son is my age, it will be exactly a hundred years since the Wannsee Conference.

6 p.m.

Walk past the Lichtenstein Palace, the Gestapo headquarters during the war.

8 p.m.

Dine with the group in a restaurant near the river. We are on the verge of what may be a gruelling journey: to Theresienstadt tomorrow, and to Auschwitz the day after. It is a nervous time. I have prepared readings for each place that we will visit. Some are hard to listen to, and hard to read. But they will give a picture of what happened during the Holocaust period in the places we visit.

10.30 p.m.

We walk back through Prague, by a winding route, to the hotel, passing the 'Heydrich' church again. It is strange that so near the hotel is so powerful a reminder of the war years, of blood shed in the fight against tyranny.

Midnight

We sit in the hotel hallway for a nightcap. The bar is closed but the concierge sells us, somewhat reluctantly, some beer and some bottled water. There is talk about the Holocaust museum that is being built in London as part of the Imperial War Museum. Jon points out that there are those in the Jewish community in Britain who fear that Jewish identity is becoming 'too much Holocaust centred'. Jewish creativity, and Jewish life, must not be eclipsed.

After midnight

A bright moon is shining over the rooftops and eaves, and on the roof and spire of the church just outside my window. I do not want to close my curtain for fear of losing such a magical sight while I drift off to sleep.

DAY 5

PRAGUE – ZILINA

'Free to walk on a pavement'

5.05 a.m.
Dawn has broken over Prague. I look out from my hotel bedroom as
the sun strikes the rooftops. Now that the city's Jews have emerged
from its double-long night of 1939 to 1945 and 1948 – after the
Communist coup – to 1989, do the ghosts of those years disappear?
Certainly those terrors are gone, except in the minds of the dwindling
number of survivors. Can the visitor – the proliferating numbers of
visitors – recapture, or even sense for a few moments, what the terrors
were: the coming of the Nazi era – so different from Prague's earlier
Habsburg era – in March 1939; the search for visas to a safe haven;
the suicides; the early stillness, silence and isolation; the first incidents;
the first murders; and then, in October 1941, the first deportations?

The survivor, the historian, the teacher and the student, each from
their own perspective can try to invest streets, individual buildings,
wall plaques, with meaning. The historian, the teacher and the student
can retell, through readings and through the written word, the recorded
atmosphere of the time, the detail, the poignant moment, the end of
hope; but even the recorded atmosphere, as set down by eye-witnesses
in letters and diaries, or by survivors in their memoirs, comes close to
defying the most vivid imagination. If one really could 'imagine' what
one reads and studies, would one not go mad?

6.15 a.m.
I leave the hotel and walk through the silent, empty streets, down to
the river, the glory of Prague (or at least one of its glories). It is hard
to know what word to use for what is now called the Holocaust. There
are historians who object to the word, as it relates to destruction by
fire, not to so much wider and vaster a destruction. After the war the

word used was 'extermination', but books which told of the extermination of the Jews – even in their titles – were objected to because of the link with rats. Before 1914, the British government in India exterminated millions of rats in an attempt to halt the ravages of plague. When rats (or cockroaches) invade a house, the person to call in is the exterminator. Others want to use the word 'genocide'. But the American television series based on the novel *Holocaust* by Gerald Green (whose book *The Artists of Terezin* I will read from later today) gave the word its universal application, which will surely always be linked now with the murder of the 6,000,000 Jews.

For Israelis, and for many other Jews, the word 'shoah' – catastrophe – has gained a wide usage. Claude Lanzman's nine-hour film has that title, and it continues to make a strong impact. Steven Spielberg's remarkable effort to record all the survivor testimonies goes under the name of the Shoah Foundation. For Yiddish speakers, the word that had been in use since 1945 is 'churban', the destruction. But Yiddish speakers, like survivors, are a dwindling band.

As well as what to call it, there is the question of numbers. How does one cope with such an enormous death toll? In our mind's eye, when we focus on individuals, we can begin to grasp the scale, but it is so vast that the mind is numbed. I felt that numbness after going through the Holocaust Museum in Washington. Everything was so vivid, and the cumulative effect was overwhelming. At the end I felt quite ill.

The impact of an individual experience does not necessarily require horror to convey the realities that existed in those times. I think of how Anne Frank's diary makes such an enormous impact on generation after generation, yet there is not even a deportation in it, let alone Auschwitz. But it is, of course, in the context of Auschwitz, and of her subsequent deportation, that we read it.

6.55 a.m.

I go into the breakfast room. Yesterday, as we sat in the morning by the banks of the Vltava (Moldau), I read the accounts of various expulsions from Prague throughout the Middle Ages. There were so many echoes, so much resonance, with what was to come, and yet there is no real comparison. The expulsion of those days was usually followed by return. Not so from 1941 to 1945. So few returned; those who did return were a tiny fragment, a remnant, and, for the most part, a broken remnant. 'Yet a remnant of them shall return.' The Psalmist was talking of the Jews expelled from Jerusalem to Babylon.

A far larger percentage returned from that expulsion, to rebuild Jerusalem, than from the Second World War deportations from Prague. And those who did not return from Babylon were able to survive along the Tigris and Euphrates as a diaspora, and even, after 2,000 years and more, to return to the land from which their ancestors were exiled, with their belongings and culture intact, and even enhanced. Those deported to their deaths from this city, as from every city, were the last in the line of a thousand-year-long exile that Hitler decreed was to come to an absolute end, to total destruction. As far as the Jews of Czechoslovakia were concerned, he succeeded. Of the 277,000 Jews who were deported from Czechoslovakia, only 44,000 survived.

Ben points out that even this small percentage of survival is much larger than that of the survival of Lithuanian and Polish Jews.

7.10 a.m.

A Swedish choir group arrives in the breakfast room. They are to sing in a church in an hour's time. Sweden, after long years of expressing no interest, is now basking in the reflected glory of Raoul Wallenberg, whose protective passes saved so many thousands of Hungarian Jews in Budapest. But the Wallenberg story, which is such an impressive example of courage and persistence, has also spawned exaggeration and myth. Although he arrived in the Hungarian capital shortly after the last deportation from Hungary to Auschwitz, he is more and more credited with having saved Jews from deportation to Auschwitz. What he saved them from was savage attacks by Hungarian Fascists, and, in many cases, from deportation to slave labour camps; but not to Auschwitz. The number of those whom he protected soars wildly in different accounts. Nor is much credit, if any, given to two other foreign consular officials, Charles Lutz of Switzerland and Carlos Perlasca of Spain, who also worked to save Jews by issuing them with protective documents, as did the special emissary to Hungary of the International Committee of the Red Cross, Dr Robert Schirmer.

All simplifications and misrepresentations trouble us. So does the way in which a fictional episode in a novel – Leon Uris's magnificent *Exodus*, which inspired tens of thousands of Soviet Jews in their dark hour, and the film version of which starred Paul Newman – is now paraded as fact: that the King of Denmark threatened to wear (or even wore) a yellow star in order to stop it being imposed on the Jews of Denmark. No such threat ever took place. The King, and his people, courageously arranged for most Danish Jews to be smuggled across the water to Sweden on the eve of the planned deportation. But the episode with the yellow star never took place.

Another myth that we discuss is that of the soap; the allegation that the Nazis used the fat from Jewish corpses to make soap. No evidence that such a thing happened has come to light. But the myth goes on. It had powerful origins. Ben tells us (as we finish our breakfast) that, immediately after the war, when he was here in Prague, there was a bar of soap in the museum which was labelled as made from Jewish corpses. 'The Poles used to say, of the Germans, "They will turn you into soap." We laughed. We didn't believe it. How was it possible to make soap out of human beings? In the glass factory in Piotrkow where I used to work, every time a transport of Jews went past during the deportations in October 1942 the Poles would say, "Jada na midlo" (They travel on the way to soap).'

7.25 a.m.

We are about to leave for the former Theresienstadt ghetto, about an hour's drive away. Rachael does not think she can continue with the journey. 'I don't feel I can make it,' she tells me. Her father's parents were both deported to Theresienstadt. They survived the war, but many other relatives on her mother's side did not. We sadly say goodbye to her. She will fly back to Britain in a few days' time. We will make the journey to Theresienstadt, and walk through its streets, without her.

7.40 a.m.

A minibus takes us from the hotel. Our driver, George, drives through the city.

7.45 a.m.

We cross the River Vltava, and drive underneath the hill on which Stalin's thirty-metre-high statue used to stand, dominating the city, visible from the central square. It was blown up many years before the end of Communism. We discuss Stalin and the Jews, and the plan he is believed to have devised, shortly before his death, to deport the Jews of Russia to camps in Siberia. Apparently the camps were all prepared for them. He had become convinced that Jewish doctors were trying to poison him.[1]

---

[1] When I was preparing this diary for publication, the newspapers reported that the plinth of the Stalin statue in Prague had been used to erect an equally large papier-mâché statue of Michael Jackson, the pop star, who was making his first visit to Prague at that time.

7.47 a.m.

We reach the Park Hotel. A plaque on the roadside wall records that this was the site of the deportation of the Jews of Prague to Theresienstadt. We stand for a few moments in the forecourt of the hotel, where, fifty-five years ago, a railway spur joined the main railway line, which ran less than a hundred yards away. The assembly place is now a pedestrian concourse and car park. The hotel, facing the buildings of nineteenth-century Prague, is in ultra-modern style. From this innocuous forecourt, beginning on 16 October 1941, 5,000 Jews were deported within the following three weeks to the Lodz ghetto. Most of them were murdered in the nearby Chelmno death camp a few months later.

The saga of the deportations from Prague did not end there. On 24 November 1941 the first train left here for Theresienstadt, taking Jews to the ghetto that had just been established there. Almost all of those who did not die of starvation in Theresienstadt were deported to Auschwitz and other camps, including Treblinka, and killed. From the outset, however, Theresienstadt was publicised by the Germans as a place where elderly Jews could live out their remaining years in comfort. In fact, Jews of all ages, including many thousands of children, lived in appalling conditions, suffered and died there.

As we drive away from the Park Hotel we go under the railway bridge which, today as then, took the railway around Prague.

8 a.m.

We reach the spot where Reinhard Heydrich was mortally wounded in May 1942. As the traffic roars by (for it is a busy main road now), and wanting to remember, not a tyrant, but one of the tens of thousands of people whose life in Prague was broken off – for ever – by Nazism, I read Saul Friedländer's memories of his childhood here before the war. Today he is a professor of history in Tel Aviv and Los Angeles:

'I started school in the month of September 1938, only a short time before the Munich Conference. People nowadays forget that during those few days, on the eve of the final abandonment of Czechoslovakia, war seemed imminent. In Prague, alerts followed one after the other; I remember sirens, shelters, and above all the gas masks that everyone carried about like a talisman, in a cylindrical box slung across the shoulder. I thus went about with my schoolbag on my back and my gas mask at my side. I have no idea whether these gas masks would have been effective in case of an attack, but I do remember that in our family they almost brought about the death of one of us: my Aunt Martha. Like everyone else, she tried her mask on, was unable to see how to open the breathing tube, couldn't get out of the rubber envelope, and barely escaped suffocation.'

Saul, whom I first met at a scholars' conference in London in the mid-1960s, learned that he was Jewish during a weekly class in religion. His memoir continues: 'I imagine that classes such as this were held in all Czech schools at the time. That might seem to involve no problem, but for the four or five of us who were Jews it was a repeated humiliation: once a week, when the catechism teacher came into the main study hall, we were obliged to leave the room, beneath the gaze of classmates that today I suppose was either mocking or amused, but one that I distinctly remember as being attentive.

'We went to join a rabbi at the end of the hall, in a sort of little nook that was more like a storeroom than an office, to hear Bible stories. The rabbi quite naturally began with the creation of the world, and after that we made rapid progress: Adam and Eve, Cain and Abel, the hapless builders of the Tower of Babel and those who happily escaped the Flood. I couldn't say whether we listened to these stories eagerly or were bored; all I remember is having heard them. We took up the story of Abraham and the sacrifice of Isaac: "Take now thy son, thine only son Isaac, whom thou lovest, and get thee into the land of Moriah; and offer him there for a burnt offering upon one of the mountains which I will tell thee of ..."

'The rabbi told us the story but didn't explain anything; Vlasta could shed only very dim light on the subject; as for my parents, biblical questions seemed to occupy them very little at this moment, when the need to flee the country was becoming increasingly obvious. I imagined Abraham journeying into the desert, bowed down by the weight of years, with his son Isaac at his side, and behind them the donkey loaded down with the wood for the burnt offering and the sword of the sacrifice. On the third day they saw Mount Moriah looming up before them.

'Then for a long time I forgot the question raised by the awesome text, only to see it arise again later, and with what forcefulness! Why is this one of the first stories of our people? Why was it preserved in the Bible? I have read all sorts of interpretations and explanations of it, but this text does not leave me in peace: "Take now thy son, thine only son ... and offer him for a burnt offering."

'Abraham's obedience explains our entire history. Today most Jews no longer obey God's injunctions, yet they still obey the call of some

1. The courtyard of Hitler's Chancellery in Berlin. Today it is a children's playground (see page 27).

2. Goering's Air Ministry in the Wilhelmstrasse, built in 1936, and surviving until today (page 27).

3. Books being sold today in Berlin, at the place of the book burning on 1 May 1933. The railings are those of the Humboldt University. The building across the Unter den Linden is the Opera House (page 29).

4. Memorial stones to German Jews murdered in the Holocaust, Heerstrasse Jewish Cemetery, Berlin (page 42).

5. Wannsee: the entrance to the villa at which the 'final solution' was discussed in January 1942 (page 43).

6. Theresienstadt: the railway spur used to bring Jews into the camp, and also to deport them to Auschwitz and elsewhere in the East. The street along which it ran was known as Bahnhofstrasse (Station Street). The railway line ran in front of the Hamburg Barracks – to the right (page 95).

7. Skalite: the single-track railway line leading from Zilina to Auschwitz, along which Jews from Theresienstadt, as well as Slovak, Hungarian, Italian, Greek and Yugoslav Jews were deported (pages 123–33).

8. The author reading to the group by the railway line at Birkenau. Just beyond the track are the entrance gate and ruins of Crematorium III (pages 149–52).

9. (above) Birkenau: former
Gestapo headquarters,
subsequently a convent (page 159).

10. (right) Cracow: Oskar
Schindler's factory in Lipowa
Street (pages 191–2).

11. Cracow: a remnant of the ghetto wall, which had been designed in the shape of
Jewish tombstones. The former ghetto is behind the wall (page 194).

12. Lancut: the house of the Polish-Jewish patriot, Filip Sanbra-Kahane, built just before the First World War, now a restaurant and hotel (pages 202–4).

13. Lancut: the exterior of the synagogue, built in 1761 (pages 204–5).

14. Lancut: restored decorations in the interior of the synagogue.

15. Lancut: at the site of the Ark in the synagogue, Paul says afternoon prayers.

16. Belzec: the memorial set up after the war near the site of the gas chamber (pages 209–18).

17. Belzec: a path inside the camp, leading to the pits where the bodies of the victims were dumped, and later disinterred and their ashes scattered.

mysterious destiny. Why this fidelity? In the name of what?'

I read one more paragraph from Saul Friedländer's account. 'On 12 March 1939,' he writes, 'it had become blindingly clear, even to us, that Hitler would occupy Czecho-Slovakia (the hyphen marked the change that had taken place in six months) at any moment. My parents decided to flee across the Hungarian border by car. All I remember of the first part of the journey is how uncomfortable I was on a back seat piled full of suitcases that left very little room.'

Saul Friedländer's parents eventually reached France. From there, they sought safety in neutral Switzerland, but were turned back from the border by the Swiss police. 'That is why it is so important to mention the bystanders and the collaborators,' says Ben. Once back in France, they were deported to Auschwitz and killed. Saul survived, placed by his parents with Catholic nuns. Prague, and the world of his childhood, became a graveyard for so many of those whom he had known and loved and played with.

8.15 a.m.
We enter our minibus and drive away, out of Prague, along the motorway leading north.

8.30 a.m.
Veltrusy. We look down into the valley of the River Vltava (Moldau in German) and across the valley to the River Elbe. An incredible yellow pancake of pollution stretches to the horizon. Apparently, according to European experts on these matters, this is one of the most polluted valleys in Europe. The beautiful conical hills of the Sudetenland, which we saw two days ago from the train, peek out above the yellow haze.

8.53 a.m.
Doksany.

9.02 a.m.
We reach Bohusovice, and leave the minibus in Masaryk Street. At last the democratic Czechoslovakia of the inter-war years is being remembered in freedom instead of fear. Throughout the Communist years, Thomas Masaryk, the founder of modern Czechoslovakia, and its first President, was a non-person.

We walk to Bohusovice station. This is where we came through, two evenings ago, on our train journey from Berlin to Prague; it is the place to which tens of thousands of Jewish deportees were brought by train between 1941 and 1945. Those who arrived before the summer of 1943 were forced to leave the trains and walk the remaining two miles to Theresienstadt. Ben reflects on the piece of luggage that each person had been allowed to bring at the time of the first deportation from his or her home town, when taking a piece of luggage was still allowed. What a burden that piece of luggage became, he comments, as the walk from the station began. 'You just want to be rid of it. You are being whipped. You are being shouted at. Your piece of luggage is bearing you down. You think, "What the hell do I do with it?" So you let it drop. You abandon the last of your possessions.'

Paul is indignant that the local inhabitants must have seen it all. Ben says: 'They looked on helplessly. There was nothing they could do. If they had done anything, they would have been killed.'

As deportees were brought in to Theresienstadt, so some of those who had arrived earlier were taken out. On 9 January 1942 the first of a number of trains left Bohusovice, taking deportees away from the ghetto. They were sent from here to Riga, having been brought back on foot, or in trucks, from Theresienstadt to the railway station here. Most of them were taken by rail to Riga and from there to the nearby Rumbuli forest, where they were shot.

Starting on 26 October 1942, the first trains left Bohusovice for Auschwitz. This small wayside station, of no particular significance in the Central European rail system, neither a junction nor a sizeable town, had taken on a sinister importance. For seven months it was the starting point of the rail journey from Theresienstadt to Auschwitz for tens of thousands of deportees. Others were put on trains here and sent to destinations even further east, some to the village of Maly Trostenets, a camp just outside Minsk, where they too were murdered – tens of thousands of them. It was not until 1 June 1943 that a railway spur was built, by Jews from the ghetto under SS supervision, linking Bohusovice station with Theresienstadt itself (work on the spur had begun the previous August).

As the trains of today rush through this unimpressive little station, on the main line linking Berlin with Prague, Budapest and Bucharest, and with connections in Prague for Warsaw, Moscow and Kiev, their modern passengers can have no inkling of the terrifying scenes and torments that were enacted daily at this place fifty-five years ago. And we, gathered here under the shadow of a large, gabled railway shed, looking along the railway embankment to the signal box, and at two goods wagons that have been shunted on to a grassy siding, feel collectively savaged by the burden of knowledge. We are impotent to do more than try to envisage the multitude of human beings whose lives were to be destroyed within months of reaching this place, or within days of leaving it.

9.12 a.m.

We leave Bohusovice, and return to our minibus to drive slowly towards Theresienstadt, thinking of those who were being driven so relentlessly along the same route in the year and a half before the rail spur was built.

According to one of the reference books, the journey from Bohusovice to Theresienstadt was just over a kilometre. 'It's a long kilometre,' comments Ben. It is in fact almost three kilometres.

9.20 a.m.

We reach Theresienstadt. It is so normal a town that we drive through it before we realise we have gone past it, and crossed the River Ohre (in German, the Eger). We stop, consult the map, and turn round. Theresienstadt today, as it was during the war, is on the main Dresden–Prague road, which runs through a corner of the town. We drive back to it. The red-brick buildings of the ghetto were the red-brick buildings of the eighteenth century, and are the red-brick buildings of today.

9.25 a.m.

We get off the bus by the former Stadtpark (Town Park) and I give a short account of the history of the town. The future ghetto was once a garrison town, built at the end of the eighteenth century, inside strong fortifications, with high walls and imposing bastions. It was intended by the Habsburg monarchy as protection against Prussian attack. In the event it was never attacked, and had become, by the late nineteenth century, a provincial garrison town of no great military significance. Across the River Ohre, one of its fortifications, known as the Small Fort, was used as a military prison.

9.30 a.m.

I give a brief account of the chronology of the ghetto. I read from the order signed by Heydrich on 2 October 1941: 'The Jews from Bohemia and Moravia will be concentrated for evacuation ... in one transit camp. For this purpose Theresienstadt has been completely evacuated by all units of the army ... The Czechs have been advised to move somewhere else ... 50,000 to 60,000 Jews can easily be housed in Theresienstadt ... From there the Jews will be taken to the East.' The formal decision to establish a ghetto here was taken in Prague eight days later, on 10 October 1941, at a meeting attended by Heydrich and Adolf Eichmann, a lieutenant-colonel in the SS, and the head of the subsection (IV-B-4) of the Reich Security Main Office (RSHA) that was responsible for Jewish affairs. Following this meeting, the first 342 Jewish deportees, all men, were brought here to Theresienstadt from Prague on 24 November 1941. They were at once put to work making the town ready for an enormous influx of deportees. On 4 December 1941 a second train brought 1,000 men, who were to form the basis of the Jewish self-government envisaged by Heydrich and Eichmann: self-government behind tightly guarded walls and with the absolute minimum of rations and medication. To make room for some 30,000 to 40,000 Jews, the local Czech population was cleared out (today, it is again a small Czech town).

At the instigation of the Germans, a Jewish Elder (Judenältester) was appointed. He was Jakub Edelstein. He made particular efforts to try to improve the living conditions for the teenagers and children. In November 1943 he was deported to Auschwitz, where he was later shot, together with his wife and son. Some months before Edelstein's deportation, he had been succeeded as Elder by Dr Paul Eppstein, who was also later taken to the Small Fort across the River Ohre from Theresienstadt, and shot. Eppstein had been a young official in Berlin in 1933, working for the Representation of German Jewry, under Leo Baeck, a fellow-prisoner here in Theresienstadt.

Various names were used by the Nazis for the ghetto here. At an early stage it was known both as Theresienbad (Spa Terezin) and Reichsaltersheim (State Old People's Home). For most of its existence it was called, equally enticingly, to make it seem both a plausible and acceptable destination, the Jüdische Selbstverwaltung (Jewish Self-Administration). Statements that it was also called the Paradiesghetto (Paradise ghetto) by the Germans are apparently a legend.

The first commandant, until mid-1943, was SS-Obersturmführer Dr Siegfried Seidl. Later he served in Belsen. After the war he was sentenced to death in Vienna, and executed.

Hunger in the ghetto was such that, in the month of September 1942, almost four thousand people died, especially the very old. It was to relieve themselves of the 'burden' that was caused by the death of so many old people inside the ghetto that, between 19 September and

22 October 1942, the Germans deported more than forty-four thousand mostly elderly inmates to the East, in eleven trains. Each train left Bohusovice station with as many as two thousand people locked on board. Of these 44,000 deportees, only three are known to have survived.

On 24 August 1943, a black day well remembered by those who were incarcerated here then, and who survived the war, there arrived in the ghetto 1,260 children who had been brought here from the Bialystok ghetto. They were the few child survivors of the destruction of that ghetto. They were kept in strict isolation, and then sent out, with fifty-three volunteer doctors, nurses and attendants from Theresienstadt. As they left, on 5 October 1943, the Germans said that they were going to be exchanged for German prisoners-of-war in Allied hands. The exchange would take place in neutral Switzerland (some said, in Palestine). Instead, they were taken to Auschwitz and murdered.

The precise German records give the number of those who were brought into Theresienstadt between 1941 and 1945 as 139,654. The number of deportees who died while in the ghetto was 33,430. The number of Jews who were deported to their deaths from here, starting with the Riga deportation in January 1942, and including many deportations to Maly Trostenets near Minsk, and to Auschwitz, was 86,934.

It is a grim set of statistics.

9.25 a.m.
We begin our walk. My principal guide book is Ludmila Chladkova's *The Terezin Ghetto*, published here in 1991, with a detailed map which I had photocopied in London, and now hand out to everyone in the group. As Terezin is still today a garrison town, now serving the army of the Czech Republic, many of the buildings of the former ghetto are still used by the army as barracks and stores. While it is possible to walk anywhere, most of the barracks that we shall be looking at cannot be entered by the public.

The first building we look at (No. 1 on the map) was 17 Haupt Strasse (High Street). It was also – according to the notation introduced throughout the ghetto in July 1942 – building L 417. It is the former children's house. Before the war it was a school. Some of the downstairs rooms were Home One, for teenage boys. Children secretly attended school in the attic of this building, and gave theatrical performances in its gymnasium. On 28 November 1942 they gave the Theresienstadt 'premiere' of Smetana's *The Bartered Bride* here.

The gymnasium has been converted into a lecture hall. Elsewhere in the building, a museum of the ghetto has been established. It includes many examples of the drawings that these children made, which were hidden in the building, and discovered after the war. In almost every case, these drawings are the only evidence of the existence and activities of these children in Theresienstadt.

The boys who lived in Home One in this building, who were from ten to fifteen years old, lived forty boys to a room, in three-layer bunk beds. Each room was headed by a *madrich* (the Hebrew for a leader), someone in his twenties. 'Each of these outstanding men,' John Freund has recalled, 'ideologically inspired the boys. Several of them – ranging from Czech assimilationists to Zionists to Communists, survived and are still alive. Walter Eisinger did not survive.' It was he who, downstairs, in Room One, encouraged the boys to set up, in secret, their own system of self-government, which they called the Republic of Shkid – from the Russian, **Shkola imeni Dostoyevskovo**, the school in the name of Dostoyevsky; a school for orphans in post-revolutionary St Petersburg. The idea of a children's parliament, and of children's responsibility for each other's well-being, had its earliest Jewish origin with the Polish-Jewish educator, Janusz Korczak, who was deported with his orphans from Warsaw to Treblinka in the summer of 1942. Eisinger was inspired by a Soviet experiment in youth self-government. Shkid was kept a secret. To strangers who would ask what the word stood for the boys would say, in Czech, **Skola 1. Domov** – *School, Home No.1).*

The boys also secretly published a magazine, *Vedem* (In the Lead). The editor was Petr Ginz, born in 1928, and among those boys – the vast majority – who were deported to Auschwitz and killed. One of the few survivors of Home One, Kurt Kotouc, later recalled Ginz: 'I can still see him, sitting cross-legged on his lower bunk, surrounded by pens, pencils, engravers, brushes and paints, and sheets of paper of all sizes, along with what was left of a parcel from his parents. Well, here you are, Petr. *Vedem* is coming out again. But it took us a long time, didn't it? Petr is smiling. "Mey-fah-zu," he says. He used to claim that this was an expression in the language of the proverbially apathetic Manchu people, which means, "There's nothing to be done about it." I still don't know if this is true, or whether Petr just made it up. I never had the chance to ask him. "Well, get on with it," he'd say. "Go round to all the boys so we get it out on time"...'

I read from *Vedem* a poem by a twelve-year-old Czech boy, Zdenek Weinberger, who was deported to Theresienstadt on 24 April 1942:

Broken people,
Walking along the street.
The children are quite pale.
They have packs on their backs.
The transport is leaving for Poland.

Old ones go,
And young ones go.
Healthy ones go,
And sick ones go,
Not knowing if they will survive.
Transport 'A' went,
And more went too.
Thousands died
And nothing helped.
The German weasel
Wants more and more blood.

Zdenek Weinberger was sent from Theresienstadt to Auschwitz on 6 September 1943. He was thirteen years old. He did not survive.

Above the doorway of this pleasant, late-nineteenth-century building, has recently been embossed the Hebrew word 'Yizkor' (Remember).

We walk around the corner to 17 Rathaus Gasse (Town Hall Street), No. 2 on the map. In ghetto notation it was building Q 619. On the lintel above the building is a monumental inscription, giving (in Latin numerals) the year of its construction – 1839. In the days when Theresienstadt was an Austro-Hungarian, and later a Czech, town, this building was the Town Hall. In the ghetto years it was used for concerts and theatrical performances. During the time of the ghetto, the building also housed a post office, a bank (where the specially printed ghetto money could be deposited, and drawn), and a ghetto court. Some of the ghetto dwellers were given permission to live in the attic, the so-called 'garrets' of the ghetto.

Today, the building is once again the Municipal Office, as it was before the war. Next to it is 17 Rathaus Gasse, No. 11 on the map. Today it is the Post Office. It was an infant school in the ghetto. The children returned to their mothers in the evening. There were also a kitchen and a bakery here, which supplied food to the young people's homes. Some theatrical performances were also held here.

Facing us is Marktplatz (Market Square), No. 5 on the map. From May 1943 it was covered with a circus tent divided into three parts, and used for slave labour. In one section, the inmates of the ghetto assembled wooden crates. In another they packed equipment, which had been made nearby, designed to protect motor engines from freezing, an essential component of army vehicles on the Eastern Front. In all, 1,000 prisoners worked here. The tented area was surrounded by a high fence, and closed to anyone who did not work there.

In the early months of 1944, when for the purpose of the Red Cross visit and propaganda film, the ghetto was transformed (the 'Improvement Action' as it was called), the tents were taken down and the square turned into a park, with a music pavilion in front of the café at 18 Neue Gasse (New Street). Today the lawn is manicured, and the central area bordered with red flowers. In case the Red Cross should also have asked to visit the place to which the Jews of Theresienstadt were being deported, a special 'Family Camp' (*Familienlager*) was created in the barracks at Birkenau, where men, women and children from Theresienstadt were kept together, classes held, and a semblance of normality maintained (the area was within sight and smell of the crematoria). After the Red Cross visit to Theresienstadt, those in the Family Camp at Birkenau were sent to the gas chambers.

The block of buildings facing the corner of the square, Block F III in ghetto notation (No. 12 on the map), contained homes for children and apprentices. Some theatrical and cultural performances were held here, and there was also a library for young people (in L 216). Next to this building, on the Lange Strasse (Long Street) side of the square, is the block – No. 10 on the map, known in the ghetto as L 315 – which housed more than a hundred Jews who served in the Ghetto Guard (Ghettowache). Their task was to maintain order inside the ghetto. Only able-bodied young men were members of this guard, but the second camp commandant, SS-Obersturmführer Anton Burger – who disappeared after the war, having later served in Greece – fearing that the guard might serve as a focus of revolt, although they were unarmed, sent most of them to their deaths on the first 'transport' to the East, the deportation to Riga. The guard was then dissolved. It was later reconstituted with men over forty-five.

Inside this building was a hall in which theatrical performances were given in the ghetto years. Today it is the town's Culture House.

The next building along Lang Strasse – L 311 (No. 9 on the map) still facing the square – was an army barracks in the Austro-Hungarian and Czech periods. In the ghetto, elderly Jews were housed here, in conditions of great privation. There was a small hospital with wards for those with heart disease. Cultural programmes and lectures also took place here. In the attic, its services conducted in the greatest secrecy, was a small synagogue.

Reaching the far corner of the square, we turn into Neue Gasse. The corner building, No. 8 on the map, was the headquarters, from August 1942, of the SS Camp Command (SS-Lagerkommandatur). In the cellars were specially built 'bunkers' where the Gestapo imprisoned and tortured those whom they wanted to punish or interrogate, often before they were sent to the Small Fort across the River Ohre and executed there. At the level of the pavement, we can see the tops of the windows of the bunkers.

We walk along the side of the square to No. 18 Neue Gasse (No. 7 on the map). This was Q 418 in the ghetto. In December 1942 a café was opened here. A hundred people could sit in it at any one time. Each admission ticket was valid for two hours. Ersatz coffee and tea were served – made without a single grain of coffee or tea leaf. An orchestra performed here for the clientele, and there were also cabaret shows.

The juxtaposition of the café and the prison was the subject of a poem by Josef Taussig, a Czech–Jewish journalist who survived Theresienstadt and Auschwitz, but who died in Flossenburg just before the war ended. He called his poem 'Would you care for dessert?':

> A clean tablecloth, tasteful tables –
> Gentlemen in dark suits –
> Girls painted scarlet –
> Witty repartee –
> Swinging jazz –
> Coffee served in the salon –
> You can even get whipped cream –
> Or just get whipped – but that's next door.

Next door to the café, on one side, the prison; on the other side – the corner building, 15 Haupt Strasse (No. 6 on the map) – one of three ghetto shops. This one sold used clothing and underwear. Most of the items sold here, as in the other two shops, had come from the luggage of the deportees which was confiscated when they arrived (the better items would go to the SS, or were shipped off to Germany).

We move back along the Haupt Strasse side of the square. No. 10 (No. 4 on the map), also known as L 410, was the home for girls between the ages of eight and sixteen. Girls who were too young to go out to the various labour tasks imposed on inmates of the ghetto were taught here. Older girls, who went out to work, were given lessons

when they returned from work. Drawing lessons were given by Friedl
Dicker-Brandejsova, and there was concert practice in the cellar.

We cross in front of the eighteenth-century church, which was
closed during the war. Next to it is No. 14 Haupt Strasse (No. 3 on
the map, L 414), a large, imposing, three-storey building. Here, until
August 1942, was the SS Camp Command (SS-Lagerkommandatur).
When the SS Camp Command moved to the far corner of the square,
most of this building was given over to house young people, mostly
those deported from Germany. There was also a home for Czech girls
here, where they published another clandestine magazine, *Bonako*.

We walk across the Stadtpark (Town Park) – No. 20 on the map.
During the Improvement Action which began in 1944 a playground
for children was built here, and also an attractive wooden pavilion.
Beyond the park, one of the few buildings destroyed at the end of the
war was Block G VI (No. 19 on the map). Here mothers with children
under three years old were housed. The block contained a hall for
theatrical performances and concerts, a library and a reading room.

We continue along the park side of Rathaus Gasse to the corner of
Wall Strasse (Wall Street) which is just inside the bastion. The barracks
on the corner, the Vrchlabi Barracks, Block E VI in the ghetto (No. 21
on the map), had been a military hospital before the war. It was used
in the ghetto period as the central hospital, and also for public baths
and showers. Food for the hospital patients was prepared in the kitchen
in this building.

We look up at a building which is part of the bastion, Block E VI in
the ghetto, the Kavalir – Cavalry – Barrack before the war (No. 22 on
the map). Those deportees who were old, or insane, were brought here
and left to die. John Freund later recalled: 'Some boys would go to see
the most horrible sights of insane people who were in the Kavalir
Barrack.'

Walking between two bastions, we cross the moat (No. 36 on the
map). Here, during the so-called 'Improvement Action', impressive
gardening work was done, and allotments created; they were seen,
worked by Jews stripped to the waist in the hot sun, by the Red Cross
delegation of four – two Danes and two Swiss – whom the Nazis invited
to visit the ghetto on 23 June 1944. The 'Improvement Action' ensured
that everything looked just right; a band of inmate musicians played
on the specially erected bandstand in the square (where the labour
camp had been until a short time before). Children, dressed in clean
clothes, rode on a merry-go-round. The Ghetto Elder, Dr Paul Eppstein,
was given a car and a chauffeur. The Red Cross visitors saw the

chauffeur open the door, bow, and let him in. A day before, this same chauffeur, in fact an SS man, had beaten Eppstein without compunction; and was to do so again in the days to come, many times.

The Red Cross visitors were not shown the barracks crowded with the old, the sick and the dying. Nor were they shown the storerooms filled with the belongings taken from the Jews on their arrival.

The allotments we are looking at, and which the Red Cross visitors did see, also appear in a film that was about to be made, using the same deception, entitled: 'Der Führer schenkt den Juden eine Stadt' (known today in film circles as 'The Führer Gives the Jews a Town').

I speak about the film. The last commandant of Theresienstadt, SS-Obersturmführer Karl Rahm, who had been put in charge of the 'Improvement Action', was told by his masters in Berlin to commission a film to be made that would impress anyone who saw it with the merits and virtues of the ghetto. The making of the film was begun on 16 August 1944 and completed on September 11.

The film does not appear to have been shown during the war. After the war no print of it could be found. A copy was later discovered at the Staatsarchiv in Koblenz. A well-known German-Jewish actor, Kurt Gerron, who in his time had directed films at the UFA studio in Berlin, was promised his freedom if he made the film. His reward was not the promised freedom, but death. In the film, a well-known Czech-Jewish sportsman, a world-class diving champion, was shown diving into a swimming pool. It was not explained that, except when the film was being made, this pool was the preserve of the SS. Two of the Jewish youth teams who regularly played football (soccer) at Theresienstadt, as members of the ghetto's Jewish Football League, were shown in action in the film. The referee wore the yellow star.

I read Gerald Green's description of the film-making, once Kurt Gerron had submitted a script to the commandant: 'The connecting tissue, the leitmotif of his effort was water – the rivers, bathtubs, faucets, showers, irrigation ditches,' Green writes. 'Evidently Berlin liked this aqueous view of Terezin, and approval was given to start filming. A team of documentary cameramen was sent from Berlin, and under watchful SS guards the project got under way.[2]

'A prisoner who worked as Gerron's assistant later wrote that only a handful of people were willing to appear in the film. The majority of the fifty thousand Jews[3] would drift away when cameras appeared,

---

[2] The film crew was actually a Czech one – Aktualita Praha.
[3] In fact, somewhat fewer by that time.

find excuses to avoid the enactments of camp life. There was an additional problem. Berlin had decreed that only prisoners who *looked* like Jews could appear. They were to be hook-nosed, dark-haired, dark-eyed, and preferably furtive in manner. This presented a problem for the assistant director. Terezin was filled with blue-eyed, blond-haired Jews, and they were automatically excluded. A sequence showing a track meet presented a crisis – the woman high-jump champion of Czechoslovakia, a Jew, was forbidden to participate. She had blonde hair.

'The "bank" was filmed. So was the post office, where prisoners received fake packages. On the riverbank, a swimming meet was held. The national high-diving champion performed. Just out of range were boats filled with armed SS men in the event that any of the contestants decided to swim to freedom.

'For days the cameras whirred, the lights were focused on the stunned prisoners. A meeting of the Jewish Council was moved from a dingy room in the Magdeburg Barracks to a bright room in the gymnasium. Herr Eppstein addressed his colleagues, but no sound was recorded. His speech was dubbed in Berlin. To this day no one knows what the tormented man was forced to say. Two months later, Dr Eppstein, a brave man who faced up to the SS with courage and humour, was shot dead at Rahm's orders. Rahm had long wanted to be rid of him. The circumstances of his death were as follows: at Rahm's order, relayed by an underling, Eppstein went to a location normally off limits to get some sacks. Rahm saw him there, accused him of attempting escape, and had him hustled off to the Kleine Festung – the Small Fort – where he was executed. (The dog had a bite.)

'Gerron's film grew with a life of its own. Firemen in new uniforms put out a fire. One day food rations were tripled for the filming. In the gym, *The Tales of Hoffmann* was performed. An especially touching scene was filmed at the VIP barracks. Like misty ghosts from a Europe long dead, Rabbi Baeck, Field Marshal von Sommer, the Mayor of Lyons, M. Meyer, and several Czech ministers participated in a pleasant garden party, chatting, sipping coffee.

'When a train bearing Jewish children from Holland arrived, Rahm himself was there to welcome them, lifting the youngsters from the wagons. It was dutifully recorded. Then, abruptly, the filming ended. The technicians were ordered back to Berlin. Gerron was discharged. Band concerts were terminated; dancing was forbidden. The camp slipped back into its cruel, starved routine. The old and the ill died and were cremated. The same children whom Rahm took from the train were sent to Auschwitz.

'As for the film, it was never shown, and was apparently never even edited. Several still photographs made from it do survive, and must have been distributed at one time. One shows a meeting of the man appointed by the Germans as *Judenältester* (Elder of the Jews), Dr Eppstein, who stands at a long table addressing his colleagues. His face is strained, as if the horrid fake in which he is forced to take part weighs heavily on his mind. His mouth is drawn, his eyes are frowning, and a perplexed vertical crease separates his eyebrows. Dr Murmelstein, his aide and successor, squints up at him, he too surfeited with disbelief. On Eppstein's left breast pocket is a cloth Jewish star. The Nazis left a morsel of truth in the film.'

We walk back towards the town, and turn down Park Strasse (Park Street). The first building on our right (No. 24 on the map) was a military riding school in the eighteenth century. It is now dilapidated. In the ghetto it was used as a joiners' workshop. Turning left along Badhaus Gasse (Bathhouse Street) we come to Block D VI (No. 23 on the map), a pre-war brewery, which was used as a disinfection centre, laundry, and shower room. Part of it was also turned into living accommodation. Above the small extension is inscribed the year 1941.

11.05 a.m.

Reaching Wall Strasse again, we turn right, to the far north-east corner of the camp. Here is one of the largest buildings in Theresienstadt, the three-storey Magdeburg Barracks, Block B V in ghetto usage (and No. 25 on the map). Here the Jewish Council of Elders, and the man appointed by the Germans as *Judenältester*, had their offices. Members of the Council, and other employees of the Council, had small rooms here in which to sleep. Leo Baeck, one of the leading figures of inter-war German-Jewish spiritual life, was also given a room for himself. But there was simply not enough room for the hundreds of other distinguished rabbis, cantors, writers, artists, teachers, surgeons, former senior officers in the Austro-Hungarian and Czech armies (such as Field Marshal Friedländer) to have a room to themselves.

The work of the Council of Elders here in the Magdeburg Barracks covered every branch of activity in the ghetto. The secretariat maintained the statistical records. An economics department was in charge of labour details, nutrition, laundry, and the allocation of space. A financial department was responsible for the book-keeping side. A technical department supervised water and power supplies, construction, maintenance, and the fire brigade. There was also a health and social welfare department, in charge of the health centres, the youth homes, old people's homes, and burials. All this work was done under a cloud of constant hunger and repeated deportations.

Among the things which were strictly forbidden in the ghetto until June 1942 was any contact between men and women, the sending or receiving of letters, the possession of cigarettes or cigarette lighters, the use of light, the possession of musical instruments, and walking on pavements. Jews had to walk in the gutter or in the road. Cameras were never allowed in Theresienstadt.

At the Magdeburg Barracks was a hall in which theatrical performances were held. The children's opera *Brundibar* was performed in the auditorium here – more than fifty times. It was written a year before the war by a Jewish composer, Hans Krasa, who was also imprisoned at Theresienstadt, and who died in Auschwitz. The first performance of *Brundibar* was in a Jewish orphanage in Prague, in 1941. The Germans had forbidden all public performances.

The story of *Brundibar* is the story of good and evil. Two children, Aninka and Pepicek, need to buy milk for their sick mother. Because they are poor, they decide to earn the money they need by singing, like the organ-grinder, Brundibar. As Brundibar and the local policeman are not sympathetic, the two children enlist the help of three animals: a dog, a cat and a sparrow. The neighbourhood children join them, and sing a lullaby. Passers-by give money, but Brundibar takes it away. Finally the organ-grinder is defeated, and the children celebrate with the Song of Victory.

For the children in Theresienstadt, the Song of Victory was a clarion call of hope – one which they sang on 23 June 1944, at the time of the visit of the International Red Cross, at the specially prepared Sokol gymnasium – but it was hope not destined to be fulfilled.

One of those who saw *Brundibar* performed in Theresienstadt, in 1943, was the thirteen-year-old John Freund, who was subsequently deported to Birkenau, and who survived there with some ninety other boys aged between thirteen and fifteen. On his initiative, *Brundibar* was performed in Toronto fifty-three years after he saw it in Theresienstadt.

From the Magdeburg Barracks we walk on to another large, solidly constructed pre-First World War building, the Hanover Barracks, Block B IV (No. 26 on the map). Men were accommodated here. Just across Bäckergasse (Baker Street), built against one of the bastions, was Block A IV, the ghetto bakery and central food store (No. 27 on the map).

We walk on, past a small park, to Süd Strasse (South Street). This pleasantly named street was a site of great suffering. It was here that the deportees who had been driven or forced to walk from Bohusovice station reached the ghetto. And it was here, from 1 June 1943, that the railway entered the ghetto. A little way down the street, in the bastion itself, is the place (No. 34 on the map) beyond which mourners were not allowed to go when the corpses of the dead were taken out of the ghetto to a cemetery and crematorium a hundred yards further on, out of sight of the bastion. After September 1942, all those who died in the ghetto were cremated; there were no more burials.

Mourners were not allowed to go to the cemetery. It was here, in the fortifications themselves, that the last rites had to be held. There are two inscriptions on the wall, both in Hebrew. One of them reads: 'For not in his death will he take everything; his glory does not go down after him.' A person's glory survives, unlike his body.

The second quotation, which is between two Stars of David, is from the Jewish burial service. A quotation from Isaiah, it reads: 'He maketh death to vanish in life eternal; and The Lord God wipeth away tears from off all faces; and the reproach of His people shall He take away from off all the earth: for The Lord hath spoken it.' These are the words that a Jew says when leaving a cemetery, and in the home of a mourner.

In the facing wall of the fortifications a columbarium was built, number 35 on the map. It was here that urns with the ashes were placed. In November 1944 the ashes were taken away. Some were buried near an underground factory at Leitmeritz (now Litomerice). Others were thrown into the waters of the River Ohre.

There is not time to walk on to the cemetery, where 9,000 of those who died in the ghetto were buried, and more than 30,000 cremated. I remember it from when I was here about three years ago: a sombre place, with the crematorium – which the Jews had been forced to build – still intact, and several monuments to the dead of the ghetto. There is also a monument to those Russian prisoners-of-war who were held in Theresienstadt in the First World War, and who died in the camp.

We retrace our steps along the railway line, which has been preserved at the point where it enters the ghetto. The railway, like the crematorium, was built by ghetto labour. We are at the start of Bahnhof Strasse (Station Street). The railway line ran right into the ghetto at this point (No. 28 on the map). Standing by the tracks, which have been retained as a memorial, one can see, in the distance along the street, one of the tall conical hills of the Sudeten Mountains; those incarcerated here in the ghetto could see that free and open hillside every day.

11.10 a.m.
To the right of the railway line is the Hamburg Barracks, Block C III (No. 29 on the map). It is a long, stark, three-storey building, painted in a dull yellow. Before the railway was built, this was the main women's barracks. Dutch Jews were also brought here, the first transport arriving on 22 April 1943. When the German propaganda film was made to show how normal, and indeed pleasant, life was in Theresienstadt, one of its sequences showed the arrival here of a transport from Holland.

After 1 June 1943, when the railway line to Bohusovice was completed, part of the Hamburg Barracks was set aside for those Jews who were about to be deported to Auschwitz: the railway line ran in front of this building and for one block beyond. No one in the ghetto would see people being led through the ghetto to the trains; they were simply taken out of the front door of the building and pushed on board the train that was lined up in front of it.

In the last weeks of the war, thousands of young Jews who had survived the death marches and death trains were brought to Theresienstadt, some to the Hamburg Barracks. I read what one of them, Moniek Goldberg, from the far-off, small Polish town of Glowaczow, wrote to me about arriving there on 5 May 1945, his seventeenth birthday, carrying with him some wheat which he had managed to salvage from a deserted storehouse on the journey. While the Hamburg Barracks was an 'improvement' on the journey, he recalled, 'it soon turned into a nightmare. People were dying like so many flies. A lot of people had dysentery and were too weak to use the toilets. We could barely distinguish the living from the dead. But the worst of all was the stench. It was unbearable. On the transport people ate grass and whatever else they could lay their hands on. Now it was taking its toll and there were very few who were not ill. I was one of the very few, thanks to the wheat and the tough Russians who protected me from having it taken away.'

There were few remaining inmates of the original ghetto still alive in Theresienstadt when the transports arrived from Buchenwald and other concentration camps in April 1945. One of them was fourteen-year-old Eva Ginzova, the sister of Petr Ginz, who wrote in her diary on April 23: 'Dear God, what is happening here, I can't even describe it. One afternoon (Friday, April 20) I was at work, when we saw a freight train passing. People stuck their heads out of the window. They looked simply awful. Pale, completely yellow and green in the face, unshaven, like skeletons, sunken cheeks, their heads shaved, in prisoners' clothes ... and their eyes were glittering so strangely ... from hunger.

'I immediately ran into the ghetto (we are working outside) to the station. They were just getting out of the trucks, if you could call what they did getting out. Only a few managed to keep on their feet (their legs were just shanks covered with skin); the rest were lying completely exhausted on the floor of the trucks. They had been on the road for a fortnight and had been given almost nothing to eat. They were coming from Buchenwald and from Auschwitz. They were mostly Hungarians and Poles. I thought I would go mad with excitement, because all the time I was looking for Petr among them. A few of them had left from here, but Petr was not among them.

'Then one transport after another began to arrive. Hungarians, French, Slovaks, Poles (they had been in the concentration camps for seven years) and some Czechs as well. None from our lot. And the corpses among them! A heap in every truck. Clothed in rags, barefoot or in broken clogs. They were taking them away from the concentration camps because the Russians were supposed to be approaching. Such a terrible sight as few can have seen. If only I could express everything on paper. But I haven't enough talent to do it properly. And how these poor creatures threw themselves at any food they got, whatever it was. And how they fought for it – awful! Some of them have paratyphoid and many other terrible diseases.

'And those who came from Litzmannstadt[4] and Birkenau, what they had to tell! Auschwitz and Birkenau are really the same. They were two adjoining camps. All that is now occupied by the Russians. Everyone who arrived by transport in Birkenau was immediately stripped and classified. Children under fourteen and people over fifty went immediately into the gas chambers and then were cremated. They also constantly selected some from those remaining to gas. And the miserable food! Coffee, soup, coffee, etc. I wouldn't have believed it if those who had lived through it hadn't told me themselves.'

Eva Ginzova added: 'I am so worried about what has become of our Petr. Is he still alive at all?' Petr Ginz was dead.

We reflect on how the first news about the reality of Birkenau

---

[4] The German name for Lodz.

reached his sister in Theresienstadt at such a late date. The hiding of the truth about Birkenau had been the most skilful of all the Nazi deceptions.

We walk on to the southernmost corner of the camp, Block A II, the barracks (No. 30 on the map) where elderly prisoners – in their seventies and eighties, some even in their nineties – were forced to live in terrible conditions of overcrowding, and where the delousing of clothing took place. Behind this barracks is the Südberg (South Hill), on which, in 1943, a sports area was built (No. 31 on the map), which children as well as adults were allowed to use.

11.40 a.m.

We walk down West Gasse (West Street), outside the fortifications, to the pre-war Sokol sports club gym building, Block C I in the ghetto (and No. 33 on the map). It was built between the wars and is still in use as a sports club, though somewhat run down. The building was used during the time of the ghetto to house Jewish deportees who were suffering from encephalitis. For the propaganda film and the Red Cross visit, the building was transformed for a few weeks into a social club, complete with a library, a synagogue, a 'relaxation area' on the terrace, and a culture hall, in which the children's opera *Brundibar* was performed.

Just beyond the clubhouse is a sports field. Beyond it, in the distance, can be seen more of the conical peaks of the Sudeten Mountains. It was in this field, and in the fields beyond, that one of the grotesque events of Theresienstadt took place – a census. Gerald Green has described it thus: 'It took place on a misty drizzling day, 11 November 1943. All forty thousand prisoners were marched to a muddy field, a low meadow lying between mountains. There this great host stood all day, without food or water, with no toilets, bending, weeping, murmuring, fainting. Planes circled overhead; machine guns bristled on the mountains, as a lunatic attempt at a full count of heads was begun. Toward evening the prisoners' endurance crumpled, and panic broke out. Children shrieked; women fainted. The old and ill collapsed. Many died. From seven in the morning until midnight, the census went on, and it established nothing at all – merely that there were approximately forty thousand people in the camp. When, after midnight, the Jews were allowed to stagger back to the camp, over three hundred corpses remained on the muddy field.'

John Freund writes: 'I remember that day, and how happy we all were to be back in the Ghetto again.'

11.50 a.m.

We walk back down West Gasse and along See Strasse (Sea Street). On our left, built into a bastion, is the Sudeten Barracks, Block E I in ghetto numbering (and No. 32 on the map). It is a formidable-looking building, with an inscription to the Emperor Joseph II, dated 6 October 1780. This was where the first transport of Jews came to Theresienstadt, on 24 November 1941. Several more transports followed in the next two weeks. Then the women and children were separated, and taken to the Dresden Barracks.

As we walk down See Strasse we come, on our right, to the pre-war officers' club, Block G II in the ghetto (and No. 13 on the map). In the period of the ghetto it was the barracks of the Czech gendarmes guarding the borders of the ghetto, and keeping watch over those prisoners who were taken outside the ghetto on work details. Today it is the Garrison Army House. We walk around it. The façade, on Bahnhof Strasse, is quite handsome, with tall windows facing the park.

12 noon

We return to See Strasse and continue along it to the end, to another bastion, Block H II in the ghetto years (and No. 14 on the map). Here, various craft workshops were housed. We look through a fence at the group of outbuildings, which nestle just inside the outer wall of the fortress. It was here, at the beginning of 1945, that a gas chamber was built in an underground passageway. According to rumours circulating at the time, orders came from Berlin that no prisoners should be left alive when the Russians arrived, but Commandant Rahm disobeyed these orders. It is more likely that Rahm made up the story of these orders in order to try to gain credit for having disobeyed them. He was already in touch with representatives of the International Committee of the Red Cross, told them of these orders, and then handed the camp over to them. In return, he was allowed to leave unmolested, on the very eve of the arrival of the Russians.

Rahm's participation in this charade did not save his life. For his cruelty here at Theresienstadt he was sentenced to death by a Special People's Court in nearby Litomerice after the war, and executed in 1947.

We all look at Ben, who was brought here at the very end of the war, one of 13,000 survivors of the death marches of those final months who were dumped here, starving, sick and bewildered – in wooden barracks on the outskirts of the ghetto, which were pulled down soon after the war. We shudder to think that he could so easily have been one of those killed in the final hours of the war had the gas chamber been activated. With that thought in our minds we are silent as we walk away from the fence. Once more there is a sort of collective sense of the awfulness embodied in the places around us.

12.05 p.m.

We walk across the Brunnenpark – Fountain Park, though it has no fountain today – to Lange Strasse, and the Podmokly Barracks, Block H IV in the ghetto (and No. 16 on the map). An inscription above the entrance door gives the date of the building as 1792. This is where the deportees were brought to be registered.

When the Allied air raids on Berlin began to intensify in 1943, the archives of the Reich Security Main Office (RSHA) were transferred here, as well as to other locations in the ghetto. Jews were moved out of the Podmokly Barracks so that documents could be stacked and preserved there. The SS felt that their voluminous archives would be safe here in Theresienstadt, and indeed they were, until the Russians drew near. Then, to prevent them falling into enemy hands, they were consigned to the flames.

We discuss the phenomenon of the archives of mass murder being preserved by the perpetrators. Was this not the sort of evidence that one would want to destroy? In answer, Ben comments: 'To the last minute they believed that they would overwhelm the world – and they wanted their archives safe.'

We walk to the far end of Lange Strasse. Here is another bastion (No. 17 on the map). At first it was used for registration of deportees, but soon became the central clothing store, where belongings confiscated from the luggage of the deportees were housed. It was from here that items considered of good quality were sent to Germany. The remainder were offered for sale at the three shops in the ghetto.

Two executions took place here at the beginning of 1942: nine prisoners were hanged on January 10 for having violated an order not to send letters out of the ghetto. Seven more were hanged on February 26,

We turn down Post Gasse, a short street which leads to the Dresden Barracks, Block H V in the ghetto (and No. 18 on the map). Women were housed here from 6 December 1941. Part of the building was set aside for theatrical performances and concerts. Leagues were allowed to play football in the yard. In the cellar was a prison for those who infringed the ghetto regulations.

At the Dresden Barracks, as elsewhere in Theresienstadt, the sporting activity for the young was organised by Fredy Hirsch. Aged twenty-six when he arrived in the ghetto, he committed suicide two years later at Auschwitz, having led a protest on the eve of the destruction of the Czech 'family camp' there.

John Freund, a survivor of Theresienstadt and Auschwitz, later wrote of Hirsch: 'His good looks, dark hair and deep, probing eyes, tall and erect, confident and arrogant; those were the physical qualities of the new Jew. He was an ardent Zionist, who inspired all near him. Fredy came from Germany in 1933 at the age of twenty to Czechoslovakia. He became deeply involved with the Jewish Youth Movements. He spoke with a German accent, which some of us thought funny.'

In Theresienstadt, Fredy Hirsch had the nominal function of 'building maintenance superintendent', John Freund recalled, 'but he was, in fact, the leader of children and youth activities. He believed that education should begin with strengthening the body, discipline, cleanliness and self-esteem. These were the qualities which lead to productive lives. Israel needed youth. All training was directed towards the future, but Fredy also wanted the children to be spared the daily terror, which was life in the camps. He abhorred brutality.'

Hirsch's activities in Theresienstadt, and later at Auschwitz, wrote Freund, 'were not frustrated by the authorities, who felt he was at least preventing trouble from the young'. In Theresienstadt (where there is a plaque to Hirsch on the wall of L 417, which can be seen from the yard behind the building) 'he organised games in the large grassy valley between the walls of the ghetto. Up to 6,000 children and youth took part in these well-organised games of athletic pursuit. There he stood, handsome and confident, at the top of the hill overseeing the activities.'

It was here at the Dresden Barracks, the scene of so many sports activities organised by Fredy Hirsch, that, when the war was over, the Russian military governor of Theresienstadt, Major Kuzmin, addressed the survivors of the death marches who had been brought to the camp in its final weeks under German rule. I read out the account of one of those survivors, Simon Klin, from the Polish town of Zdunska Wola. Major Kuzmin, he recalled, 'assembled all the Jews in the courtyard of the Dresden Armoury in Theresienstadt, and addressed us from the balcony. A Jewish delegate from the Polish government was standing at his side. He began his address: "Polish Jews and Jewesses! Return to your homeland, to your own soil, to your houses, to your property." The Polish delegation continued in much the same vein. I felt that I had no reason to go back. There was already a strong Zionist movement in Germany, preparing groups for Hachsharah[5] in Germany to be followed by emigration to Palestine. Children's houses were formed at Theresienstadt where we were taught a little Hebrew. We were left undisturbed by the Russians.

'At first there were rumours that the youth groups were going to Switzerland, but after a while it became quite clear that we were going to England. On hearing this, the Polish–Jewish delegate raced round on his motorbike, and warned us that anyone caught wandering outside the camp gates would be sent back to Poland. Major Kuzmin took us to see an anti-capitalist film demonstrating the exploitation of workers in America. Czech soldiers, meeting us in the street, asked whether it was true we were going to England, telling us, "Russia is much better".'

Simon Klin was among several hundred teenage survivors who made their way, not to Russia, but to Britain. A few others returned to Poland, among them Lucjan Dobroszycki, whose edition of the Lodz Ghetto Chronicle is one of the important texts of the Holocaust. After the Polish anti-Semitic upsurge in 1968 he emigrated to the United States.

There is a further distressing link with the story of the Zionist inclinations of so many of those who were deported to Theresienstadt. On 5 March 1943, among those who died of hunger here in the ghetto was the fifty-two-year-old Trude Neumann. From 1918 until 1942 she had been a mental patient in an institution near Vienna. In 1942 all the patients were taken from that institution, and from all the mental homes in the region, and deported to Theresienstadt. Trude Neumann was the daughter of Theodor Herzl, the founder of political Zionism.

12.15 p.m.

We retrace our steps down Post Gasse and turn along Lange Strasse towards the centre of the ghetto. At No. 24 Lange Strasse was the SS dormitory, the Kameradschaftsheim, later known as 'Victoria' (No. 15 on the map). It was one of the few buildings in Theresienstadt that was destroyed at the end of the war. On the ground floor were the restaurant and recreation rooms. Above them were flats for the SS. Jews were not allowed to enter the building. The building constructed on the site after the war is now the Park Hotel (the same name as the

[5] Agricultural training: preparation, in every European country, for life in Palestine, a central feature of pre-war Zionism.

hotel built on the deportation yards in Prague which we saw a few hours ago).

In the park facing the hotel, the Brunnenpark, a mother and child are playing. The park is a pleasant prospect of trees and grass. Ben recalls that when he was here in the last weeks of the war, it was a desolate open space, with no trees and no grass. 'All the trees had been cut down,' he tells us. 'All available wood was being used for heating during that period when we existed, rather than lived, in Theresienstadt.' Once more, we are made aware of what a difficult act of imagination – how many such acts of imagination – we must make, even to get a glimpse of what must have been.

12.25 p.m.

We return to the main square. A mother, holding her child by the hand, is leaving the square by the clothes shop, where once the clothes taken from the Jews as they arrived, and from Jews who had died, were sold. The ghetto had its own paper money, worthless except in the internal world of barter.

We still have the museum to go round, but the group want to go to the restaurant a block to the north. We are all drained. To walk around a museum does not appeal. In the restaurant we can behave 'normally', and not be overwhelmed by what is to the left and the right of us, as on the walk. Ben leads the way in showing just what normality is when he complains to the waiter that there are not enough noodles in his soup. He gets quite indignant.

I wonder that any of us can eat anything. I suppose it is an imperative for all of us that somehow life must go on, and that we must not allow ourselves to become depressed by the past, overwhelming though it has seemed during the past three hours.

It seems such a compact area for so much suffering.

While some of us are finishing lunch, Caroline, Marie and Petra visit the museum, which is located in L 417, the former children's home.

1.50 p.m.

Ben was lucky that his arrival in Theresienstadt at the end of April 1945 coincided with the decline of German control and the arrival of the Red Cross. 'For the first time in five months we got fresh clothing,' he recalled. 'We could sleep. For so many years we had been deprived of sleep.'

We leave Theresienstadt and drive back to the main road, the road to Litomerice. A road sign indicates that the town is only two kilometres away. This was the road along which, on the day of liberation, Ben went in search of food, and was successful. I read his account of that day:

'As I went towards Leitmeritz, there were German women and children walking on the road. They had been chased out of their homes. Two Hungarian–Jewish survivors, young girls of seventeen or eighteen – older than I – were beating up a German woman who had two children with her, a baby in a pram, and a boy not much older than my own sister was when she was killed by the Germans, nine years old. The baby was crying. I told them to stop it. They said "But she's German. Germans beat us up. Now we will beat them." I asked them to stop, and when they ignored me I got hold of them and pushed them away. I threw them into a ditch.

'In Leitmeritz, former camp inmates were running, grabbing whatever they could get hold of. Some, the older ones especially, were looking for jewellery and other valuables. I looked for food. I was fifteen years old. I was naïve. In a shop I saw rice and sugar. People were just raiding everything. Some people ran into banks and were grabbing money, but the money was no longer valid currency. I took some rice and sugar in a sack, about twenty kilograms, as much as I could carry. The three weeks in Theresienstadt, not being driven to work, and having sufficient sleep, restored my strength enough to enable me to carry this weight for more than a kilometre.

'When I got back to Theresienstadt I heard people crying out, "Kill him, kill him." There was a big circle. In the middle was an SS man. Anyone who could get into the circle was kicking him and hitting him. He got up. They kicked him and pushed him down. I stood there. I felt sick. The man was literally beaten to death, and yet people were still beating him up. I was very upset. I had a burning sense of justice, because of the many injustices I had experienced against myself, against my family, against the Jews of my town. Although I knew that this SS man was guilty, I felt that this was not the way to deal with him.'

2.02 p.m.
We drive across the River Ohre. Just to the north is the spot where 22,000 urns with the ashes of those Jews who died in the Theresienstadt ghetto were thrown into the river in November 1944.

2.03 p.m.
The road runs past the Small Fort of Theresienstadt, originally built to defend the River Ohre flood gates, and water traffic on the Elbe. In

Habsburg times, and in inter-war Czechoslovakia, the fort was a prison. Gavrilo Princip, the assassin of the Archduke Franz-Ferdinand, was imprisoned here in 1914. During his incarceration he was tended by a Jewish doctor (Jan Levit) but died of tuberculosis in 1918. Dr Levit was among the Czech Jews brought to Theresienstadt in 1942 – in his case, brought back. Between the wars Dr Levit had been a Professor of Military Surgery. He was also a second-generation practising Christian, but, under the Nazi racial laws, he was a Jew. In 1944 he was deported from Theresienstadt to Auschwitz, where he was killed.

From 1940 to 1945 the Small Fort was used as a prison by the Prague Gestapo. At its entrance is a large memorial cemetery. Among those buried here are Jews who were taken from the Theresienstadt ghetto and shot for disobedience, or supposed disobedience, or for some other trumped-up charge. But most of the Jewish graves here are of those who died during the epidemics of typhus and spotted fever at the end of the war and shortly after liberation. Among the field of crosses, their graves are marked with a Star of David.

2.10 p.m.

George is driving us speedily back south through the rolling Bohemian countryside. Some of us are dozing, others are writing up their diaries. After three hours walking around Theresienstadt, looking at so many buildings and talking about what happened in each of them, one has a strange sense of the multitude who once suffered there. I had originally thought of writing 'lived' there, but it hardly seems appropriate. Even in Ben's presence, who was here for so very short a time in the end – a few weeks – and survived, there is a sense of helplessness. There is also a sense of immediacy, as he recognises, and points out with animation, the houses between which the railway used to run, and where he arrived; and tells us of those who arrived after him – a day or two before liberation – who were too emaciated to survive even those few days.

We discuss how, when one sees the bastions, and feels the sense of isolation, being cut off from the outside world, with only the hills across the Elbe as evidence that the outside world existed at all, one is brought very close to the reality, even if one can never fully grasp it.

The journey back to Prague is taking us past fields of yellow mustard seed. On the left is Mount Rip, 459 metres (1,514 feet) high. It looks like Mount Tabor in the Galilee. According to Czech legend, Mount Rip is the place where the patriarch Cech, the founder of the Czech nation, stopped to place his people 'in that beautiful land' (writes John Freund) 'full of milk and honey'.

In March 1939 many hundreds of Czech Jews were in possession of Palestine Certificates, entitling them to emigrate to Palestine, a journey which, for many of them, seemed imminent. But the coming of war made it impossible for them to use these certificates; the only journey the Nazis would allow was to Theresienstadt, or to the camps and ghettos in the East.

The road climbs a hill. In the valley are small villages with red-roofed houses.

2.20 p.m.
We drive through Straskov.

2.30 p.m.
We cross the Dresden–Prague railway at Novy Ouholice. Railway lines are gaining a significance for all of us we did not think possible. They look so harmless, lines of metal stretching into the distance.

2.35 p.m.
We are about halfway between Theresienstadt and Prague. These two cities existed between 1941 and 1945, each ignorant of the other: Prague, with its Jews gone; and Theresienstadt, which the citizens of Prague could no longer visit, and whose own citizens had been taken away. The power of the totalitarian state to order men's lives even before total destruction – indeed, the process of separation at the time of deportation, and then the further separation after deportation, and the perpetual isolation – were themselves important features of the destructive goal: to lull and deceive to the bitter end.

We are passing a field of gorgeous poppies – the flower for soldiers fallen in battle.

The German method in Theresienstadt, as in every ghetto, was to make deprivation normal, to make isolation normal, to make disappointment normal, so the old people who were given a signed contract setting out the benefits which they would find when they reached Theresienstadt were aggrieved (understandably) when they arrived. The grievance at not receiving what had been promised – a room of one's own, sheets, a regular evening meal – became more important, more real, than the reality of the destructive process. The so-called contract was simply an instrument of deception.

2.50 p.m.
We see the spires of Prague in the distance.

2.52 p.m.
Two plaques at the roadside record the execution of Czech partisans by the Germans.

2.56 p.m.
As we approach the station there is a fine view of Prague Castle across the Vltava. As the bus stops in front of the station forecourt George warns us to beware of thieves: 'The homeless are on the watch for what they can grab.'

3 p.m.
We enter the magnificent hall of Prague station. The vaulted dome is decorated with statues and coats of arms. We go to the waiting room, and find ourselves at the various food stalls. A man and woman walk by, looking at the train departure board. They are both wearing military uniforms and bandanas around their heads. He has a large knife in his belt. She has various accoutrements hanging from hers. A few moments later two Czech skinheads come to look at the board. They have Mohican-style hair – a strip of hair on a shaven head. A drunk passes, and two prostitutes. A Gypsy woman begging, with her daughter in her arms, arrives. I buy a phone card and manage to get through to my son in London to tell him I am safe in Prague and shortly to leave by train for Slovakia.

4.15 p.m.
We board our train, the Zilina express.

4.22 p.m.
The train draws out of the station.

4.55 p.m.
Cesky Brod. Two kilometres to the south-east is the village of Pristoupim, where three Jewish families were living in 1724. By 1890 this had grown to 200 Jews in the religious congregation known as 'Cesky Brod-Pristoupim'. In 1930 there were ten Jews in Pristoupim and seventy-four in Cesky Brod. Unlike their community, their synagogue, built in 1842, survives. Today it is a library (which preserves the

building as a structure). The eighteenth-century Jewish Community House also survives; today it is a private dwelling.

In the former Jewish cemetery here are several remarkable baroque and classical tombstones. Also in the cemetery is a small mass grave of eight Jewish women who died while being deported along this railway line from Auschwitz in January 1945 on one of the 'death trains' which brought tens of thousands of Jews from east to west in those last months of the war. The bodies of those who died during the journey – sometimes as many as half of the deportees – were often just tossed out of the carriages to the side of the track.

5.15 p.m.

Kolin. Here was one of the oldest Jewish communities in Bohemia, dating from the fourteenth century. Ancient Jewish buildings survive here, including the late-seventeenth-century synagogue, whose ornate baroque décor on the walls and ceiling vaulting includes delicate frescoes of grapevines and bunches of grapes. There are also many eighteenth-century Jewish houses and a Jewish school. The cemetery dates from 1418. Among the graves are those of Rabbi Bezalel – Rabbi Loew's son – and of Mordechai Maisel's nephew Samuel.

I read from Ruth Ellen Gruber's description in her *Jewish Heritage Travel* guide book to East-Central Europe: 'Much of the cemetery is fantastically overgrown with ivy, trees, and bushes; tombstones and tree trunks alike are covered by carpets of vines – but this adds to the impressive sight and imparts a sense of timeless age quite different from that felt at the Prague Old Cemetery. In season, pear trees among the gravestones produce delicious fruits.'

It is a pity that we have no time to stop here for an hour or two, and catch a later train east, but ours is the last train that can get us to Zilina tonight.

Many famous rabbis and writers lived and worked here in Kolin. Among them was the Czech-Jewish poet and literary historian, Camill Hoffman. In 1942 more than two thousand Jews were deported from here to Theresienstadt. Only a hundred survived the war. Hoffman was among those who perished in Auschwitz.

Among the Kolin Jews who survived the war was Hana Lustig (now Greenfield). 'We had such a wonderful rabbi,' she recalled, when I told her about this journey. 'These were the most wonderful memories I had, because I grew up in the most wonderful democratic and prosperous days.' I read from her memoirs:

'Lovely baroque houses frame the town's piazza, many of which were owned by Jewish merchants in my youth: a general store by the Eisner family, where I was always treated to some exotic nuts whenever I passed by, the Ornstein family, my mother's lawyer, the Kodicek family, where we got our new shoes for each Jewish holiday, Aunt Heller, where I collected a few coins for an ice-cream cone whenever I was nearby, the Roubicek family, whose son studied Hebrew and Jewish history with me, taught by Dr Feder, our esteemed rabbi, every Saturday afternoon, in his home.

'I had many friends amongst my schoolmates, who came to our house to play with my toys. I would rarely go to theirs. I wondered why? Being the only Jewish pupil in my class, I never felt any anti-Semitism, it was probably there, but suppressed, in the democracy we lived in. Every season had its excitement. In winter we skied and skated, in summer we bicycled and swam in the famous River Labe (Elbe) that flows through the town.

'Loved by my parents and grandparents, never having missed a meal or any other of life's necessities, I attended local schools, looking forward with excitement to each new day, learning and laughing at the wonderful world I lived in. Until the day when clouds gathered over my country and Hitler marched into Czechoslovakia and occupied it.

'It didn't take long until signs "Jews are not wanted here" were seen everywhere. I could no longer continue my studies, participate in the Scouts movement, Sokol or other activities. A dictator put an end to my freedom, injected hate and fear, by his terrible tactics, into the majority of the population and I became an outcast.

'After the assassination of Heydrich the town of Lidice was eliminated as a reprisal: 173 men were shot, 60 women were sent to concentration camps and eighty-eight children were re-educated by the Nazis. Lidice is a world-known episode, commemorated until today. The fact that a thousand of Kolin's Jewish residents were also rounded up and sent to their death, as reprisal for the assassination, has never been acknowledged.

'And while the Kolin population watched the deportation, nobody dared to protest. This brought to an end the 600-year-old Jewish community of Kolin.'

On 10 October 1996 Hana Lustig returned to Kolin from her home in Israel, with other survivors of the town who now live in Israel, Britain, Australia, and the United States. They brought with them some of the twenty-five Scrolls of the Law which had belonged to the Kolin synagogue before the war. After the deportation of the Jews of

Kolin to Theresienstadt, these scrolls were taken by the Germans to Prague, to be catalogued for the proposed Museum of the Lost Jewish Race. After the Nazi era, the scrolls were inherited by the Communists who, not appreciating their value, allowed them to moulder in a cellar. One day, they were seen by an English art dealer who was visiting Prague, and who persuaded the Communists to sell them to him. He gave them to the Westminster Synagogue in London, which painstakingly restored them. Those scrolls that could be restored were given to synagogues in Britain, Australia, the United States and Israel. One of them found its way to Hana Greenfield's synagogue in Tel Aviv. Now it is back in its original home.

5.45 p.m.
Pardubice. Another town which once had a vigorous Jewish life, all destroyed by the Nazis. The first record of Jewish settlement here dates from 1492, the year (as Ben reminds us – it is one of his favourite comparative dates) when Columbus discovered America. In the Jewish cemetery is another of those collective graves of Jews who died while being brought by train at the beginning of 1945 from Auschwitz back into Czechoslovakia. Seven are buried here.

As the train continues, we see in the distance many villages and small towns in which there were once Jewish communities.

6.40 p.m.
Usti nad Orlici (in German, Wildenschwert). Here too was a small Jewish community in the pre-war years. The Czech-Jewish satirist and librettist, Fritz Beda-Löhner, was born here in 1883. He perished in Auschwitz in 1942. A British physicist, Professor Felix Weinberg, who was born here in 1928, and came to Britain after the war, recalled (in a letter to me): 'One of the consequences of the many successive restrictions was that we had a great deal of spare time, so that I got to know every path in the beautiful forests on the hills around Usti. Sometimes the whole family went on fungi-collecting expeditions (I am still expert in recognising edible fungi). Right at the peak there is a hut where it was possible to buy bread thickly spread with real butter, long after butter became just a memory in the town, but that was a very long haul. More often my brother and I were out in the woods and meadows looking down on the roofs of the small town. We spent days just walking with me telling him stories I made up. No one ever spoke to us, perhaps because of our yellow stars, but we never experienced any unkindness from the Czechs. However, the time was

rapidly running out for the little Jewish community of about a dozen individuals. First everyone had to move into my uncle's house which was just about big enough to accommodate us all. Shortly thereafter the house was requisitioned by the German administration and we all had to move into the flat of the Weiners – a retired couple, who had lived opposite the church. There were many of us to each room and I remember sleeping on a bed of blankets on the floor. It did not last long before we got our Wehrmacht escort to the cattle trucks waiting at the station. There was a delay while the soldiers went to collect one old couple who had not turned up. They never did turn up, having taken an overdose the night before. In the years that followed I came to think of that as a sort of victory.'

The train is travelling through rolling countryside, cultivated fields, wooded hills, and wide rural vistas.

7.25 p.m.

Zabreh na Morave (in German, Hohenstadt). The birthplace of the painter, sculptor and poet, Gertrud Groag, who survived Theresienstadt and emigrated to Israel after the war. She died in Haifa in 1979, at the age of ninety.

7.30 p.m.

We make our way in relays to the restaurant car, which belongs to Slovak Railways. Drinks and snacks keep us going. We are still much under the influence of the morning in Theresienstadt. Ben tells us of the moment of liberation. 'The first thing I did, I danced on the pavement. It was the first time that I had walked on a pavement for more than three years. Before that, we walked and marched in the road. I was overjoyed – just the fact that I was free to walk on a pavement.'

7.50 p.m.

Stepanov. Ben speaks of how, after he had been liberated in Theresienstadt in May 1945, he made his way back to Poland. On reaching the city of Czestochowa, he, then aged fifteen, and his twelve-year-old cousin Gershon, who was with him (and who was also a survivor), were approached at the station by two Poles who said they were policemen and had to check their documents at the police station. The Poles led the two youngsters away, and took them, not to the police station, but to a secluded, deserted street. There the Poles ordered them against a wall, and prepared to shoot them. As Ben recalled, with an intensity as if it were yesterday:

'Both my cousin and I felt rooted to the ground unable to move. When, at last, I recovered my composure, I emitted a torrent of desperate appeals and entreaties. I pleaded with them, "Haven't we suffered enough? Haven't the Nazis caused enough destruction and devastation to all of us? Our common enemy is destroyed and the future is ours. We have survived against all the odds and why are you intent on promoting the heinous crimes that the Nazis have unleashed? Don't we speak the same language as you? Didn't we imbibe the same culture as you?"

'I went on in the same vein speaking agitatedly for some time. Eventually, one of the officers succumbed to my pleading and said, "Let's leave them. They are after all still boys." As they put away their pistols, they made a remark which still rings loud in my ears. "You can consider yourselves very lucky. We have killed many of your kind. You are the first ones we have left alive." With this comment they disappeared into the dark of the night.

'That was the nearest I came to death in all those years. Under the Nazis I was lucky enough never to be ordered to go to the wall. Many years later, in 1988, at an academic conference on Polish-Jewish relations in Jerusalem, one of the Polish academics showed a video about the post-war pogrom in Kielce, in which forty-three Jews were killed. One of those interviewed in the video told the story of how, after the war, Jews returning from the concentration camps were taken away from the station at Czestochowa and killed. If ever I needed confirmation, this was it. It made me shudder. They would have left me there without a name. They would have left me naked. My sister would never have known what happened to me, or to my cousin. She would have been told that I survived the camps and the war, but that we had disappeared, that there was no trace of me.'

8 p.m.

Olomouc. Robin O'Neil is on the platform. He had left us in Prague to go to Svitavy, Oskar Schindler's home town. He has much to tell us about what he saw there. Here is his account: 'I met the museum staff where we exchanged a number of research documents. One interesting document I was given was a contract between Schindler and a local family named Butchovsky for the rent of a piece of ground at Brunnlitz. The ground was to be used as an allotment to produce food for Schindler's Jewish workers. There were a number of conditions: the allotment had to be fenced, rent would be 47 Reichsmark per year for as long as the war lasted, the lease would run from 1 November 1944 and continue as long as the war lasted. Finally both sides of the contract had to confirm that they were "Aryan".

'I visited the Jewish cemetery that has been in a desolate state for many years. I have for some time been trying to persuade the local council to tidy the cemetery and perhaps commemorate the site. In 1939 there were 1,600 Jews living in Svitavy. Today there are none. I contacted the Mayor, Jiry Bridyle, and asked how the cemetery tidy-up was progressing. I received the usual negative reply, "No cash".

'Sitting on a wall overlooking the Schindler memorial, which was covered in graffiti, my attention was drawn to a motor-cycle and side-car coming down the road. It was a very old machine and was making a lot of noise. At its approach I saw that it was being ridden by two males wearing Nazi-style helmets. On the front of the machine was a broom handle protruding from the front (machine gun?). On both arms of the sidecar were swastika emblems. It passed before I could use my camera. This was so unreal, I had to ask myself, did I see what I saw?'

We are all delighted to see Robin again. 'What a reception!' is his comment.

8.20 p.m.
Prosenice. We have reached the Beskid Mountains, where Czech and Slovak partisans, fighting in the mountains on either side of the Jablunka Pass – through which the train will travel – linked up and worked together to cut German rail communications. There are hop fields alongside the railway.

8.43 p.m.
Hranice nad Morava. The defile of the Moravian Gates is closing in on either side of the railway; high, wooded hills, that in distant times barred the route of the barbarians pouring into Central Europe from the east.

9.15 p.m.
Vsetin. The railway wends its way to the top of the Jablunka Pass, 1,855 feet above sea level.

9.30 p.m.
We reach the top of the pass. Then the train begins the long descent.

9.46 p.m.

Horni Lidec. This is the border between the Czech and Slovak Republics. Sitting in the restaurant car as we cross the border, I speak of the country we have just entered. Jews first settled in Slovakia in Roman times. By the beginning of the twentieth century there were more than five hundred towns and villages in Slovakia with former or existing Jewish communities. By the time of the outbreak of war, 136,737 Jews lived here. The Fascist government, which was set up in March 1939, allied itself with Germany, and deported 'its' Jews to German-occupied Poland with zeal.

I speak of the Jewish participation in the Slovak revolt in the autumn of 1944. More than 1,500 Jews joined the 16,000 Slovak soldiers and partisans who took part in the revolt. Of the 2,100 partisans who were killed in action, 269 were Jews. One Jewish partisan battalion commander, Edita Katz, covered the retreat of her unit with a machine gun, until her ammunition ran out. She then used hand grenades to hold off the Germans and the Hlinka Guard, until she was hit and killed.

Within four weeks of the outbreak of the Slovak revolt, the Jewish units, and the Slovak fighters, were joined by Jewish parachutists sent from Palestine, among them Havivah Reik, who, after fighting in the hills with a small group of Slovak Jews (she had herself been born in Slovakia in 1914, and emigrated to Palestine in 1939), was captured by the Germans at the end of October 1944, imprisoned, and executed on 20 November 1944.

Among the Jews who were in Slovakia during the uprising, and survived, were two men who had escaped from Auschwitz, Rudolf Vrba (who escaped in April 1944) and Czeslaw Mordowicz (who escaped a month later). During the Slovak uprising Mordowicz was captured and, together with several thousand surviving Slovak Jews, deported to Auschwitz. The existing Auschwitz number tattooed on his forearm would, if discovered by the camp authorities, have meant the torture and execution always meted out to an escapee. On reaching the tattoo barracks, Mordowicz had a magnificent multi-scaled fish tattooed over and around the original number. A new number was then tattooed elsewhere, and his previous sojourn in the camp was never discovered by the SS.

The Germans reacted savagely to the Slovak uprising. Tibor Cifea, a Jewish partisan, was shot, and left hanging for three days as a warning. Pavel Ekstein was executed less than two months before his eighteenth birthday. In all, 722 Jews were 'specially handled' on the spot, mostly shot, or hanged. A Swiss Red Cross official, Georges Dunand, who was in Bratislava, tried to ameliorate the Jewish suffering (it was he who, in the first week of May 1945, went to Theresienstadt and persuaded the German commandant to hand over the town to the Red Cross).

Despite Georges Dunand's efforts on behalf of the surviving Jews of Slovakia, Adolf Eichmann sent an emissary to Bratislava to ensure that the deportations were carried out, and 8,975 Slovak Jews were deported that autumn to Auschwitz.

Trekking southward from Slovakia, one of the parachutists from Palestine, the twenty-four-year-old Abba Berdichev, hoped to bring some succour to the Jews of Roumania, his birthplace. 'I hope,' he had written before leaving Palestine, 'that this time luck will be with me, because the desire and determination to fulfil my duty as a Jew is still strong.' Berdichev was captured while still in Slovakia, charged with spying and sabotage, and shot.

10.20 p.m.
Puchov. It is dark. There is nothing to see but the yellow glow of the station arc lights.

10.30 p.m.
Povazska Bystrica. We are getting near our journey's end. It cannot be more than half an hour before we reach Zilina. I give a short account of the Jews of Zilina. Jews were first invited to settle here by the kings of Hungary after the Tatar invasion had been repulsed in the thirteenth century. In the early nineteenth century, however, Jews were not allowed to live in the town, although they could attend its fairs and markets. The first organised Jewish community was formed in 1852. When the town became an important Habsburg railway centre linking east and west and north and south, the Jewish population increased. Jews were active in creating a textile industry here, and also in making Zilina the centre of the timber trade of the region. Zionist activity was strong here.

From 1902 until his death in 1934, a leading Jewish scholar, David Friedmann, was the rabbi. The new synagogue, built in 1934, was regarded as one of the most beautiful in the whole of Czechoslovakia. Hugo Stransky, who succeeded Rabbi Friedmann, emigrated to England in 1938. His successor, Martin Klein, a noted Talmudic scholar, returned to Zilina after the war, but died soon afterwards.

When war came, there were 3,500 Jews in Zilina. About seven hundred survived the war. Of these, 400 left, mainly for Israel, before

1950. Most of those who remained left either for the Slovak capital, Bratislava, or for abroad, after the Soviet invasion of Czechoslovakia in 1968.

We look at a map of the wartime railway network. Zilina was one of the main railway hubs for the despatch of Jews to Auschwitz. The railway lines came through here from Italy, Croatia, Greece, Bohemia, Moravia, western Slovakia and western Hungary. So many Jews were brought through this town that a transit concentration camp was set up. Thousands of Jews passed through it. In the *Encyclopaedia Judaica*, Elieser Beck has called it the 'anteroom to hell'.

10.55 p.m.
Zilina. We arrive in black darkness. We leave the station, and walk across the square to our hotel, the Hotel Polom.

11.10 p.m.
Distribution of keys. I check that there will be breakfast tomorrow. It turns out that it has 'not been requested'. I negotiate for a while, and breakfast is promised. I then sit in the lobby, discussing with Jon (who has been to Auschwitz before with a group) how to deal with the difficulties and problems that a visit can create. How should I do my readings? How should the walk be 'structured' to avoid insensitivities and combine the memorial and sombre aspect with the historical aspect? Should we go first to Auschwitz I, the mainly political prisoners' camp, where mostly Poles suffered, but which has all the exhibitions, including the Jewish one? Or should we go first to Auschwitz II (Birkenau) which was the site of the mass murder of more than a million Jews? I feel a heavy responsibility, and nervousness, about how best to 'introduce' Auschwitz. I also wonder whether it was wise to have decided to go there by train, along an actual wartime deportation railway line. I fear this might seem something of a gimmick, or in bad taste – or too emotionally disturbing.

11.40 p.m.
In my room, I sort out the material that will be the readings tomorrow. Robin gives me a helping hand.

11.55 p.m.
Across the small square outside my window, the station announcer is giving the midnight arrivals and departures. The occasional train whistle blows.

12.04 a.m.

Lights out, nineteen hours after waking up this morning in Prague.

DAY 6

ZILINA – CRACOW

'The most desolate tracks'

7 a.m.
Outside my window, a line of people are waiting for a bus. I can hear the Zilina train station announcer whose voice was the last voice I heard last night.

7.15 a.m.
Before breakfast I leave the hotel and walk along the street leading from the station to the centre of town. It is a precinct area of two-storey, late nineteenth- and early twentieth-century houses. One is dated 1904. They are in pastel shades: mostly yellow, blue and pink.

7.20 a.m.
Reach the town square and see an expanse of paving with a pine tree in the middle, next to an almost empty ornamental pond. There is a partisan war memorial below the steps that leads up to the imposing spire and bell-tower of the cathedral. At one side of the square is a statue of Father Hlinka, the leader of Slovak nationalism in the pre-war years, and indeed before the First World War. Since the recent independence of Slovakia he has become the national hero again. The inscription says: 'Andrej Hlinka, Father of the People.'

7.55 a.m.
Return to the hotel and join the group at breakfast. In response to my negotiations last night, something of a feast is laid out, including large pork sausages in a rich sauce. Most of the group cannot eat these: either they are too rich, not kosher, or far from vegetarian. Luckily there is also bread and jam, and a sweet pastry.

Our plan is to take the morning Bratislava–Cracow express which follows one of the main deportation railways north to Auschwitz, and will bring us to Auschwitz station at noon. Everyone is rather nervous about this journey. I talk over with Jon some of the problems, as I did last night. Was it too much to have decided to make this journey by rail?

8.35 a.m.

We leave the hotel and cross the street to the station. I go to the departure board and cannot see the 8.52 train. My first thought is that for some reason the timetable is changed by an hour and that we have missed it. We could easily have come across here for the 7.52 if we had known of the change. I then look to see if there is a later train to Cracow but there is nothing until after five o'clock this afternoon. Sending the group to wait on the platform, I go with Ben to try to find the stationmaster or someone who can advise us about what has happened to the 8.52.

At the ticket office they are emphatic that the 8.52 train does not exist. I take out my Thomas Cook *European Timetable* and there it is, but that is, of course, from the London perspective. Here in Zilina itself there is no doubt that it will not be running, that no train is making its way this morning from Bratislava to the north). In my mind I see the whole trip unravelling as we are unable to leave this remote Slovak railway junction. Studying the departure board I contemplate the possibility of taking a train to some other, more westerly, part of Poland, and entering Poland from another direction. But, this would mean missing the long – if somewhat nervously – awaited journey along the deportation route. It seems that now instead of two trains a day, only one train a day makes the journey along the single track across the Slovak–Polish border.

9.15 a.m.

After considerable difficulty, as was so common in Communist days – with much waiting and negotiating with the Post Office clerk – I manage to telephone to the travel agent in Cracow and tell them the earliest we can reach Cracow will be midnight tonight. That the minibus that was to meet us at Auschwitz at midday will have to meet us at Cracow late tonight. I have decided that we will go up to the border on the first possible local train and wait there until the express comes through. In this way we can at least spend a relaxed day in the mountains.

9.45 a.m.

I explain the plan to the group. There is a train to Cadca in forty minutes' time. We will take that and see what emerges. From the map it looks as if it might be a pleasant mountain town. Having been geared up by the thought of being at Auschwitz at noon there was a sense of anti-climax and disappointment, but also perhaps of relief. I tell the group that if we can get to Cracow by midnight, we will go to Auschwitz the following morning. Meanwhile, the sun is shining, while around us is the bustle of the busy station, and to the north, the wooded hills of Slovakia.

10 a.m.

We sit in the warm sunlight, facing the goods yard at the entrance to Zilina station. It is interesting that an unexpected delay does not mean a gap in our historical survey. So much happened in each place on our itinerary that one could spend hours rather than minutes, and days rather than hours, wherever we pass through, or come to rest. I tell the group of an episode here at Zilina station. On 3 July 1942, 1,000 Jews from Sered were forced on board a train and brought northward. Vlasta Kladivova has written (in a speech in Banska Bystrica in March 1992, later published in *The Tragedy of Slovak Jews*):

'The transport of July 3 was brought up to a thousand persons with people from the Sered hospital. They transported them by train to Zilina where they were transferred to a transport rolling stock. During the transfer the guardians treated them very badly and ruthlessly, taking the blankets on which they lay or were covered by. The transport of July 11 was also completed with the insane persons who were transferred from all mental hospitals in Slovakia. Ervin Steiner, a social care clerk at the Central Jewish Office who was in Zilina before the departure of both transports, testified before the National Court that both transports were the most terrible which had ever passed through Zilina.

'Dr Eugen Kunstadt, a physician from the health department of the Central Jewish Office, testified in the National Court that on about 10 July 1942, by order of the Fourteenth Department of the Slovak Ministry of the Interior, all the ill, the lame, the blind and the old were taken away from the old people's home in Edlova Street in Bratislava and were driven by ambulance to Patronka. From there they were transported in carriages to Zilina where they were joined to the transport. "As a physician I can claim that only few of them survived the transport and reached Auschwitz alive." This was repeated a short time later at the Jewish home at No. 43 Goering Street in Bratislava.

'Eva Neumannova from Ochodnica was included in the transport of July 17 and 18 in Zilina. She was arrested on charges of illegal activity. Nothing was proved, however, and after interrogation she was sent to the collection centre in Zilina. She was cleaning there for ten to fourteen days and she could see what was happening. She remembers a small concrete shelter, which was called a bunker, where those prisoners who were intended to complete the transport were placed.

'Eva Neumannova describes the departure from Zilina and the selection after the arrival of the transport of July 17 and 18 as follows: "Preparations for the transport of July 17 started early morning as was usual on other days. Everything was organised and supervised by members of the Hlinka Guard. Gendarmes stood around the train and further from it to prevent anybody visiting the deported. They got into each carriage in groups of forty. We were allowed to take luggage up to fifty kilograms from our homes which we had to lay off at a certain place on the platform and take only a small hand case or a handbag into the carriage.

'The train left Zilina at about noon. Next day, when it stopped at a station inscribed with Auschwitz, accompanied by shouting SS men, we all had to quickly get out of the carriages ...'

10.15 a.m.

Another episode took place here in August 1944, during a deportation from the distant island of Rhodes (the first land seen by air travellers flying today from Israel to Europe). The 1,712 Jews deported from Rhodes were first taken by sea to Athens, then by train northwards through Yugoslavia and Hungary. For seventeen days the train continued on its journey northward. One of those on board was a Slovak Jew, Sidney Fahn. In 1940 he had escaped from the Slovak capital, Bratislava, with his family, and made his way, slowly and perilously, southward through Europe to the Aegean Sea and Rhodes. For more than three years he was safe there, the island being under Italian rule. When Italy surrendered to the Allies in 1943, Germany took over all her possessions.

Sidney Fahn was deported with the Jews of Rhodes. As the deportation train went northward from Hungary, he realised that the train would shortly pass close to the town of Ruzomberok in the Tatra Mountains, where his parents were still living. When the train stopped at Sered, Fahn saw through a crack in the carriage wall a man whom he had known before the war, and was able to call down to the man, and to ask him to telephone his father, Arnold Fahn, to say that the train was heading his way.

Receiving the message, Arnold Fahn went at once to the goods yard at Zilina – which is in front of us as I tell this story. It was here that he learned that the train carrying his two sons, Sidney and Rudolf, as well as his daughter-in-law Regina and his nine-month-old grandson, Shani, whom he had never seen, would be passing through Zilina in a few hours' time.

A British writer, John Bierman, who uncovered this unusual story, has recorded how, here at Zilina, the last encounter took place between the Fahn brothers and their father: 'Through the cracks in their car, as the train stood at rest, they could see the old man searching frantically for them. They called out to him – "Here, Papa, here." The old man ran forward. "The child," he cried, "let me see the child!"

'An SS man jumped down on the track. "Get back," he shouted. "Keep away from the train." Frantic to see his sons and grandson, the old man found the courage to ignore him. Pressed close to the car he had time – before the SS drove him off at gunpoint – to get his longed-for glimpse of Shani, held in the arms of his mother, and to tell Sidney and Rudolf that he had bribed the relief engineer to slow down and give them a chance to jump from the train at a spot some miles up the track. But Arnold Fahn had wasted his money. The train did not slow down, and even if it had, there was no way the prisoners could have got out of the sealed cattle car.'

10.25 a.m.
We leave Zilina on the express train to Ostrava (in the Czech Republic), which will go as far as Cadca on line towards Poland, before branching away westward. We are on the same line as that taken by Sidney Fahn and his family, and many hundreds of thousands of Greek, Hungarian, Italian and Croat Jews. After a few moments there are high hills on both sides of the line. We will either stop in Cadca until about six o'clock, or go on (perhaps there is a local train) to the border, at Zwardon (which was shown on the train departure board).

I distribute the baguette sandwiches that I bought when walking back from the main square.

10.27 a.m.
Ochodnica. The beauty of the scenery – grassy meadows in the valley, pine-clad hills above – is in extreme contrast to the grimness of the journey fifty-two years ago. We are making this journey during the

exact month of the start of the Hungarian–Jewish deportations in 1944. Greek Jews were also being deported on this line at the same time.

10.35 a.m.
The valley opens up to the west. On the east are high pine-clad hills.

10.55 a.m.
Cadca. We leave the train, which is going on into the Czech Republic. But we will not stop here. Instead, walking along the gravel platform, we cross the tracks to where a two-carriage train is waiting to go on to Skalite.

11.12 a.m.
Leave Cadca. Tens of thousands of deportees were sent in cattle trucks along this route. It is unbearable to think about.

11.17 a.m.
Svrcinovec. The train leaves the main line and crosses on to a single track which is leading up into the mountains. At this point the deportees were on the railway line that would take them to a border manned by German guards.

11.27 a.m.
Cierne. A tiny village, in the hills to the north of which three countries meet: the Slovak Republic, the Czech Republic, and Poland. To the south, alpine meadows, with wild flowers on the embankment. The hay has been harvested and small haystacks stand in the front gardens of the cottages. As the train goes slowly around a curve four geese waddle towards the line.

11.30 a.m.
We are in the Beskid Mountains. The highest one visible, about five miles away, goes up to 3,200 feet.

11.35 a.m.
We reach Skalite. This is as far as our train goes. We haul our luggage out and drag it to the station. I go into the small waiting room and look at the departure board. There will be a train quite soon to the border station of Zwardon. In my enthusiasm to continue I suggest that we take this train so that we are on the Polish–Slovak border

when the evening train comes through and can spend the rest of the day on the border, which must be hilly and wooded. This is not a very welcome suggestion, as it is a hot morning. Even dragging the bags from the train to the station has caused some displeasure. Ben gets upset. He starts telling the group, as he did at Bohusovice yesterday morning, of the terrible burdens of carrying luggage and the imperative of discarding luggage during the deportation journeys and what a tiny unimportant irritant our journey's disruption is.

We decide to stay here, at Skalite, until the evening train. After successfully negotiating with the stationmaster, we leave our bags in a locked room in the station building, and then set off up the hill into the village. Within a few minutes we reach a hotel, the Hotel Kolonial, which has a bar and restaurant. We sit down at tables in the sun. Below the hotel, down a short slope, is the single-track railway from Skalite to the border, and then on to Auschwitz, the railway along which so many hundreds of thousands of Jews were deported.

12.30 p.m.
Some of the group decide to walk through the village, others stay at the hotel. In the village, we find a small shop selling local cherries: small and tart and refreshing.

We come to the church, and to the First World War memorial. Its base is a marble woman with her head in her hands. There are fifty-three names on the memorial, all killed fighting in the Austro-Hungarian army. Six of the dead have the same surname, Canecky. We wonder if J. Feuermann might have been a Jew.

As we walk on, Ben asks an old woman who is walking towards us about the war. 'I don't remember anything,' she says. 'I was only ten.'

'I was also ten,' says Ben, 'but I remember a lot.'

The woman shrugs and walks off. We think of the contrast between their two lives. The young girl living in a village through which, day after day and night after night, sealed trains pass taking people to their unknown destination across the mountains, and the young boy working in a slave labour camp along the perimeter of which trains are leaving, taking his nearest and dearest, family and friends, on a journey from which almost none of them will return.

1.45 p.m.
We rendezvous for lunch at the hotel. The cherries are a culinary bonus.

3 p.m.

We leave the hotel, walk through the village, pass the cemetery and reach the railway. It is a beautiful hot summer afternoon in the mountains of Slovakia. We walk along the railway for a kilometre. There is a profusion of dandelions by the railway line, and lush alpine greenery. In a field below the railway two elderly peasants, a man and a woman, are preparing haystacks. We sit on the grassy embankment between the railway and their field. A single-carriage train goes by, in its mauve and yellow livery, on its way from Skalite to Serafinov, the last Slovak station before the Polish border. As we look at the peaceful rural scene, I read out a description by Arek Hersh, who now lives in Britain, of his enforced journey to Auschwitz by rail in 1944, from the Lodz Ghetto. He was fifteen at the time:

'As the train progressed, it gradually grew hotter and hotter in the wagon. Little children began to cry, elderly people began to feel faint, and many people started getting desperate to go to the toilet. I was standing on a bucket, looking out of the tiny window, but had to get down when one of the men asked if he could use the bucket for a makeshift toilet. He fenced off a corner of the wagon with a blanket, then put the bucket behind it. That way people could go behind the blanket and thus retain what little dignity they still had left.

'After a while the stench from the bucket became unbearable. However, we had to live with it, as the doors were locked and the window was too high and narrow to empty out the bucket's contents. The heat, too, continued to build, and little children continued to cry. We could not sit down as the wagon was too cramped, and we were all very hungry. Fortunately a few people had brought bottles of water with them which they began to pass round.

'All at once an old woman collapsed, and within minutes was dead. Now, as well as all our other problems, we had a corpse in the wagon with us. I began to pray as never before. "Please God, let us reach our destination soon." My prayers, however, went unheeded; the long day dragged on and on, heading slowly towards night.

'Eventually one reaches a stage where one resigns oneself to a certain situation. During that long, terrible day, I believe that I reached that stage for perhaps the first time since the war had begun. I began to care little about my own fate; I just wished that this horrendous ordeal would end, one way or another. Perhaps the only thing that stopped me from giving up completely was the responsibility I felt towards Genia and her brother.

'Genia was nervous and trembling with fear. She had never been in a camp before and did not know what to expect. I stroked her face and held her hand, the sweat slippery between our palms. I assured her that we would be all right, that I had been in a camp before and I was still alive. She squeezed my hand tightly, and gradually I was able to calm her down a little.

'Every so often I asked Heniek and Szymek to lift me up so that I could look out of the window. When the train curved I could see the guard on the running-board outside our wagon, brandishing his machine gun. I wondered how close the Russians really were, whether they would ever release us from this ordeal. Most of all I wondered where this train was taking us.

'At last night fell and it began to get cooler, but it also grew steadily darker until it was pitch-black. We slept what little we could, half-standing, leaning against one another, but our sleep was punctuated by the smell of sweat and death and human waste, and by the moans and groans of the people. The darkness, like the heat, seemed to go on and on; a night that lasted a year. When, finally, dawn came it brought very little hope. The train was still speeding on towards its destination, but where that destination was, none of us could say.

'We travelled a little further and then, abruptly, the train began to slow down. Once again I asked Szymek and Heniek to lift me up to the window so that I could see what was going on. The sight that met my eyes was what I had been expecting, yet my spirits plummeted all the same. I saw a camp, barracks, high wire fencing, guards in towers, people walking about in striped suits. The train slowed down gradually and then came to a stop. After a journey that had seemed to go on for ever, we had finally arrived at our destination.

'We waited a further ten minutes, then we heard German voices, the noise of the doors being pulled open.'

After the reading, silence. For what seems many minutes no one speaks. We look at the railway tracks curving past us up into the hills. Across the field, the two elderly peasants have continued preparing their haystacks. I am reminded of Thomas Hardy's poem, 'In Time of "The Breaking of Nations"':

> Only a man harrowing clods
>   In a slow silent walk
> With an old horse that stumbles and nods
>   Half asleep as they stalk.
>
> Only thin smoke without flame
>   From the heaps of couch-grass;

> Yet this will go onward the same
>> Though Dynasties pass.
>
> Yonder a maid and her wight
>> Come whispering by:
> War's annals will cloud into night
>> Ere their story die.

When we arrived at Skalite station this morning, I remembered that it was here at Skalite that Rudolf Vrba had crossed from Poland to Slovakia after his escape from Auschwitz. He was the first escapee to bring to the West – with his fellow-prisoner Alfred Wetzler – news of the mass murder process at Auschwitz.

I had .brought his memoirs on this journey, intending to read the story of his escape from Auschwitz when we reach the camp itself. But it also contains an account of his arrival here, at this very village, and, as we settle down again by the roadside, I read from his memoir. I take up the story while Vrba and Wetzler were still on the Polish side of the border. These are Vrba's words:

'We kept to the most desolate tracks, for the thought of a last-ditch capture was unbearable and people were dangerous, sometimes deliberately, sometimes by accident, but dangerous nevertheless. Yet people unfortunately have a habit of appearing in the most unlikely places and a day later, as we worked our way through a field, we stumbled across an old Polish peasant woman.

'For quite a while we stood in silence, gazing at each other, trying to assess the situation. The old woman showed no fear, but she knew we meant trouble, that we were on the run. If she helped us, the Germans might kill her. If she did not help us, we might kill her. It was as simple as that.

'At last I said: "We're heading for the Slovak border. Can you show us the way? We've escaped from a concentration camp, from Auschwitz."

'It was pointless trying to deceive her; and suddenly I realised that, for the first time, I was talking about Auschwitz to someone outside the camp. It meant nothing to her, of course, but I felt that, if I died that moment, at least I had told one person.

'"You'll have to wait here," she said slowly, never taking her eyes off our faces. "Tonight I'll send a man who will help you. And I'll send you some food right away."

'I realised then that we were starving. Food had been scarce on the mountain, but tension had blunted our appetites after our encounter with the German patrol. We had drunk from streams and hardly eaten a bite for several days.

'We thanked her, but we did not trust her. As she walked away, we studied our position and saw that she would have to cross a bridge about a thousand yards away. About two hundred yards away in the opposite direction was a forest. If she tipped off the Germans, we would see them crossing the bridge and would have plenty of time to reach shelter before they even saw us.

'Two hours later we saw someone approaching the bridge, not a soldier, but a small boy of about twelve. He skipped up the hill to us and with a shy smile handed us a big parcel. We opened it, found it contained a kilogram of cooked potatoes and some meat, and gobbled it greedily. The boy's grin broadened as he watched us and he said when we had finished: "My grandmother will be back when it is dark."

'The food appeased our hunger, but did little to lull our suspicions. If she returned when it was dark, we would not be able to see who was with her, when she crossed the bridge. For a while we debated whether we should press on, but in the end we decided that we would be able to gauge from the sound of the footsteps how many were with her and whether we should bolt for the trees.

'For hours we waited. I shivered without my overcoat as the sky darkened and the chill of evening seeped into my bones. I soon forgot the cold, however, when, peering through the deepening dusk, I saw the old woman returning with a man who wore the rough clothes of a peasant.

'Still we did not relax, for this, too, could be a trick. We waited without speaking until they were quite close to us; and then we saw a pistol in the man's hand.

'Instinctively we closed our hands on the knives in our pockets. The situation was dangerous, but by no means hopeless, for, if he were taking us back to the Gestapo, we still had a long road to travel and both of us were desperate. We knew we could kill him before he fired in the dark; and we were prepared to do so.

'The old woman, however, behaved just as she had that morning, calmly and without fear. She gave us another big parcel and said: "Here's some more food. You look as if you need it."

'The man with the gun never spoke and our eyes never left him, as we crammed the food into our mouths. Because we were still famished, we finished it in a few minutes; and then, to our amazement, he roared with laughter.

'Shoving the gun into his pocket, he said: "You're from a concentration camp, all right. Only really hungry men could eat like that.
But at first I thought you might be Gestapo agents."

'"Gestapo agents?"

'"Yes. Sometimes they try to trick us. They know we help the
partisans and so they dangle decoy ducks in front of us, hoping that
we'll show our hands. But it's easy enough to tell the real from the
sham.

'"Now you'd better come with me. You can stay the night in my
place and tomorrow night I'll see you safely across the border."

'We rose to our feet, grinning like children. The border ... people
who spoke Slovak ... friends ... safety ... home. It seemed too good
to be true.

'As we moved off, however, I wondered if I would make it. My feet,
which had been giving me trouble for a long time, were now so swollen
that I could not walk properly, I could only hobble.

'He took us to his home, a small, neat cottage in the valley. There I
flopped into a chair and tried to ease off my boots. They would not
budge. I tugged at them, wincing with agony, while Fred and our host
watched me anxiously.

'"There's only one thing for it," said Fred. "You'll have to cut them
off. You'll get nowhere if you wear them."

'He was right. Once inside Slovakia I felt confident I could lay my
hands on a pair of boots or shoes; and I was determined to cross that
border, even if it meant walking on my hands.

'From an inside pocket I took my razor blade, the suicide blade that
Volkov – a Russian prisoner-of-war at Auschwitz – had told me I must
carry. Carefully I cut through the fine Dutch leather and my feet
expanded with relief, as the boots fell away.

'"You can't travel in your socks," grunted the Pole. "Here ... take
my carpet slippers. They're all I can spare."

'That night we knew the luxury of sleeping in a bed. All next
day we stayed in the cottage, while our friend went off to work.
When he returned, we had supper and then he said: "It's time to go.
But first let me tell you what you're facing. This border is patrolled
fairly well. The guards, however, stick to a routine, the idiots, and
that means that I can gauge fairly accurately where they are at
any given time. So long as you do exactly what I say, I'll get you
across."

'Ten minutes later we left. The old man moved surprisingly swiftly
and silently for his age and I had quite a job keeping up with him in

my carpet slippers. At last, however, he stopped and consulted a heavy gun-metal watch.

'"A German patrol passes here every ten minutes," he said casually, as if he were announcing the time of the next train. "We'll have to let the next one go by."

'We hid in the bushes. Soon we heard the crunch of marching feet; and, as we peered cautiously through the branches, the soldiers passed, so close to us that we could have touched their green uniforms.

'The journey lasted longer than we had anticipated, two hours in fact. At last, however, we came to a clearing and our guide stopped.

'"See that forest over there?" he said. "That's Slovakia. At this point the German patrols pass every three hours. So you'd better wait until the next bunch appears before you move on."

'We gazed at the forest fifty yards away, dampening down the urge to dash for it right away. Then we turned to the tough old Pole and thanked him.

'"I'm glad I could help," he said with a grin. Then he glanced at my feet and added: "I hope the slippers hold out!"

'He disappeared without another word. We hid in the trees on the edge of the clearing until the patrol came and went; and then we dashed for Slovakia. For the first time since we had climbed from the pile of wood, we felt really free, even though the country was still ruled by Monsignor Tiso with his Hlinka Guards and was well populated with Quislings.

'Freedom, however, was not enough. It was not the primary reason for our escape. We still had to contact the Zionists, the Jewish committees with whose help the Germans were able to arrange the deportations. We had to tell them that resettlement areas really meant gas chambers and we knew that making this vital contact was not going to be easy.

'It meant walking into a town without papers, exposing ourselves to spot checks by the Hlinka Guards or the Germans, asking our way, seeking the addresses of the Jews, revealing ourselves, in fact, as strangers from God knew where.

'It would have been safer, indeed, to stay in the forests, to join the partisans, to fight with them; but that was a luxury which would have to wait until we had finished the job we had set out to do.

'After marching through the forest for about two hours, we came to open country. A peasant working in a field straightened himself and stared at us as we approached. Now I was on more familiar ground, for I knew my own people; and as I studied him carefully, I had a feeling that I could trust him.

'Bluntly, for deception would have been pointless, I said: "Where are we?"

'"Near the village of Skalite. Not far from the town of Cadca."'

I stop reading. Everyone is silent. Here we are, at the very village to which Vrba and Wetzler came, after their extraordinary escape, bearing with them the information about Auschwitz that was to shake the world, and lead to such a strong and immediate outcry – not only from the Allies but also from the Pope and the King of Sweden – that the Germans were forced to halt the Hungarian deportations before they could encompass the Jews of Budapest.

Vrba knew both Skalite and Cadca from his earlier days as a Slovak student. I continue reading his account:

'I took another good look at the man in the field. He was tall and hardy with dark brown eyes and an inscrutable face. My instincts still insisted that he was reliable, though my suspicious mind, tempered by Auschwitz, warned me to be careful. Fred, I knew, was thinking much as I was; and after a while we both came to the conclusion that now we had to trust him anyway. Obviously he was no fool. He knew we were strangers; and he knew that we wanted to reach the nearest town or village. Even if we left him, he could still betray us and have us picked up within the hour.

'"We need help," I said. "We must get to Cadca."

'He looked us up and down and grinned. Then he said: "You'd better come to my place first because you're not going to get far in those clothes. By the way, my name is Canecky."

'We looked at each other and saw how right he was. We no longer looked like two impeccably dressed Dutch businessmen, which would have been bad enough. We looked like two Dutch businessmen who had been rolled in the mud and torn through a very large bramble bush. Without another word we followed him to his cottage. There he fed us; and while we ate he searched his own sparse wardrobe and came back with some peasants' clothes which would give us a veneer of respectability in that farming community. We changed quickly and then sat down to give him a brief outline of our story.'

4 p.m.

The reading is over. We sit for a while looking up at the hill down which Vrba had come, and wondering which was Canecky's house. A local train, just a single carriage, passes by, on its way up to the Polish border. We have about two hours before our 'morning' train makes its appearance. At the station I had checked most carefully to make sure the evening express existed. And there it was, the one and only train shown in red (express) lettering on the indicator board.

4.14 p.m.

We break up into small groups and wander off, some back to the village, some to the hotel, others across the fields. I walk with Herut across the river and along a narrow country lane with stooks in the meadow. At the end of the lane is a cottage. An old lady comes out of the front door. Thinking of the farmer who had given succour to Vrba, I ask, 'Is Canecky here?'

'No,' she says. 'He's up the hill.'

Herut and I retrace our steps along the path, across the river and then walk up a steep slope. We pass another man and woman cutting hay in a tiny sloping meadow. A man overtakes us walking up the slope on his way home. Does Canecky live up here, I ask him. He laughs. There are six Caneckys, he says, 'one up here, one over there' (across the valley), 'another there' (he continues to point).

I have no doubt that if one had a whole day here it would be possible to find Vrba's Canecky or his sons, and certainly the farm.

Herut and I walk on past well-kept houses and fields: potatoes, onions, carrots; each house has a plot of vegetables, often across the road from the house, and a fruit garden. We pass some gooseberry bushes. In one garden a kid is tethered. In another are a goose and its goslings, which Herut photographs for her grandson. Far below little trains (mostly of only one carriage) are passing to and fro on the Skalite–Zwardon line.

5.30 p.m.

We return to Skalite village, passing on the way down the steep hill path the two farmers in their little field. They are still making hay, and wave and laugh as we pass, and are staggered to learn that we have come from London.

We return to the Hotel Kolonial, where the group is gathering. I sit with a bottle of mineral water and a cup of coffee, eating a creamy yogurt I had bought in the village. It has been a strange and unexpected afternoon, something not planned during all those months of preparation in London. Much was unexpected, not only the place itself, but the silence during the Arek Hersh reading; and then the long silence afterwards. I had been unable to say anything for quite a while as everyone was so deep in thought. And then, during the Vrba reading, the same silence. We are in the same hills and then – the same village.

Everyone, including me, was beginning to feel nervous about Auschwitz. These apprehensions were being expressed, and I was uncertain how to handle them. But this enforced change of schedule may have given us a necessary break, an afternoon of calm reflection together – and singly – on what is to come. For tonight we will sleep in Cracow, and tomorrow morning we will reach Auschwitz.

6.15 p.m.
We leave the Hotel Kolonial and walk down the road to the railway station. It is a bright, sunny evening. The mountain air is cool and fresh.

6.45 p.m.
The train to Bratislava arrives, having come down the single track from the Polish border. Because it is a single track, the train must wait until ours comes in alongside. Then both trains – and we – can move off.

6.53 p.m.
The Bratislava—Cracow express draws in from the south. We clamber on board.

6.55 p.m.
Our train draws out of Skalite station and wends its way up the valley towards the Polish border. The evening sun is shining brightly on the fields. All over the hillside, as in a medieval painting, men and women are scything the grass, haymaking in the evening sun. At a railway crossing, a man is standing with his scythe.

7 p.m.
We go through Serafinov, the last station on the Slovak side of the border.

7.05 p.m
Zwardon. The station is on the Polish side of the border. Slovak frontier police come on board and briefly examine our passports.

7.14 p.m.

A Polish officer looks into our compartment and wishes us 'good travel'.

7.15 p.m.

A train pulls in alongside us which has come up from Katowice. There is a second Polish passport control.

7.20 p.m.

The train descends through thick pines. I read from Primo Levi's memoirs. At the age of twenty-four, and a partisan in northern Italy, he was captured by the Italian Fascist Militia on 13 December 1943. After being held in a camp at Fossoli with more than six hundred other Jews, the day came when, on 22 February 1944, he was deported. The passage that I read begins with the moment when that deportation began, and brought him to the very pine forest we are going through now:

'With the absurd precision to which we later had to accustom ourselves, the Germans held the roll-call. At the end the officer asked "Wieviel Stück?" ("How many pieces?") The corporal saluted smartly and replied that there were six hundred and fifty "pieces" and that all was in order. They then loaded us on to the buses and took us to the station of Carpi. Here the train was waiting for us, with our escort for the journey. Here we received the first blows: and it was so new and senseless that we felt no pain, neither in body nor in spirit. Only a profound amazement: how can one hit a man without anger?

'There were twelve goods wagons for six hundred and fifty men; in mine we were only forty-five, but it was a small wagon. Here then, before our very eyes, under our very feet, was one of those notorious transport trains, those which never return, and of which, shuddering and always a little incredulous, we had so often heard speak. Exactly like this, detail for detail: goods wagons closed from the outside, with men, women and children pressed together without pity, like cheap merchandise, for a journey down there, towards the bottom. This time it is us who are inside.

'Sooner or later in life everyone discovers that perfect happiness is unrealisable, but there are a few who pause to consider the antithesis: that perfect unhappiness is equally unattainable. The obstacles preventing the realisation of both these extreme states are of the same nature: they derive from our human condition which is opposed to everything infinite. Our ever-insufficient knowledge of the future opposes it: and this is called, in the one instance, hope, and in the other, uncertainty of the following day. The certainty of death opposes it: for it places a limit on every joy, but also on every grief. The inevitable material cares oppose it: for as they poison every lasting happiness, they equally assiduously distract us from our misfortunes and make our consciousness of them intermittent and hence supportable.

'It was the very discomfort, the blows, the cold, the thirst that kept us aloft in the void of bottomless despair, both during the journey and after. It was not the will to live, nor a conscious resignation; for few are the men capable of such resolution, and we were but a common sample of humanity.

'The doors had been closed at once, but the train did not move until evening. We had learnt of our destination with relief. Auschwitz: a name without significance for us at that time, but it at least implied some place on this earth.

'The train travelled slowly, with long, unnerving halts. Through the slit we saw the tall pale cliffs of the Adige Valley and the names of the last Italian cities disappear behind us. We passed the Brenner at midday of the second day and everyone stood up, but no one said a word. The thought of the return journey stuck in my heart, and I cruelly pictured to myself the inhuman joy of that other journey, with doors open, no one wanting to flee, and the first Italian names ... and I looked around and wondered how many, among that poor human dust, would be struck by fate. Among the forty-five people in my wagon only four saw their homes again; and it was by far the most fortunate wagon.

'We suffered from thirst and cold; at every stop we clamoured for water, or even a handful of snow, but we were rarely heard; the soldiers of the escort drove off anybody who tried to approach the convoy. Two young mothers, nursing their children, groaned night and day, begging for water. Our state of nervous tension made the hunger, exhaustion and lack of sleep seem less of a torment. But the hours of darkness were nightmares without end.

'There are few men who know how to go to their deaths with dignity, and often they are not those whom one would expect. Few know how to remain silent and respect the silence of others. Our restless sleep was often interrupted by noisy and futile disputes, by curses, by kicks and blows blindly delivered to ward off some encroaching and inevitable contact. Then someone would light a candle, and its mournful flicker would reveal an obscure agitation, a human mass, extended across the floor, confused and continuous, sluggish and aching, rising here and there in sudden convulsions and immediately collapsing again in exhaustion.

'Through the slit, known and unknown names of Austrian cities, Salzburg, Vienna, then Czech, finally Polish names. On the evening of the fourth day the cold became intense: the train ran through interminable black pine forests, climbing perceptibly. The snow was high. It must have been a branch line as the stations were small and almost deserted. During the halts, no one tried any more to communicate with the outside world: we felt ourselves by now "on the other side". There was a long halt in open country. The train started up with extreme slowness, and the convoy stopped for the last time, in the dead of night, in the middle of a dark and silent plain.'

We will be reaching that 'dark and silent plain' in about two and a half hours' time: time to reflect, time to read, time to be silent.

7.30 p.m.
The train has emerged into a valley with meadows full of wild flowers.

7.35 p.m.
Sol. I read, as I told him I would, from Elie Wiesel's memoirs, *All Rivers Run to the Sea*, in which he recalled his deportation along a parallel track further east:

'Life in the cattle cars was the death of my adolescence. How quickly I aged. As a child I loved the unexpected: a visitor from afar, an unforeseen event, a marriage, a storm, even a disaster. Anything was preferable to routine. Now it was just the opposite. Anything was preferable to change. We clung to the present, we dreaded the future.

'Hunger, thirst, and heat, the fetid stench, the hysterical howling of a woman gone mad – we were ready to endure it all, to suffer it all. So much so that a "normal", structured social life soon took shape in the car. Families stayed together, sharing whatever came their way: hard-boiled eggs, dried cakes, or fruit, respecting strict rules about drinking water, allowing each member a turn near the barred openings or at the waste pail shielded by blankets. People adjusted with disconcerting rapidity. Morning and evening we said our prayers together. I had brought some precious books along in my pack: a commentary by Rabbi Haim David Azoulai (the Hida), and the *K'dushat Levi* of the Berdichever rebbe. I opened them and tried hard to concentrate. A phrase of the *Zohar*, a major work of the Kabala, haunted me: "When the people of Israel set out into exile, God went with them." And now? I wondered. How far would God follow us now?

'On the last day, when the train stopped near the Auschwitz station, our premonitions resurfaced. A few "neighbours" devoured more than their rations, as though sensing that their days were numbered. My mother kept entreating us: "Stay together at all costs." Someone, I can't remember who, asked, "What if we can't? What if they separate us?" My mother's answer: "Then we'll meet again at home as soon as the war is over."

'Certain images of the days and nights spent on that train invade my dreams even now: anticipation of danger, fear of the dark; the screams of poor Mrs Schechter, who, in her delirium, saw flames in the distance; the efforts to make her stop; the terror in her little boy's eyes. I recall every hour, every second. How could I forget? They were the last hours I spent with my family: the murmured prayers of my grandmother, whose eyes saw beyond this world; my mother's gestures, which had never been more tender; the troubled face of my little sister, who refused to show her fear. Yes, my memory gathered it all in, retained it all.'

7.45 p.m.
Rajcza. We wend our way down the valley of River Sola. High pine-clad hills stretch on either side of the railway. On the right is Sucha Gora, 1,000 metres high. A farmer with his horse-drawn cart goes by laden with hay.

7.55 p.m.
Milowka. This is where Vrba and Wetzler were helped by Polish partisans with food and shelter.

8.05 p.m
Wegierska Gorka.

8.25 p.m.
We are travelling through the valley where, in 1981, the British filmmaker Rex Bloomstein came with me and a Polish camera crew to film the story of Vrba's escape. It was still the Communist era. I remember how worried we were that this might turn out to be a military zone, or otherwise an area in which filming was not allowed. In the event, the hundreds of hours of film which Rex had taken all over Poland, including at Chelmno and Auschwitz, were deliberately fogged when he passed through East Germany. Not one minute was

transmittable, and he had to start all over again. The hills and fields have a much less ominous air about them today.

8.30 p.m.
Zywiec. There was a Jewish community here from the mid-nineteenth century. No community survives, only some two hundred gravestones in the Jewish cemetery.

8.50 p.m.
Wylkowice.

9.05 p.m.
Bielsko-Biala, known to most of its Jewish inhabitants by its German name, Bielitz. Jews are recorded living here in 1765. There were 4,700 Jews when war broke out in 1939; most of them were deported to Auschwitz and murdered there in 1942.

On 3 September 1939 the German army entered Bielsko-Biala. The town had a substantial German minority at that time. As our train waits in the station, I read Kurt Klappholz's recollections of the arrival of the Germans here. Kurt, who was then twelve years old, had gone with his father into the centre of town to view the scene:

'We gazed at their columns in amazement. Never before had we seen an army so well equipped. Moreover, the troops were not only trained for fighting – a training which on that occasion proved redundant, they had obviously also had good training in making propaganda. They rose from the benches in their troop-carriers, bench by bench, gave the Hitler salute, and chorused one or another of their well-known slogans – "Ein Volk, ein Reich, ein Führer" ("One People, one Nation, one Leader"), "Wir danken unserem Führer" ("We thank our Leader"), etc. While the day before the town centre had been almost empty, now it was thronged with frenziedly jubilant crowds, most of them the German inhabitants, who not only loudly repeated the soldiers' slogans, but showered their liberators with flowers, cakes and sandwiches. The crowd's jubilant enthusiasm was infectious. I still remember that even my father offered a cigarette to a German soldier. Even so, we did not stay to see the end of the "parade" but returned home, where several of our neighbours were talking excitedly.

'While my father joined in the conversation, I distanced myself from the little group, and started to brood over what I had just seen, and began to cry. My father noticed this and came over to ask why I was crying. I wiped my tears and began to mumble that Poland was lost.

Then I paused, looked him in the eyes and said: "Papa, ich glaube, dass wir diesen Krieg nicht überleben werden" ("Father, I fear that we will not survive this war"). He patted me on the head gently, smiled, and tried to calm my outlandish, childish fears.'

9.19 p.m.
The train passes the Vacuum Oil factory. This was one of the slave labour camps where Jews from Auschwitz worked.

9.23 p.m.
Czechowice-Dziedzice. The train stops here for ten minutes. In several of the factories around here Jewish slave labourers were employed.

9.33 p.m.
We leave Czechowice-Dzedzice and join the main line travelling eastward. The train speeds up considerably.

9.50 p.m.
We pass, on the right of the train, the industrial town of Jawiszowice, the site of another wartime slave labour camp. We are now within a few minutes of Auschwitz. We stand by the window as the train travels along a righthand curve. It is dark and the lights from the train windows are shining on the track. When this righthand curve straightens out we will be running towards the perimeter and rail spur of Birkenau. The line straightens and the train slows down, then speeds up again, travelling very fast. We enter what was once the Auschwitz concentration camp zone.

Angela later writes to me of this moment: 'One thing I recall vividly is how cold it was, and the shiver both Caroline and I felt as we looked out of the window.'

9.56 p.m.
The train continues at a rapid pace, straight as a die. Suddenly, outside the window, we see the outline of the huts in the women's camp. Then quickly we pass the line of the spur railroad into Birkenau, and then slow down as we reach Auschwitz station. We will be here again tomorrow morning.

10 p.m.
The train stops at Auschwitz station. Everyone is surprised at how close to the station the camp is.

10.02 p.m.
The train draws out. It is all passed within five minutes: camp, spur and station. German officers, sitting in the restaurant car of the Vienna–Cracow express saw, as we did, the line of the huts in the women's camp. They also saw the flames and smoke belching from the chimneys.

10.10 p.m.
Two Polish conductors arrive. They tell us that as we are not on the morning train, the supplements we paid are not valid, and we must pay new supplements. We point out that the morning train had not existed, and wonder why. 'They cancel trains regularly,' explain the conductors. 'They were going to cancel this one too.'

10.35 p.m.
Trzebinia. We join the main Silesia–Cracow railway hurtling westward at what seems to be an increasing speed. A massive oil refinery here was one of the main targets of several Allied bombing raids in the autumn of 1944.

10.40 p.m.
The two conductors return. They are trying to work out how much money they can extract from us for the supplement. I suggest thirty dollars. 'This is a Jewish group then?' they ask. Ben explains that we are not, in fact, all Jewish. 'You see that blonde one over there,' he says, pointing to Marie, 'she is Swedish.' Petra is German. Robin is a good Anglican. Suzanne, likewise, not Jewish.

   This seems not quite what the conductors had expected, and they reduce their surcharge to twenty dollars accordingly. They seem thrilled with their bonus. They then explain to Ben that quite a number of Jewish groups travel this section of the line, from Auschwitz to Cracow, providing them with a useful income.

11.07 p.m.
Cracow. We leave the train and make our way through the almost deserted main station. Luckily my phone call from Zilina had worked and the minibus is awaiting us.

11.20 p.m.
The bus sets off and takes us along the Planty; this pleasant green circuit of the city is where my grandmother used to walk, almost exactly a hundred years ago. She studied here in Cracow as a young

girl. When I was ten or so, she used to tell me about walking along the Planty.

11.25 p.m.
We reach the hotel, the Dom Turysty, and I distribute the room keys. As 'tour leader' I deal with a dozen details to try to ensure a smooth start to what is most certainly going to be a difficult day – early-morning calls, arrangements with the bus driver tomorrow, ensuring that breakfast will be available and when.

11.45 p.m.
Room. Shower. I read an article I have brought with me, written in 1984 by Mikhail Salman, a Leningrad Jew who was then refused permission to leave the Soviet Union (he lives today in Israel). As a 'refusenik' he did research into the 'blood libels' in the Middle Ages, and even in more modern times, that so often led to pogroms, and to the execution of Jews accused of using Christian blood to make Passover bread. Two of these blood libel accusations were made here in Cracow, one in 1407, the other in 1637. Looking through Mikhail Salman's list, I see that we will be visiting four other places where this charge was made: Lublin (in 1598 and 1636), Leczyca (1637), Wlodawa (1816) and Poznan (1736–40) – which we will be going through on the train on our last night.

Midnight
Bed.

DAY 7

CRACOW – AUSCHWITZ – CRACOW

'Paralysed by this mournful weeping'

6.45 a.m.
The sun is shining over the trees and grass of the Planty. I look out over my grandmother's city. Memories come back of her bedside in London where I sang my Barmitzvah portion for her. She was too frail to go to the synagogue. I remember how emphatic she was when I was a young schoolboy that I should do well at Latin.

7 a.m.
In the hotel breakfast room I introduce Kathy Jones to the group. She is working in Poland for the Imperial War Museum, collecting material for a Holocaust exhibition which is to open in three years' time. She will travel with us for the rest of our journey.

   As a result of having being unable to spend yesterday afternoon at Auschwitz, I work out a new programme today whereby we will go to Auschwitz this morning and try to do during the afternoon everything we would have done in Cracow today.

8.08 a.m.
We board the minibus and are driven through Cracow, reaching Wawel Castle and driving along the Vistula.

8.25 a.m.
We pass the first 'Oswiecim' signpost (Oswiecim is the Polish for Auschwitz). It is fifty-six kilometres from here.

9 a.m.
In the hills to the south of us is Wadowice. It was here, after the war, that Karol Wojtyla, the present Pope, who was then in training for the

priesthood, was asked by a Polish Catholic woman, Mrs Jachowicz, for guidance with regard to the Jewish child she had been hiding and protecting during the war. Neither of the child's parents, Moses and Helen Hiller, survived the war. Mrs Jachowicz, meanwhile, had become very attached to the little boy, took great pride in her 'son', and took him regularly to church. Soon, he knew by heart all the Sunday hymns.

A devout Catholic, Mrs Jachowicz decided to have Shachne Hiller baptised. It was then that she went to see the young parish priest Karol Wojtyla. Revealing the secret of the boy's identity, Mrs Jachowicz told the priest of her wish that Shachne should become a 'true Christian' and devout Catholic like herself.

Wojtyla listened intently to the woman's story. When she had finished, he asked: 'And what was the parents' wish, when they entrusted their only child to you and to your husband?' Mrs Jachowicz then told him that Helen Hiller's last request had been that the child should be told of his Jewish origins, and 'returned to his people' if his parents died. Hearing this, Wojtyla replied that he would not perform the baptismal ceremony. It would be unfair, he explained, to baptise Shachne while there was still hope that, once the war was over, his relatives might take him.

Shachne Hiller not only survived the war, but was eventually united with relatives in the United States.

9.10 a.m.
We reach a crossroads at which there is a sign: 'Oswiecim Museum Auschwitz'.

9.15 a.m.
To the left of the road is a view of Buna, the vast industrial complex at nearby Monowitz (known as Auschwitz III) where so many Jewish slave labourers from Birkenau worked to produce the synthetic oil vital to the German war effort in the autumn of 1944. There were also British prisoners-of-war working here. One of them, Charles Coward, was awarded after the war one of the first medals of the 'righteous gentiles' by the State of Israel, for his work in saving Jewish lives at Buna while himself a prisoner.

9.20 a.m.
We are driven through Auschwitz town – which appears in the 1943 Baedeker guide book for German travellers as 'an industrial town of

12,000 inhabitants', with one recommended hotel – and reach the station which we had passed by train last night.

9.25 a.m.
We cross the railway bridge from which can be seen the rail spur curving into Birkenau.

9.28 a.m.
I ask the minibus driver to stop some way short of the gate of Birkenau. We get out, and walk slowly towards the gate. It is a stunningly beautiful sunny day with a light refreshing breeze. The mountains in the distance – which we came through yesterday on the train – can be seen through a light mist; just as the prisoners here could have seen them.

Two groups enter the gate in front of us. We decide to wait for a few moments before entering, and by then, as the place is so vast, the other groups have disappeared from view. We walk slowly along the railway line with the huts of the camp to the left and right of us. On our left, stretching into the distance, is the women's camp (B I a and B I b). On our right, we pass first the registration office (B II a), then the Czech family camp (B II b), then the men's camp (B II c and B II d), then the Gypsy camp (B II e) and finally the medical camp (B II f) where Dr Mengele, Dr Wirths, Dr Kremer and others – men trained in the profession of healing – carried out their appalling experiments.

As we begin this walk we see, almost immediately, to our left, the first of several small water tanks. These were built here in the late summer of 1944, when the Germans feared that Allied bombing raids might lead to huts being set on fire. American bombers did strike at the nearby Buna synthetic oil plant several times. But when the truth about Birkenau, and the request to bomb the railway lines leading to it and the crematoria, reached Washington, the War Department official to whom it was sent gave instructions to 'kill' the request. The result was that the request was rejected several times. But when it reached London a few weeks later, Winston Churchill wanted action to be taken. He wrote to Anthony Eden, the Foreign Secretary, 'Get anything out of the Air Force you can, and invoke me if necessary.'

Within a few days of Churchill giving this instruction, there was a widespread outcry in the United States at the news about Birkenau which became public knowledge as soon as the report by Rudolf Vrba and Alfred Wetzler reached Switzerland. As a result of this outcry, the deportations from Hungary (to impede which the bombing had been requested) were stopped, on direct orders of the Hungarian government. From that moment the urgent appeals from the Jewish leaders became, not further bombing (they did not realise that deportations had begun from elsewhere, including the Lodz ghetto), but protective documents for the hundreds of thousands of Jews who were still in Hungary. These appeals were immediately taken up by several foreign diplomats in Budapest. These included the Swedish consul Raoul Wallenberg, the Swiss consul, Charles Lutz, and the Spanish consul, Perlasca, each of whom issued thousands of protective documents.

During the American raid on Buna on 13 September 1944 several bombs fell wide of their target. One of them hit a bomb shelter that had been constructed alongside the railway siding leading to the crematoria (where we are walking now) and thirty Polish civilian workers sheltering there were killed. Other bombs during this raid were dropped, also in error, on Auschwitz Main Camp (Auschwitz I). One of these bombs hit the SS barracks and killed fifteen SS men. Another bomb hit a clothing workshop and killed twenty-three Jews.

We sit at the end of the ramp along which the deportation trains came. Here, between Crematorium II and Crematorium III, I read out the description of arriving here by Arek Hersh, whose recollections of the train journey we read yesterday afternoon by the railway line at Skalite: 'The train had stopped. It had remained still for ten minutes and then those inside the carriage had heard German voices and the noise of the doors being pulled open. Despite our fear, we were urging them to hurry up, to get to our door. All of us were anxious for that precious moment when we would feel sunlight on our faces again and smell the scent of fresh clean air. At last we heard voices outside our wagon, the rattle of the door being unlocked. I smiled nervously at my friends and gathered my few belongings together, ready to disembark.

'We screwed up our eyes as the brightness of the day hit us, gulped in lungfuls of the wonderful air. However, we did not have much time to appreciate it as the Germans began to shout at us, "Raus! Schnell!" ("Out! Quick!"), and started herding us into lines. All around me was commotion. I heard the shouts of the Germans, the screams of lost, frightened children, the cries of mothers frantically searching for their own sons and daughters. The SS, the same kind of men who had taken my friends away in those closed lorries to their deaths, were very brutal, kicking and beating people into line. There were five thousand people on the platform, which meant there was bound to be some disorder, yet the Germans liked things to be orderly, even when they were taking you to your death.

'There was a long concrete ramp leading from the station into the camp, along which streamed an endless line of people. We had to wait in a queue for our turn to ascend the ramp, all of us nervous, terrified, trying to keep out of the way of the German soldiers. I saw one young mother screaming and clinging to her children as the SS tried to take them away from her. A number of SS waded in and began to thump and kick her, smashing her nose, knocking her to the ground. She lay, screaming horribly with pain, but even then they didn't stop their beating and kicking. I turned away, sickened and shocked, feeling horribly guilty for not going to her aid, but knowing there was nothing I could do, that we simply had to keep quiet and remain unobtrusive, and hope that by some miracle we would survive this nightmare.

'Eventually our line began to move, was herded towards the long concrete ramp. As we got closer I realised that the Germans were separating people into two rows, one row going to the left, the other to the right. I saw that the lefthand row was full of children and old people, and I knew I must avoid that one at all costs. As I neared the two high-ranking SS officers who were dividing the people into these rows, I drew myself up to my full height and tried to give an impression of strength and fitness.

'To my horror the SS men barely glanced at me before indicating that I should join the lefthand row. There was nothing I could do or say; my mind was numb, but racing. I saw that all the children from the orphanage were in this row, shuffling forward, and I joined them, my numbness gradually giving way to an awful sense of terror.

'Suddenly behind us a commotion began, perhaps another small attempt at resistance, accompanied by much scuffling and screaming. With the attention of our guards on this commotion, I instinctively stepped across the dividing line into the righthand row. I merged in with the people in this row, my heart beating fast, my eyes focused downwards on my shoes. I was certain that I must have been spotted, but no guard appeared to tell me to rejoin the children and the old people. I shuffled in through the gates of the camp, still not fully realising what I had done, still not fully aware that I had just saved myself from certain death in the gas chambers. A man in a striped suit working at the side of the road looked up and said very quietly in Yiddish that we were lucky to be in this group. He informed us that we were in "Birkenau, Auschwitz", which didn't mean very much to me as I had never heard of the place before.'

After the reading there is silence. We are standing on the spot where these terrible events took place. It is hard to focus on the scene around us, the sunlight, the grassy platform, the huts across the track (the women's camp), the row after row of chimneys on our side of the track (all that is left after most of the huts were burned down after the war).

There are relatively new memorial plaques at the end of the ramp. When I was last here, in 1981, there was no mention in any of the plaques that Jews had been murdered here. The word chosen was 'people'. The new plaques, in many languages, read (there is one in English):

> For ever let this place be
> a cry of despair
> and a warning to humanity,
> where the Nazis murdered
> about one and a half
> million
> men, women, and children,
> mainly Jews
> from various countries
> of Europe.
> Auschwitz-Birkenau
> 1940–1945

There is one more reading that I want to do here, from Primo Levi, whose recollections of the deportation journey we read yesterday in the train, a few hours after we had read Arek Hersh's recollection, and just after the train had crossed the Slovak–Polish border. In his book *If This Is A Man*, Primo Levi recalled how the train finally stopped at a place where rows of red and white lights could be seen on both sides of the track 'as far as the eye could see', and how those in his wagon fell silent. 'The climax came suddenly,' Levi wrote. 'The door opened with a crash, and the dark echoed with outlandish orders in that curt, barbaric barking of Germans in command which seems to give vent to a millennial anger. A vast platform appeared before us, lit up by reflectors. A little beyond it, a row of lorries. Then everything was silent again. Someone translated: we had to climb down with our luggage and deposit it alongside the train. In a moment the platform was swarming with shadows. But we were afraid to break that silence: everyone busied himself with his luggage, searched for someone else, called to somebody, but timidly, in a whisper.

'A dozen SS men stood around, legs akimbo, with an indifferent air. At a certain moment they moved among us, and in a subdued tone of voice, with faces of stone, began to interrogate us rapidly, one by one, in bad Italian. They did not interrogate everybody, only a few: "How old? Healthy or ill?" And on the basis of the reply they pointed in two different directions.

'Everything was as silent as an aquarium, or as in certain dream sequences. We had expected something more apocalyptic: they seemed simple police agents. It was disconcerting and disarming. Someone dared to ask for his luggage: they replied, "luggage afterwards". Someone else did not want to leave his wife: they said, "together again afterwards". Many mothers did not want to be separated from their children: they said, "good, good, stay with child". They behaved with the calm assurance of people doing their normal duty of every day. But Renzo stayed an instant too long to say good-bye to Francesca, his fiancée, and with a single blow they knocked him to the ground. It was their everyday duty.

'In less than ten minutes all the fit men had been collected together in a group. What happened to the others, to the women, to the children, to the old men, we could establish neither then nor later: the night swallowed them up, purely and simply. Today, however, we know that in that rapid and summary choice each one of us had been judged capable or not of working usefully for the Reich; we know that of our convoy no more than ninety-six men and twenty-nine women entered the respective camps of Monowitz-Buna and Birkenau, and that of all the others, more than five hundred in number, not one was living two days later. We also know that not even this tenuous principle of discrimination between fit and unfit was always followed, and that later the simpler method was often adopted of merely opening both the doors of the wagon without warning or instructions to the new arrivals. Those who by chance climbed down on one side of the convoy entered the camp; the others went to the gas chamber.

'This is the reason why three-year-old Emilia died: the historical necessity of killing the children of Jews was self-demonstrative to the Germans. Emilia, daughter of Aldo Levi of Milan, was a curious, ambitious, cheerful, intelligent child; her parents had succeeded in washing her during the journey in the packed car in a tub with tepid water which the degenerate German engineer had allowed them to draw from the engine that was dragging us all to death.

'Thus, in an instant, our women, our parents, our children disappeared. We saw them for a while as an obscure mass at the other end of the platform; then we saw nothing more.

'Instead, two groups of strange individuals emerged into the light of the lamps. They walked in squads, in rows of three, with an odd, embarrassed step, head dangling in front, arms rigid. On their heads they wore comic berets and were all dressed in long striped overcoats, which even by night and from a distance looked filthy and in rags. They walked in a large circle around us, never drawing near, and in silence began to busy themselves with our luggage and to climb in and out of the empty wagons.

'We looked at each other without a word. It was all incomprehensible and mad, but one thing we had understood. This was the meta-morphosis that awaited us. Tomorrow we would be like them.

'Without knowing how I found myself loaded on to a lorry with thirty others; the lorry sped into the night at full speed. It was covered and we could not see outside, but by the shaking we could tell that the road had many curves and bumps. Are we unguarded? Throw ourselves down? It is too late, too late, we are all "down". In any case we are soon aware that we are not without a guard. He is a strange guard, a German soldier bristling with arms. We do not see him because of the thick darkness, but we feel the hard contact every time that a lurch of the lorry throws us all in a heap. At a certain point he switches on a pocket torch and instead of shouting threats of damnation at us, he asks us courteously, one by one, in German and in pidgin language, if we have any money or watches to give him, seeing that they will not be useful to us any more. This is no order, no regulation: it is obvious that it is a small private initiative of our Charon. The matter stirs us to anger and laughter and brings relief.'

Primo Levi had been taken, not to a section of Birkenau, but to the slave labour camp at Buna. From where we are standing on the ramp at Birkenau we can see the chimneys of the factory at Monowitz; it operates to this day.

10.30 a.m.

We walk from the end of the ramp a few short yards to the gate of Crematorium III. Here I read the account given by Claude Vaillant Couturier. Deported from Paris for her part in resistance activity, she had been put in a block opposite the notorious Block 25, the 'Waiting Block'. She had seen Jewish women brought naked from the other barracks to Block 25. These were women who had been judged too sick or too frail to work, or even chosen at random. From Block 25, after being kept for up to a week without food and water, they were all sent, invariably from that hut, to the gas chamber.

Of the fate of the women who had been brought to Block 25 that particular Christmas, 1943, Madame Vaillant Couturier recalled how uncovered trucks were driven up to the block, and then, 'on them the naked women were piled, as many as the trucks could hold. Each time a truck started, the famous Hessler ran after the truck and with his bludgeon repeatedly struck the naked women going to their death. They knew they were going to the gas chamber and tried to escape. They were massacred. They attempted to jump from the truck and we, from our own block, watched the trucks pass by and heard the grievous wailing of all those women who knew they were going to be gassed.'

At the Nuremberg Trials, less than two years after the events which she had witnessed, Madame Vaillant Couturier recalled what she saw from her block directly facing the special rail spur that came right into Birkenau, 'practically right up to the gas chamber': 'We saw the unsealing of the coaches and the soldiers ordering men, women and children out of them. We then witnessed heart-rending scenes, old couples forced to part from each other, mothers made to abandon their young daughters, since the latter were sent to the camp whereas mothers and children were sent to the gas chambers.

'All these people were unaware of the fate awaiting them. They were merely upset at being separated but they did not know that they were going to their death. To render their welcome more pleasant at this time – June, July 1944 – an orchestra composed of internees – all young and pretty girls, dressed in little white blouses and navy blue skirts – played during the selection on the arrival of the trains, gay tunes such as "The Merry Widow", the "Barcarolle" from *The Tales of Hoffmann*, etc. They were then informed that this was a labour camp, and since they were not brought into the camp they only saw the small platform surrounded by flowering plants. Naturally, they could not realise what was in store for them.'

Those selected to be killed, Claude Vaillant Couturier added – the old people, mothers and children – were 'escorted' to a red-brick building. They were not tattooed. 'They were not even counted.' They were all gassed.

We stand in the bright sun and look across the almost deserted camp. In the far distance towards the gate another small group is making its way along the railway line. There is an air of total desolation. There is nothing here but a few huts, the ruins of the gas chambers and crematoria, a few monuments, and an incredible silence. There is a sense of total oppressiveness which the readings seem only to deepen.

One of those who survived here was Dr Gisella Perl. She later recalled the arrival of a train from Holland in September 1944. Just over a thousand Jews were on that train. It reached this ramp on September

5; from the train half the deportees were taken straight to the gas chamber where we are standing. In her recollections Dr Perl later recalled how 'a group of well-dressed, white-bearded gentlemen go by, fully dressed, with hats and gloves and well-cut overcoats. They carried fine plaid blankets and small overnight cases in their hands, like diplomats going to some important conference.' These were 'rich people', Gisella Perl was later told, 'who had been able to hide until now, thanks to their money and connections'. Most were gassed. 'Only a very few came out of the selection alive,' she recalled, 'dressed in rags like the rest of us.' Her account continued:

'A few days later I spoke to one of these newcomers. He worked on the refuse heap near the crematorium. In that short time, the elegant, well-groomed man, who had looked like a diplomat, had become a dirty, lice-infected, human wreck, his spirits broken. He was a Dutchman and he spoke German.

'I saw him go over to one of the camp foremen and whisper to him under his breath, anxiously, hurriedly. The foreman looked at him expectantly, and the new prisoner reached under his rags and brought out a small leather pouch, the kind which usually holds tobacco. He opened it with trembling hands and shook the contents into his palm.

'Like a million little suns the diamonds shone and sparkled in his dirty, broken-nailed hands. Grinning broadly, the foreman nodded and held out three miserable uncooked potatoes, and the elderly man, shaking with impatience, tore them out of his hand and put them to his mouth, chewing, swallowing, as if every bite gave him a new lease of life. The little pouch full of diamonds already rested in the pocket of the foreman and he kept his hand on it, caressing the stones almost tenderly.

'Here, in this Stock Exchange of Hell, the value of a bag of diamonds was three uncooked potatoes. And this value was the real one. Three potatoes had positive value, they prolonged life, gave strength to work and to withstand beatings, and strength meant life, even if for a short time only. The bag of diamonds itself was good for nothing. For a while, a short while, it might delight the eyes of a ruthless murderer, but when the day of reckoning came – it would not save his life.'

We are standing where, between 1942 and 1944, hundreds of able-bodied Jewish men – members of the Sonderkommando, or 'special squad' – many of them teenagers, were forced to take the bodies out of the gas chambers, to the crematoria, afterwards scattering the ashes in one of the dozens of nearby pits. I read from the notes of one of these men, Salmen Gradowski, who had been brought to Auschwitz in February 1943. On 6 September 1944, shortly before he himself was murdered, he buried the notes which he had managed to write over the previous nineteen months, and in which he described his own deportation and subsequent events in the camp. Having put his notes in a metal canister, he buried them in one of the pits of human ash. The canister was discovered after the war. I read from his letter which was found with his notes: 'I have buried this under the ashes, deeming it the safest place, where people will certainly dig to find the traces of millions of men who were exterminated.'

Gradowski dedicated his notes to the members of his family 'burnt alive at Birkenau', his wife Sonia, his mother Sara, his sisters Estera-Rachel and Liba, his father-in-law Rafael and his brother-in-law Wolf. In his letter he also wrote: 'Dear finder, search everywhere, in every inch of soil. Dozens of documents are buried under it, mine and those of other persons, which will throw light on everything that was happening here. Great quantities of teeth are also buried here. It was we, the Kommando workers, who expressly have strewn them all over the terrain, as many as we could, so that the world should find material traces of the millions of murdered people. We ourselves have lost hope of being able to live to see the moment of liberation.'

11 a.m.

The readings over, some sit silently nearby, others drift silently away, some holding hands. We will reassemble only when we feel that we can. The ruins of the crematoria are so near. Around Crematorium III are tall poplar trees. They had been planted as saplings in 1944 in an attempt to mask the crematoria and the camp.

11.30 a.m.

We gather at Crematorium III. A few yards away across the end of the ramp are the ruins of Crematorium II. A thousand yards to the north are Crematoria IV and V. These four crematoria were the centre of the killing process at Birkenau. They were also the site of the revolt of October 1944. The German records show that there were 169 Sonderkommando forced to work at Crematorium III, where we are standing, on 3 October 1944. At Crematorium II there were also 169 and at Crematorium IV, 154. I read from my account of the revolt; of how, with the gassing at Birkenau coming to an end, the men and boys of the Sonderkommando were alert to any indication that their days too might be numbered, they who in their gruesome task were given the privilege of ample food and blankets, and such 'comforts' as they might need in their barracks.

On the morning of Saturday, October 7, the senior Sonderkommando man at Crematorium IV was ordered to draw up lists for 'evacuation' of 300 men at noon that same day. Fearing that this was a prelude to destruction, he refused. The SS ordered a roll call for noon. The purpose of the roll call, the Jews were told, was that they were to be sent away by train to work in another camp. As the SS Staff Sergeant called out their numbers, however, only a few men answered.

After repeated calls and threats, Chaim Neuhof, a Jew from the nearby Polish town of Sosnowiec who had worked in the Son-derkommando since 1942, stepped forward. He approached the SS Staff Sergeant, talked to him, and gesticulated. When the SS man reached for his gun, Neuhof, loudly yelling the password, 'Hurrah,' struck the SS man on the head with a hammer. The SS man fell to the ground. The other prisoners then echoed Neuhof's 'Hurrah' and threw stones at the SS.

Reporting these events at Crematorium IV, Salmen Lewental noted, of his fellow Sonderkommando: 'They showed an immense courage refusing to budge [from the spot].[1] They set up a loud shout, hurled themselves upon the guards with hammers and axes, wounded some of them, the rest they beat with what they could get at, they pelted them with stones without further ado. It is easy to imagine what was the upshot of this. Few moments had passed when a whole detachment of SS men drove in, armed with machine guns and grenades. There were so many of them that each had two machine guns for one prisoner. Even such an army was mobilised against them.'

Some of the Sonderkommando at Crematorium IV attacked the SS so viciously with axes, picks and crowbars that several SS men fell wounded and bleeding to the ground. Other SS men sought cover behind the barbed-wire fence, shooting at the prisoners with their pistols.

Some of the prisoners then managed to run into their empty barracks, where there were hundreds of straw mattresses on the wooden bunks. They set the mattresses on fire. The fire spread at once to the wooden roof of Crematorium IV. 'Our men,' Lewental noted, 'seeing they were brought to destruction, wanted to set fire to Crematorium IV at the

---

[1] The words in square brackets in the Sonderkommando manuscripts are passages that were too badly damaged to be read clearly. The words in square brackets have been suggested by the editors of the manuscripts.

last moment and perish in battle, fall on the spot under the hail of bullets. And in this way, the whole crematorium went up in flames.'

The arrival of SS reinforcements on motorcycles, from the SS barracks inside Birkenau, brought the revolt at Crematorium IV to an end. All those who had acquired implements, and all who had set fire to the crematorium roof, were machine-gunned.

The blazing roof of Crematorium IV was seen by the Sonderkommando of Crematorium II. They took the flames as a sign that the revolt, for which they too had been preparing, had begun. Before they could act as planned, however, their well-prepared scheme was foiled by an accident of fate. At that very moment, a group of Soviet prisoners-of-war who were working in Crematorium II saw armed SS men coming towards the crematorium. The Russians, Lewental noted, thought that the SS were coming 'just to take them away'. It was 'impossible', he added 'to restrain them in this last moment'.

In panic, the Russians seized the leading Kapo, a German, 'and in a flash threw him alive into the burning furnace'. The Jews of the Sonderkommando, Lewental wrote, 'seeing that they were faced with an accomplished fact, and realising that retreat was no longer possible, decided to begin their revolt. Distributing such tools as they had been able to assemble, they cut the wire near their crematorium, and fled into the nearby countryside.' During the escape, the Jews killed three SS corporals: Rudolf Erler, Willi Freese and Josef Purke.

The men at Crematorium II had used neither arms nor grenades. Some of them hoped to find an escape route through the adjoining area in which the 'Cleaning Installations' Commando was living. They were joined there by Sol Schindel, a Jew from the southern Polish city of Rzeszow, who worked in the 'Cleaning Installations' Commando. Schindel later recalled how 'as we ran past the watchtower, I saw the SS men shooting with machine guns. I saw many dead already lying on the ground. I threw myself to the ground and crept through a hole in the barbed-wire fence into the women's camp.' There, Schindel met a Kapo from the 'Canal Cleaning' Commando, with whom he was on friendly terms, joined the squad, and managed to get back to the barracks. The Sonderkommando men continued beyond the wire, in search of somewhere to hide in the fields and farmsteads between Birkenau and the River Sola.

Within minutes of the break-out through the wire near Crematorium II, the alarm siren had sounded. Almost immediately, SS men with dogs drove up in trucks and surrounded the whole area of the break-out. Catching up with those who had managed to get beyond the wire, the SS gave no quarter. Most of the escapees were shot. The rest found brief sanctuary in a barn. Not wishing to take risks, the SS set fire to the barn, then shot the escapees as they ran out.

Only twelve of those who had escaped were still outside the wire, and alive. About two hundred and fifty had been killed outside the wire, among them their leader, Jozef Dorebus, known in the camp as Jozef Warszawski. Later that day, a further 200 men of the Sonderkommando were shot inside Birkenau.

There had also been preparations for revolt among the Sonderkommando of Crematorium III, immediately across the ramp from Crematorium II. There, explosives had also been hidden, thanks to the Jewish women at the Union factory who were sent out each day from Birkenau to make munitions there for the German army.

Most of the Sonderkommando prisoners were in the attic of their barracks when the break-out from Crematorium II took place. Coming out as they heard the sirens, they saw that SS troops had surrounded 'their' crematorium. A few moments before the SS entered their barrack, they were able to move the explosives from their hiding place and pour them down the latrine. The leader of the SS troops ordered all prisoners locked up in one room and the barracks searched, but the explosives were not discovered. The men of Crematorium III were then marched across the ramp to Crematorium II and ordered to burn the 600 corpses that were still lying in the gas chamber. Later that afternoon, the bodies of those who had been shot trying to escape from Crematorium II were brought to Crematorium III, stripped, and burned in the ovens.

Twelve men from Crematorium II had not yet been recaptured. SS patrols with dogs found them, exhausted, in an empty building on the other side of the river. They were killed, and their bodies brought back to Birkenau.

There were several reprisals for the revolt of the Jewish Sonderkommando at Birkenau. One was the execution of four Jewish women – Roza Robota, Ella Gartner, Toszka and Regina – who were working as slave labourers in the Union factory. It was they who had smuggled explosives into Birkenau in preparation for the revolt. All four were hanged in the women's camp of Birkenau. A second repercussion was an act of vengeance against 650 boys aged between fourteen and sixteen. Most of the boys were from Hungary, and had been deported to Birkenau in the summer. On October 20 they were forced to undress and a selection of the fittest was made. Only fifty were 'selected' to live. The rest were to be killed.

An account of their fate survives, written by another of the Sonderkommando, and hidden by him shortly before he himself was murdered. His notes were not discovered in the ground here until 1962. Part of them was damaged by water, but the Polish editors reconstructed the few missing words or letters – which appear here in square brackets.

I read out his account. 'In the middle of a bright day,' he wrote, 'six hundred Jewish boys aged from twelve to eighteen, dressed in long striped clothes, very thin; their feet were shod in worn-out shoes or wooden clogs. The boys looked so handsome and were so well built that even these rags did not mar their beauty. They were brought by twenty-five SS men, heavily burdened [with grenades]. When they came to the square the Kommandoführer gave the order for them to undress in the square. The boys noticed the smoke belching from the chimney and at once guessed that they were being led to death. They began running hither and thither in the square in wild terror, tearing their hair [not knowing] how to save themselves. Many burst into horrible tears, [there resounded] dreadful lamentation.

'The Kommandoführer and his helper beat the defenceless boys horribly to make them undress. His club broke, even, owing to that beating. So he brought another and continued the beating over the heads until violence became victorious.

'The boys undressed, instinctively afraid of death, naked and barefooted they herded together in order to avoid the blows and did not budge from the spot. One brave boy approached the Kommandoführer [standing] beside us [. . .] and begged him to spare his life, promising he would do even the hardest work. In reply he hit him several times over the head with the thick club.

'Many boys, in a wild hurry, ran towards those Jews from the Sonderkommando, threw their arms around the latter's necks, begging for help. Others scurried naked all over the big square in order to escape from death. The Kommandoführer called the sergeant with a rubber truncheon to his assistance.

'The young, clear, boyish voices resounded louder and louder with every minute when at last they passed into bitter sobbing. This dreadful lamentation was heard from very far. We stood completely aghast and as if paralysed by this mournful weeping.

'With a smile of satisfaction, without a trace of compassion, looking like proud victors, the SS men stood and, dealing terrible blows, drove them into the bunker. The sergeant stood on the steps and should anyone run too slowly to meet death he would deal a murderous blow with the rubber truncheon. Some boys, in spite of everything, still continued to scurry confusedly hither and thither in the square, seeking salvation. The SS men followed them, beat and belaboured them, until they had mastered the situation and at last drove them [into the bunker]. Their joy was indescribable. Did they not [have] any children ever.'

Robin later wrote to me: 'This reading provoked much distress amongst us, especially those who have families.'

11.45 a.m.

We walk in silence through the birch trees – the nearby forest of which gives Birkenau its name – to 'Canada'. This is the extraordinary hutted area in which the belongings of those who had been brought here were sorted for despatch to Germany: the belongings of those who had been taken to the barracks and put in the striped uniforms, and the belongings of those who had been murdered. It was known as 'Canada' because this was a country which was considered to be a place of wealth and comfort.

Rudolf Vrba worked here in 'Canada' in 1943. By a strange irony he lives today in Canada – in Vancouver. I read his account of the place where hundreds of Jews, mostly women, were made to sort such wealth and possessions as more than a million Jews had managed to bring with them to what they were told was a 'labour camp in the East' or 'help with the harvest'. Vrba remembered being lined up outside his hut in Birkenau with a number of other men, and then the order was given, 'Clearing Command! forward':

'With that we marched into "Canada", the commercial heart of Auschwitz, warehouse of the body-snatchers where hundreds of prisoners worked frantically to sort, segregate and classify the clothes and the food and the valuables of those whose bodies were still burning, whose ashes would soon be used as fertiliser.

'It was an incredible sight, an enormous rectangular yard with a watchtower at each corner and surrounded by barbed wire. There were several huge storerooms and a block of what seemed like offices with a square, open balcony at one corner. Yet what first struck me was a mountain of trunks, cases, rucksacks, kitbags and parcels stacked in the middle of the yard.

'Nearby was another mountain, of blankets this time, fifty thousand of them, maybe one hundred thousand. I was so staggered by the sight of these twin peaks of personal possessions that I never thought at that moment where their owners might be. In fact I did not have much time to think, for every step brought some new shock.

'Over to the left I saw hundreds of prams. Shiny prams, fit for a firstborn. Battered prams of character that had been handed down and down and down and had suffered gladly on the way. Opulent, ostentatious, status-symbol prams and modest, economy prams of those who knew no status and had no money. I looked at them in awe, but still I did not wonder where the babies were.

'Another mountain, this time of pots and pans from a thousand kitchens in a dozen countries. Pathetic remnants of a million meals, anonymous now, for their owners would never eat again.

'Then I saw women. Real women, not the terrible, sexless skeletons whose bodies stank and whose hearts were dead.

'These were young, well-dressed girls, with firm, ripe figures and faces made beautiful by health alone. They were bustling everywhere, running to and fro with bundles of clothes and parcels, watched by even healthier, even more elegant women kapos.

'It was all a crazy jigsaw that made no sense to me and seemed sometimes to verge on lunacy. Beside one of the storerooms I saw a row of girls sitting astride a bench with zinc buckets on either side of them. One row of buckets was filled with tubes of toothpaste which the girls were squeezing out on to the bench and then throwing into the other, empty buckets. To me it seemed thoroughly anti-German, an appalling waste of labour and material; for I had yet to learn that perhaps one tube in ten thousand contained a diamond, a nest egg that some pathetic trusting family had felt might buy privilege or even freedom.'

The huts of 'Canada' have gone. There is only a vast open field surrounded by a wire fence. Some people coming away from the centre of the field say that there are some remnants of belongings there. I do not have the strength to go and look.

To our left, and just across the path from 'Canada', is a long, low brick structure, with four tall brick chimneys, which was once the 'sauna', the building where those deportees who were to be put to slave labour were undressed, deloused and tattooed, and given their striped uniforms and wooden clogs before being sent to their barracks. Everything is within sight of everything else. From the edge of the sauna one looks straight into 'Canada', and through 'Canada', to what was the men's camp. From here, too, the more distant huts of the women are clearly visible. They lie beyond the railway, and immediately beyond us on the path, its foundations also visible, is Crematorium IV and beyond it, across a path, at the edge of the woods, is Crematorium V.

We walk past Crematorium IV to Crematorium V. To the left, beyond the perimeter fence, are fields and pits in which bodies were burned. Someone has set up a Star of David as a memorial in one of these fields, and also two or three crosses. When I spoke to Elie Wiesel shortly before setting off on this journey he expressed his concern about those crosses.

From Crematorium V we walk along the path to the former SS barracks. To our right is the men's camp. To our left, no longer part of the Auschwitz site, is the area of the enormous extension that was being prepared in the summer and autumn of 1944. It was known to the prisoners as 'Mexico'.

As we set off from Crematorium V we can see at the end of a long path a large cross. It is on the roof of the former SS barracks. The building was used recently as a convent, but the nuns have now gone elsewhere. Only the cross remains.

To our right is a pond in which the ashes from Crematorium IV were dumped. There are four memorial stones at the edge of the pond, inscribed in Polish, English, Hebrew and Yiddish. Curiously there is no mention of Jews in the inscription, which reads:

> To the memory of the men women and children
> Who fell victim to the Nazi genocide
> In this pond lie their ashes
> May their souls rest in peace

It is midday. Paul leads us in prayers. One of the memorial prayers that he reads says that the Jews died for 'Kiddush Hashem', for the Sanctification of God's name. Ben says that those who were killed did not choose to die for God, they had no choice in the matter.

We move off down the road to the former SS barracks. A tall cross can be clearly seen over the entrance tower. Beyond the fence and across the field to our right is the site of the medical huts where the Nazi doctors performed their experiments, including those performed by Dr Mengele on twins. Among the inmates who were sent to work in this section was a French Protestant doctor, Adelaide Hautval, a practising psychiatrist. She had been deported to Auschwitz in January 1943 because, while living in France, she had insisted on wearing a yellow star in sympathy with the Jews.

At Auschwitz, Dr Hautval was asked by SS Dr Wirths to participate in forcible sterilisation, but had refused to do so. 'He was surprised,' she later recalled, 'that a doctor practising psychiatry could condemn a method which aimed to improve and preserve the race. I answered that it brought grave abuse. He talked to me about the Jewish question and I answered that we had no right to dispose of the life and destiny of others.' Later she was asked to sterilise a seventeen-year-old Jewish girl from Greece. When she refused, Dr Wirths said to her, 'Cannot you see that these people are different from you?' to which she replied, 'There are several other people different from me, starting with you!'

Dr Hautval survived. Her courageous refusal to do what she believed to be wrong was a beacon of light in the darkest of storms.

To our left are the woods in which Jews were forced to wait before being taken to Crematorium V. It was here that the Hungarian Jews of one deportation, from Beregszasz, including Jews from several surrounding Carpathian towns and villages who had passed through the ghetto at Beregszasz, were photographed waiting, bewildered and uncertain, before being taken to their deaths. These photographs, part of what are known as the Auschwitz Album, are the only known pictures of people arriving at Birkenau. The album was found in Nordhausen concentration camp on the day of liberation in May 1945 by eighteen-year-old Lili Jacob, from the Sub-Carpathian town of Bilky who had earlier been deported to Auschwitz from the Beregszasz ghetto. She fainted when she found the album: for among the 193 photographs was one of the rabbi, Rabbi Weiss, who had married her parents. On continuing to look through the album, Lili Jacob found photographs of two of her five brothers, eleven-year-old Zril and nine-year-old Zeilek. They had both been gassed shortly after the picture was taken, as had her parents, her other three brothers, her grandparents, and her aunt Taba and her five children (who also appear in the album).

It emerged that the photographs had been taken on a single day (quite illegally), most probably by SS Second-Lieutenant Bernhard Walter, Director of the Identification Service at Auschwitz. After the war he was a film projectionist in Fürth, Bavaria. His assistant, SS Sergeant Ernst Hoffman, himself a photographer (who disappeared after the war), may also have taken some, or indeed all of them. The pictures were put in the album with neatly inscribed introductory captions, the first of which read: 'Umsiedlung der Juden aus Hungarn' (Resettlement of Jews from Hungary). Several months later, it would seem that a guard at Auschwitz named Heinz (his surname is unknown) sent the album to a guard at Nordhausen, perhaps his girlfriend, and probably someone who had earlier served with him at Auschwitz. He inscribed the album: 'As a remembrance of your dear, unforgettable, faithful Heinz.'

These photographs are often reproduced to illustrate very diverse periods of Birkenau's history, and to show deportations from different lands, many of which arrived not in summer but in winter. They are terrible pictures, since we know the fate of those seen standing about, sitting with their bundles, or walking along the fence. But they are only the photographic record of a single day out of the camp's more than eight hundred days on which deportees arrived, some of whom were usually sent to their deaths. We discuss how extraordinary it is that from this single day, so many different days, different circumstances, and even different camps, have been illustrated.

Two small exhibition boards have been set up showing some of the photographs taken on this spot. One can almost match up the trees in the photographs (fifty-two years ago) with the trees today.

On our left, now outside the area administered by the museum, is 'Mexico', the vast hutted area which was being prepared in the spring of 1944 for a mass extension of the camp. The huts are now gone. Among those working here preparing the new huts were Rudolf Vrba and Alfred Wetzler. Their escape plan, which was fraught with exceptional danger, involved them in hiding in a pile of timber in which their friends rubbed a rag smeared with oil and tobacco. The tobacco made it impossible for the dogs – bloodhounds – which would be searching the area for three days after any escape, to smell any human being.

I read Vrba's account of his and Wetzler's escape. Polish prisoners working in the same area, and apprised of their purpose, helped to prepare the hiding place, and, at the last moment, when the SS guards were looking elsewhere, moved the planks and, as Vrba recalled, 'gave us an almost imperceptible nod'. His account – which I am reading out – continues:

'This was it. For a moment we both hesitated, for we knew that, once we were covered up, there was no going back. Then together we skipped quickly up on top of the wood and slid into the hole. The planks moved into place over our heads, blotting out the light; and there was silence.

'Our eyes soon got used to the gloom and we could see each other in the light that filtered through the cracks. We hardly dared to breathe, let alone to talk. It was fifteen minutes, in fact, before we relaxed a little...

'I took out my powdery Russian tobacco and began puffing it into the narrow spaces which separated some of the planks, while Fredo sat, watching me in the gloom.

'It took me at least an hour to impregnate our temporary prison

thoroughly with dog repellent. Then I sat down, leaned against the
rough, wooden wall and concentrated on some positive thinking. I
forced my mind away from all thoughts of discovery and told myself
over and over again: "There'll be no more roll calls. No more work.
No more kow-towing to SS men. Soon you'll be free!"

'Free – or dead. I felt the keen blade of my knife and swore to myself
that, if they found me, they would never get me out of the cavity alive.
Time stood still. I glanced at the watch ... and saw that it was only
half past three. The alarm would not be raised until five thirty and
suddenly I realised I was longing to hear it. I felt like a boxer, sitting
in his corner, waiting for the bell, or like a soldier in the trenches,
waiting to go over the top.

'I feared the wail of that siren. Yet I could not bear the waiting. I
wanted the battle to begin.

'We could not stand up and became cramped sitting. We did not dare
to talk and that made time hang even more heavily. The movements of
the camp, movements we both knew by heart, drifted faintly into our
hole in the wood, but somehow it all seemed far away in time, as well
as in distance, for already my mind was free in advance of my body.
For the next hour I kept glancing at my watch, holding it to my ear
occasionally to see whether it had stopped. Then I disciplined myself
to ignore it, grinning in the dark as I thought fatuously of my mother
in her kitchen back home, shaking her finger at me and saying
solemnly: "A watched pot never boils!"

'In fact it was never necessary for me to look at my watch, for the
noises in the camp outside told me roughly what time it was. At last,
after what seemed a week, I heard the tramp of marching feet and at
once every fibre was alert. The prisoners were coming back from work.
Soon they would be lining up in their neat rows of ten for roll call.
Soon we would be missed; and then there would be the siren, the
baying of the dogs, the clatter of SS jackboots.

'We heard the distant orders, faint, disembodied, like lonely barking
at night. We saw in our minds the entire scene which would never be
part of our lives again. The rigid rows of the living. The silent piles of
the dead. The kapos and block leaders, snapping at their charges,
fussing, panicking. The SS, aloof, superior, totting up their units.

'I thought of what lay ahead and suddenly I realised that, if
everything went well, I would be free on April 10.

'I permitted myself the luxury of a glance at my watch. It was five
twenty-five. Five minutes from siren time. Already they must have
missed us. Already they must be debating what to do, whether we had

been delayed somehow or whether we had escaped, whether they should raise the alarm and risk ridicule, if we turned up, or whether they should wait and risk the rage of Hoess and Schwarzhuber, if it turned out that we had gone.

'Five thirty. And silence. Fredo and I stared at each other; and, though we did not speak, we shared the same thoughts. Five forty-five and still not a sound. I felt a tremor of panic, for this was ominous. It could mean big trouble, the end in fact.

'Someone, for instance, could have squealed. In a few minutes, perhaps, we would hear the planks being dragged back and see the muzzles of sub-machine-guns. Instinctively my grip tightened on my knife and I strained my ears for some sound, any sound that might give me a hint of what was going on.

'Six o'clock. The silence was torturing our nerves now. I whispered to Fred: "They're toying with us, playing with us. They must know where we are."

'He said nothing, but I knew he agreed with me. Someone walked by. We both started and held our breath. The footsteps faded in the distance. We heard voices, German voices, but they were too far away for us to understand what was being said. The walls of our wooden home seemed to grow smaller, pressing in on us, crushing our minds, our morale, wrapping us up in a neat little box that would be handed over with mock ceremony to some sneering Oberscharführer. I heard the drums. I saw the notices: "Because they tried to escape..." My mind squirmed at the humiliation of it, recoiling from the jeers and the laughter and the smug triumph that would greet our capture.

'Then the siren split my thoughts asunder, scattering them, pulverising them, whisking away fear, sweeping the cavity clean of depression, thrusting a challenge into my heart and into my mind.

'The wail rose triumphantly to its thin apex, clung there for a few minutes then died sadly. I could see Fred's eyes gleaming and I could hear chaos being born, maturing, pounding all around us. A hundred, two hundred, five hundred feet beat a tattoo. A thousand voices shouted and two thousand answered them. Orders ricocheted from barracks to barracks and the dogs gave anxious, plaintive tongue.

'The search was on. The long, meticulous, painstaking search that would continue for three days until every inch of Birkenau had been examined, every known hiding place upended. We felt something very near to exhilaration as we heard it drawing near and visualised the scene we knew so well.

'The voices were close now. I heard Unterscharführer Buntrock rasp:

"Look behind those planks! You're supposed to be searching this place, not taking the air. For Chrissake, use your heads as well as your eyes!

'Boots scrabbled up over the planks above us, sending a little shower of grit down on top of us. The pounding raised the dust and we covered our noses in case we sneezed. More boots and the heavy breathing of men. Then the dogs, snuffling, panting, their nails scraping the wood as they slithered and tumbled from plank to plank. My knife was out and I could see Fred poised, his teeth clenched in a smile of tense anticipation.

'Then the cacophony faded. Distance mellowed the grating discord, and silence filled our hideout, a silence that carried with it a strange sense of security. We had won the first round. Our nerves had been hacked against the wooden walls; and they had not failed us.

'The viciousness seeped out of Fred's grin. He winked at me and said: "The stupid bastards!" Soon, of course, they were back, sweeping ground already swept, scraping in corners, probing a little more desperately now. Again we heard the boots, again the dogs and the exasperated curses of frustrated men.

'So it went on all through the night, the noises rising and falling, fading, returning, reverberating around us. We had bread and margarine, but we could not bring ourselves to eat; wine, but we could not drink. Even when the searchers moved away, we dozed, but we did not rest, for our minds chased the fantasies of dreams, then were jerked back to the reality of our twilight by noises we had never noticed before.

'We could hear the sentries on the outer ring being checked, passwords being exchanged. Then the lorries began roaring by, forty, fifty, sixty of them on their way to the gas chambers with their victims, for outside our wooden walls, it was business as usual in Birkenau. We thought of them, filing quietly into the "showers", and after an hour or two we heard the harsh clanking of the iron grills, as they rattled into the ovens with load after load of dead flesh, twisted and sent it cascading into the flames.

'It was a monotonous sound, a sinister sound; yet it was a challenge to us, for we knew that only by escaping successfully could we do anything to silence it.

'The second day was a crucial period. The camp authorities knew that time was against them now and were whipping their men on mercilessly. They swirled around us and over us. The voices were harsh and strained, the intervals of silence shorter; and, as the tension increased outside, it filtered through to us in a gross distorted fashion because we could not see what was happening. Our nerves were frayed and hypersensitive and our stomachs were knotted with strain. Again we could neither eat nor drink, though we had had neither food nor liquid for over twenty-four hours.

'Night brought no relief. The stumbling, hurrying men kept rumbling overhead and it was only with the dawn that the pressure seemed to ease. "Just a day and a half more," said Fred. "And it shouldn't be too bad. By now they must be sure we're miles away." In a way he was right, for this third day was more relaxed, the quietest we had known, in fact. In another way, however, he was very wrong.

'At about two o'clock that afternoon we heard two German prisoners, talking outside. One said: "They can't have got away. They must be in the camp still." For a while they swapped wild theories about where we might be hiding. Then the second prisoner said: "Otto ... how about that pile of wood? Do you think they might be hiding under there somehow? Maybe they built themselves a little alcove or something."

'"The dogs have been over it a dozen times," said Otto. "They'd have smelled them ... unless, of course, they've some way of killing the scent."

'There was a long silence. Fred and I crouched motionless and heard Otto say slowly: "It's a long shot ... but it's worth trying. C'mon!"

'We heard them climbing onto the pile of wood and we drew our knives. They heaved one plank aside, then a second, a third, a fourth. Only about six inches of wood separated us from the enemy now and we stood poised to lunge, not daring to breathe. I braced my back against one wooden wall, crouching because there was not room to stand.

'Suddenly there was uproar on the other side of the camp. We could hear excited shouts and the quick patter of scurrying feet. The two Germans above us were silent now and motionless. Then Otto said: "They've got them! C'mon ... hurry!"

'They slithered off the planks and dashed off to answer a false alarm that had saved our skins.

'"One thing about Auschwitz," muttered Fred bitterly. "You meet a nice class of person. The dirty swine!"'

The next twenty-four hours passed 'quietly enough', Vrba recalled. 'The search went on,' he explained, 'but there was little heart left in it. The hours creaked by and our tension rose as we waited for the signal which for us meant action; for the dismissal of the outer cordon.

'We knew just how it would happen. An SS man would take the order to the nearest watchtower. It would be shouted from tower to tower, circling the camp, an admission of temporary defeat. The towers would empty. The guards would march back to the camp. The coast would be comparatively clear.

'Then we heard it, the first sing-song shout: *"Postenkette abziehen!"* ("Pickets withdraw!") from tower to tower. It grew fainter and fainter until we could hear it no more; but soon we picked it up again, as it completed its circle of the camp. It grew louder and louder as it came nearer and then at last it stopped.

'It was six-thirty on 10 April 1944. We heard the tramp of marching feet; then nothing more except the drone of mild activity in Birkenau. Officially we were out!

'Yet still we did not move, for isolation had magnified our suspicions and our fears. I said to Fred: "We'd better wait a while. It could be a trick. They could be foxing, just waiting for us to show ourselves."

'So we waited. Seven o'clock came ... eight ... nine. Without a word we stood up simultaneously and began pressing cautiously against the wooden planks that formed our roof. Then a moment of panic. They would not move! Grunting, straining, sweating, we used every ounce of our combined strength. Gradually, almost painfully, the planks rose an inch and now we could grip their rough edges. We heaved them sideways; and suddenly we could see stars above us in the black, winter, moonless sky.

' "Thanks be to God those bloody Germans nearly found us!" whispered Fred. "If they hadn't moved those other planks, we were trapped!"

'We scrambled out into the cold air and replaced the planks carefully in case someone else might be able to use the escape chamber later; and for a moment we sat on the pile of wood, motionless, invisible, gazing at the inner camp which we were determined never to see again.

'For the first time I was seeing Auschwitz from the outside, viewing it as its victims viewed it. The brilliant lights painted a soft yellow patch in its darkness, giving the whole place a mysterious aura that was almost beautiful. We, however, knew that it was a terrible beauty, that in those barracks, people were dying, people were starving, people were intriguing and murder lurked around every corner.

'We turned our backs to it, slid to the ground, flung ourselves flat and began to crawl slowly on our bellies, foot by careful foot, away from the toothless watchtowers and towards the small forest of birch trees that hid the old-fashioned pits of fire and gave Birkenau its name. We reached it, rose, and ran, stooping, through it until we came to open ground again and began to crawl once more.

'As I wriggled forward, I remembered Dmitri Volkov. The battle was just beginning.

'I remembered something else he said, too. Beware of mines.

'This was a chance we just had to take, for it was dark and, if we did not keep going, the dawn would catch us in the open. We moved on; and then, when we least expected it, we came to an entirely unexpected obstacle.

'At first I thought it was a river. It was about eight yards wide, a whitish ribbon stretching as far as I could see on either side. I knelt to examine it, put down my hand and found sand ... yard after yard of smooth white sand which presumably surrounded the entire Auschwitz-Birkenau camp. It was worse then water, for once we trod on it, our footsteps would be arrows for the patrols to follow as soon as it was light. As I gazed at it, in fact, I realised that it could be even more menacing than it seemed. It could easily conceal the mines of which Dmitri Volkov had spoken.

'Nevertheless that was another risk we had to take. Together we plunged across the miniature desert and found ourselves on open moor-land, thick with bracken. Here and there there were signposts which I thought might be warnings about mines; but it was too dark to read them and too risky to strike a match. So we just kept walking steadily until at last we could see the outline of another forest ahead of us just as the sky began to lighten. We quickened our pace instinctively because we had no cover, though I paused for a moment close to one of the signposts to see what it said.

'I read: "Attention! This is Auschwitz concentration camp. Anyone found on these moors will be shot without warning!"

'We were still within the confines of the camp; and the forest seemed just as far away. By that time it was quite light, in fact, we were still exposed. The moor had ended, giving way to a field of young corn. We paused to get our bearings, glanced around quickly – and flung ourselves to the ground.

'Five hundred yards away we could see a band of women prisoners, heavily escorted by SS men!

'For a moment we lay there, panting. Then cautiously we raised our heads. The column was on its way to work somewhere and obviously they had not seen us.

'Nevertheless we did not dare to stand up. Instead we wriggled along on our bellies, making use of every hollow, every dip, every ditch we could find. To hurry would have been madness and it was another two hours before we reached the safety of the trees.

'We rested briefly, then pushed on through the thick firs. The green umbrella soothed our taut nerves – until suddenly we heard voices; the voices of dozens of children.

'We plunged behind some bushes, peered cautiously through the heavy branches and saw a huge party of Hitler Youth, making their way through the forest, rucksacks on their backs. To our horror they sat down beneath the trees less than thirty yards away and began to eat sandwiches. We were trapped, not by the SS this time, but by their children!

'We must have lain behind that bush for an hour; but then our luck changed dramatically. Heavy drops of rain began to fall. The Hitler Youth glanced up and went on eating; but the shower became a downpour and at last they rose and scampered off, squealing at each other.

'We resumed our march. The ground was soggy beneath our feet, but our boots were strong. The rain beat down through the trees onto our bare heads, but it could not penetrate our fine Dutch overcoats. We felt almost happy as we ploughed on and not even the sight of an SS patrol with another band of women prisoners could depress us. We simply hid in a ditch until they had passed out of sight.

'At last I said to Fred: "It's time we slept. Let's find somewhere to hide, somewhere that not even the SS would bring women."

'For half an hour we searched until we found a large clump of bushes. We wormed our way into the centre and lay down in the bracken, confident that we could not be seen.

'A watery April sun filtered through the branches. The more enthusiastic birds twittered over our heads; and Fred lectured me amiably on the finer points of chess until we fell asleep.'

Vrba and Wetzler were free, ready to embark on a journey that would take them through the German-occupied and patrolled countryside to the Polish–Czech border (where we read about them yesterday at Skalite) and beyond.

Escape and revolt were so difficult, so rare, and so remarkable. The passages we have read inspire all of us. We ask how any of us could possibly have had the courage of those two men, who took such terrible risks?

12.25 p.m.

Continuing along the perimeter road at Birkenau, we reach the former SS headquarters, a substantial pre-1914 brick building with a three-storey tower. It is now a Catholic convent. The two crosses which adorn the building, the one on the top of the tower being visible from afar, seem extraordinarily out of place.

We sit for a while on the steps and I read from the diary of one of the SS doctors who worked here: Dr Johann Kremer. The first entry I read is dated 5 September 1942: 'This noon was present at a special action in the women's camp ("Moslems") – the most horrible of all horrors. SS Obersturmführer Thilo, military surgeon, is right when he said to me today that we are located here in "anus mundi" (anus of the world). In the evening at about 8 p.m. another special action with a draft from Holland. Men compete to take part in such actions as they get additional rations – one fifth litre vodka, five cigarettes, one hundred grams of sausage and bread. Today and tomorrow (Sunday) on duty.'

Thilo's equivalent army rank was that of Lieutenant.

The second entry that I read from Dr Kremer's diary is from the following day, 6 September 1942: 'Today an excellent Sunday dinner: tomato soup, one half of chicken with potatoes and red cabbage (20 grams of fat), dessert and magnificent vanilla ice-cream. After dinner we welcomed the new garrison doctor, Obersturmführer Wirths ... It is a week since I came to camp and I still have not been able to get rid of the fleas in my room in spite of using all kinds of insecticides, such as Flit, Cuprex etc.'

'Muselmänner' (Muslims) was the German name given to emaciated, apathetic, somnolent prisoners who no longer had the physical or mental ability to survive. Heinz Thilo was one of the Auschwitz camp physicians (he was a doctor of medicine). The 'special action in the women's camp' referred to by Dr Kremer on September 5 was the selection and gassing of 800 women.

When Dr Kremer was being cross-questioned during his trial in Cracow on 18 July 1947, he explained what his diary entry of September 5 had meant. 'The action of gassing emaciated women from the women's camp was particularly unpleasant,' he told the court. 'Such individuals were generally called "Muselmänner" (Moslems). I remember taking part in the gassing of such women in daylight. I am unable to state how numerous that group was. When I came to the bunker they sat clothed on the ground. As the clothes were in fact worn-out camp clothes, they were not let into the undressing barracks but undressed in the open. I could deduce from the behaviour of these women that they realised what was awaiting them. They begged the SS men to be allowed to live, they wept, but all of them were driven to the gas chamber and gassed. Being an anatomist I had seen many horrors, had dealt with corpses, but what I then saw was not to be compared with anything ever seen before.'

I end the readings here on the steps of the SS headquarters with Kremer's diary entry for 18 October 1942. After the arrival of 1,710 deportees from Holland, of whom 1,594 were immediately gassed, and only 116 sent to the barracks, he wrote of 'terrible scenes when three women begged to have their lives spared. They were young and healthy women but their begging was to no avail. The SS men taking the action shot them on the spot.'

12.50 p.m.

We walk slowly along the outer fence of the camp, now a busy road. Some of the photographs taken by the SS guard for his girlfriend in 1944 are on a display stand here. They show the deportees from Beregszasz and the surrounding area walking along this very road. Now the road is busy. When I was here in 1980 I do not remember a single car, only a horse and cart.

To our left, across a cornfield, is the gravel pit where the two escapees who followed Vrba and Wetzler, Czeslaw Mordowicz and Arnost Rosin, hid before their escape. It was they who witnessed the first ten days of the destruction of Polish Jewry and then on 27 May 1944, after hiding for three days in this gravel pit only 300 metres from the perimeter fence, managed to follow the route taken by Vrba and Wetzler, and like Vrba and Wetzler bring their story to the West. The pit had a hiding place in it which had been prepared by Russian prisoners-of-war. As with Vrba and Wetzler, after the three-day alert and sealing of the outer perimeter, they had been able to make their way out of the camp.

1 p.m.

We stand at the entrance to Birkenau. Most of the group go back in through the gate to look inside some of the huts that have been preserved. I remember my first visit here, in 1959, when the doors of the huts blew stutteringly in the wind, and all was desolation. Inside the huts were mounds of rubbish left by later, post-war dwellers there, Gypsies perhaps.

Standing by the gate, I think of all those whose memoirs and testimonies of Birkenau we have read during the year, and which have been a part of my own work for so many years. Every story is harrowing, every story is different. New stories are being published virtually every day. Through his Shoah Foundation, Steven Spielberg is recording tens of thousands of such stories on video. We all agree that it is quite right that this should be so. Angela is one of those doing interviews for the Shoah Foundation in London.

From Hilda Schiff's volume, *Holocaust Poetry*, I read aloud Primo Levi's poem 'Shema', a rendering of the principal Jewish prayer, 'Hear O Israel, the Lord our God, the Lord is One' (from Deuteronomy):

You who live secure
In your warm houses,
Who return at evening to find
Hot food and friendly faces:

Consider whether this is a man,
Who labours in the mud,
Who knows no peace,
Who fights for a crust of bread,
Who dies at a yes or a no.
Consider whether this is a woman,
Without hair or name,
With no more strength to remember,
Eyes empty and womb cold
As a frog in winter.

Consider that this has been:
I commend these words to you.
Engrave them on your hearts
When you are in your house, when you walk on your way,
When you go to bed, when you rise.
Repeat them to your children.
Or may your house crumble,
Disease render you powerless,
Your offspring avert their faces from you.

1.10 p.m.

We gather in the small gravel car park just outside the gate and board the bus to leave Birkenau. We leave in comfort, in our minibus, not like Vrba and Wetzler, or Mordowicz and Rosin, in fear and trembling, with their terrifying message to smuggle to the West; or to an even more frightening unknown, like those slave labourers – Primo Levi among them – who were marched out, accompanied by shouts and blows, to some other camp, with at least the possibility of survival, however slim.

1.12 p.m.

We drive past the Union factory, where 800 Jewish women worked at munitions manufacture. It is from there that the spark of revolt was lit in October 1944. In a recent book, *The Union Kommando in Auschwitz*, Lore Shelley has brought together the recollections of twenty-six of the women who worked here, as well as five of the men who worked in the machine section. I read a short extract from one of these recollections, by a Roumanian woman, Etelka Tusa, who was then eighteen years old: 'By pressing raw material, we produced bakelite-like pieces containing holes. It was rumoured that gunpowder would be placed inside. We had to work twelve hours a day, always standing on our feet, making I don't know how many pieces. When one lot was ready, we gathered the pieces and put them into metal boxes of the same size, each containing an identical amount of finished items. Then we took them to a girl named Gerda, a German prisoner, who counted the boxes and ordered us to empty them onto a heap. The Meister circulated among us, controlling what we did, checking that we worked fast enough and that the bakelite pieces were not burned. When he was not satisfied, he often shouted "Sabotage, sabotage!" – threatening, but never punishing us. I was very afraid of him then, but now, looking back, he seems to me like a dog who barked but did not bite.

'We had to work very hard in the Presse Abteilung. It was not easy staying on our feet all day and lifting heavy hot plates containing bakelite pieces. In the beginning, we got white cotton gloves and at noon we had a glass of milk or some soup. Later, those amenities ceased to be supplied.'

The conditions in which the women worked in the Union factory did improve when they were transferred from the barracks at Birkenau to Auschwitz Main Camp (Auschwitz I). Ilse Michel, from the Baltic region of Memelland, recalled the transfer of their sleeping quarters to a barracks in the Main Camp: 'The camp was clean, had electricity and washrooms. We slept in bunk beds. At that time we had no more selections and the threat of death was not so close. We could keep ourselves clean, but we never had enough to eat. We clung to life, hoping that one day someone in the wide world would help us. I say someone, since many of us had lost our belief in God, in humanity or justice.'

1.14 p.m.

We reach Auschwitz Main Camp. There are a lot of tour buses in the car park, and quite a lot of people milling around. Refreshments are on sale at the entrance.

The first group of Jews to be brought to the Main Camp and murdered by gassing were from the Upper Silesian town of Beuthen. They arrived, under Gestapo escort, on 15 February 1942, when the gas chambers at Birkenau were still under construction. Danuta Czech, the chronicler of Auschwitz, writes: 'They are unloaded on the platform of the camp siding. They have to leave their bags on the platform. The standby squad takes charge of the deportees from the Gestapo and leads them to the gas chamber in the camp crematorium. There they are killed with Zyklon-B gas.'

Neither the number of the deportees from Beuthen, nor any of their names, seem to be known, only the fact of their destruction. That same day, twenty-eight Polish prisoners and nine Russian prisoners-of-war also died in the Main Camp.

I go to see Teresa Swiebocka, whom, as Teresa Ceglowska, I knew fifteen years ago, when she came to London, together with Franciszek Piper (who joins us in Teresa's room), with an exhibition about Auschwitz which was shown in the crypt of the Bishop of Stepney's church in London. She is now in charge of publications and exhibitions at Auschwitz. She tells me of her plans for Birkenau – to enlarge the parking and build a small by-pass road around the main gate, to remove the toilets which are now inside the main gate, and to build opposite the main gate a reception centre with books, flowers, registration of visitors, refreshments. The sauna, which is now one of the few buildings surviving intact at Birkenau, other than the huts, will be opened up as a museum, with 'photographs brought by the victims' displayed there. She means the photographs which were taken away with everything else before the deportees were killed; it seems that the family photographs had no value for the German military machine.

The spur railway will be opened up as a route for visitors to walk along. Teresa is pleased to say this area belongs to the museum. In the Main Camp, the building at the entrance will be restored and turned into an exhibition. The refreshments area will be moved outside.

I listen somewhat bewildered to this professional presentation, no doubt admirable from the museum curator's perspective, but incongruous after what we have just seen. I was going to mention the crosses in the field beyond the sauna building, as Elie Wiesel would have wanted me to do, but it seems a million miles (and a hundred hours) from the office in which we are sitting, and the plans over which we are poring: plans to expand and improve, and to make sites and locations more accessible.

Teresa explains the need, as she sees it, with her professional exhibition director's eyes. Half a million people come here – like us – every year. Half of them are Poles. Many others are from Germany, Denmark, Holland, France and Italy, and, she says, 'many more from Israel'. Each year, the Israeli government helps to sponsor what is called 'The March of the Living'. Young Jews from all over the world gather here, march through Birkenau, and then go on to Israel. It has become an annual pilgrimage.

The site and museum of Auschwitz-Birkenau now have an international focus. What happens here can be politically explosive, as was the transformation a few years ago of the former SS barracks into a Catholic convent, or the recent proposal of a local Polish entrepreneur to open a supermarket just outside the entrance to the Main Camp. The crosses in the field at the far edge of Birkenau are an example of how sensitivities can be stirred. Last year the Polish skinhead (anti-foreigner) movement had wanted to hold a rally here, but the Polish government refused to give permission for it.

Whilst Birkenau was almost deserted (but will not be if Teresa's expansion plans are put into effect), Auschwitz Main Camp is teeming with visitors. The group finds this disturbing. I have no chance to experience it. In a bizarre episode, Teresa tells me that she has told a group of American students that I am here, and they have asked if I can speak to them. I can hardly say no, though it means abandoning my group for a while; Ben is already showing them the Main Camp, including the execution wall and Crematorium I, while I talk to Teresa.

2.10 p.m.
I go into one of the former barracks of the Main Camp, where a room has been turned into a lecture hall, and speak to the American students. I am uncomfortable at having had to leave the group. Ben is following, as I would have done, the route on the map which I had prepared. They see the Wall of Death, the first gas chamber, and the various relics of the victims that are displayed in different rooms: hair, clothing, suitcases, reading glasses, artificial limbs.

2.47 p.m.
I hurry from the lecture hall and rejoin the group: we get into our minibus and drive out of Auschwitz Main Camp.

We discuss what we have seen. The contrast between Birkenau and

Auschwitz Main Camp is almost too much to take. Birkenau – vast, silent, linked along each yard with stories we have read and studied, with the terrifying final moments of so many Jewish deportees from all over Europe – and Auschwitz Main Camp, primarily a site of murder and torture of many thousands of Poles: brave men and women, most of them Catholic, who challenged the Nazi regime, or fell foul of it in many different ways, including trying to save Jewish life.

Birkenau is a vast space with wooden huts and enormous empty areas where huts once stood. Auschwitz Main Camp is confined and cramped: large brick buildings, close together, with the heavy architecture of an Austro-Hungarian cavalry barracks. In 1940 they were turned into a prison camp and a place of torture and execution. But the Crematoria II, III, IV and V, with their gas chambers – where almost all the Jewish deportees were killed – are at Birkenau.

To travel from the emptiness of Birkenau to the bustle of Auschwitz was disturbing. The few, small groups at Birkenau had the air of pilgrims or even of mourners. We agree, as we talk for a few minutes in the car park, that it will be sad if Birkenau succumbs to the tourist aspect of Auschwitz Main Camp. But perhaps it is inevitable.

I speak of my own first visit here in the summer of 1959. Everything was so empty, so deserted. The Main Camp was quite empty, eerily so. In Birkenau doors banged on their hinges in the wind. There were no exhibition stands or memorial plaques.

3.05 p.m.

As we begin the drive back to Cracow we again see the Buna factory in the distance. And it has to remain in the distance, for when I ask the driver to take a side turning and go past it – it is very much in the itinerary I had planned during the last three months – he refuses. He says it is 'not in his instructions'. This insistence on instructions annoys Ben, but the driver will not take the turning, and continues doggedly on the main road.

3.30 p.m.

We are driven round Cracow and make our way through heavy traffic across the Vistula.

3.55 p.m.

We pass Wawel Castle, beautiful in the sunlight, overlooking the river. Across the river is the former Jewish quarter of Cracow, Kazimierz. We will visit it, if all goes well, this evening.

4.06 p.m.

Plaszow. We leave the bus and walk to the top of a large hilly mound. It is all that is left of this former slave labour camp. From the top we can make out three factories in the valley below: Wola Duchacka, Prokocim and Biezanow, which employed large numbers of Jewish slave labourers.

It seems difficult after Birkenau to take in another camp at all, let alone on the same day, but tens of thousands of Jews were deported here and worked as slave labourers. Among them were Moses and Helen Hiller who had given their two-year-old son to Josef Jachowicz and his wife for safe keeping.

Mojsze Bejski, who was later a witness in the Eichmann Trial, was among those who were slave labourers here. I read his recollection of an occasion when all 15,000 Jewish prisoners at Plaszow 'were called to witness a double hanging', of a boy named Halbenstock and an engineer, Krauwiert. 'The boy Halbenstock was hanged and something happened. The rope snapped. The boy was put up again on a high chair under the rope; he started begging for his life; he was ordered to be hanged again, and he did go up to the gallows once again and was hanged. And then he was shot at. The engineer was on the second chair and here the perfidy reached even further – the SS men came with their machine guns and ordered the man to gaze upon the hanging as it was being carried out, and the engineer, Krauwiert, cut his veins with a razor and thus he was hanged. Bleeding.'

Robin has made a special study of Plaszow and tells us about it. The camp was first established in 1940 for Polish prisoners. The same was true of Auschwitz. In 1941 the camp was extended and the first Jews deported here. Mojsze Bejski and his brother were chosen for Plaszow when their parents were deported to Belzec, from their home town of Dzialoszyce. Indeed most of the slave labourers brought here were the so-called 'able-bodied' minority chosen for slave labour – after the majority of the Jews of Dzialoszyce were deported to Belzec and killed.

Those who were brought here to Plaszow were the remnant that would survive, though in so many cases only for a short while. In January 1943 Amon Goeth was appointed commandant here, his 'reward' for 'having successfully' liquidated the Lublin ghetto. In March 1943, when the last Jews of the Cracow ghetto were sent to Belzec, the bodies of those who were killed during the deportation were brought to Plaszow in trucks. Robin points out the pit at the bottom of the valley in which the bodies were dumped.

During the period of the Hungarian deportations to Auschwitz there

18. Izbica railway station, the scene of almost indescribable torments in 1942 (pages 228–37).

19. The railway line and field at Izbica. Some of the group are on the platform on the left.

20. Chelm: the main synagogue, now a bank (pages 239–46).

21. Chelm: a pre-war Jewish courtyard.

22. Borki: a mass murder site where Soviet prisoners-of-war, Italian soldiers, and Jewish children, were murdered (pages 246–8).

23. Sobibor: the rectangular memorial inside the death camp site (pages 249–54).

24. Sobibor: the sandstone memorial, a woman and child.

25. Wlodawa: the exterior of the
synagogue, built in 1764 (pages
255–8).

26. Wlodawa synagogue:
two Polish girls, a boy, and the
librarian, in the synagogue
entrance hall, now a library.

27. Wlodawa: the group in front of the house of prayer, in the synagogue square.

28. Wlodawa: the interior of
the synagogue, decorations,
including a drum.

29. Wlodawa: a synagogue
decoration, including
a violin.

30. Wlodawa: the road along the River Bug on which deportees from Wlodawa were taken, for deportation to Sobibor (pages 258–9).

31. The Parczew forest (pages 264–8).

32. Majdanek: the SS women's barrack, and beyond it the SS doctor's house (page 277).

33. Majdanek: the pits of the 'Harvest Festival' (pages 278–9).

34. Majdanek: the crematorium chimney – original – and the gas chamber –
restored after the war (page 279).

was a time when even Birkenau could not cope with the numbers being brought in. (The planned extension which we saw this morning was never completed.) So 10,000 Hungarian Jews were brought here to Plaszow. Two terrible selections took place here, one on 7 May 1944 and the other a week later. In the first selection, 25,000 inmates were lined up. In the second, 12,000. Those who could not pass some notional fitness test were taken away and killed.

I read aloud an account by Mojsze Bejski of the evacuation of Plaszow on 15 October 1944. It was then that Oskar Schindler ensured that more than a thousand Jews were taken from Plaszow to a munitions factory which he had just opened in the Sudetenland. Several hundred women prisoners at Plaszow had also been chosen to work for Schindler. At the time of the deportations from Plaszow that October they were sent to Auschwitz. 'Schindler at once sought their release,' Bejski recalled, 'going personally to Auschwitz and bribing the Nazi officials there to let him take the three hundred women to his Sudetenland factory. There, they were able to rejoin their menfolk. Thus wives, daughters and even mothers were saved.'

Plaszow camp was built on the site of an inter-war Jewish cemetery. Fragments of a dozen headstones are scattered about the ground. Only one headstone is still upright, that of Jakub Chaim Abrahamer, who died in 1932.

There are two monuments here in Plaszow, one enormous, one small. The large monument was unveiled at the height of the Communist era, on 4 September 1964. Typically for Communist monuments on sites of predominantly Jewish concern, the inscription makes no mention of Jews, but refers instead to 'those murdered', not saying who they were. The small monument, which was put up by the few survivors of Cracow Jewry shortly after the war, is all the more poignant in how it describes who the victims were: 'Here in this area have been tortured, murdered, turned into ashes, several tens of thousands of Jews in the years 1943–1945, driven here from all over Poland and Hungary. We do not know the names of the murdered. Let us replace them with one word only – Jews.'

Ben tells us that before the war the commandant here, Amon Goeth, was working in a publishing house in Vienna. 'He was an intelligent man. At his trial he praised Polish justice for the fair treatment he was receiving. If this was to be the standard of post-war Poland, he said, it boded well for Poland. He thought that this speech would help him, and that he would be found not guilty. In his defence he said that all those whom he had shot at Plaszow had "broken the rules".'

Paul says a memorial prayer. We walk back to the bus. On the highest ground of the camp, two haymakers are at work.

4.40 p.m.

We leave Plaszow, drive back down the hill and join the main road back into Cracow. As we reach the city, Caroline tells us that her uncle, Michael Raye, went to school in Cracow, and lived as a young boy in a house on the Planty. She has the address and reads it out. By chance, only a few moments later, we pass the very building.

5.05 p.m.

We reach our hotel. Ben tells us a delightful story of a crossword puzzle which he found while in the ghetto in a Polish-language Jewish newspaper that was published in the Cracow ghetto in 1941. From time to time the paper reached the Piotrkow ghetto. 'It made me so happy to work the puzzle out. I was only eleven years old. I was so thrilled. I didn't know the word "Eureka" then – had I done I would have cried out the word "Eureka".'

The clues that Ben had unravelled were, one, 'A place where animals inhabit' and, two, 'A river in Germany'. The answer was, one, 'Nora' – a burrow' – and, two, the River Main; making the word 'menorah' (a lamp).

7 p.m.

I prepare the material for our visit to Kazimierz, the former Jewish quarter of Cracow. We will not have time to see everything I had wanted to. Among the streets which we will not reach, alas, are Orzeszkowa and Koletek Streets. They are both mentioned by the Cracow-born Rafael Scharf, now a Londoner, whose recollections include a passage that sums up, for me, an aspect of pre-war Jewish life that is often overlooked. In Orzeszkowa Street, he writes, 'was situated the *Nowy Dziennik* (New Daily), a Jewish daily newspaper in the Polish language, one of three such newspapers in Poland – the others being *Nasz Przeglad* (Our Review) in Warsaw and *Chwila* (A Moment) in Lvov. The newspaper served the Jews of Cracow as the main source of information, reporting events in the wider world, in Poland, in Palestine. The leading articles were often written by Dr Osias Thon, the pride of Cracow Jewry, a member of the Polish Parliament, the chairman of the Jewish Parliamentary Club, the Rabbi of the Progressive synagogue, the 'Tempel', and an ardent Zionist. The *Nowy Dziennik* was an institution without which the life of Cracow

Jewry was unthinkable. I started my journalistic career there and became its foreign correspondent in London.'

Rafael Scharf also writes of how, on a recent visit to Cracow, he visited the reading room of the Jagellonian Library, 'locus of many happy memories and – on an impulse – requested to be shown the bound folios of *Nowy Dziennik* from the year 1938. I wanted to cast a glance over those pages, re-read the articles which I then wrote to the joy of my father and, perhaps, some other readers. The folio was put on my desk. With trembling hands I started to turn the flimsy pages. I was overcome with memories. Every headline, every name, every advert ("Buy lottery tickets from Safir Brothers – every other ticket wins"), every small ad ("You will speak English like a native Englishman – Karmel, Koletek Street, 3") brought forth a flood of images, faces, scenes, events. Immersing myself entirely in that old world, slowed down by the turning of the pages, I did not get to my own articles before closing time. I had paused too long over a notice, one day in January 1938, which read: "On Wednesday, at the premises of the Massada youth-group – of which I was then the leader – at 8 pm, Felek Scharf will give a talk titled: How to get rid of the British in Palestine."

'One day, on another visit, I shall get to see the correspondence "From Our Own Reporter in London". I happen to remember one article, in particular, the last one I wrote, in August 1939, wherein there was a passage saying that "I stake my journalistic reputation (sic) on the prediction that there will be no war." At the time when this article would have reached the editor's desk – the Germans were already in Cracow.'

7.30 p.m.

We gather outside the hotel. Caught up in the preparation of my readings, I am the last to appear. The bus driver takes us to Kazimierz. Having hoped to be able to spend a whole day here, we must be content with two hours. On the bus I have time to give a very brief survey. The first documentary record of Jews living in Cracow dates from 1304. After nearly two hundred years of varying fortunes, from commercial prosperity to a ritual murder charge (in 1407) and several expulsions, the village of Kazimierz, just outside the city walls, was granted to the Jews by King Casimir the Great, who loved his Jews and was said to have had a Jewish wife, Esther. There was already a Jewish bath-house here, built in 1485, and a Jewish market, opened three years later. A synagogue built at that time is today known as the Old

Synagogue. When a fire broke out in Cracow in 1494 the Jews were, as usual, blamed, and set upon; it was this which led to the expulsion of all Jews living inside Cracow to Kazimierz.

The Jewish town, granted its own charter, flourished. A Hebrew printing press was set up here in 1534. Distinguished rabbis lived and taught here. During the second half of the nineteenth century, under Austrian rule, Jews lived throughout Cracow, Kazimierz being one of many suburbs that were an integral part of the city; there was also a poor quarter inhabited largely by Jews. Its name was Podgorze. It lay across the River Vistula.

The 1905 Baedeker guide book, *Austria-Hungary, Handbook for Travellers*, notes that Cracow had a population that year of 91,300, 'one-fourth Jews'. By 1938 the city had grown considerably in size, and there were 64,348 Jews living there. They still constituted a quarter of the city's inhabitants. Jewish life in Cracow was a vivid and lively part of the city scene, with many well-known rabbis, cantors, writers, teachers, historians and poets. The 1943 Baedeker guide book, *Das Generalgouvernement*, refers to Kazimierz as 'the former place of residence of the Jewish population of Cracow, now free of Jews'.

We leave the bus and walk into Kazimierz, down Krakowska Street. At No. 13, with its ornate nineteenth-century neo-classical façade, and tall pediment with coat of arms, was the Susser family house. Between the wars the ground floor was Thorn's restaurant.

We reach Wolnica Square. In the fourteenth-century town hall a Jewish state primary school was opened in 1830. Seven years later it was turned into an industrial and commercial school for young Jews. A bas-relief of King Casimir the Great receiving the Jews of Poland, set up here between the wars, was destroyed by the Germans.

Continuing down Krakowska Street, we come to the corner building, No. 45 (which is also No. 2 Skawinska Street). Built in 1911, this was the seat of the Congregation of the Judaic Faith in Cracow. The ground floor was the Jewish library. The second floor was the offices of the community board. And the third floor was a large room for meetings, and the archive room. Much of the rest of the building was used by a Jewish clothing co-operative. There was also a dining room here, and a kosher kitchen.

Going down Skawinska Street, we come to No. 8, which was the Jewish hospital (Szpital Izraelski) for more than a century, from 1822 to 1939. In the inter-war years, when it was much enlarged, it was known all over Poland for the quality of its medical equipment and personnel. Many famous doctors worked here, including the laryngologist Adolf Schwarzbart and the neurologist Bernard Bornstein. A leading cancer specialist, Marcel Spitzer, also worked here between the wars; he was awarded the much-valued Jozef Pilsudski Prize for his achievements.

From Skawinska Street we go down Bochenska Street. No. 4 was the Bet Midrash Sherit Bnei Emunah, where the more Orthodox Jews of Kazimierz came to pray. No. 7 was the Jewish theatre. It was inaugurated on 13 October 1926. In 1933 a great celebration of the works of Shalom Aleichem was held here.

We walk to Jozefa Street. Ben rushes into a courtyard – No. 12 – and we all follow. The courtyard is empty. Some washing is hanging on a clothes-line. It is a pre-war image with cobbled yard and wooden balconies all around. Ben describes what it must have been like before the war, with children playing in the yard and their mothers calling to each other from balcony to balcony. We go on to No. 36 where, until the end of the nineteenth century, stood a Renaissance house built in 1536 by an Italian architect from Siena for a Jew, Jonasz the son of Abraham. In 1790 it belonged to Eljasz Herszkowicz, who used the income from its rent to support the Tall Synagogue.

At No. 38 Jozefa Street is the Tall Synagogue. It was built between 1556 and 1563 and is standing in all its splendour before us. The prayer room was on the second floor. The first floor was used for shops. In 1863 it was renovated for the use of the community at that time. During the Second World War the Germans stripped it of all its fittings and decorations. It was restored in 1966, not as a place of worship, but to suit the needs of the local Historical Monuments Restoration Workshop. The cavity where the Scrolls of the Law were kept (the Aron Ha-Kodesh, the Holy Ark) has survived, but without its dais, its ornamental doors, or any Scrolls.

We move on to No. 42 Jozefa Street. This was a house of prayer founded in 1810 and renovated in 1912. The dates appear as part of the Hebrew inscription, and two Stars of David, on the façade of the building. Today it is a dwelling house. The inscription, from *Ethics of the Fathers*, reads: 'Fix a time for Torah study.'

The last house in Jozefa Street, No. 33, is the oldest Hassidic Jewish prayer house in Cracow. It was founded in 1815. From here it is but a few dozen steps to Szeroka Street, a large, rectangular square, and the centre of Jewish life in medieval Kazimierz. Since it was used in the film *Schindler's List* to represent the Podgorze ghetto (which is elsewhere, across the river, and which we will visit tomorrow), it has become a centre of revitalised tourism, and a considerable amount of commercialism.

There are three synagogues here on Szeroka Street: the Old Synagogue, built in the second half of the fifteenth century, and now a museum; Storch's Synagogue, built in 1620; and the Remuh Synagogue, built in 1553, and massively restored and remodelled in 1933. The old Jewish cemetery is also here, at No. 40, next to the Remuh Synagogue.

There are some fine old houses in Szeroka Street. No. 18 belonged to Rabbi Izaak Lewita, the Chief Rabbi of the community and the rector of the Yeshiva (Jewish Religious Academy) from 1776 to 1799: his tenure spanned both the American and French Revolutions. Inside No. 16, but hardly visible from Szeroka Street, are the high walls of Storch's Synagogue – they are best seen from Dajwor Street. This is the synagogue built in 1620 by a wealthy Jewish merchant, Wolf Bocian. None of its once highly prized wall paintings and decorations have survived.

We walk on to No. 6 Szeroka Street. This was the community bathhouse and mikveh (ritual bath). In 1806 the building was owned by Jekele Felczer, who paid the Jewish communal treasury an annual sum for the right to manage it, and to charge an entrance fee. Today it is used by the Cracow branch of the Polish Historical Monuments Restoration Workshop. Some relics of the mikveh are kept in the basement, but we have arrived too late to visit them (nor could we get into the Old Synagogue and see its treasures: the guard was just locking up when we arrived).

At the opposite end of Szeroka Street to the Old Synagogue was a group of buildings, now amalgamated into a single block, which date back to the seventeenth century. Rabbi Joszua Heszel, who was the Chief Rabbi from 1654 to 1663, lived in one of them; as did Samuel Kac, a Jew from Padua, who, in an even earlier period, was head of the Kazimierz Jewish community. In the nineteenth century the building, in which more than a dozen families lived, belonged to the Landau family, one of whose members, Rafal Landau, was the last Chairman of the Cracow Jewish Community before the Second World War.

As we stand outside the Remuh Synagogue and the cemetery wall, Paul tells us of the importance of the Remuh (or Rema) in Jewish thought. Rabbi Moses Isserlis, known by his Hebrew acronym as the Rema, was a towering figure in the sixteenth-century world of religious interpretation. He was a leading advocate of allowing custom to be given weight in matters of religious performance. Isserlis had written a commentary on Rabbi Joseph Caro's Code of Jewish law (*Shulhan Arukh* – the Prepared Table) in which Isserlis disagreed with Caro on issues of custom versus law. The Code was published in Venice in 1594 with Isserlis's commentaries included.

His grave is in the cemetery in front of us, as are the graves of his grandmother, his father, his brother and his sister. He was born in Cracow in either 1525 or 1530. His first wife died in 1552, when she was only twenty years old. It was in her memory that he built the Remuh Synagogue in 1553. He died in 1572. Until the outbreak of the Second World War, thousands of Polish Jews would make a pilgrimage to his grave here on the anniversary of his death.

It is said that the Nazis used the tombstones here for target practice, but that when the bullets they fired at Isserlis's tombstone apparently rebounded, they were so disturbed that they did not return. The wall of the cemetery is made out of shattered tombstones.

I had hoped to walk on a few hundred yards to the two other remarkable synagogues of Kazimierz, the Ajzyk Synagogue, built in 1638, and the Kupa Synagogue, built about ten years later, but we need to take a rest. Our original plan was to have spent five hours here, not twenty-five minutes, and to do so at the beginning of a new day, not at the end of a physically and emotionally exhausting one. But we have seen enough to grasp what Kazimierz must once have been. The Tempel Synagogue is still in regular use.

7.55 p.m.

We enter the Ariel restaurant on the east side of Szeroka Street and collapse around the tables. We have somehow managed to fit two days into one. We were lucky that the day we had originally thought of as lost, and which we spent in the mountains of Slovakia, did not force the cutting out of Cracow altogether.

The square buzzes with Jewish and crypto-Jewish restaurants. The card of the Ariel, where we are sitting, states: 'The Jewish artistic café in the heart of Kazimierz. The only place of its kind in Poland.' The menu proliferates with Jewish dishes. The owner is proud of the fact that Steven Spielberg ate here during the filming of *Schindler's List*. He shows us a framed message from Spielberg on the wall.

As we choose our items from the menu, I reflect how far we have come within a few hours, from the world of Birkenau with its evil memories and terrifying shadows, to a modern world of food and entertainment.

10.15 p.m.

We leave the Ariel restaurant and walk along Starowislna Street (in Communist times it was named Fighters of Stalingrad Street). We continue to the Old Town, and to Market Square, the centre of Cracow. From 1940 to 1944 it was named Adolf-Hitler-Platz. In various times in the seventeenth and eighteenth centuries, many Jewish merchants had their houses here. We find a café and drink and talk about the events of the day. The contrast between Birkenau and Auschwitz, and the commercialisation and bustle of Auschwitz, have made the greatest impact.

11.45 p.m.

Hotel and bed.

DAY 8

CRACOW – ZAMOSC

'Someone to relate our story'

6.15 a.m.

Wake up to the sound of church bells, and to the rattle of a tram passing by. I leave the hotel (the woman who took my washing yesterday is in the lobby, and says my clean clothes will be ready in an hour). I walk across the Planty. As I walk, I try to picture my grandmother walking here, an educated woman of about twenty, in love with a shoemaker who wants to emigrate. Perhaps he does not want to have to serve in the Austro-Hungarian army. Perhaps he wants to go to a country where he can better himself. He can see what the world has to offer, and then his brothers and sisters can join him. He is the oldest of many brothers and sisters (there were at least eight by the time he decided to leave, and, eventually, seventeen in all).

By 1896 my grandmother and grandfather were in England – their first child, my uncle, was born in London in 1897. Perhaps my grandfather and grandmother (Aron and Anna) walked arm in arm just here, where I am walking. It is sad to know so little about their time here, in what was then Western Galicia, a part of Austria-Hungary. And yet, in the mystery of their early lives lies a certain satisfaction, in that the privacy of their lives is protected for ever.

I walk into the Old Town. It is, as always, an impressive sight. The great square, the cloth hall and the spire from which the bugle plays each hour the first notes that the young bugler had played to arouse the citizens as the Tatar invaders approached, enabling them to defend their city. The young bugler had been killed halfway through his tune, and that broken sound became the great clarion call of Polish courage and resistance.

I reach No. 38 Szpitalna Street, now a Pizzeria on one side and a 'Laser Disco' on the other. In 1940 it was the Cyganeria café. During the Second World War it was for use only by Germans. There was a historic episode here, on 22 December 1942, when members of the Jewish Fighting Organisation (ZOB in its Polish initials), their numbers much weakened by earlier arrests and executions, decided that the time had come when they must act. Led by Adolf Liebeskind, the group attacked this very café, then frequented by the SS and the Gestapo. Seven Germans were killed. Yitzhak Zuckerman, who had come from Warsaw that day, took part in a second attack, in order, he later recalled, 'to save what could be saved, at least honour'.

Wounded in the leg, Zuckerman succeeded in returning to Warsaw. The Germans moved rapidly against the other members of the group, tracking them down to their hiding place. Judah Tenenbaum, snatching a pistol from a German, killed one of his attackers before he was shot by bursts of machine-gun fire. Liebeskind was also killed. His sister-in-law, Miriam, managed to reach Radom, where she hoped to organise a ghetto uprising. But she was captured there, tortured and shot. A few weeks before his death, Liebeskind had remarked bitterly, 'We are fighting for three lines in the history books.'

Decimated, Liebeskind's group nevertheless survived his death. Some of them managed to escape altogether from 'Aryan' Cracow, intending, as Liebeskind's wife Rivka later recalled, 'to set up hide-outs, to work in forests, and to enable Jews to hide – because they still hoped that the war would end'. Their aim, she added, 'was to save at least someone to relate our story'.

There is a plaque on the café wall: 'On the night of 24–25 December 1942, a group of soldiers of the Armia Ludowa and the Jewish Fighting Organisation carried out an operation on the Cyganeria hall, which was full of Germans, and inflicted heavy losses upon the conqueror.' The inscription, which was put up in Communist times when the Armia Ludowa was the only fully recognised resistance army, does not say that all those who took part in the attack were in fact Jews. And the date is three days out. Two other cafés were also attacked, the Esplanada and the Zakopianka. It is a little-known episode of Jewish defiance. A clandestine Jewish newspaper, published in Cracow on 13 August 1943, declared with great bitterness, and anger: 'Nobody lent a hand to the dying Jews, no one even tried to help to the extent that would make it possible for individuals to escape from the danger of destruction. They looked upon our annihilation as crushing worms, and not like the loss of a people with high cultural values.

'Their hatred towards the Germans diminished, since the problem of the extermination of the Jews came up. They expressed full solidarity with the enemy only to see the Jews' defeat. Only very few kept any shred of humanity, and even those dared not give this any external expression. This time it was proven anew how isolated we are. We shall carry the heavy yoke of this isolation to our dying day.'

Almost all the members of the Jewish Fighting Organisation in Cracow were hunted down and executed during 1943. Many of them were betrayed while in hiding. Among those caught and killed – gun in hand – was Heszek Bauminger, whose brother Arieh, who survived the war, wrote a book commemorating their heroism, and from which the above quotation is taken.

There is just a moment, before returning to the hotel, to walk from the Cyganeria café along Szpitalna Street, to No. 24. Between the wars there was a Jewish prayer house here, Ahavat Haim (Love of Life), which was used by Jews living in the centre of the city. Its choir was conducted by a noted local cantor and teacher, Baruch Szperber. After the war the building was taken over by a Christian parish.

7.05 a.m.

Return to the hotel. Herut is in the lobby. Reflecting on the plans we heard at the Auschwitz museum yesterday, she feels as I do that Birkenau should be kept as it is, not 'developed' any more. She also found the crosses on the former SS barracks quite disturbing. The one on the roof was visible from Crematorium IV. It is strange that such an important building as the SS barracks should be outside the area administered by the museum, and not within their jurisdiction as far as changes, such as the erection of large crosses, is concerned.

8.10 a.m.

We board the minibus and are driven about half a mile, to the site of the Cracow ghetto. It is a much more run-down area than the Jewish quarter of Kazimierz. Someone comments that Steven Spielberg chose the scenic main square of Kazimierz rather than the drab streets of the ghetto to represent the ghetto in his film.

At what was Zgody Square, and is now named Ghetto Fighters' Square (Plac Bohaterow Getta), we leave the bus. In March 1941, between 15,000 and 17,000 Jews were forced into the confines of a ghetto here. Twice, after the deportations of June 1942 and October 1942, its already small size was reduced. The final deportation took place on 13 and 14 March 1943; that was the end of the ghetto, and the end of Cracow Jewry as one of the great centres of Jewish life across four centuries.

The headquarters of the Jewish Fighting Organisation in the ghetto, at No. 6 Ghetto Fighters' Square, is marked with a plaque. Unusually for Poland, this plaque was put up in the Communist era, on 13 March 1948, the fifth anniversary of the final destruction of the ghetto (I always feel uneasy at the word 'liquidation', which seems too clinical and businesslike for something that was so horrific).

We have begun to spend time looking at wall plaques and reading inscriptions; they are the silent but often poignant reminders of what happened to the Jews of Poland. Almost all of them were put up after the fall of Communism. For almost half a century, the identification of specifically Jewish sites was officially frowned upon. It was made difficult in those days to identify anything with certainty; there were far fewer guide books, and much less detail was recorded in those that there were. The Jewish aspect was often totally absent. Nor did locals always want to volunteer what they knew.

At the building which was once a pharmacy owned by a Christian Pole, but situated just inside the ghetto, I read aloud from the diary of the pharmacist, Tadeusz Pankiewicz. His pharmacy was called Apteka pod Orlem (Pharmacy under the Eagle). The reduction of the size of the ghetto – an even tighter confinement that took place in almost all ghettos as the deportations continued – placed the pharmacy on the very border of the ghetto. Pankiewicz used his position astride the new boundary to smuggle Jews out, and to smuggle in food and medical supplies. His efforts to help Jews were enormously risky, and deeply appreciated inside the ghetto. Nor were those efforts forgotten; when Robin was in Cracow in 1992 he visited Pankiewicz, who was dying of cancer in hospital, and thanked him for his humanity during the ghetto occupation.

In his wartime diary, Pankiewicz wrote of what he saw of the start of the main deportation from the square in front of his windows: 'The scorching sun is merciless. The heat makes for unbearable thirst, dries out the throats. All wait, frozen with fright and uncertainty.'

Pankiewicz went on to describe how armed Germans arrived, shooting at random into the crowd. Then the deportees were forced out of the square, amid what he called the 'constant screaming of the Germans, mercilessly beating, kicking and shooting'. Old people, women, and children, he wrote, 'pass by the pharmacy windows like ghosts. I see an old woman of around seventy years, her hair loose, walking alone, a few steps away from a larger group of deportees. Her eyes have a glazed look; immobile, wide open, filled with horror, they stare straight ahead. She walks slowly, quietly, only in her dress and slippers, without even a bundle, or handbag. She holds in her hands something small, something black, which she caresses fondly and keeps close to her old breast. It is a small puppy – her most precious possession, all that she saved and would not leave behind.

'Laughing, inarticulately gesturing with her hands, walks a young deranged girl of about fourteen, so familiar to all inhabitants of the ghetto. She walks barefoot, in a crumpled nightgown. One shuddered watching the girl laughing, having a good time. Old and young pass by, some dressed, some only in their underwear, hauled out of their beds and driven out. People after major operations and people with chronic diseases went by ...

'Across the street from the pharmacy, out of the building at No. 2 Harmony Square, walks a blind old man, well known to the inhabitants of the ghetto; he is about seventy years old, wears dark goggles over his blind eyes, which he lost in the battles on the Italian front in 1915 fighting side by side with the Austrians. He wears a yellow armband with three black circles on his left arm to signify his blindness. His head high, he walks erect, guided by his son on one side, by his wife on the other. "He should be happy he cannot see, it will be easier for him to die," says a hospital nurse to us. Pinned on his chest is the medal he won during the war. It may, perhaps, have some significance for the Germans. Such were the illusions in the beginning.

'Immediately after him, another elderly person appears, a cripple with one leg, on crutches. The Germans close in on them; slowly, in dance step, one of them runs towards the blind man and yells with all his power: "Schnell!" "Hurry!" This encourages the other Germans to start a peculiar game.

'Two of the SS men approach the old man without the leg and shout the order for him to run. Another one comes from behind and with the butt of his rifle hits the crutch. The old man falls down. The German screams savagely, threatens to shoot. All this takes place right at the back of the blind man who is unable to see, but hears the beastly voices of the Germans, interspersed with cascades of their laughter. A German soldier approaches the cripple who is lying on the ground and helps him to rise. This help will show on the snapshot of a German officer who is eagerly taking pictures of all scenes that will prove "German help in the humane resettlement of the Jews".

'For a moment we think that perhaps there will be at least one human being among them unable to stand torturing people one hour before their death. Alas, there was no such person in the annals of the Cracow ghetto. No sooner were they saturated with torturing the cripple than they decided to try the same with the blind war invalid.

They chased away his son and wife, trapped him, and rejoiced at his falling to the ground. This time they did not even pretend to help him and he had to rise by himself, rushed on by horrifying screaming of the SS men hovering over him. They repeated this game several times, a truly shattering experience of cruelty. One could not tell from what they derived more pleasure, the physical pain of the fallen invalid or the despair of his wife and son standing aside watching helplessly. The shots are echoing all over the ghetto.'

Among those shot in Cracow that day was the Yiddish songwriter and poet, Mordechai Gebirtig. I read aloud his poem 'Our village burns', which was written after the Przytyk pogrom of 9 March 1936, in which two Jews had been killed. The Jews of the village had then driven off further attacks, killing a Polish peasant in the process. Gebirtig fears much worse will occur:

> It burns, brothers, it burns,
> The time of anguish – God forbid – now churns,
> When the village and you in one blow
> Turns to ashes, to flames all aglow.
> Nothing will remain at all –
> Just a blackened wall –
> And you look and you stand,
> Each with folded hand.
>
> And you look and you stand,
> At burned village and land.
>
> It burns, brothers, it burns,
> To you alone this agony turns.
> If you love your town, its name,
> Take the vessels, quench the flame.
> Quench it with your own blood too:
> Show what you can do.
> Brothers, do not look and stand,
> Each with folded hand.
> Brothers, do not look and stand
> While town burns and land,
> While town burns and land.

In one of his last songs, written a month before his death, Mordechai Gebirtig had expressed his hope that, 'from too much gorging, the invader's end would result, Amen'.

The Germans, dissatisfied by the number of Jews who had been assembled during the Cracow deportations, and critical of the 'technique of delivery' to Harmony Square, arrested the Chairman of the Cracow Jewish Council, Dr Aharon Artur Rosenzweig, and deported him together with his family.

At No. 42 Limanowskiego lived, among others, the Liebling and Abrahamer families. One of those who survived in the dark basement during the ghetto years, Janina Martinho, wrote to me before our journey here of an artisan's sign, made of small stained-glass panes, which the Polish family living on the ground floor showed her during a recent visit. Dated 1913, it is the sign of Maurycy Krautwirt, Decorator and Painter – a tiny remnant of the once full Jewish commercial life of Cracow. Although a poorer area than Kazimierz, across the Vistula, Podgorze likewise exuded the pace and pattern of Jewish life. There were, and still are, many fine shops and houses here.

8.45 a.m.

Our minibus drives out of the ghetto area the short distance to Oskar Schindler's Emalia factory in Lipowa Street. It is still a factory, the 'Krakowskie Zaklady Elektroniczne "Telpod"'. Robin, who told us so much about Plaszow yesterday, tells us about this factory. For more than ten years he has made a detailed study of Schindler. Long before he came to me as a pupil last autumn he had corresponded with me about his Schindler researches, which are considerable.

We stand at the entrance, and Robin tells us that the Emalia factory was Jewish-owned before the war, located in an area of Jewish factories. Schindler took the property after the German occupation. It employed about 150 workers at that time, of whom only seven were Jews. He started to employ more Jews, not through altruism, but because Jews were cheaper to employ. By March 1943, Schindler was employing 900 Jewish workers, who were prisoners from Plaszow camp. Every day they had to march the four kilometres from Plaszow to the factory, and then back again at night. Schindler had an idea, to build his own barracks at the back of the factory. In November 1943 he was allowed to move his workers from Plaszow to the Emalia barracks.

Schindler took into his workforce family members and friends of those already working in the factory. It became a haven. But in August 1944 it was disbanded, and 600 of the workers were sent by the Gestapo back to Plaszow camp. Three hundred remained at Emalia, and dismantled it, for transfer to a new site, far away (or at least farther away) from the Russian front. The new factory was located at Brunnlitz, in the Sudetenland; it was then that Schindler persuaded the Gestapo to let him take the 300 workers with him.

Schindler also persuaded the Gestapo to let him include some of those who had been sent back to Plaszow, the famous 'Schindler's list'. Robin tells us of those who 'bought themselves into the list'. Ben speaks of those who were 'excluded from the list because others had bought themselves into it'. Ben becomes emotional. 'It was a dirty business. It is an untold story. It is very difficult to tell, what people did to save their own lives.'

We take a last look at the factory, struck by its curving inter-war design of the most modern, almost art-deco style of the day. Along the outside wall, in the direction of the railway and the ghetto, is a plaque. It has nothing to do with the Jews or with Oskar Schindler. It recalls a plane crash on 17 August 1944. Of the three-man crew, one baled out and was captured on landing. The other two crashed with their plane and were killed. They were buried by the Germans with full military honours, in Cracow cemetery. Their names are recorded on the plaque:

> F/Cdr John P. Liversidge RAAF
> Ft/Lt Pilot William D. Wright, RAF
> F/Sgt A/G John D. Clarke.

Flight-Sergeant Liversidge, of the Royal Australian Air Force, was the navigator. Flight-Lieutenant Wright was the pilot. Flight-Sergeant Clarke was the rear gunner. Two other crew members, the flight engineer, Sergeant L. J. Blunt and the mid-upper gunner, Sergeant F. W. Holme, parachuted out and were taken prisoner. The sixth member of the crew, the wireless operator and air gunner, Flight-Lieutenant A. H. Hammet, evaded capture. Later he set down for Air Ministry intelligence an account of the flight, and of his subsequent adventures. The flight had begun from the main Allied air base in southern Italy:

'We took off near Foggia in a Liberator aircraft at 1800 hours on 16 August 1944 on a special mission to near Warsaw. Our mission was successful and on the return journey to base we are attacked by an unidentified aircraft. The aircraft was set on fire and the pilot gave the order to bale out. He died from bullet wounds a few moments later. I was wounded by bullets in the arms, legs, hand and right side.

'I baled out about 0200 hours on August 17 and landed in a field about twenty kilometres east of Cracow. I buried my parachute, harness and "mae west" and began walking North East. About dawn I hid in a clump of bushes until evening, when I resumed walking North and hid in a wood during August 18.

'That evening I approached a farmhouse and asked for dressings for my wounds. About two hours later a nurse, accompanied by a partisan, arrived. I was able to converse with them in French. My wounds were dressed and I was given food. About 0300 hours on August 19, I was taken by horse-wagon to a house on a large estate ... I was attended by a doctor at this house and I remained there until August 20. I was supplied with civilian clothes. On that day I was taken by horse-wagon to Slaboszow where I stayed with a group of Armia Krajowa for about six weeks.

'About September 20 I was engaged with the partisans on a raid for arms, ammunition and clothes in Miechow. We obtained them from a small party of Germans at the railway station without a fight. About September 23 I was engaged with the partisans in a raid on a sugar factory at Kazimierza. We killed eight German guards and removed all the sugar from the factory. This was distributed at a later date to Poles by the manager of the factory.

'About September 30 I was taken to a place near Warsaw escorted by partisans in stages. I had learned of a Miss Walker there, but I was unable to make contact with her, owing to the attitude of the Poles. After staying at a house there for about ten days, I asked to be sent back to Slaboszow. I arrived there about October 20 and rejoined the partisan group.

'About the end of October I was engaged with the partisans in the shooting down, by rifle and machine-gun fire, of a German Storch aircraft. The pilot was killed. A few days later the Germans sent out a reprisal force of about one hundred Ukrainians from Miechow. A partisan force, including myself, met and opposed them east of Swiecice. Nineteen Ukrainians were killed. The partisan forces lost nine killed including two Britishers (escaped prisoners-of-war, further details unknown). I did not know that these two Britishers were included in the partisan force until several days later, when it was impossible to obtain information.

'Some days later I learned that three Ukrainians in the German forces were in a peasant's hut in Slaboszow. I threw a mills bomb into the room they were in. I did not wait to see the results, but I heard later that they had been killed.

'About November 6 I went to a large house on the outskirts of Swiecice. I remained there until the arrival of the Russian forces about 20 January 1945.'

After his liberation, Flight-Lieutenant Hammet was given charge of about eight hundred British prisoners-of-war. After three days they were sent by train to Odessa, and then by boat to Britain.

9.05 a.m.
We leave the Emalia factory and drive back under the railway to the ghetto.

9.09 a.m.
Drive down Lwowska Street, where there is a small surviving section of the ghetto wall. It is on a busy main road, and the driver is reluctant to stop, but we persuade him. Between No. 25 and No. 29 Lwowska Street is a wall three metres high, decorated with arches which have been modelled on the rounded tops of Jewish tombstones. There is a commemorative plaque here, put up in 1983, after the Solidarity revolution in Poland. The plaque reads, in Yiddish and Polish: 'Here they lived, suffered and died, murdered by the Nazi hangmen. From here they went on their last way to concentration camps.'

9.12 a.m.
We drive out of Cracow, along Wielicka Street to the E. 40. Our route will take us the whole length of Western Galicia. We should have visited the ghetto and the factory yesterday, and left Cracow this morning an hour earlier, but the driver is confident that before nightfall he can go everywhere that we had planned to go today.

9.35 a.m.
On the north-eastern horizon we see the edge of the Puszcza Niepolomicka forest. It was to this forest, the nearest to the city, that many young Jews made their escape from the Cracow ghetto at the time of the deportation. More than eight thousand managed to reach the forest. Very few of them survived the repeated German military attacks against them. One of those who had planned to be with this group was a twenty-four-year-old Jewish girl, Matilda Bandet.

As our bus drives closer to the wood, I speak of how, while waiting for my daughter one evening at Ben-Gurion Airport, about fifteen years ago, I found myself sitting next to a man who told me his story. He had emigrated to Palestine from Poland shortly before the outbreak of the war. His sister had hoped to follow him in a year or two's time. Before she could do so, war broke out. Later, he learned from a family friend what had happened to her. One morning in 1943 her friends came to her in the ghetto and told her that a German 'action' was imminent. The time had come, they said, for them to try to escape to the woods. Matilda Bandet hesitated. 'My place is with my parents,' she told her friends. 'They need me. They are old. They have no means of defending themselves. If I leave them, they will be alone. I will stay here with them.'

The friends made their escape. Matilda Bandet remained in the ghetto, and was deported with her parents to Belzec, where she and they were murdered. Which deportation it was, we do not know. There are no written records of the names of those deported to Belzec, either from the towns from which they were sent, or in the camp.

There were two main deportations from Cracow to Belzec. The first took place on 1 June 1942, when 2,000 Jews were deported, and the second, four days later, when 5,000 were deported. There were no survivors of either of these two deportations.

We are on the road to Belzec.

9.50 a.m.

Bochnia. On 25 August 1942, from this small town, 2,600 Jews were deported to Belzec. There were no survivors. The deportation was done according to the carefully prepared, detailed plan of deportations, which took one or two communities every day, working through East and West Galicia in strict rotation, usually taking about half of those in the ghetto, before coming back for the rest. This is what happened here. On 3 September 1942, nine days after that first deportation – and on the third anniversary of Britain's declaration of war on Germany, while the German army was still master of Europe from the Atlantic to the Urals – a second deportation took place.

Two thousand Jews were taken to the railway station here at Bochnia and put in one long train for Belzec. There were no survivors. Six hundred of Bochnia's Jews – mostly the old and the sick, and many children – were marched out of the town that day and shot in a nearby wood, near the village of Baczkow. That same day, the first 2,000 of 8,000 Jews were deported from the ghetto at Dzialoszyce, thirty miles north of Bochnia. Within a week the ghetto there was emptied. The deportees from Dzialoszyce were also sent to Belzec and murdered. A thousand of the Jews of Dzialoszyce were shot in the street, or taken just outside the town to be killed. A few hundred of the able-bodied younger men in both towns were taken away for slave labour, mostly to Plaszow.

As we drive through Bochnia, I speak of the Jewish life in the town before the war. A Jewish cemetery was opened here in 1872. In the local cemetery are the graves of twenty Jews who fought and fell in the ranks of the Austro-Hungarian army between 1914 and 1918. By 1932 there were three synagogues in the town. The ghetto was set up on 15 March 1941. Jews from a dozen villages around Bochnia were deported into it; the population of the ghetto was 15,000, its inmates working as slave labourers for the Germans in tailoring, shoemaking and dressmaking factories. Others were sent out each day to work on the roads: one of the main German military roads leading from Silesia to the Eastern Front ran through Bochnia; indeed, it is the road we are on.

The deportation and the killings of 3 September 1942 were not the last. Eight days later, the Gestapo raided the Jewish hospital and killed all forty-four sick people who were in beds on the wards. They also killed the doctors and nurses. A year later, in September 1943, the ghetto was, in the German terminology, 'liquidated' (that is, 'wound up'). Three thousand Jews were sent to a labour camp that had been set up at Szebnie, further to the east. Four thousand were sent to Auschwitz. The remaining sixty were shot in the deserted ghetto, probably after being made to carry out some clearing tasks.

10 a.m.
We drive on through a wonderful, peaceful, pastoral scene, of gentle rolling hills and cultivated fields. To our left, just to the north of the road, runs the railway that in those days led to Belzec. Today, as then, it is the main line from Cracow to Lvov and Kiev.

10.15 a.m.
Brzesko. Another Western Galician town which had a substantial Jewish population before the war. In the ghetto here, which was opened in 1940, all 4,000 Jews were confined. Brzesko's cemetery was founded in 1846, and the most recent of the three synagogues in 1904, at the height of the Habsburg era, when the Jews of this region embarked upon the twentieth century with parliamentary representation and an ever-widening sense of citizenship and participation in national life. To a large extent, those hopes persisted during the inter-war years, within independent Poland. They were swept away with the arrival of the German army in the first week of September 1939.

In September 1942 there was a substantial deportation from here to Belzec of more than two thousand Jews. When the ghetto was emptied a year later, those who had survived the year of hardship were sent – 3,000 in all – to Auschwitz.

Ben speaks of the contribution of the Jews to Polish life. He is proud
of the fact that the leading Polish philologists ('not Yiddish philologists
and not Hebrew philologists, but Polish philologists') were Jewish. As
Jews, he explains, they expounded and enriched the Polish language.

10.20 a.m.

We drive through Wojnicz. Here a Polish drama unfolded in the war.
There was also a prison here, for Poles arrested in the region. There,
in 1943, two Poles were shot. In the autumn of 1944 a slave labour
camp was established in this small town where 360 Poles, a third of
them women, were made to work on anti-tank fortifications, in a vain
German attempt to slow down the imminent advance of the Russian
army.

10.30 a.m.

We reach Tarnow, a great Jewish centre before the war, and, earlier,
in Austro-Hungarian times. Jews were first recorded here in the fifteenth
century – 500 years ago. At the end of the eighteenth century the
majority of Tarnow's Jews were Hassidim, but in the nineteenth century
the spirit of the Enlightenment (Haskalah) became the dominant force,
followed by an active Zionist movement: a Lovers of Zion Society was
set up here in 1891, to encourage emigration to Palestine, then under
Turkish rule.

On the eve of war in 1939 there were 25,000 Jews in Tarnow,
almost half the population of the town, a substantial Jewish community.
The German army entered the town on 8 September 1939.

It was from Tarnow that the first deportation to Auschwitz concentration camp took place. Auschwitz was then being used as a
punishment camp for Poles; it was not originally planned for the mass
murder of Jews. Those chosen for deportation were 708 Poles, then
held in Tarnow prison. Some were in prison because they had been
caught trying to escape southwards into Slovakia. Others had been
arrested because they were community leaders: priests and school-
teachers. About twenty Jews were also deported to Auschwitz in this
first deportation, among them Maximilian Rosenbusz, the director of
the local Hebrew school, and two lawyers, Emil Wieder and Isaac
Holzer.

As the passenger train in which the deportees were being taken to
Auschwitz passed through Cracow station, the deportees heard an
excited station announcer trumpet the fall of Paris. On arrival in
Auschwitz, the prisoners were put to work digging ditches and moving

earth. Of the first 728 deportees, 137 survived the war. All the Jews among them perished.

As we drive through Tarnow, I read an account of the deportation from there on 28 July 1942. Early that morning the Jews of Tarnow were ordered out of their houses. All had to remove their shoes, and, barefoot, were driven with rifle butts and whips into the market square. There, everyone was ordered to kneel down, after which, as one eye-witness recalled, 'Gestapo men walked among the kneeling people and took away the children.' The children were taken to a shed at the edge of the square, and shot. 'Indescribable lamentations, sobbing and weeping filled the market,' the eye-witness recalled.

'One could go mad,' the eye-witness wrote, and he added: 'In the corner of the square a thin, white-haired man was kneeling, and at his side his daughter, a slim brunette. A fat Gestapo man stopped near them, drew his revolver and killed the Jew. His daughter then leaped to her feet and cried to the Gestapo man in German: "You scoundrel! What did my father do to you that you shot him?" The Gestapo man flew at her, hit her and threatened to kill her, too. The girl looked at him with a penetrating gaze. When he turned away, avoiding her eyes, she insulted him again, called him a mean coward who shot defenceless people, and shouted that he dared not look into her eyes. "Look straight into my eyes, you coward," she cried, "and shoot! These eyes will pursue you and haunt you all your life!" The Gestapo man winced, turned away from the girl, as if to muster his courage, and after a moment aimed his revolver at her and shot her.'

A few Jews, the eye-witness among them, were taken off as forced labourers. The Jews of Tarnow were then deported, to Belzec, and to their death.

Several hundred Tarnow Jews were given refuge by non-Jews. Among those who were saved in this way from deportation were the wife and daughter of Maximilian Rosenbusz, the director of the local Hebrew school who had been taken to Auschwitz in June 1940 at the time of the camp's construction, and had perished there. The man who gave shelter to the two women was Wladyslaw Horbacki, a former regional school inspector of the Polish Ministry of Education. Both women survived the war.

On 25 and 26 March 1943, at the time of the liquidation of the Cracow ghetto, a factory owner in Tarnow, Julius Madritsch, from Vienna, had taken 232 Jews – men, women and children – from the Cracow ghetto into his clothing factory at Tarnow. He did not ill-treat them there, and, as Oskar Schindler was doing in Cracow, he protected them from deportation. Five months later, on 31 August 1943, Amon Goeth went specially from Plaszow to Tarnow to prepare for the destruction of the Tarnow ghetto. That night he ordered Madritsch to pay a large sum of money to protect 'his' Jews. Madritsch did so.

The final deportation from Tarnow took place on 2 September 1943, when 5,000 Jews were forced from the places where they were housed in the ghetto and ordered to march to the railway station. A report by the Polish underground tells of the Jews resisting these orders, and of the Germans using hand grenades to break up the resistance. Those Jews who survived the explosion of the grenades were loaded into cattle trucks, the floors of which had been covered with carbide and lime, which, if mixed with water, would give off poisonous fumes. According to the Polish report, the trucks were then 'sealed, inundated with water, and sent off to extermination'. Their destination was Auschwitz.

The 'Madritsch Jews' survived. Robin is researching into the story, piecing it together. He has made contact with Madritsch's widow, who lives in Vienna.

After the war, less than seven hundred of the 25,000 pre-war Jewish population of Tarnow returned, and most of them left soon afterwards to live in the United States or Palestine. Today there are associations of former Tarnow Jews in Israel, the United States, France and Canada.

We are driving through a country that had a Jewish population of more than three million before the war. 'We are driving through a graveyard,' Ben remarks, 'and with memories of a vibrant world that has gone.'

10.52 a.m.
Pilzow. There was a small Jewish community here before the war, probably two or three hundred people.

11 a.m.
Debica. There is an eighteenth-century synagogue here, one of the oldest in this part of Poland. The Jewish population by the end of the nineteenth century was just over three thousand. When the ghetto was established in 1942, 4,000 Jews were incarcerated in it, several hundred from the villages around it, including Pilzow, through which we drove less than ten minutes ago. Every one of the towns we are driving through not only had a large Jewish population, but was linked across the fields between with a dozen villages where Jews lived and worked, mostly as farmers and small shopkeepers. All were rounded

up and sent to the ghettos in the larger towns, the towns that lay, for the most part, on the railway lines.

In early 1942 a concentration camp was set up in the town. There, 1,600 Polish Jews were brought, to work on the railway line. But during a typhoid epidemic many of them were shot. There were also executions in the Jewish cemetery. Then, in July 1942, 4,000 Jews were deported from the ghetto here to Belzec. Those who were too old or too sick to board the trains were taken to the nearby Woliki forest and shot there. A few hundred able-bodied youngsters were taken to the slave labour camp at Rzeszow airport, one of the main German Air Force centres in southern Poland.

German records suggest that there were Poles in Debica who tried to help Jews. On 19 November 1942 a notice was posted on walls in the town stating that, from December 1, any Pole 'helping to lodge, feed or hide a Jew will be punished by death'.

The ghetto was finally emptied in April 1943, when most of the surviving inmates were shot. Those who were not shot were sent to slave labour camps elsewhere.

11.15 a.m.
As we drive on beyond Debica, the landscape becomes more hilly. To the north, we have a view across a wide plain.

11.35 a.m.
Ropczyce. Another small town, again with a long Jewish history, and a tragic end to that history. The end, as in so many other hundreds of towns in Poland, was the same: a ghetto established, some men sent to a slave labour camp – about a hundred and fifty – then the day of deportation, with the old people, and many children, being taken to the cemetery and shot. The remaining Jews of Ropczyce, numbering two or three hundred men and women, were not to be put on a deportation train by themselves; they were sent instead to the nearby town of Sedziszow, to share the fate of the Jews there.

It takes us only another five minutes to reach Sedziszow.

11.40 a.m.
We are driving through beautiful rolling countryside, and look down on the peaceful town of Sedziszow, its gardens and wooden roofs, from the by-pass road. Together with the Jews from Ropczyce, there were 1,900 Jews confined in the ghetto here. In July 1942, 400 Jews were killed in the streets. The rest – 1,500 in all – were sent by train to

Belzec. A single train took these two Jewish communities to their death. There were no survivors. In the cemetery here, only a few fragments of headstones survive.

11.46 a.m.
We cross the main deportation railway line (Cracow–Tarnow–Rzeszow– Belzec) at the village of Kleczany.

12.05 p.m.
Rzeszow. A major town in southern Poland with a long tradition of Jewish life and achievement, which came to an end in the war years. The first recorded Jewish residence here goes back to the fifteenth century. In the mid-nineteenth century the town was known as 'Little Jerusalem'. Among the leading citizens here was Rabbi Aaron Lewin. Before the war, while head of the Rzeszow rabbinical court, he was also a Deputy in the Polish Parliament. Zionism was strong here; the Hebrew language was taught in the kindergartens and in the Hebrew high school.

When the war began, there were 14,000 Jews living in Rzeszow, more than 35 per cent of the total population. Under German rule (when the city was renamed Reichshof), it became the centre of a labour camp region. There were ten slave labour camps in the area. All Jewish males between the ages of fourteen and sixty were liable to be seized on the streets, or summoned by order of the local Jewish Councils – at the Gestapo demand – and sent to work in conditions of the utmost hardship. Many did not return from these camps. The military airport just to the north of Rzeszow was taken over by the Germans and quickly became the main workplace for Jewish slave labourers in the region.

During the war, the Warsaw-based Jewish Fighting Organisation, which had a branch in Cracow, also had a small branch here. In October 1942 six of its members, having acquired a few pistols and knives, set off for the woods and hilly ground (which we can see to the north). There, they were betrayed by local peasants. When the Germans came to get them, they fought back, escaping deeper into the woods. But a second German search flushed them out, and five of the six were killed.

A Jew from Rzeszow, Sol Schindel, was an eye-witness of the blowing up of Crematorium II at Auschwitz during the Sonderkommando revolt in October 1944. Yesterday we read out his testimony, by the ruins of the crematorium itself.

The 1944 edition of Baedeker's *Generalgouvernement* guide book describes Rzeszow as 'formerly dominated by numerous Jews'. Of the city's 14,000 Jews on the outbreak of war, only 400 remained in a slave labour camp in the city by the summer of 1944, when most were deported to camps in Germany. A few dozen managed to escape and hide in the nearby forests.

12.15 p.m.
We are driving eastward from Rzeszow, with rolling hill country both to the north and the south.

12.20 p.m.
We reach Lancut (pronounced, approximately, 'wine-soot'). The synagogue here was built in 1761. We leave the bus in the municipal car park and set off up the hill into the town, in search of the synagogue, and somewhere to eat. We have been on the road for more than three hours.

Walking through a bustling market town, we come to a striking yellow-ochre building, with several tall windows on the upper floor, and an ornamental entrance leading up to the second floor. 'This,' we say, as if by a collective will, 'is the synagogue.' It is (or was). A notice on the door gives the opening hours, for it is now a museum. At the moment it is closed, but will be open in the afternoon. We go off in search of a restaurant.

12.50 p.m.
We reach No. 18 Paderewski Street. It is a private house, converted into a restaurant and small hotel, the Pensjonat Palaczyk (Pension Little Palace). We sit down in a palatial dining room and wait to be served. I recount the story of the Jews of Lancut. They are first recorded in the town more than four hundred years ago. In 1865 the 1,200 Jews here made up 40 per cent of the population. In 1918 a Jewish self-defence group was active, and successful, during a spate of attacks by local anti-Semites. Between the wars, Hebrew language studies flourished here, as did Jewish education generally. The Jews were still 40 per cent of the population – perhaps slightly more – when war came in 1939. They then numbered 2,753.

The German army entered Lancut on 9 September 1939. Thirteen days later, most of the Jews were expelled across the River San into Russia. Some Jews later returned. A Polish survivor of the Holocaust who came to London after the war, Charles Shane (formerly Chaim

Szlamberg), told me how, at the end of 1939, his parents had travelled from Lodz to Lancut, hoping to cross the Soviet border. 'A Jewish smuggler – a woman – offered to take us over the border to Russia. She wanted everything she could lay her hands on, everything we had. My parents said no.' Charles Shane's parents did not survive the war.

Some of the Lancut Jews who had been expelled into Russia returned after several months. They found a thousand Jews in the town, who had been expelled from Cracow. A ghetto was set up, and all were confined in it. On 1 August 1942 almost all the inmates of the ghetto were driven to the village of Pelkinie, nine miles away, where all the elderly, the sick, and the children, were shot. The fifty Jews still remaining in Lancut were taken on 17 September 1942 to the Szeniawa ghetto, where they were murdered in May 1943 in the local cemetery, together with several hundred other Jews who had been concentrated at Szeniawa.

The most feared Nazi official in Lancut, Joseph Kokut, was discovered in 1957 in Czechoslovakia and sent back to Poland, where he was tried, sentenced to death, and executed that same year.

I leave the dining room and wander off into another, smaller dining room. In the corner is a large brass menorah – the candelabra which Jews light for the eight nights of the festival of Chanukah. I carry it into our room. Caroline produces a lighter and lights the candles in it. Although it is not Chanukah (which normally falls near Christmas), we somehow feel it is appropriate to light it. I recall, from the prayer book of the Reform Synagogues of Great Britain, Hugo Gryn's account of a wartime Chanukah, and of the lesson of faith:

'I did not learn this lesson about faith in a theological college, that came much later, but in a miserable little concentration camp in German Silesia grotesquely called Lieberose – Lovely Rose. It was the cold winter of 1944 and although we had nothing like calendars, my father, who was my fellow prisoner there, took me and some of our friends to a corner in our barrack. He announced that it was the eve of Chanukah, produced a curious-shaped clay bowl, and began to light a wick immersed in his precious, but now melted, margarine ration. Before he could recite the blessing, I protested at this waste of food. He looked at me – then at the lamp – and finally said: "You and I have seen that it is possible to live up to three weeks without food. We once lived almost three days without water; but you cannot live properly for three minutes without hope!"'

1.20 p.m.

We ask the waiter about the building. It belonged to a Jew, Filip Sanbra-Kahane, who had fought in the Polish uprising of 1863, when he was twenty-four years old. During the fighting he lost his right hand, hence his extra name, Sanbra (sans bras). After the uprising he was arrested by the Austrians and imprisoned for half a year in Lvov. Later he graduated from the local agricultural academy, and married the daughter of a local Christian landowner. They had this house built for them in 1904, and it was here that Filip Sanbra-Kahane died in 1915, aged seventy-six. A Polish hero, he was buried among the insurrectionists of the November 1863 uprising.

Sanbra-Kahane was a co-founder of Sokol, the Austro-Hungarian youth movement. His wife was a Catholic. He moved in the world of Catholic Poland. 'He carried on in both worlds,' comments Ben. The menorah, the one surviving Jewish artefact in the house, belonged to him. Each year, his descendants in the United States come here for a celebratory reunion with those of his descendants who live here. The families who come from abroad are Jewish, the families who live here are Polish.

2.40 p.m.

We return to the Lancut synagogue. Its interior has been restored, by volunteers from the nearby art academy, to its pristine pre-war – and eighteenth-century – glory. The painted panels are magnificent: lions, deer, goats, eagles, snakes, and Jerusalem. One scene shows Noah's Ark on the flood waters, with the dove sitting on a branch floating in the water; another shows Abraham about to sacrifice Isaac, with the ram caught in the thicket, and the words, 'Do not put your knife on the boy.' There are also two magnificent horned stags with fishes' tails, holding up a crown.

In the war, the synagogue building remained intact because it was used by the Germans as a grain store. The one thing a grain store needs is a waterproof roof. Apparently there was a moment when the Germans wanted to destroy it, but the Lord of Lancut, Count Zamoyski, intervened to prevent this. He was related by marriage to several members of the German aristocracy, and his intervention succeeded.

The synagogue is now a museum, and is maintained by the municipality. On the wall near the entrance are photographs of pre-war and wartime scenes in Lancut. One of the photographs shows four Jewish soldiers from Lancut serving in the Austro-Hungarian army; one of them has a magnificent beard.

In the entranceway are some forty headstones, or parts of headstones, brought from the site of the former Jewish cemetery. Some are more than a hundred and fifty years old.

A plaque informs us: 'Renovation of the synagogue is sponsored partly by Lancut distillery.'

Paul prays at the site of the Ark.

3 p.m.
We leave the synagogue and return down the hill to the car park.

3.08 p.m.
As we drive away from Lancut, our spirits are uplifted by the beauty of the synagogue, and at the same time downcast at the thought that almost all those who had worshipped there on the eve of war had been murdered, and that several centuries of Jewish life before then, so much of which had centred around the synagogue, have no continuation.

3.30 p.m.
Przeworsk. The Jewish cemetery here dates back to the mid-nineteenth century. In July 1942 most of the Jews of the town were deported to Belzec. The railway to Belzec runs through the town.

3.45 p.m.
Jaroslaw. For more than a hundred years this was a bustling Jewish town in Western Galicia. The first synagogue recorded here was established in 1640. Even earlier, when Jews were not allowed to live in the town, but were allowed to attend the annual fair as cattle dealers and itinerant pedlars, they would hold prayer meetings here.

A great fire in 1663 destroyed the Jewish part of the town. Ben points out that it was three years before the Great Fire of London.

The Council of the Four Lands, the Jewish self-governing authority in the sixteenth and seventeenth centuries, often met here (as well as in Lublin). Today, the sole graffiti at the station states, 'Jews stink.'

The oldest surviving synagogue in Jaroslaw, built in 1807, is now an art school. There is also a fine nineteenth-century synagogue. The first cemetery was established in 1699. In the eighteenth century, the town was the centre of ox trading, in which Jews played a leading part. In order to resolve disputes that broke out among the Jews themselves, the Jews of the town were allowed their own judges.

In the nineteenth century, Jaroslaw was one of the main towns on the border between Austria-Hungary and Tsarist Russia. Thousands of

Jews, leaving Russia for the West, crossed the River San just to the east of the town, and came up the hill to this haven: the first town in which they were free from Tsarist restrictions and the fear of pogroms, from whose railway station they could continue to Cracow, Vienna, and the ports where ships would carry them to the United States – the Goldene Medine (the Golden Country) of their dreams and hopes.

In 1921, at the start of the independent Polish years, there were more than six thousand Jews living here. By the outbreak of war the number was 10,000. We are travelling through Poland with our thoughts on the destruction of Jewry, but in Jaroslaw, even without Jews, it is Jewish life that impresses our minds and imagination – the three centuries during which Jewish life flourished and proliferated.

The bus takes us through the town. There are many fine buildings from the Jewish times, including a Tarbut (Hebrew) school and the nineteenth-century synagogue. These are the buildings of Jewish life, of the Jewish continuity of those days. Then Germany invaded Poland, and the Red Army advanced to take up its position in eastern Poland, as agreed a few weeks earlier in the Nazi–Soviet Pact.

From the end of September 1939 the Soviet border ran along the River San, only four kilometres from the centre of Jaroslaw. The Jews were ordered out of their homes, forced down the hill, and pushed at rifle point across the bridge into Russia. Despite the sudden and crude nature of their expulsion, they were the lucky ones. Once in Russia, they were dispersed, many of them to Central Asia, and when Poland and the Soviet Union signed their treaty on 30 July 1941 – five and a half weeks after the German invasion of the Soviet Union – they became allies. Many of the former Jews of Jaroslaw joined the Polish army being recruited on Soviet soil, and were later stationed in Palestine (where some slipped away to join the underground Jewish army). Others fought with the Polish army in Italy and Normandy.

The fate of Russian soldiers captured by the Germans is part of the history of Jaroslaw. In the summer of 1941 a prisoner-of-war camp, Stalag 327, was opened here. As many as a thousand Russian soldiers captured as the German army moved eastward across the San were incarcerated here. It is not known if any of them survived.

The 1905 Baedeker guide for Austria-Hungary tells us that a branch line of the main railway line runs north-east from here to Sokal, with a 'branch to Belzec'.

4 p.m.
We leave Jaroslaw, driving down the hill to the River San.

4.02 p.m.
The River San. We are at one of the great Jewish geographic divides. Across the river was Tsarist Russia, where Jewish legal and political disabilities during more than a century and a half were offset by a flourishing of Jewish cultural and spiritual life; on this side of the river, the Austro-Hungarian Jews were more easily accepted and far more able to participate in almost every sphere of national life. From Napoleonic times until the First World War this was the border between Austria-Hungary and Russia; and also part of the line which divided German-occupied Poland and the Soviet Union between September 1939 and June 1941.

It was across this line that the German army launched its attack on Russia on 22 June 1941. To the south of us, along the River San, was an area of dense Jewish village settlement, reaching to the Carpathian Mountains. In front of us, stretching eastward, was the Pale of Settlement in Tsarist times, the area of the most populated Jewish region of Europe at the turn of the century.

4.03 p.m.
We cross the River San and drive eastward. There is a sense of another, less prosperous, less 'modern' world.

4.08 p.m.
We pass a goose farm. Geese in groups are waddling to and fro. This is a common sight in rural Poland.

4.20 p.m.
The road enters the forest. It is dark and uninviting, row after row of tall pines, densely packed together.

4.25 p.m.
Oleszyce. A small Jewish community was here, dating back 200 years. There are a hundred gravestones in the Jewish cemetery. In 1942 just over a hundred Jews, the whole community, were taken from here to the ghetto in Lubaczow, five miles away, and shot. There is a memorial to them in the Oleszyce cemetery.

4.30 p.m.

In the valley below we can see the town of Lubaczow. In 1880 there was a Jewish community of 1,500 here. They constituted a third of the town's population. A high point of their life came in 1899, when Baron Edmond de Rothschild, the patron of so many Jewish villages in Palestine, paid for the rebuilding of the synagogue here (it had been burned down). Between the wars the town boasted a well-known Hebrew school. All this suffered the same fate with which, during this one day's journey, from town to town, we have become familiar. In October 1942 the Jews from Lubaczow, and from all the neighbouring towns and villages, were concentrated here, and then deported by train to Belzec. Those who were not deported were taken to the cemetery and shot.

4.35 p.m.

The village of Dachnow: a village square, horses, geese and a pond.

4.40 p.m.

We drive through Cieszanow, passing the town's fine brick synagogue built in 1889. In this area, which was just on the German side of the German–Soviet border between 1939 and 1941, the Germans built massive anti-tank fortifications. Eight hundred Jewish slave labourers were brought from Tomaszow Lubelski and 500 from Mielec. In all, 5,000 Jews were put to this task. A thousand of them came from my great-grandfather's town, Czestochowa, in August 1940. After their task was done, those of the slave labourers who had survived were then interned in the Cieszanow ghetto, until Belzec death camp was operational, and they were taken there and killed.

Belzec is only twenty-eight kilometres from here.

4.50 p.m.

We are driving along the same road on which the 5,000 deportees from Cieszanow to Belzec would have been forced out of their town, perhaps on trucks, perhaps on foot. We are in one of the most densely wooded areas of Poland, the Puszcza Solska. The road is straight, through another forest of dense pines, their trunks rose-coloured in the declining sun. We are getting nearer and nearer to Belzec.

5 p.m.

We go through a village, Plazow, which is surrounded by pine forests.

5.12 p.m.

We reach the western outskirts of Belzec village, and cross the railway. On one side of the road is a small railway station, a mere halt, with the station name 'Belzec II'. This is the railway line that leads from several hundred towns south and west of Lublin whose Jewish inhabitants were deported along this (single-track) line to be murdered.

5.18 p.m.

We reach the main Warsaw–Lvov highway, the centre of Belzec village. We turn south and drive through the village. We are only ten miles from the Ukrainian border.

Among the local Ukrainians living in Belzec village before the war, and also in the villages around here, were those who collaborated with the Germans. The Ukrainian Uprising Army (the UPA) was both anti-Polish and anti-Jewish. The population of Belzec at the outbreak of war was about two thousand. A third were Ukrainians, a third Poles and a third Volksdeutsche: so-called 'Ethnic Germans' whose ancestors had settled in this area – as in many other areas of Eastern Europe – many generations ago, but who still spoke German, and considered themselves ethnically, or racially, German. There were also eighty Jews living here.

Mike Tregenza, a Cornishman who now lives in Lublin, and who knows more than anyone else about Belzec, told me on the telephone when I spoke to him from London a week ago: 'The Belzec camp was a cottage industry. Everybody made something out of it.'

Except of course the Jews. The Jews of the village, and Jews from throughout Galicia, as well as from Slovakia and Germany, were brought here only to be murdered.

5.22 p.m.

Driving south from the village, along the main Warsaw–Lvov highway, we reach Belzec station. Just behind the station is a large red-brick building. At the time of the deportations, this was the building in which the clothes of the victims were first sorted and stored.

5.24 p.m.

We turn off the road to the entrance of the camp. It is just across the railway tracks. Outside the camp gate (which I remember well from my journey here sixteen years ago) is a forester's cottage built in the 1960s as a local Militia post. In the garden two children are playing. Their mother is calling them. The kitchens and laundry of the camp were behind the forester's house, in what is now his garden. The house itself is on the site of the Jewish work brigade compound.

I find the same difficulty at Belzec now as I did on my earlier visit. The site is smaller than the original camp area, dilapidated, and desperately sad.

The monumental entrance gate – built after the war on a spot inside the original camp – has a strong barbed-wire motif in metal, and is highlighted with the dates '1942–1943'. There is also a metal notice affixed to the gate, in white lettering on a blue background, informing the passer-by: 'This is where a monument in commemoration of the slaughter of Jewish children (who died between 1939–1945 in Poland) will be built.' Those who will contribute to the monument are described on the notice as 'People of Good Will'.

The monument just inside the post-war entrance is inscribed with the stark facts, recording, in Polish, that 600,000 Jews 'from Poland and other countries of Europe' were murdered here and also 1,500 Poles 'who tried to save Jews'.

We read the plaque, and look at a map which has been set up just inside the gate to show the wartime layout of the camp. The map identifies nine locations within the site. We then begin our walk. The camp lies on a slope. The entrance where we stand is where one of four watchtowers stood. We pass the place where the deportees were ordered to undress and leave their clothes, and on, up the slope, to a monument that has been built near the site of the gas chamber. It is a large block set at the top of four low steps. An inscription asks us to remember the victims of Hitlerite terror 'murdered in the years 1942– 1943'. There is no mention of Jews. In front of the monument, an emaciated sculpted figure tries to hold up another, who cannot stand.

From the gas-chamber monument, which is at the edge of the wood in which the ashes of the victims were dumped, we turn towards the barracks of the Ukrainian guards, at the northern edge of the camp, and then walk up a path that runs along the northern edge of the camp into the wood, where there is a series of concrete slabs on the site of the mass graves.

There seems nothing to say.

Just outside the upper perimeter of the camp, through the fence there, we look down on a series of ditches. These are part of the ditches dug by Jewish prisoners in the original Belzec camp, which operated then as a slave labour camp, and to which, between May and December 1940, several thousand Jews were brought to build anti-tank ditches for the German defenders of the Reich. Of the 2,000 Jewish slave labourers brought from Radom in 1940 almost none survived. Other towns in the Radom region were also forced to send many of their young men here. Many of them died as they were beaten and subjected to great brutality while they worked. They too should be remembered as among the victims at this horrific site.

I have said that I will do my reading outside the camp after we have walked around it; it seems almost a desecration to read anything, or even to say anything on the site itself. Slowly, each of us makes our own way back to the entrance. As I arrive, I am startled out of my reflections by a train coming along the railway from the direction of Lvov; it passes literally fifteen yards from the camp entrance.

Ros lights a memorial candle in front of the monument on the site of the gas chamber. Slowly we gather at the gate. I have with me a copy of the diary of a German non-commissioned officer who travelled on this railway line on 31 August 1942. His name was Wilhelm Cornides. The diary entry from which I read is headed: 'In the train from Rawa Ruska to Chelm, 5.30 p.m.', and reads:

'When we boarded at 4.40 p.m. an empty transport had just arrived. I walked along the train twice and counted fifty-six cars. On the doors had been written in chalk: "60", "70", once "90", occasionally "40" – obviously the number of Jews that were carried inside.

'In my compartment I spoke with a railway policeman's wife who is currently visiting her husband here. She says these transports are now passing through daily, sometimes also with German Jews. Yesterday six children's bodies were found along the track. The woman thinks that the Jews themselves had killed these children – that they must have succumbed during the trip.

'The railway policeman who comes along as train escort joined us in our compartment. He confirmed the woman's statements about the children's bodies which were found along the track yesterday. I asked: "Do the Jews know then what is happening with them?" The woman answered: "Those who come from far won't know anything, but here in the vicinity they know already. They attempt to run away then, if they notice that someone is coming for them. So, for example, most recently in Chelm where three were shot on the way through the city."

' "In the railway documents these trains run under the name of resettlement transports," remarked the railway policeman. Then he said that after Heydrich was murdered, several transports with Czechs passed through. Camp Belzec is supposed to be located right on the railway line and the woman promised to show it to me when we pass it.

'5.40 p.m. Short stop. Opposite us another transport. I talk to the policemen who ride on the passenger car in front. I ask: "Going back home to the Reich?" Grinning, one of them says: "You know where we come from, don't you? Well, for us the work does not cease." Then the transport train continued – the cars were empty and swept clean; there were thirty-five. In all probability that was the train I saw at 1 p.m. on the station in Rawa Ruska.

'6.20 p.m. We passed camp Belzec. Before then, we travelled for some time through a tall pine forest. When the woman called, "Now it comes," one could see a high hedge of fir trees. A strong sweetish odour could be made out distinctly. "But they are stinking already," says the woman. "Oh nonsense, that is only the gas," the railway policeman said, laughing. Meanwhile – we had gone on about two hundred yards – the sweetish odour was transformed into a strong smell of something burning. "That is from the crematory," says the policeman.

'A short distance farther the fence stopped. In front of it, one could see a guardhouse with an SS post. A double track led into the camp. One track branched off from the main line, the other ran over a turntable from the camp to a row of sheds about two hundred and fifty yards away. A freight car happened to stand on the table. Several Jews were busy turning the disk. SS guards, rifle under the arm, stood by. One of the sheds was open; one could distinctly see that it was filled with bundles of clothes to the ceiling. As we went on, I looked back one more time. The fence was too high to see anything at all. The woman says that sometimes, while going by, one can see smoke rising from the camp, but I could notice nothing of the sort. My estimate is that the camp measures about 800 by 400 yards.'

My next reading is from the recollections of the thirty-seven-year-old chief of the Waffen-SS Technical Disinfections Services. His name was Kurt Gerstein. The organiser of the Polish death camps, SS Brigadier – later Major-General – Odilo Globocnik, an Austrian Nazi whose headquarters we will visit in Lublin in two days' time, had sought Gerstein's help in disinfecting what he called 'large piles of clothing coming from Jews, Poles Czechs, etc'.

On 18 August 1942, thirteen days before Wilhelm Cornides went past the camp in the train, Globocnik took Kurt Gerstein to Belzec. With them was SS Lieutenant-Colonel Dr Wilhelm Pfannenstiel, Professor of Hygiene at the University of Marburg. Two and a half years after this visit, Gerstein recalled: 'We saw no dead bodies that day, but a pestilential odour hung over the whole area. Alongside the station there was a "dressing" hut with a window for "valuables". Farther on, a room designated as "the barber". Then a corridor 150 metres long in the open air, barbed wire on both sides, with signs: "to the baths and inhalants". In front of us a building like a bath-house; to the left and right, large concrete pots of geraniums or other flowers. On the roof, the Star of David. On the building, a sign: "Hackenholt Foundation".'

Gerstein and Professor Pfannenstiel stayed at Belzec village overnight, as the guests of the camp commandant, Christian Wirth. Then, as Gerstein recalled: 'The following morning, a little before seven, there was an announcement, "The first train will arrive in ten minutes!" A few minutes later a train arrives from Lemberg: forty-five cars arrive with more than six thousand people; two hundred Ukrainians assigned to this work flung open the doors and drove the Jews out of the cars with leather whips.

'A loudspeaker gave instructions: "Strip, even artificial limbs and glasses. Hand all money and valuables in at the 'valuables' window. Women and young girls are to have their hair cut in the 'barber's hut'." (An SS Sergeant told me: "From that they make something special for submarine crews.")

'Then the march began. Barbed wire on both sides, in the rear two dozen Ukrainians with rifles. They drew near. Wirth and I found ourselves in front of the death-chambers. Stark naked men, women, children and cripples passed by. A tall SS man in the corner called to the unfortunates in a loud minister's voice: "Nothing is going to hurt you! Just breathe deep and it will strengthen your lungs. It's a way to prevent contagious diseases. It's good disinfectant!"

'They asked him what was going to happen and he answered: "The men will have to work, build houses and streets. The women won't have to do that. They will be busy with the housework and the kitchen."

'This was the last hope for some of these poor people, enough to make them march toward the death-chambers without resistance. The majority knew everything; the smell betrayed it! They climbed a little wooden stair and entered the death-chambers, most of them silently, pushed by those behind them.

'A Jewess of about forty with eyes like fire cursed the murderers: she disappeared into the gas-chambers after being struck several times by Captain Wirth's whip. Many prayed; others asked: "Who will give us the water before we die?"

'SS men pushed the men into the chambers. "Fill them up tight!"

Wirth ordered. Seven to eight hundred people in ninety-three square metres. The doors closed. Then I understood the reason for the "Hackenholt" sign. Hackenholt was the driver of the diesel, whose exhaust was to kill these poor unfortunates.

'Hackenholt tried to start the motor. It wouldn't start! Captain Wirth came up. You could see he was afraid because I was there to see the disaster. Yes, I saw everything and waited. My stopwatch clocked it all: fifty minutes. Seventy minutes and the diesel still would not start! The men were waiting in the gas chambers. You could hear them weeping, "as though in a synagogue", said Professor Pfannenstiel, his eyes glued to the peephole in the wooden door.[1]

'Captain Wirth, furious, struck with this whip the Ukrainian who helped Hackenholt. The diesel engine started up after two hours and forty-nine minutes by my stopwatch. Twenty-five minutes passed. You could see through the window that many were already dead, for an electric light illuminated the interior of the room. All were dead after thirty-two minutes.

'Jewish workers on the other side opened the wooden doors. They had been promised their lives in return for doing this horrible work, plus a small percentage of the money and valuables collected. The people were still standing like columns of stone, with no room to fall or lean. Even in death you could tell the families, all holding hands. It was difficult to separate them emptying the room for the next batch. The bodies were tossed out, blue, wet with sweat and urine, the legs smeared with excrement and menstrual blood. Two dozen workers were busy checking mouths which they opened with iron hooks ... Dentists knocked out gold teeth, bridges and crowns with hammers.

'Captain Wirth stood in the middle of them. He was in his element and, showing me a big jam box filled with teeth, said, "See the weight of the gold! Just from yesterday and the day before! You can't imagine what we find every day, dollars, diamonds, gold! You'll see!" He took me over to a jeweller who was responsible for all the valuables. They also pointed out to me one of the heads of the big Berlin store, Kaufhaus des Westens, and a little man whom they forced to play the violin, the chief of the Jewish workers' commandos. "He is a captain of the Imperial Austrian Army; Chevalier of the German Iron Cross," Wirth told me.

---

[1] Pfannenstiel later denied that he uttered these words. In a post-war deposition he said that the peepholes in the doors were quickly steamed up and that nothing could be seen inside the chambers.

'Then the bodies were thrown into big ditches near the gas chambers, about 100 by 20 by 12 metres.[1] After a few days, the bodies swelled...

'When the swelling went down again, the bodies matted down again. They told me later they poured diesel oil over the bodies and burned them on railway lines to make them disappear.'

Kurt Gerstein went on from Belzec to Treblinka. Then, on August 22, he took the express train back to Berlin (along the Warsaw–Berlin line on which we will be travelling in a few days' time). Also travelling on the train was a Swedish diplomat, Baron von Otter. Less than an hour from Warsaw the train stopped in open country. 'We both got down to get a breath of air,' Otter later recalled. 'I offered him a cigarette. He refused. There were beads of sweat on his forehead. There were tears in his eyes. And his voice was hoarse when he said, at once, "I saw something awful yesterday – can I come and see you at the Legation?"'

Otter suggested that they talk on the train. Gerstein agreed. 'Is it the Jews?' Otter asked. 'Yes, it is,' Gerstein replied. 'I saw more than ten thousand die yesterday.'

There were almost no survivors of Belzec. Of the 600,000 men, women and children who were murdered here, only five are known to have survived. They were among those who had been taken away from the incoming trains to work at the various labour tasks inside the camp. The work brigades in Belzec totalled a thousand men. They too were murdered at regular intervals, or by sadistic guards.

One of the five known survivors is a woman, Sara Ritterband. She worked in the laundry and kitchens. She was badly beaten on at least twenty occasions. When she reached Belzec she was with her four-year-old daughter, who was smuggled out of the camp and hidden in the village. When Belzec was closed down, Sara Ritterband was transferred to Trawniki, and from there to Auschwitz. She survived the 'death march' from Auschwitz to Bergen-Belsen, where she was liberated by the British army on 15 April 1945. Today she lives in Israel. Her daughter also survived the war, and lives in Israel.

Another of the survivors of Belzec, Chaim Hirszman, was living in Lublin after liberation. On 19 March 1946 he gave his testimony to the Jewish Historical District Commission in Lublin. As we stand just inside the entrance of the camp, I read from his account. He had been brought by train from the town of Zaklikow. At the selection in

---

[1] Gerstein's estimated measurements were wrong; the ditches measured about thirty metres by twenty.

Zaklikow, he, like several hundred other able-bodied men (he was then twenty-nine years old and a metal worker) was selected for forced labour. But, he told the Commission, 'since my wife and my half-a-year-old son were sent to the opposite side, I asked to join them and was permitted to do so.' His account continued:

'We were entrained and taken to Belzec. The train entered a small forest. Then, the entire crew of the train was changed. SS men from the death camp replaced the railroad employees. We were not aware of this at that time.

'The train entered the camp. Other SS men took us off the train. They led us all together – women, men, children – to a barrack. We were told to undress before we went to the bath. I understood immediately what that meant. After undressing we were told to form two groups, one of men and the other of women and children. An SS man, with the strike of a horse-whip, sent the men to the right or to the left, to death – to work.

'I was selected to death, I didn't know it then. Anyway, I believed that both sides meant the same – death. But, when I jumped in the indicated direction, an SS man called me and said "Du bist ein Militärmensch, dich können wir brauchen." ("You are a military man, we could use you.")

'We, who were selected for work, were told to dress. I and some other men were appointed to take the people to the kiln. I was sent with the women. The Ukrainian Schmidt, an Ethnic German, was standing at the entrance to the gas chamber and hitting with a knout – a knotted whip – every entering woman. Before the door was closed, he fired a few shots from his revolver and then the door closed automatically and forty minutes later we went in and carried the bodies out to a special ramp.[1] We shaved the hair off the bodies, which was afterwards packed into sacks and taken away by Germans.

'The children were thrown into the chamber simply on the women's heads. In one of the "transports" taken out of the gas chamber, I found the body of my wife and I had to shave her hair.

'The bodies were not buried on the spot, the Germans waited until more bodies were gathered. So, that day we did not bury ...'

There are a number of other passages which I had intended to read. But when I brought them out of my bag, and looked through them, I did not feel able to do so. There is a limit to how much one can take

[1] Heinz Schmidt was in fact an Ethnic German (Volksdeutscher) from Latvia, not the Ukraine. He committed suicide in Italy in 1944.

in, even on the spot; perhaps it is harder on the spot than in the classroom or in the study, for here one is on the actual ground where these terrible events took place.

My final reading was to have been from an official wartime report in which Lieutenant Westermann, a German police officer in the reserve, describes the deportation of 8,000 Jews from the Eastern Galician towns of Horodenka, Sniatyn and Kolomyja. These Jews were sent to Belzec in a single (thirty-wagon) train in September 1942. These are the sentences I would have read, but the last reading was so devastating that I decide not to read it. Westermann wrote:

'The slow journey was time and again used by the strongest Jews to press themselves through the holes they had forced open and to seek their safety in flight, because in jumping from the slow-moving train they were scarcely injured. Despite the repeated requests to the engineer to go faster, this was not possible, so that the frequent stops on open stretches became increasingly unpleasant.

'Shortly before Lemberg the commando had already shot off the ammunition they had with them and also used up a further two hundred rounds that they had received from army soldiers, so that for the rest of the journey they had to resort to stones while the train was moving and to fixed bayonets when the train stopped.

'The ever greater panic spreading among the Jews due to the great heat, overloading of the train cars, and stink of dead bodies made the transport almost unworkable.'

When, on September 10, after more than three days on this journey without food or water, the train reached Belzec, 2,000 of the 8,000 deportees were dead. Westermann then handed over the transport personally to Wirth.

6.20 p.m.
We wander about over the rough ground. Some are silent, some are crying. All are disconsolate.

Some of us return to the area in front of the gas-chamber memorial. Paul leads a small group in prayer: first, 'El Maleh Rachamim' (God of Mercy); then, 'The Lord is my Shepherd', then Psalm 120:

> In my distress I cried unto the Lord, and he answered me.
> Deliver my soul, O Lord, from a lying lip and from a deceitful tongue.
> What shall be given unto thee, and what shall be done more unto thee, thou deceitful tongue?
> Sharpened arrows of a mighty man, with coals of broom.

Woe is me, that I sojourn in Mesech, that I dwell among the tents of Kedar.

My soul hath full long had her dwelling with him that hateth peace.

I am all peace; but when I speak, they are for war.

Paul ends with the Kaddish (extolling God's name).

There are five of us saying the prayers. Not everyone felt able to bring God into the equation. We stand at the edge of the field, facing up the gentle slope towards the site of the main graves and cremation pyres, across the brick-red earth. As we turn away we are shattered.

Paul says, 'If we could take in what happened here we could not go on living.'

6.35 p.m.

I stand for a few moments just outside the gate looking again at the forester's house, which has been built there since my last visit. A young child plays at the front gate facing the entrance to the camp. A turkey and her chicks cross the yard. A small boy comes out of the house and chases the turkey with a stick. His mother gathers the young chicks with a broom. There is a water pump in the yard. There are pretty potted plants around the house, and lace curtains in the window.

Marie later wrote to me of what she called 'my feeling of disgust, or was it pity (?) for the children in the house who were playing in the garden. I didn't even want to imagine what it would be like to grow up next to a death camp.'

6.40 p.m.

Across the railway is the commandant's house. We get into the minibus and drive across the railway, and turn north, back into Belzec village. A passenger train passes along the railway, going south. Cows graze between the road and the railway. A toddler rides beside the track on a tricycle. We cross the single-track former deportation railway line going north. Just beyond the crossing is a sign on a gate, 'Belzec sports stadium'.

As we leave Belzec village I read an account by a Polish eye-witness who recalled that the wartime Polish inhabitants of Belzec 'were complaining about the stench which increased day by day. Everyone understood that in some way the Jews were being killed there. In the end, passengers travelling through Belzec by train also started to complain that the stench of rotting bodies was unbearable and was even penetrating the interior of the carriages through tightly shut windows.'

6.45 p.m.
The bus drives us northwards through a prosperous farming landscape. To the right of the road, looking eastward, across the cultivated fields, is a line of dark woods. Everyone's thoughts are on what we have seen.

6.50 p.m.
Tomaszow Lubelski. We remain too shattered to do any more reading, even though there is much to tell here, as everywhere. This was a town where the Jewish community was wiped out during the Chmielnicki massacres of 1648 – when as many as 100,000 Jews were murdered throughout the Ukraine by Bogdan Chmielnicki's Cossack soldiers on the rampage. After that catastrophe, Hassidism later gained many adherents here, as it did throughout the region where the killings had taken place.

Before the outbreak of the Second World War, the 6,000 Jews of Tomaszow Lubelski made up 43 per cent of the population. In late September and early October 1939 as many as 4,500 of them were able to escape across the newly established Soviet border, which ran just to the south, on the outskirts of Belzec. Those who remained were taken to Belzec and killed two years later.

The two brick synagogues here were both pulled down during the war. The cemetery was also demolished, the Germans using the headstones to pave the streets of the town, and to create a pavement around Gestapo headquarters. Only a dozen tombstones, the oldest dating from 1724, remain: a physical reminder that this was a town where Jews lived and flourished.

We drive through streets which were once full of Jewish activity. But it is Belzec that is on everyone's mind.

Caroline later told me how shocked she was, as Marie had been, that a family could live today so close to the camp, only a few paces from the main entrance. The forester's house had in fact been built not outside, but inside the area of the original camp, on the site of the Jewish work brigade compound.

In the letter which she wrote to me after our journey, Marie reflected on how remote Belzec was. 'How many people actually know about it?' she asked 'How many people visit? Will it be forgotten?'

We are to have many such reflections and conversations after our return home. But as we drove north from Belzec we travelled in silence.

6.55 p.m.

A road sign indicates that Zamosc, where we will stop tonight, is only thirty-one kilometres away. There are forests on either side of the road and small meadows. A tethered cow has her grazing patch on the narrow grass verge by the roadside.

7 p.m.

As the road rises, we see to the left a vast wooded landscape below us. We are looking across a region which had the greatest wealth and proliferation of Jewish towns and life, including Bilgoraj, where two of the leading Yiddish writers of recent times, Israel Joshua and Isaac Bashevis Singer, were born (the latter winning the Nobel Prize for Literature).

Still no one is speaking. It has been a long, often distressing day, and its end is inevitably a sombre one.

7.02 p.m.

As we drive through the tiny village of Budy, Robin, who has just about regained his composure, tells me of a dentist, whose name was Bachner, who was deported from Cracow to Belzec on 3 June 1942. Bachner, having been put in a work squad, managed to escape from the camp on 28 October 1942. He somehow managed to leave the work squad and make a dash for a cesspit. He hid in it, up to his neck in human excrement, until he was able to get away. When he reached Cracow he gave a full description of what was going on in Belzec. It seemed so unbelievable that no one accepted it.

7.12 p.m.

Labunie village. Four small children are playing in front of a house. I cannot get Chaim Hirszman's description out of my mind.

As we continue towards Zamosc along a long straight road, I reflect on the triple scene that has been presented to us today, during eleven hours of almost non-stop travelling: first the world that was, as typified by the Lancut Synagogue and the buildings of Jaroslaw; then the places of destruction, culminating in Belzec; and finally the scene today as we drove through so many towns in which there had once been a full and vibrant Jewish life. Poland was a heartland for the Jewish people up to 1939. They had been an integral part of town and village life for several hundred years. Today we have driven through several dozen of those towns and villages, where the Nazi intention has been in every case fulfilled.

7.20 p.m.
We reach the outskirts of Zamosc, and drive to our hotel, the Hotel Jubilat. It is a modern hotel, built on the ruins of what was the Jewish quarter before the war.

7.25 p.m.
We will have an hour's break. I go to my room.

8.25 p.m.
We leave the hotel by minibus, and drive into town. Zamosc was founded in 1580 as the private town of Count Jan Zamoyski. It was built, in the form we see it today, between 1610 and 1618, in the Renaissance style of the cities of Italy, and is known as the 'Padua of the north'.

8.35 p.m.
We arrive at the Zamosc city car park. It is getting dark. We walk through one of the gates in the city walls and along the streets of a delightful old town, to the synagogue. The building is closed, but its crenellations are silhouetted magnificently against the evening sky. It was built between 1610 and 1618. Today it is the public library.

We discuss how many of the surviving synagogues in Poland are preserved precisely because they have been turned into libraries: which need to have waterproof roofs to protect the books, and generally can be designed so as not to alter the synagogue layout.

I give a short account of the history of the Jews of Zamosc. The Jewish community was founded in 1588 by Sephardi Jews who came here from Lvov (where there was also an Armenian Christian community). They were later joined by Sephardi Jews from Turkey, Italy and Holland. But within fifty years they were outnumbered by Ashkenazi Jews.

In 1648 Chmielnicki's troops besieged the town, but failed to break through its fortifications. However, several thousand Jews died of hunger and disease during the siege, most of them having sought shelter here from neighbouring towns and villages.

By 1857 the 2,490 Jews here made up just over sixty-one per cent of the population. The town was a centre of the Jewish Enlightenment movement (Haskalah). The writer I. L. Peretz, as well as Ludwig

Zamenhof, the founder of Esperanto – the international language – and Rosa Luxemburg, the revolutionary socialist, were each born in the town. Between the wars Zamosc boasted three Yiddish newspapers: *Unzer Gajst, Zamoszczer Wort* and *Zamoszczer Sztyme*.

We reflect on how remarkable it is that two internationalists, Rosa Luxemburg and Ludwig Zamenhof, were both born here: seeking from such different perspectives to unite the world that they were convinced could be best united under a single theme: for the one, universal brotherhood, for the other, a universal language.

I. L. Peretz was born in Zamosc in 1851. For ten years he worked here as a lawyer. In Prague, when we were at Rabbi Loew's statue, I read his story about the Golem. Many of his tales, so loved by the Jews of Poland, and Jews far beyond Poland, at the turn of the century, were based on the sights and scenes that he witnessed here in Zamosc, and in the villages nearby.

Almost all the Jewish-owned houses of the seventeenth and eighteenth century survive here; they are an integral part of the town. Most of them are around the Rynek Solny (Salt Market). The former mikveh (ritual bath-house) is at No. 3 Zamenhofa Street, in a high-vaulted cellar. It is now a jazz club. The Jewish cemetery on Prosta Street, established in 1907, was destroyed in the war, but five years after the war the surviving headstones were made into a tall obelisk, on which the Tablets of the Law were inscribed (in Hebrew and Polish) with one only of the Ten Commandments: Thou Shalt Not Kill.

The ghetto was set up not only for the Jews of Zamosc but for Jews deported to Zamosc in 1941 and 1942 from Germany, Czechoslovakia, and western Poland. Those held in the ghetto were later deported to Belzec, the first 3,000 on 11 April 1942, the last 4,000, including the entire Jewish Council, on 15 November 1942.

A prisoner-of-war camp was set up here in Zamosc in 1943 to incarcerate captured Soviet officers. Shortly after their arrival the Jewish officers among them were taken away and shot.

For the Poles, Zamosc is notorious for the German attempt during the war to clear the whole region of Poles and to turn it into a German reservation. The town, with its fine seventeenth-century buildings, and attractive rural vistas, was renamed by the Germans 'Himmlerstadt'.

9.10 p.m.

In the main square of Zamosc we choose a restaurant and descend into the ornate brick cellar for dinner. It takes a while to put the events of the day far enough behind even to look at the menu.

After dinner we walk back, along the street named after I. L. Peretz, to the car park where the minibus is waiting to take us back to the hotel. We drive back past the Polish military cemetery, in which are buried those Polish soldiers who fell in action in the Zamosc region in the battles against the Germans in September 1939. There are several Jews among them (alas, it is too late for us to stop and find their graves, nor will we have time to do so tomorrow). I mention Hilel Nusymowicz, an engineer, and Dawid Vogelfanger, an infantryman, both privates.

We discuss Jewish participation in previous wars. Here in Zamosc was born (in 1788) Dr Filip Lubelski, who served as a volunteer physician for two years with Napoleon's armies. Later he fought in the Polish insurrection against Russia of 1831, being awarded the Golden Military Cross. Another doctor, Dr Leon Goldsobel, who organised a partisan division during the insurrection of 1863, was imprisoned here in Zamosc. After his release he became a departmental chief in the Jewish hospital in Warsaw.

11.30 p.m.
Bed.

DAY 9

ZAMOSC – LUBLIN

A day of tears and laughter

6.15 a.m.

I leave the hotel and walk to the road that runs behind it, M. Reja Street. A hundred years ago this was the centre of the then 'new' Jewish quarter. The most impressive building on the street is a large brick building, now a kindergarten. It was once the synagogue. Built in 1872, and reconstructed in 1914, it was badly damaged in the Second World War, but the heavy structure has survived the ravages of war and time. It still stands, a mute testimony to the once flourishing Jewish life of this street, and this area.

I walk around the corner to the bus station. It is next to the market. Known as Nowy Miasto (New Town), this whole area was the centre of the nineteenth-century Jewish town. Where the buses draw in, there are a number of Gypsy women with small children, begging.

The bus destinations give an echo of pre-war Jewish life. The bus just leaving is going to Zwierzyniec, one of fifty towns in this region which had age-old Jewish communities.

Another bus is awaiting its passengers for Szczebrzeszyn, which has a magnificent synagogue, first reconstructed in 1659, after the Chmielnicki depredations of 1648, set on fire by the Germans in 1940, and now superbly restored.

There is a bus about to set off for Tyszowce, a shtetl whose Jewish shops and houses survived the Second World War intact. I visited it in 1980 with a pre-war map; none of the buildings had been pulled down or enlarged; it was only the Jews who were no more. The Jewish cemetery had become the town sports field.

A bus pulls in on the Chelm–Rzeszow line, stopping here for a few minutes. It will be going on via the town of Bilgoraj, 1,000 of whose Jews managed to cross into the Soviet Union with the Red Army, when it withdrew in October 1939 from the area it had briefly occupied. The remaining 4,000 Jews were confined to a ghetto. The main deportation was to Belzec, on 2 November 1942 – 'Balfour Day', the twenty-fifth anniversary of Britain's Balfour Declaration, promising the Jewish people a National Home in Palestine. A group of young Jews from Bilgoraj managed to escape to the nearby woods at the time of the November deportation, and fought against the Germans until they were wiped out. On 15 January 1943 the Germans discovered twenty-seven Jews still in hiding in Bilgoraj. They were shot.

Other buses are leaving for towns which once had flourishing Jewish communities which were destroyed in the war – Hrubieszow, Turobin and Zolkiewka. There is a bus preparing to leave for Chelm. At ten past nine the daily express bus will leave for Lodz, via Kielce, the town where forty-two Jews were murdered by Poles more than a year after the war was over.

So many Jewish towns without Jews. The list of destinations on the departure board is like a roll call of their lost communities. From the Jewish perspective, even the bustling Zamosc bus terminal is dead. It is part of a ghost town. Yet during the first three years of my own life in London, it was populated by thousands of Jews and vibrant with Jewish life.

Polish peasants are sitting on the benches in the bus station where once Jews sat. Polish shopkeepers are trading in the booths where once Jews traded.

There is an unusual 'special offer': a bus will leave the bus station here in Zamosc at eight o'clock this morning, for (of all places) Paris. It will go via Lublin, Piotrkow and Kalisz, and having driven through the night, will stop in Lille and Lens before reaching Paris at four o'clock tomorrow afternoon. In a few days' time, a similar 'special' will leave for Cologne.

8.15 a.m.
I return to the hotel, and have some breakfast. Mike Tregenza arrives by bus from Lublin. He left London four years ago and now lives, with his Polish wife, in Poland. He is the expert on the Operation Reinhard death camps (Belzec, Sobibor and Treblinka) which were organised by SS Brigadier Odilo Globocnik after the assassination of Reinhard Heydrich in Prague. He will come with us to Sobibor today, and will be with us in Lublin tonight and tomorrow.

8.20 a.m.

We drive from the hotel, down Partyzantow Street, into Zamosc. This is the route by which the Jews were forced to the station fifty-four years ago. I have in my ears a ringing that one sometimes hears, almost like a continuous high-pitched radio signal. But now it seems like cries of anguish from the time when the Jews of Zamosc were being driven along this road into the unknown: they would never see their homes or their synagogue again, or go to market or catch a bus. That terrifying unknown was murder.

At the bottom of Partyzantow Street we pass one of the medieval town bastions. In this bastion, Mike tells us, some Jews who had been driven down the road from the ghetto were kept overnight, before being taken to the railway station, and from there to the death camp. We drive on past the synagogue, and along the road to the railway station: at the time of the deportations the local Poles macabrely called this the Via Dolorosa.

I read from the diary of a Polish doctor, Zygmunt Klukowski, from the town of Szczebrzeszyn, twenty kilometres away. The date was 11 April 1942: 'Towards evening came the news that Zamosc was surrounded. Everyone is sure that now the round-up and transportation of the Zamosc Jews to their deaths will begin. In our town, the fear is indescribable. Some are resigned, others are going around the town insanely looking for help. Everyone is convinced that any day now the same thing will happen in Szczebrzeszyn.'

As feared, the round-up of Zamosc Jews took place. Another eye-witness, David Mekler, later recalled: 'On April 11 1942, the SS, SD and the mounted police fell like a pack of savages on the Zamosc Jewish quarter. It was a complete surprise. The brutes on horseback in particular created a panic; they raced through the streets shouting insults, slashing out on all sides with their whips. Our community then numbered ten thousand people. In a twinkling, without even realising what was happening, a crowd of three thousand men, women and children, picked up haphazardly in the streets and in the houses, were driven to the station and deported to an unknown destination. The spectacle which the ghetto presented after the attack literally drove the survivors mad. Bodies everywhere, in the streets, in the courtyards, inside the houses; babies thrown from the third or fourth floors lay crushed on the pavements. The Jews themselves had to pick up and bury the dead.'

News of the Zamosc deportation reached Szczebrzeszyn on the following day, April 12. 'Several hundred people were killed on the spot,' Klukowski noted in his diary. 'Apparently some tried to resist. However, we don't have any details and we don't know anything for sure. Among our own Jews there is a great panic. Some old Jewish women were sleeping in the Jewish cemetery, they would rather die here in their own town – among the graves of their own people – than in Belzec, among horrifying tortures.'

8.25 a.m.

We reach Zamosc railway station. It was from here that several thousand Jews were deported to Sobibor, which is one of our destinations today. Other Jews were deported from Zamosc to Belzec. Yesterday we followed one of the main deportation routes to Belzec.

Today we will be in the area where many Jewish communities were sent to the death camp at Sobibor and murdered there. Zamosc lies on the edge of two deportation areas. For the purpose of an orderly, systematic, efficient deportation policy, Poland was divided up by the Germans into regions for each camp, so that more than two million people could be uprooted and killed within fifteen months.

The departure board here at Zamosc station, unlike the destination board at the bus station which recalled lost Jewish communities, is a roll call of Holocaust locations. To Belzec three trains leave each day, departing at 8.44, 15.35 and 21.01. To Plaszow another three trains leave each day, at 4.45, 21.01 and 21.37.

8.30 a.m.

A train is waiting in Zamosc station. On the side of the carriages is its destination board: 'Belzec-Lubartow'. An eerie glimpse of one of the deportation routes of 1942. 'They believed it was a labour camp,' says Ben, 'because without such a belief there was no other way of survival. There was no help from the outside world, even from the world across the street; so there was no other way but to believe in the German assurances. Had there been an alternative, they would have taken it. The alternative – to try to run away from the ghetto – meant almost immediate death.'

Mike recounts the story of a German-Jewish boy, Wolsztejn (his first name is not known, his surname has been rendered in the Polish spelling), who had been deported to Zamosc from Leslau, in Silesia, and then deported from Zamosc to Belzec. As the boy's father was employed in a Jewish slave labour gang here at Zamosc station, he, the father, was not deported.

On reaching Belzec the boy managed to hide in a latrine pit. From there he saw the whole killing operation. When all those who had been deported with him had been murdered, he managed to leave the pit and escape from the camp. In the town of Belzec, a Pole, Eugeniusz Goch, found him wandering in the main street, took him in, and then showed him the way back to Zamosc. There, the boy told his story to the deputy head of the Jewish Council, a man by the name of Garfinkel. The boy was not believed. It did not seem possible that the deportees, so many men, women and children, could have been murdered. The German assurance that they were going to a labour camp in the east seemed far more plausible than the story of mass murder, even if the story of mass murder was told by someone who claimed to be an eye-witness.

The Wolsztejn boy and his father were killed during a later round-up for Belzec. Garfinkel escaped from Zamosc and survived the war. Later he lived in London.

8.40 a.m.
We leave Zamosc station, and drive north. The story of the boy Wolsztejn, the good Pole, Goch, and the disbelieving Garfinkel, gives us pause for thought – not for the first time on this journey – and we are again silent.

9.08 a.m.
We reach the village of Izbica Lubelska, and turn off the main road to the small wayside railway station. It is still in use, the station name, like Belzec, unchanged. We discuss if any of these names should be changed; the general consensus is that they must remain, even if the terrible associations are not evident to most people who pass through them. Here at Izbica some of the most horrendous scenes recorded in the Holocaust, or indeed in the Second World War, took place.

I ask Mike to tell us about the place we are in. He has been here many times, and spoken to many of the locals about what happened here in the war. Izbica Lubelska was a so-called 'transit ghetto'. In addition to the ghetto, there was a large camp located in a field below the village, across the railway tracks from the local station. This was used when, as happened quite often, there were too many deportees to fit into the ghetto.

Between 40,000 and 50,000 Jews were brought here between March 1942 and March 1943, most of them from Germany. Others were German, Austrian and Czech Jews brought from Theresienstadt. Those who were taken off the trains here were held in the transit ghetto until Belzec was ready to take them in, and to kill them.

According to the orderly, systematic plan that had been prepared at the Operation Reinhard headquarters in Lublin (which we will see tomorrow), trains left here for Belzec every Tuesday and Friday. The first deportees from Theresienstadt to Belzec were brought here in March 1942. Their train, labelled 'Transport Aa', left Theresienstadt on March 11 and reached here two days later.

Two German SS men ran the camp at Izbica, Kurt Engel and Ludwig Klem. They were known as 'the lords of life and death'. Both were in their twenties (Klem was twenty-nine). They were not even officers. Their headquarters of that time is now the village police station. The town and the camp were guarded by several hundred Ukrainians under their command.

9.25 a.m.

We walk along the platform, to the very end, looking back along the curving railway line, and overlooking the field which was turned into a 'ghetto'. A member of the Polish underground, Jan Karski, was asked to come here in 1942 by the Jews of Warsaw, to report on what he saw, and to take his account back with him on his clandestine and dangerous journey to Britain (and subsequently to the United States). He did so, arranging to see what was happening here at Izbica in the disguise of an Estonian guard, accompanied by an Estonian who, he later wrote, 'gave me a brief, dissatisfied, critical scrutiny and then began to order me about like a martinet. I was told to polish my boots, fix my tie, and tighten my belt. He even informed me that my posture was too relaxed and undignified. I said nothing and did as I was told but with a slightly grudging air, striking a pose of exaggerated military stiffness. He relented a little and excused himself on the grounds that the Germans were very severe about such matters and did not like to see "their Latvians, Estonians and Ukrainians" negligently dressed.'

In his book *Story of a Secret State*, Jan Karski described what he saw here at Izbica, in this very field below us. I begin to read from his book, and slowly continue for fifteen minutes. It is one of the most difficult of all the readings; it brings us as close as we will ever get, having not experienced it, to the reality of what happened here, to the reality of the Holocaust. It is a long account, but so poignant that no one wants me to stop reading. In Karski's words:

'As we approached to within a few hundred yards of the camp, the shouts, cries, and shots cut off further conversation. I noticed, or thought I noticed, an unpleasant stench that seemed to have come from decomposing bodies mixed with horse manure. This may have been an illusion. The Estonian was, in any case, completely impervious to it. He even began to hum some sort of folk tune to himself. We passed through a small grove of decrepit-looking trees and emerged directly in front of the loud, sobbing, reeking camp of death.

'It was on a large, flat plain and occupied about a square mile. It was surrounded on all sides by a formidable barbed-wire fence, nearly two yards in height and in good repair. Inside the fence, at intervals of about fifteen yards, guards were standing, holding rifles with fixed bayonets ready for use. Around the outside of the fence militia men circulated on constant patrol. The camp itself contained a few small sheds or barracks. The rest of the area was completely covered by a dense, pulsating, throbbing, noisy human mass. Starved, stinking, gesticulating, insane human beings in constant, agitated motion. Through them, forcing paths if necessary with their rifle butts, walked the German police and the militia men. They walked in silence, their faces bored and indifferent. They looked like shepherds bringing a flock to the market or pig-dealers among their pigs. They had the tired, vaguely disgusted appearance of men doing a routine, tedious job.

'Into the fence, a few passages had been cut, and gates made of poles tied together with barbed-wire swung back, allowing entrance. Each gate was guarded by two men who slouched about carelessly. We stopped for a moment to collect ourselves. To my left I noticed the railroad tracks which passed about a hundred yards from the camp.

'From the camp to the track a sort of raised passage had been built from old boards. On the track a dusty freight train waited, motionless.

'The Estonian followed my gaze with the interest of a person seeing what kind of an impression his home made on a visitor. He proceeded eagerly to enlighten me.

' "That's the train they'll load them on. You'll see it all."

'We came to a gate. Two German non-coms[1] were standing there talking. I could hear snatches of their conversation. They seemed to be talking about a night they had spent in a nearby town. I hung back a bit. The Estonian seemed to think I was losing my nerve.

' "Go ahead," he whispered impatiently into my ear. "Don't be afraid. They won't even inspect your papers. They don't care about the likes of you."

'We walked up to the gate and saluted the non-coms vigorously.

[1] Non-Commissioned Officers (NCOs), that is, corporals, sergeants or sergeant-majors.

They returned the salute indifferently and we passed through, entering the camp, and mingled unnoticed with the crowd.

' "Follow me," he said quite loudly. "I'l take you to a good spot."

'We passed an old Jew, a man of about sixty, sitting on the ground without a stitch of clothing on him. I was not sure whether his clothes had been torn off or whether he, himself, had thrown them away in a fit of madness. Silent, motionless, he sat on the ground, no one paying him the slightest attention. Not a muscle or fibre in his whole body moved. He might have been dead or petrified except for his pre-ternaturally animated eyes, which blinked rapidly and incessantly. Not far from him a small child, clad in a few rags, was lying on the ground. He was all alone and crouched quivering on the ground, staring up with the large, frightened eyes of a rabbit. No one paid any attention to him, either.

'The Jewish mass vibrated, trembled, and moved to and fro as if united in a single, insane, rhythmic trance. They waved their hands, shouted, quarrelled, cursed, and spat at each other. Hunger, thirst, fear, and exhaustion had driven them all insane. I had been told that they were usually left in the camp for three or four days without a drop of water or food.

'They were all former inhabitants of the Warsaw ghetto. When they had been rounded up they were given permission to take about ten pounds of baggage. Most of them took food, clothes, bedding, and, if they had any, money and jewellery. On the train, the Germans who accompanied them stripped them of everything that had the slightest value, even snatching away any article of clothing to which they took a fancy. They were left a few rags for apparel, bedding, and a few scraps of food. Those who left the train without any food starved continuously from the moment they set foot in the camp.

'There was no organisation or order of any kind. None of them could possibly help or share with each other and they soon lost any self-control or any sense whatsoever except the barest instinct of self-preservation. They had become, at this stage, completely dehumanised. It was, moreover, typical autumn weather, cold, raw, and rainy. The sheds could not accommodate more than two or three thousand people and every 'batch' included more than five thousand. This meant that there were always two to three thousand men, women, and children scattered about in the open, suffering exposure as well as everything else.

'The chaos, the squalor, the hideousness of it all was simply inde-scribable. There was a suffocating stench of sweat, filth, decay, damp straw and excrement. To get to my post we had to squeeze our way through this mob. It was a ghastly ordeal. I had to push foot by foot through the crowd and step over the limbs of those who were lying prone. It was like forcing my way through a mass of sheer death and decomposition made even more horrible by its agonised pulsations. My companion had the skill of long practice, evading the bodies on the ground and winding his way through the mass with the ease of a contortionist. Distracted and clumsy I would brush against people or step on a figure that reacted like an animal, quickly, often with a moan or a yelp. Each time this occurred I would be seized by a fit of nausea and come to a stop. But my guide kept urging and hustling me along.

'In this way we crossed the entire camp and finally stopped about twenty yards from the gate which opened on the passage leading to the train. It was a comparatively uncrowded spot. I felt immeasurably relieved at having finished my stumbling, sweating journey. The guide was standing at my side, saying something, giving me advice. I hardly heard him, my thoughts were elsewhere. He tapped me on the shoulder. I turned toward him mechanically, seeing him with difficulty. He raised his voice.

'"Look here. You are going to stay here. I'll walk on a little further. You know what you are supposed to do. Remember to keep away from Estonians. Don't forget, if there's any trouble, you don't know me and I don't know you."

'I nodded vaguely at him. He shook his head and walked off.

'I remained there perhaps half-an-hour, watching this spectacle of human misery. At each moment I felt the impulse to run and flee. I had to force myself to remain indifferent, practise stratagems on myself to convince myself that I was not one of the condemned, throbbing multitude, forcing myself to relax as my body seemed to tie itself into knots, or turning away at intervals to gaze into the distance at a line of trees near the horizon. I had to remain on the alert, too, for an Estonian uniform, ducking toward the crowd or behind a nearby shed every time one approached me. The crowd continued to writhe in agony, the guards circulated about, bored and indifferent, occasionally distracting themselves by firing a shot or dealing out a blow. Finally I noticed a change in the motion of the guards. They walked less and they all seemed to be glancing in the same direction – at the passage to the track which was quite close to me.

'I turned toward it myself. Two German policemen came to the gate with a tall, bulky, SS man. He barked out an order and they began to open the gate with some difficulty. It was very heavy. He shouted at them impatiently. They worked at it frantically and finally whipped it open. They dashed down the passage as though they were afraid the SS man might come after them and took up their positions where the passage ended. The whole system had been worked out with crude effectiveness. The outlet of the passage was blocked off by two cars of the freight train, so that any attempt on the part of one of the Jews to break out of the mob, or to escape if they had had so much presence of mind left, would have been completely impossible. Moreover, it facilitated the job of loading them onto the train.

'The SS man turned to the crowd, planted himself with his feet wide apart and his hands on his hips and loosed a roar that must have actually hurt his ribs. It could be heard far above the hellish babble that came from the crowd.

'"*Ruhe, Ruhe!* Quiet, quiet! All Jews will board this train to be taken to a place where work awaits them. Keep order. Do not push. Anyone who attempts to resist or create a panic will be shot."

'He stopped speaking and looked challengingly at the helpless mob that hardly seemed to know what was happening. Suddenly, accompanying the movement with a loud, hearty laugh, he yanked out his gun and fired three random shots into the crowd. A single stricken groan answered him. He replaced the gun in his holster, smiled, and set himself for another roar:

'"*Alle Juden, 'raus – 'raus!*"

'For a moment the crowd was silent. Those nearest the SS man recoiled from the shots and tried to dodge, panic-stricken, toward the rear. But this was resisted by the mob as a volley of shots from the rear sent the whole mass surging forward madly, screaming in pain and fear. The shots continued without let-up from the rear and now from the sides, too, narrowing the mob down and driving it in a savage scramble onto the passageway. In utter panic, groaning in despair and agony, they rushed down the passageway, trampling it so furiously that it threatened to fall apart.

'Here new shots were heard. The two policemen at the entrance to the train were now firing into the oncoming throng corralled in the passageway, in order to slow them down and prevent them from demolishing the flimsy structure. The SS man now added his roar to the deafening bedlam.

'"*Ordnung, Ordnung!*" he bellowed like a madman.

'Order, order!' The two policemen echoed him hoarsely, firing straight into the faces of the Jews running to the trains. Impelled and controlled by this ring of fire, they filled the two cars quickly.

'And now came the most horrible episode of them all. The Bund leader had warned me that if I lived to be a hundred I would never forget some of the things I saw. He did not exaggerate.

'The military rule stipulates that a freight car may carry eight horses or forty soldiers. Without any baggage at all, a maximum of a hundred passengers standing close together and pressing against each other could be crowded into a car. The Germans had simply issued orders to the effect that 120 to 130 Jews had to enter each car. These orders were now being carried out. Alternately swinging and firing with their rifles, the policemen were forcing still more people into the two cars which were already over-full. The shots continued to ring out in the rear and the driven mob surged forward, exerting an irresistible pressure against those nearest to the train. These unfortunates, crazed by what they had been through, scourged by the policemen, and shoved forward by the milling mob, then began to climb on the heads and shoulders of those in the trains.

'These were helpless since they had the weight of the entire advancing throng against them and responded only with howls of anguish to those who, clutching at their hair and clothes for support, trampling on necks, faces and shoulders, breaking bones and shouting with insensate fury, attempted to clamber over them. More than another score of human beings, men, women and children gained admittance in this fashion. Then the policemen slammed the doors across the hastily withdrawn limbs that still protruded and pushed the iron bars in place.

'The two cars were now crammed to bursting with tightly packed human flesh, completely hermetically filled. All this while the entire camp had reverberated with a tremendous volume of sound in which the hideous groans and screams mingled weirdly with shots, curses, and bellowed commands.

'Nor was this all. I know that many people will not believe me, will not be able to believe me, will think I exaggerate or invent. But I saw it and it is not exaggerated or invented. I have no other proofs, no photographs. All I can say is that I saw it and that it is the truth.

'The floors of the car had been covered with a thick, white powder. It was quicklime. Quicklime is simply unslaked lime or calcium oxide that has been dehydrated. Anyone who has seen cement being mixed knows what occurs when water is poured on lime. The mixture bubbles and steams as the powder combines with the water, generating a large amount of heat.

'Here the lime served a double purpose in the Nazi economy of brutality. The moist flesh coming in contact with the lime is rapidly dehydrated and burned. The occupants of the cars would be literally burned to death before long, the flesh eaten from their bones. Thus, the Jews would "die in agony", fulfilling the promise Himmler had issued "in accord with the will of the Fuehrer" in Warsaw, in 1942. Secondly, the lime would prevent decomposing bodies from spreading disease. It was efficient and inexpensive – a perfectly chosen agent for their purposes.

'It took three hours to fill up the entire train by repetitions of this procedure. It was twilight when the forty-six (I counted them) cars were packed. From one end to the other, the train, with its quivering cargo of flesh, seemed to throb, vibrate, rock, and jump as if bewitched. There would be a strangely uniform momentary lull and then, again, the train would begin to moan and sob, wail and howl. Inside the camp a few score dead bodies remained and a few in the final throes of death. German policemen walked around at leisure with smoking guns, pumping bullets into anything, that by a moan or motion betrayed an excess of vitality. Soon, not a single one was left alive. In the now quiet camp the only sounds were the inhuman screams that were echoes from the moving train. Then these, too, ceased. All that was now left was the stench of excrement and rotting straw and a queer, sickening, acidulous odour which, I thought, may have come from the quantities of blood that had been shed, and with which the ground was stained.

'As I listened to the dwindling outcries from the train, I thought of the destination toward which it was speeding. My informants had minutely described the entire journey. The train would travel about eighty miles and finally come to a halt in an empty, barren field. Then nothing at all would happen. The train would stand stock-still, patiently waiting while death penetrated into every corner of its interior. This would take from two to four days.

'When quicklime, asphyxiation, and injuries had silenced every outcry, a group of men would appear. They would be young, strong Jews, assigned to the task of cleaning out these cars until their own turn to be in them should arrive. Under a strong guard they would unseal the cars and expel the heaps of decomposing bodies. The mounds of flesh that they piled up would then be burned and the remnants buried in a single huge hole. The cleaning, burning and burial would consume one or two full days.

'The entire process of disposal would take, then, from three to six days. During this period the camp would have recruited new victims.

The train would return and the whole cycle would be repeated from the beginning.

'I was still standing near the gate, gazing after the no longer visible train, when I felt a rough hand on my shoulder. The Estonian was back again. He was frantically trying to rouse my attention and to keep his voice lowered at the same time.

' "Wake up, wake up," he was scolding me hoarsely. "Don't stand there with your mouth open. Come on, hurry, or we'll both get caught. Follow me and be quick about it."

'I followed him at a distance, feeling completely benumbed.'

9.55 a.m.
Profoundly moved, we stand on the platform of Izbica station. Jan Karski's vivid description and report of the terrifying scene are clear in our mind. The field in front of us, so lush with grass and bushes, bordered by fine trees, a light breeze cooling the rays of the morning sun, loses its appeal and its lustre. All we see is the grotesque scene of death, humiliation and terror.

It almost seems impossible to go on reading, to go on thinking. But the group say they need to know what happened here, and we are here, at the very spot of so much human suffering.

Among the documents I have brought is the deportation schedule of trains sent out of Theresienstadt. There were three known deportations from Theresienstadt to Izbica, with 1,000 people on each, leaving Theresienstadt on 11 and 17 March, and 27 April 1942. Of those 3,000 deportees, only ten survived; they were taken off the trains before they reached this hell-hole.

My second, shorter reading here on the Izbica station platform is from the diary of Zygmunt Klukowski, the Polish doctor from the nearby town of Szczebrzeszyn. He wrote, on 26 March 1942: 'There is great unhappiness and fear among the Jews. From everywhere comes the news about the incredible violence against the Jews. They are bringing trainloads of Jews from Czechoslovakia, Germany, and even from Belgium. They are also resettling the Jews from various towns and villages and taking them somewhere towards Belzec. Today I heard a story about what they did to the Jews in Lublin. It is difficult to believe it's true. Today they deported Jews from Izbica – they were also taken to Belzec, where there is supposed to be some monstrous camp.'

Jews were also taken from this station to another 'monstrous camp', Sobibor, with which Izbica is also linked by rail. A survivor of one of the Izbica–Sobibor deportations, Tom Blatt, who lives today in Seattle, comes back here every year. 'He cannot stay away,' comments Mike. After escaping from Sobibor Tom Blatt had walked back to Izbica. 'He did not know anywhere else to hide. He walked on the roads. The Germans were searching the woods. When he arrived back in Izbica, a farmer opened his door and let him in. The farmer's name was Bojarski. It had taken Tom three days to get here from Sobibor.'

It is going to take us about two hours' driving to get to Sobibor.

Bojarski later shot Blatt, whom he had hidden under his barn. He left him for dead, with a bullet in his jaw – which is still lodged there today. Blatt managed to escape to a neighbouring village.

On 14 October 1993, the fiftieth anniversary of the Sobibor revolt, eleven survivors came back, mostly from the United States and Israel.

9.58 a.m.

We drive away from Izbica station, and through the small village. Like most of the Jewish towns and villages in this region, it was a poor one; the whole region lacked the industry and the modernity of western Poland. We pass many old houses around the market place and along the highway. They were all Jewish family homes until 1939. Jews first lived here 400 years ago.

A brick synagogue was in existence here in 1819. A few years later a well-known tzaddik (righteous man), Mordechaj Josef Teiner, lived here. He was the founder of a dynasty of tzaddikim who continued to preach and teach in this town until 1942. It was always an essentially Jewish town. The 3,000 Jews who lived here in 1897 made up 95 per cent of the population. On the outbreak of war there were just over 5,000 Jews here, 85 per cent of the townsfolk. Then the town was turned into a ghetto, from which its inhabitants shared the fate of the many thousands of Jews brought here from Western and Central Europe.

Mike tells us that not so long ago a group of Jews came to Izbica's Jewish cemetery. A Polish family who saw them arrive went into the cemetery after them: the parents wanted to show their children a 'real, live Jew'. On the right side of the road as we drive towards Krasnystaw we see the hill on which the cemetery lies. There is a plaque in the cemetery which reads:

> Here rest the ashes of Jews
>   murdered by the Germans in November 1942.
> The dead ask respect to this sacred place, and a prayer.

Near the plaque is an obelisk. It was put up by two brothers, Jakub and Chaim Griner, in memory of their parents and their sisters who were murdered by the Nazis. Jakub Griner was given a hiding place by a Catholic family. After the war he converted to Catholicism and took Holy Orders. He became a priest, Father Grzegorz Pawlowski (Father Gregory) and went to live in Israel.

10 a.m.
We are driving northward, with the railway line to Lublin (and also to Sobibor) running alongside us.

10.10 a.m.
Krasnystaw. A small market town. The synagogue, built in 1900, survives (it is between the market square and the bus station), but our driver is insistent that he cannot drive into the town.

There was a Jewish community here in the early sixteenth century. An ordinance of 1554 was effectively an expulsion order; under it Jews were prohibited from living in the town. After a disastrous fire in 1811 destroyed much of the town, the inhabitants decided that the admission of Jews would help them to restore the town, although permission to reside was not formally granted again until 1824. From 1833 Jews were allowed to buy land and build houses. By the beginning of this century, the 2,000 Jews living here constituted a quarter of the population. A further 10,000 Jews lived in the villages around. Every other village in the region was, in effect, a Jewish village.

10.33 a.m.
Rejowiec. A small town with many wooden houses. 'It must have been a very primitive place by today's standards,' comments Ben, 'with no electricity or running water.'

Water came from the well. The toilets were all outdoors.

Before the war the Jewish community here numbered about five hundred. In February 1940 the first German attacks on Jews took place. Jews were also forced to dismantle the synagogue brick by brick. In 1941 a ghetto was set up in 'Jewish Street', off the main square. Jews from the surrounding villages were then brought into the ghetto, as well as Jews from Cracow, and from Germany and Theresienstadt.

In April 1942, at Passover, two hundred Jews were shot in the Rejowiec ghetto at the start of the Gestapo action. Those trying to seek safety in the nearby woods were hunted down and killed. The remaining three hundred were sent to the slave labour camp at Krychow. The two German organisers of the action were Gustav Jeski and Oster Peter.

Jeski was tried in Hamburg in the 1970s; Peter has never been tracked down.

After the first destruction, a further 3,000 Jews were then brought to Rejowiec from Theresienstadt. They were kept in the ghetto until August 1943, when they were sent – Sobibor and Belzec no longer being in operation – to Majdanek, fifty-five kilometres away, on the outskirts of Lublin. Three months later they were murdered at Majdanek, in what the German perpetrators called the 'Harvest Festival' massacre.

Most of the handful of survivors of Rejowiec live in Israel. Every Passover they gather in Tel Aviv for a commemorative meeting. In Rejowiec itself, the Jewish cemetery (in what was once Kolejowa Street, now Dabrowska Street), where many of the inhabitants of the ghetto were murdered, is partly built over by houses, partly wasteground, and partly a farmer's field. Pressed to do so by a British Jew, Sheila Pinczewski-Grossnass, whose great-grandparents lived in Rejowiec, the local municipality agreed to put a fence around the site of the mass murder, to leave the site undisturbed, to plant nothing on it, and to erect a monument.

10.50 a.m.

We reach the outskirts of Chelm. More Jewish jokes relate to the Jewish inhabitants of Chelm than have ever been assembled in one book. This is the town of 'Jewish fools'. The Chelmites are the archetypal Jewish idiots – stupid and obtuse. The stories about them were legendary throughout Russian Poland and far beyond. They are the stock-in-trade of every anthology of Jewish humour. So all-pervasive was the image of the foolish Chelmite that Jews from Chelm who made their way in the world were often reluctant to divulge the name of their town of origin.

Yet Jewish life in Chelm had a venerable and impressive pedigree. Jews were first recorded in the town in the twelfth century. Several distinguished rabbis preached and taught here, among them, in the late sixteenth century, Reb Yehuda Aron. Among the well-known teachers here at the beginning of the seventeenth century were Simeon Auerbach, Salama Zalaman, and Shmuel Leizer Ben Yehuda Edels.

Disaster struck the Chelm Jewish community in the mid-seventeenth century, when one of Bogdan Chmielnicki's armed Cossack units burst into the town, killing many Jews. Ben says: 'I grew up with stories of Chmielnicki. Although his pogrom had taken place nearly three hundred years earlier, it was such a terrible event that it was known even to little boys. His was the last great torment. After the killings, the religious zeal of Hassidism was the response of many – the search for joy through prayer and song to counter the misery Chmielnicki had brought about. Not only did I learn about Chmielnicki, I also learned about world history. I knew that Chmielnicki's pogrom was a year before King Charles I was beheaded in London.'

Jewish life recovered after the slaughter here in Chelm, as it did throughout the regions in which the Chmielnicki pogroms had taken place. When Jewish life revived, it did so with an upsurge of Hassidism, the movement that combined intense religious devotion with exuberance, singing, dancing and joy, especially the Joy of Sabbath.

By the end of the nineteenth century, Chelm was one of those Polish towns where as many as three-quarters of the inhabitants were Jews. It was in effect a Jewish town. In the census of 1931, there were 13,537 Jews recorded here. Then came the disaster. As we park in the main square, I read an account of how, in December 1939, several hundred Jews from Chelm were taken in trucks to Hrubieszow, where, together with more than a thousand Hrubieszow Jews, they were forced to walk to the Soviet border. Only a few hundred reached the border alive; the rest were shot at random on the march, or were taken out of the line and shot by the roadside. The survivors were taken to the bridge across the River Bug and ordered to march across it with their hands held high, singing 'Long Live Stalin'. The Soviet border guards let them through.

It was on 11 April 1942 that the first deportation of the remaining Jews of Chelm took place. They were sent to Belzec. Then, in the summer, the Germans laid a new railway track from Chelm to Sobibor (along the route we will be taking shortly). This linked the whole of the Lublin region with the death camp. Among the documents published by Serge Klarsfeld in Paris is one which shows a deportation train from Paris, sent, not to Auschwitz, like almost all the others that year, but to Chelm. From Chelm it is probable that the deportees were sent on to Sobibor. Among them was a German painter, Hermann Lismann, who had been on active service in the German army during the First World War. When Hitler came to power in 1933, Lismann had fled to France. There, in 1939, he had been interned, had escaped, was caught, and then deported here, to Chelm.

We walk away from the main square down a short street to the synagogue. It is now a bank. We go in but the bank manager is adamant that we cannot see the site of the Ark, as it is his office – and 'important business is being transacted here'. The interior of the synagogue has been very much modernised in accordance with banking décor. It has nothing at all in common with the magnificence of the interior of the synagogue at Lancut. Indeed, from inside one would not know it had been a synagogue except perhaps from the tall rounded windows.

From the outside, the aspect of a synagogue is clear. Down a side street is a former Jewish courtyard, very dilapidated.

After our return to England, Jon wrote to me: 'I felt a little uneasy about the synagogue in Chelm as we walked towards it. Its shell was instantly recognisable as a synagogue, but a large gold and green sign outside it identified it as a bank. The anti-Semitic association of Jews with money immediately sprang to mind – how ironic that the Poles were now utilising a Jewish house of prayer for their own financial purposes! Its interior was equally incongruous – it looked like a synagogue and I could make out where the Ark had once been, but several counters and offices had been somewhat randomly built inside it, and it was surely apparent even to the uninformed visitor that this building had not originally been designed for its current purpose. It had a high ceiling which the top of the offices and counters did not reach, so I could see across the entire room.

'I wanted to take a photograph, but it quickly became apparent that the bank manager was unhappy with this as soon as I removed the lens cap from my camera. Kathy tried to negotiate an arrangement with him, and he eventually agreed to allow us to photograph the ceiling – a picture which, to my mind, would have been meaningless and dull. Ignoring his demand, I stood in the corner and proceeded to capture the entire room, complete with the bank manager walking towards me holding his hand up, Kathy looking on, nervously chewing her pen, and Paul pointing his camera directly up at the ceiling. Of all the photos I took during the trip, that one gave me the most pleasure.

'In retrospect, I could have accepted the manager's request and taken a shot of the ceiling, or just walked out of the bank. But at that moment, in that context, I wasn't prepared to allow someone to prevent me from taking a tiny part of Polish Jewry home with me. The building felt as if it partially, in some way, belonged to me, and nobody had the right to keep it from me. I took the picture because it felt as if it were rightly mine to take.'

12.20 p.m.

We walk up the hill to the Café Pierrot, where the group gathers round and, as I look out of the window to the roof of the synagogue, I read from Isaac Bashevis Singer's children's book, *The Fools of Chelm and their History*. Chapter 1 tells of how Chelm came to be:

'There was no agreement among the scholars of Chelm on how the town came into existence. The pious believed that God said, "Let there be Chelm." And there was Chelm. But many scholars insisted that the town happened as the result of an eruption. "Before Chelm," they said, "the area was one huge chaos, all fog and mist. Then came a great explosion and Chelm appeared." At the beginning the surface of Chelm was so hot that even if Chelmites had already existed, they could not have walked on the earth because they would have burned their feet. But slowly Chelm cooled and was covered by a crust, like a pot of porridge that has been left standing. The first Chelmites, the scholars say, were not people but microbes, amoebas, and other such creatures. Later a river formed in Chelm. It contained many fish, and these were the ancestors of the Chelmites. This may be the reason why the Chelmites love fish, especially gefilte fish ...'

I continue reading for another twenty minutes. But the readers of this diary who do not know the tale must turn to Singer himself to learn what became of the Chelmites, and in particular why, and how, they made war on the Jewish villages nearest to them.

Ros writes in the flyleaf of the book, which I had borrowed from my son Joshua: 'Thanks for the loan of the book – just think of your Dad reading these stories in a strange café, with even stranger people looking over their shoulders at the eclectic group gathered and listening!'

I buy a local magazine, *Goniec Chelmskie*, the Chelm Messenger. The high point of the past week has been the visit of the Polish Health Minister to the local hospital. The Hotel Kamena advertises its restaurant, café, billiard tables and nightclub.

1 p.m.
We leave the centre of Chelm and our minibus takes us down to the station. To this day, while Jews still recount stories of their foolish Chelmites, the tradition has survived without the Jews. Mike tells us that there are Poles today who regard a person from Chelm as not quite right in the head. In the prison here in Chelm is the former Communist secret police captain who was sentenced to ten years in prison for the murder of Father Jerzy Popieluszko. On appealing in Lublin last year against the severity of the sentence, the captain was given another three years. Popieluszko, a Catholic priest, had spoken out strongly in favour of the democratisation of Poland after the banning of the Solidarity trade union in 1981. He had been kidnapped

by the Communist secret police, and was murdered in October 1984 – more than a year after the lifting of martial law.

Among the Jews born here in Chelm was Joe Finkelstone, who as a young boy left for England with his family before the war. Today he lives in London, and has recently published a book about his friendship with President Anwar Sadat of Egypt. As a cub reporter on the *Carlisle Journal* in 1945, Joe wrote almost his first journalistic article about the arrival of a group of teenage survivors of the Holocaust who had been flown from Prague to Carlisle airport that August. By a strange coincidence, one of those survivors was Krulik Wilder, whose father had been born in Chelm in 1900.

Joe Finkelstone's recollections of Chelm give a vivid picture of the world that was here before the war, of the Jewish life whose echoes we are seeking as we retrace our way through the areas so dominated by the Holocaust. Sixty years after leaving Chelm, Joe wrote to me of what he remembered. Having been born in Chelm was not a bonus. 'Fear of being mocked or laughed at, or not being taken seriously, was so intense in me,' he explained, 'that throughout my employment at the London *Jewish Chronicle* I avoided strenuously mentioning my birthplace. When the subject of a birthplace came up, I tried frantically to change the subject of the conversation, heaving a great sigh of relief when I achieved this objective. My embarrassing secret was never, I thought and fervently hoped, discovered, although I was concerned that one or two of my colleagues had their suspicions. It was only after retirement from the *Jewish Chronicle* and from the Israeli daily newspaper *Maariv* – from whom I also kept my secret – that I began gradually to "come out", though even now I feel a twinge of alarm when Chelm is mentioned. My consolation is the apparent fact that many former Jewish citizens of Chelm, now living in the United States and Israel, have been highly successful in their careers as businessmen, scholars and scientists, truly "wise men", and yet, and yet ...!

'My earliest memories concern primarily my maternal grandfather, then still a prosperous owner of forests and timber yards. In my memory he is a huge, magnificently-built white-haired man who was known in Chelm as Abysh Tichever, the man from Tichiv, apparently because he owned that village (a rare precious photograph, always near my bed, shows him to be of normal height). His surname was really Szneider (Tailor). As he got older he passed the management of his Chelm timber yards to his three sons-in-law, including my father. None of them was a real businessman – my father who was entirely engrossed in "kulisher machen" (communal Jewish affairs) hardly ever visited the timber yard. I still remember vividly my grandfather walking down the long courtyard which he owned, waving his stick, indignantly denouncing, like Moses of old, his sons-in-law for ruining the timber-yard business.

'This huge timber yard was so denuded of timber by the mis-management that it became a parking place for the hundreds of peasants from the surrounding countryside who arrived with their horses and wagons for the agricultural fairs in the town. Somehow I obtained a number of school textbooks, some of them quite torn, and persuaded the peasants to buy them for their children at a cut price. Another of my early capitalist ventures was to collect newspapers and sell them to the shopkeepers who used them for wrapping up goods, in return receiving the equivalent of a penny.

'Most of the Jews of Chelm appeared to me to be highly religious, with beards, and wearing little black peak hats, called, I think, a hitteleh. Wearing a trilby was a symbol of revolt and adoption of "goyishe" (non-Jewish) habits. My elder late brother, Shapseh (Charles) had to use subterfuges – wearing a hitteleh at home but exchanging it for a trilby, which he hid under the stairs, when going out to see friends. There was a terrible row when father discovered the shameful truth. I, too, was a bit of a rebel, refusing to wear payot (sidelocks) and giving the most preposterous reason why the barber cut them off.

'As the son of the president of the community I was allowed to have chickens slaughtered at the local Jewish abattoir, without any payment. I watched spellbound as the chickens had their throats cut. Sometimes neighbours tried to give me their chickens to avoid having to pay any fees. One day I went to one of the two cinemas in town with a big white chicken. In the middle of the dramatic performance of a film, in a moment of utter silence, as an affecting romantic scene was being enacted, the chicken, clearly a strident cockerel, suddenly crowed loudly, to my acute embarrassment and everyone else's delight.

'I remember vividly the hefty water-carriers, carrying two full pails on each side over the cobbled stones to the houses, ours included. They seemed to be giants. I recall the pungent smell of the herrings and pickled cucumbers in the shops, all of them apparently owned by Jews. But it was not at all clear where the majority of Chelmers got their "parnuse" – their living. Yet all somehow managed to have enough to eat – mostly bread, herrings, fish and potatoes.

'Oranges were always associated with illness. I was presented with only a tiny piece of orange when I fell ill. The taste was wonderful, almost worthwhile being sick. To summon a doctor – a very expensive measure – meant being very seriously, even dangerously ill. For a non-immediately life-threatening illness, a feltsher (a non-qualified medical man) was summoned, even then very reluctantly. He was far less expensive. Throughout my young life in Chelm I was never visited by a doctor.

'Chelm was full of shtieblech (small prayer houses), with a large formal synagogue in the centre of the town. On Sabbath and the festivals the town closed down, but many people loved to go "spatziren" (to go walking about, many arm in arm).

'There were, of course, no motor cars. When the first motor car was seen in the town there was great excitement and the boys ran after it.

'When Hitler came to power a young Polish boy asked me, "Why are the Jews hated?" I could not give an answer. I saw my father stand near the Town Hall and address a huge protest meeting against Hitler. Later, I heard an elderly Pole warn that after the death of the Polish leader, Marshal Pilsudski, known to be friendly to the Jews and their protector, "things now are not going to be so good for the Jews". He was right. A number of pogroms took place in Poland – never, though, in our Chelm – and anti-Semitism grew. Social contacts with Christians were frowned on, and when a Jewish girl was seen talking to a Polish boy it was considered a scandal.

'Father, seeing the worsening situation, decided to accept an invitation to settle in London, and left. From time to time he sent us a single pound sterling on which we could live for many weeks and obtain credit for many more. Once, when somehow the pound did not arrive, mother had tears in her eyes as she told us in the morning, as we prepared to go to school, "We have no bread."

'Memories of Chelm are, nevertheless, almost entirely of excitement and enjoyment – captaining boys' teams in football – the only time father smacked me in the face was when he saw me playing football on Shabbat – enjoying lively days in the Yeshiva and school, taking part in various celebrations of our huge family circles – weddings always went on throughout the night – reading voraciously Polish books – for some reason I had a slight dislike of Yiddish – and being altogether a bit of a rebel and a lobbas (an urchin), climbing up buildings and jumping off tall huts.

'As the train moved out of Chelm late in December 1936 – the main world news then was the love affair between King Edward VIII and Mrs Simpson – on our journey to England to join father, I waved at the many relatives who came to see us off, including my grandfather (grandmother had died earlier).

'I was to see only two of my close relatives again. All the others were killed by the Germans. One of the two, Velvel (the Wolf), was my best friend. He once saved me from drowning in a Mikveh (ritual bath). He saved himself by joining the Russian army, becoming a tank commander, and fighting all the way to Berlin, ending up with a huge number of medals. I was so glad, so tremendously relieved, that grandfather died, apparently close to a hundred, before the Germans started their extermination campaign, and that hundreds if not thousands walked peacefully in the funeral procession. How possibly could I have kept on living a normal life if I had learned that the Germans had hurt him and made him suffer?'

I am reading out Joe Finkelstone's recollections on Chelm station platform. As I reach the end a train draws in. It is the Berlin–Kiev express. Once a day, and once a night, this express stops at Chelm. From here the railway line continues eastward. This train will reach Kiev tomorrow morning (it started in Berlin just before midnight last night, and left Warsaw at nine this morning).

Chelm is only twenty-eight kilometres from the River Bug and the border of the Ukraine. In June 1941 it was across this border that the mass killing of Jews began with the German invasion of the Soviet Union; killings on the spot, by special killing squads, without deportations and without death camps. One of the largest of these killings was in Kiev, 300 miles to the east, at the end of this railway route, where, in three days in September 1941, more than 33,000 Jews were murdered at Babi Yar, a ravine on the outskirts of Kiev.

1.10 p.m.
We are driving out of Chelm. In the former German military cemetery here two SS men and nine Ukrainian guards from Sobibor were buried. They had been killed during the Sobibor revolt on 14 October 1943 (about which I plan to give a reading when we reach Sobibor in about an hour's time). The cemetery later became the Soviet military cemetery.

Leaving Chelm, we drive through a post-war suburb across the river and up the hill to the Borki woods. From the entrance to the wood one can see on the facing skyline the great dome and spires of the Russian Orthodox cathedral (built in 1753). It was here in 1980 that I came to find the site of the mass execution of many thousands of Soviet prisoners-of-war.

We enter the wood and within a few minutes reach the mass murder site. In 1980 it was overgrown with bushes and weeds. Today a group of a dozen local labourers are clearing the undergrowth. Some are raking, some are smoking and some are drinking. One, with three or four empty bottles in front of him, has his head in his hands.

I read an account by a Jew, Josef Reznik, a former Polish soldier who had been held as a prisoner-of-war with thousands of other Jews at the Lipowa Street camp in Lublin since November 1939. Taken to Majdanek in November 1943 he was one of 300 Jews who were taken out of Majdanek on the day of the notorious 'Harvest Festival' when tens of thousands were murdered. He and the three hundred with him were brought here to Borki.

In the earth around us are an estimated 30,000 Soviet prisoners-of-war, murdered long after they had been made captive. Also murdered in this wood were a number of Italian soldiers. Once Germany's allies, they were killed by the Germans in the summer of 1943 after Italy had abandoned the German cause, after they too had been made prisoners-of-war. Some Jewish children were murdered here as well, having been brought to Borki from Hrubieszow.

Hitler had decided that all these corpses (and the corpses of more than a million other murdered people in different mass graves throughout the East) should be dug up and burned, and their ashes scattered over the earth, and the earth planted with trees, so that no evidence of the mass murder would survive.

Most of the three hundred Jews who were forced to dig up and burn this vast necropolis were themselves murdered when their work was finished. Josef Reznik survived. He later recalled how even as he and his fellow-Jews were opening the graves and removing the corpses, trucks would arrive with more corpses in them. As he remembered, 'the new corpses would be coming all the time continuously. A truck would bring warm bodies, which would be thrown into the graves. They were naked like Adam and Eve.'

Reznik also recalled how, when one of the mass graves was opened, 'we saw a boy of two or three, lying on his mother's body. He had little white shoes on, and a little white jacket. His face was pressed against his mother's, and we were touched and moved, because we ourselves had children of our own.'

After the graves had been emptied, disinfected, and filled with earth, grass was planted over them. The bodies had meanwhile been placed on massive pyres, 1,000 on each pyre. 'There were two pyres of bodies going all the time,' Reznik recalled, 'and they burned for two or three days, each heap of the dead.'

When I came here to Borki in 1980 there was a small memorial plaque marking the site of these terrible events. Today there is a large memorial, and also a smaller memorial to the Italian dead, erected in 1989.

We watch for a while as the Poles continue to clear the ground. It is not easy to walk on this soil knowing what it contained, and what it still contains. The fate of the 3,500,000 Soviet prisoners-of-war impinges once more upon our Jewish focus. There is of course an overlap, in that among those murdered prisoners-of-war in this wood were many Jews.

1.20 p.m.
We leave Borki wood and drive back through Chelm past the Russian Orthodox church. It is used now for Roman Catholic services.

1.25 p.m.
We drive north, on the road to Wlodawa.

1.53 p.m.
Turn off the road to the village of Osowa. Between the wars this was a Jewish village, probably with a dozen families, all farmers. In the war, it became what was called a 'rural' ghetto. The farmers were not fenced in, but they were forbidden to leave the confines of the village. In 1941 the Germans set up a slave labour camp here, in the schoolhouse. Later they built a barrack on the edge of the village. To the slave labour camp, 4,000 Jews were brought from the surrounding villages and towns, some even from Western Europe. 'Transport Ax' – its German railway designation – from Theresienstadt, which left the ghetto on 17 May 1942, is known to have come here. There were 1,000 Czech and German Jews on this single train. The historian of Theresienstadt, Zdenek Lederer, writes (in *Ghetto Theresienstadt*): 'No deportee from this transport returned; hence it must be assumed that all prisoners perished in Sobibor,' and he adds: 'Number of survivors, 0.'

It is known that seventy of the Jews in the slave labour camp here were murdered by the Nazis in the village itself, and that another 170 died here from starvation and ill-treatment. At some point in 1943 all those held at Osowa were sent to Sobibor and murdered. They must have been marched through the woods. Sobibor death camp is only ten kilometres from Osowa. It was, indeed, the German police stationed here in Osowa who were the first on the scene at Sobibor when the revolt broke out there.

It is drizzling and there is an air of desolation. 'Such a God-forsaken place,' comments Ben, 'and to think that four thousand people once lived here.'

2.05 p.m.
We leave Osowa, drive back to the main road and continue northward.

2.20 p.m.
We reach the Sobibor turning and drive eastward. The road winds through a thick forest.

2.25 p.m.
Sobibor railway station. It is in a clearing in the midst of woodland. It is now, in fact, a nature reserve. Its woods and lakes are protected by law against the depredations of picnickers and wild-flower enthusiasts. When I was here in 1980, the main area of the camp was a popular picnic site, with a café at the edge of it. All that has now gone.

The village of Sobibor is four kilometres away. At the station, there are two platforms, one by the station building (which is a mere hut) and the other, where we are standing, inside the former perimeter of the camp. The only substantial building, just at the end of the platform, is the commandant's villa. It was known, for reasons which are obscure, as 'The Merry Flea'.

Very little remains of the camp itself, other than the villa. There is a tall watchtower, which used to be within the precincts of the camp, but was moved after the war closer to the station. Unlike Belzec and Treblinka, Sobibor was not completely razed to the ground, and the site disguised with trees, when the killing ceased. In 1944 many of the camp barracks were used by an SS construction unit engaged in fortifying the western bank of the River Bug beween Wlodawa and Chelm, against the imminent Russian attack. The last of the buildings were not demolished until 1947, with the exception of the com- mandant's house and the watchtower.

While the death camp was operating, thirty SS men and 120 Lithuanian and Ukrainian guards were on duty at any one time. At the end of the platform that ran inside the camp is a small section of original track, with the original buffers. The platform itself was rebuilt after the war. The station is still in use. As we are standing on the platform a train draws in, on its way south to Chelm.

Mike tells us what he has gleaned in his researches over many years. There is an elderly farmer who lives up the road who is well remembered by the locals around here for having prostituted his twelve-year-old daughter to the Ukrainian guards.

After the Jewish revolt here in October 1943 the camp was closed down. A few of the Sobibor guards who had earlier been at Belzec returned to Sobibor to clear the area and plant trees. Christian Wirth, who was then in overall charge of the Lublin death camp region, left German-occupied Poland for Trieste. His former staff members, and those working to demolish the camp at Sobibor, went home on leave. Just before Christmas, however, they received orders to report to Wirth in Trieste. He had a new assignment and they were to assist him: he had been put in charge of a concentration camp set up in a former rice factory at San Sabba. Three thousand Italian and Yugoslav partisans, including Jewish partisans and Jewish women and children, were murdered there before the end of the war. Three thousand Italian prisoners-of-war, arrested when Italy left the Axis, were also murdered here (as at Borki). Of Trieste's 1,920 Jews, 620 were deported from San Sabba to concentration camps in the Reich, most of them to Mauthausen and Flossenburg, and the women to Ravensbrück. Thus the trail of murder that encompassed Sobibor continued in distant lands long after Sobibor closed down.

Mike leads us through the site of Sobibor camp. We walk along what is now a grass path. The Germans called it 'the route to heaven'. We pass the area in which the deportees were forced to undress, then the area in which the clothing barracks stood. Then we turn through what is now thick woodland, past what was once one of the final stops on the 'route to heaven': the building where the women had their hair cut off.

When the camp was deliberately obliterated in the autumn of 1943, trees were planted all over this area. Now they are sturdy, half-century-old mature trees. We push on through the wood and reach the site of the gas chambers and the cremation pyres. In front of us is a low mound of ash, and around the mound, to the left and right, fields of ash. There is a patch of sand where men have recently been digging, trying to find the rails that were used for the crematorium pyres where the bodies had been burned. This work is being done by the regional museum at Wlodawa.

We are at the centre of the camp: the site of the gas chamber and the cremation pyres. From here a modern path leads back to the entrance. Along it, at the site of the gas chambers, are two monuments, a tall rectangular block faced with stone, and a sculpture of a woman holding a child.

As we walked from the ramp and through the camp, I tried to give a brief description of what had been at each of the places we passed. It was not easy, and once we reached the mound of ash it seemed impossible to continue with the explanations. Once more, Paul led a small group of us in prayers.

Slowly we drifted back along the modern path. Returning to the end of the ramp, we sit around for a while. There are four plaques, in English, Hebrew, Yiddish and Polish, describing the camp. The English plaque reads: 'At this site between the years 1942 and 1943 there existed a Nazi death camp where 250,000 Jews and approximately 1,000 Poles were murdered. On 14 October 1943 during the armed revolt by the Jewish prisoners, the Nazis were overpowered and several hundred prisoners escaped to freedom. Following this revolt the death camp ceased to function.' The plaque ends with a quotation from Job: 'Earth conceal not my blood.'

I am asked to read some of the passages which I have prepared about Sobibor. It is difficult to do so. Even words written by survivors seem to intrude on the awfulness of the place. And yet, without these words, the awfulness is somehow diminished.

After the revolt, the Germans hunted down those who had escaped, but there were nevertheless sixty-four survivors. One of them was Moishe Shklarek. He was not quite fifteen years old when, in May, he was deported in a train from Zamosc, with 2,500 other Jews. On its journey, the train was guarded by Ukrainians. No food or water was given to the deportees. Three days later, the train reached Sobibor: a journey in normal times of less than four hours. All the deportees were then taken, first to Camp II, the barbers' huts, and then on to Camp III, the gas chamber: all except Shklarek. This one young man, out of 2,500 deportees, was chosen to work with the hundred or so Jews in the 'Corpse Commando', the 'Work Commando', one of several work brigades in the camp. Shklarek later recalled the characteristics of some of the camp staff, among them SS Technical Sergeant Hermann Michel:

'He treated his servants decently, but his victims rudely and brutally. Because of the slippery-tongued speeches which he delivered to the arrivals at camp, we nicknamed him the "Preacher". When a new transport would arrive Hermann would deliver his lying speech, in which he assured the arrivals that this was a transit camp where they would only undergo classification and disinfection, and from here they would be taken to work in the Ukraine until the war was over.

'In his apartment in the camp there was concentrated the abundant property that the arrivals had brought with them – silver, gold, rings, watches, jewellery and various other valuables. Actually, he was the camp treasurer.

'All the transports passed into Hermann's hands; he classified the arrivals, ordered them to strip and instructed them how to arrange their clothing so they would get it back when they came out of the "bath-house". He would escort the people on the special road that led from Camp II to the barbers' huts and from there – to the gas chambers. With his tricks and his smooth tongue, Hermann was more dangerous than his comrades in crime.'

There were several recorded instances of attempted revolt at Sobibor. On 30 April 1943, 2,000 Jews from nearby Wlodawa were brought here by train. On arrival at the unloading ramp they attacked the SS guard with bare hands and pieces of wood torn from the wagons. All of them were killed by grenades and machine-gun fire.

Preparations for revolt had also been made inside Sobibor, but they too were doomed to failure. I read from the recollections of a Sobibor survivor, Dov Freiberg, who had been brought here in the first days of the camp, in May 1942:

'There was a captain from Holland, a Jew. He headed an organisation, a secret organisation. It was a period when there were difficulties among the Ukrainians and we thought maybe we could get in touch with them. We heard stories about the partisans from them and some contact was established between this Dutchman and the Ukrainians for a revolt.

'They began plotting an uprising. And then one day in a roll call they took him out, this Dutchman, and began questioning him. "Who were the ringleaders?"

'This man withstood tortures and endless blows and he never said a word. The Germans told him that if he did not speak they would give orders that the Dutch block would be ordered to move to Camp III and they will be beheaded in front of his eyes. And he said, "Anyway you are doing what you wish, you will not get a word out of me, not a whisper." And they gave the order to this Dutch block to move, all of them, about seventy people, and they were brought to Camp III. On the next day we learned that the Germans kept their word. They beheaded the people. Yes, they cut off their heads.'

Finally there was a revolt at Sobibor that succeeded. Among the Jews who were kept in Camp I, the labour camp, which held 600 slave labourers, were a number of Red Army men who had been captured in the fighting on the Eastern Front, and brought here as slave labourers. Their leader, Alexander Pechersky, was a composer. Before the war he had written music for plays in his home town, Rostov-on-Don. Twenty years ago, when we were in correspondence, he sent me an account from Rostov of the Sobibor uprising. I give the group a summary of what he told me, and of what he had written many years ago in a Russian Yiddish magazine.

To make revolt possible, several of the Jewish girls who worked in the SS quarters, polishing shoes and cleaning floors, had managed to steal a few hand grenades, some pistols, a rifle, and a sub-machine-gun. Meanwhile, the trains continued to arrive with new victims. On the morning of 11 October 1943, before the conspirators were ready with their plans, a group of new deportees, already undressed and on their way to the gas chamber, tried to run in the direction of the barbed wire. The guards began to shoot, killing many of them instantly. The others were dragged naked to the gas chambers. 'That day,' Pechersky recalled, 'the cremation pyres burned longer than usual. Huge flames rose up in the grey autumn sky and the camp was lit with strange colours. Helpless and distressed, we looked at the bodies of our brothers and sisters.'

On the night of 13 October 1943, Alexander Pechersky, and his co-conspirator, Leon Feldhendler, a Polish Jew from Lublin, distributed knives and hatchets, as well as warm clothing. Then, in the late afternoon of October 14, their plan was put into action. As individual German and Ukrainian guards entered the huts on their regular tours of inspection, they were attacked. Two SS men and nine Ukrainians were killed, whereupon, as Yaakov Biskowitz later recalled, the signal was given for the revolt to begin: the password 'Hurrah'.

Of the 600 prisoners in Camp I, 300 managed to escape. Nearly two hundred were shot by the SS and Ukrainian guards while trying to break out. The rest were killed in the camp with the arrival of police reinforcements from nearby Chelm, and from the even nearer Osowa. The local German army commander refused to assist in this round-up.

Many of the escaped prisoners joined Soviet and Polish partisan units. One of those who did so was Semyon Rozenfeld, a Russian Jew who later joined the Red Army, and was in Berlin on the day of victory.

Among the 300 Jews killed in the Sobibor revolt was Max Van Dam, a thirty-three-year-old Dutch painter. Before the war he had travelled and painted in Italy, France and Spain. In July 1942, when the deportations from Holland began, Van Dam was hidden by a Dutch friend in the village of Blaricum. Later that year he tried to reach

Switzerland, was caught, sent to Drancy, a suburb of Paris, and from there deported to Sobibor.

The story of the revolt in Sobibor is heartening, but the story of the mass murder at Sobibor is distressing in the extreme. After my readings there is silence. Petra is in tears, standing still by a tree, unable to move. People are comforting each other. Several are crying as they board the bus.

3.20 p.m.

As we set off, there is silence in the bus. A few yards along the road back, we pass the Lazarett execution site. It was here that SS Sergeant Paul Groth used to enjoy target practice against Jews. He would put a tin bucket on a Jew's head and shoot at the bucket until the Jew was dead.

We drive back through the wood to the main road. After we have been driving for a few minutes there is a ferocious rain storm. The sun is shining brightly in the west as the rain crashes down on the warm surface of the road, turning to haze.

In the bus, silence. Nobody is able to speak.

3.23 p.m.

We reach the main road, where we are to turn north, towards Wlodawa. Everyone is still silent. The only voice is the staccato (or so it seems) voice of the driver, asking, when we reach the crossroads, if he is to take the direction to Wlodawa.

We drive north. The rain stops as suddenly as it had begun; as if it had wanted to make our route away a vale of tears.

Yesterday afternoon at Belzec and this afternoon at Sobibor we have been to two places where almost a million Jews were murdered in the space of twelve months. Mike tells us that at Belzec the locals still have picnics on the site.

3.35 p.m.

We pass a signpost to Biale lake. It was here, in 1980, that some drunks who had found a permanent home in the cellar of the deserted synagogue at Wlodawa invited me to a party.

The sun is shining brightly now. We are still silent. Three children are cycling in single file towards Wlodawa. We slow down to pass them. A cow and a horse graze in a field by the roadside.

3.37 p.m.

The road runs along the shore of Biale lake. No one talks. There is nothing to say.

3.40 p.m.

We reach the city limits of Wlodawa. The silence is broken, but the members of the group whisper, rather than talk out loud.

This town, so near to the death camp, was for more than a hundred years a centre of Jewish bustle and learning.

3.45 p.m.

We drive into the Wlodawa town centre. There is a town museum here with a small exhibition about Sobibor. Mike tells us that one of the Ukrainian guards who worked (and killed) in Sobibor lives in a village not far from here. '"Why don't you go and interview him?" I ask the museum people here. They say, "We are afraid."'

Angela has heard one of the few survivors of the Sobibor revolt, Dov Freiburg, speak at Yad Vashem in Jerusalem. At one point, asked how he was able to smile after his terrible experiences, he said: 'If I don't smile, I'll just end up crying.'

Having heard Dov Freiburg speak, Angela reflected, 'made this visit very hard for me, as I could visualise Dov and his account of Sobibor as we walked around'.

3.50 p.m.

I give a brief account of the history of the Jews of Wlodawa. I would have done so on the journey into town, but the impact of Sobibor was too great to break it with a reading. Jews first settled here in the second half of the sixteenth century. In 1648 the forces of Bogdan Chmielnicki reached Wlodawa and broke into the town. Several thousand Jews, many of whom had come in from the surrounding towns and villages for safety, were massacred. By 1857 the 4,304 Jews who lived here constituted 72 per cent of the population. Between the wars Wlodawa's vigorous Jewish life included four Zionist parties and two Ultra-Orthodox parties. There was also a Tarbut Hebrew-language school. On the outbreak of war in 1939 there were 5,650 Jews in Wlodawa, just over sixty per cent of the population.

We leave the town centre, and walk to the synagogue, which is one minute's walk away. To my surprise, it is no longer desolate, and certainly no longer a haven for the local drunks. The days when it was an empty ruin are no more. The entrance wing is a children's library. At a table in the centre, two young girls are reading a book. At the librarian's desk, a young boy is taking out a book.

We walk into the synagogue hall. It dates from 1764, and has been brilliantly restored. The decorations are no longer the peeling and dusty remnants that I saw in 1980, when they looked as though they would be gone altogether within a decade. The Ark in particular is resplendent with its paintings, including colourful musical instruments, and white fluted columns, surmounted by two winged lions, representing the cherubs who stood on top of the Ark in the Temple in Jerusalem.

The hall is being used for a permanent exhibition of Wlodawa Jewry. There are more than a hundred photographs around the walls. There are photographs of the Wlodawa Jewish Dramatic Group in their costumes for two plays, *Shulamit* (1927) and *Uriel Dacosta* (1928). There is a photograph of the Jewish Working Men's Club (1929), the name of the club being 'Jutrzenka' (Dawn). Another group, of wealthier-looking worthies, are gathered to raise money for the Jewish orphans of Wlodawa (1926). A photograph next to it shows the pharmacist Erlin, and the Secretary of the Wlodawa Jewish Workers Association, Hopsler, giving food to orphans.

There are photographs of the Betar orchestra (1927) and the Trumpeldor youth group football team (1932). There was not only a strong Zionist, but also a strong Zionist-Revisionist group in Wlodawa between the wars – followers of Zev Jabotinsky and admirers of Josef Trumpeldor (who was killed in Galilee in 1921 defending a remote outpost against Arab marauders). The attraction of the Betar movement was not only political. Ben tells us that he joined Betar in Piotrkow when he was nine, because, he explains, 'They were the only ones with a table-tennis table.'

We walk around the synagogue walls examining the photographs. One of them, dated 1929, shows a discussion of a book by the Polish-born novelist and dramatist Sholem Asch (who died in London in 1957). His collected Yiddish novels were published in twelve volumes in 1932. He had begun publishing at the turn of the century, advised to write in Yiddish by his fellow novelist I. L. Peretz. The best known of Asch's work is his trilogy, *The Nazarene* (1939), *The Apostle* (1943) and *Mary* (1949).

Also on the wall is a photograph of an event organised by the Cultural Commission of the Association of Jewish Artisans. There is a photograph of Jewish youth with their leader, Szepel Kominer. They were members of the local youth organisation, *Ha-Shomer* (from the

Hebrew, The Guard). Another photograph shows Jewish wartime partisans in the Wlodawa region. We will be driving through their 'territory' in an hour's time.

In a number of display cases are the artefacts of Jewish religious life, labelled so that Poles may have some idea of what the Jews were, and what they did. There is, rather incongruously, a purple knitted skull-cap, of the sort often worn in Israel today. It is labelled 'Jarmulka' (the Hebrew for skull-cap). There is a Scroll of the Law, under glass, some prayer shawls, fifteen spice boxes, and thirty-five kiddush cups, one of which Mike found last summer lying in the grass at Sobibor, on the site of the Jewish work brigade's barracks.

There is a fine menorah on display – even more ornate than the one we lit at Lancut – and a Torah crown, as well as a shofar (ram's horn) and some phylacteries. There is also a display of a few broken tombstones. Everything on display is somewhat higgledy-piggledy, and a little dusty. Most of the exhibits have no explanations. What a weird fall from the vibrant life that used to be here, in this very synagogue hall, sixty years ago. It is like an exhibition of medieval relics, or, as Paul reflects, the type of museum that Hitler had intended to create of the vanished (that is, destroyed) Jewish world.

Ben speaks to the two ladies who are in charge of the exhibition. He has tears in his eyes. He tells them how much he appreciates that they have put on this exhibition: 'This is all that is left from the life that existed here before the war.'

We leave the synagogue and stand in the sun in the large courtyard. A smaller synagogue, and a study house (Bet Midrash), are on two sides of it. The smaller synagogue, built in the second half of the nineteenth century, was badly damaged during the fighting in Wlodawa at the beginning of the First World War, when the Russians tried in vain to defend the town against the Germans. It was rebuilt in 1916. A plaque records that this was done thanks to the generosity of Lejb ben Mosze Eliakim Lichtenberg. Today it is being turned into part of the museum complex of Jewish Wlodawa.

The study house was built in the nineteenth century. It too was badly damaged in the First World War but has recently been restored.

One must make a great leap of the imagination to fill this courtyard, and these houses, with the life and energy that once characterised them, as they did so many other such courtyards in every town we have been through.

4.23 p.m.

We leave the synagogue courtyard and go to a nearby café. The houses around the synagogue and square are mostly wooden, single-storey, pre-war (and once Jewish) dwellings. We sit for a while in the sun. Petra and Marie tell me how distressed they were by Sobibor.

Before we board the bus, I read from a description of an episode here in Wlodawa, that was recorded in the Warsaw ghetto by the historian Emanuel Ringelblum. It concerned a man by the name of Ankerman, who was among 2,000 Jews assembled in Wlodawa on 23 May 1942 for deportation to Sobibor. When all were assembled, the Germans asked, 'Where is the rabbi?' Thinking that the Gestapo wished to take the rabbi out of the deportation, Ankerman pointed him out, hoping thereby to save the rabbi's life. The Gestapo at once shot Ankerman. The rabbi was deported to Sobibor with the rest.

Ankerman's action, and his death, were an example, Ringelblum believed, of Kiddush Hashem, the sanctification of the Name of God through martyrdom.

I read a second story, a recollection by Aizik Rottenberg, one of the few Jews of Wlodawa who survived the war. In October 1942, a further 8,000 Jews from Wlodawa and the surrounding villages were assembled here and deported to Sobibor. Rottenberg, a bricklayer before the war, later asked: 'You may also wonder why eight thousand people did not fight the Nazis. But a hundred men armed with machine guns are more powerful than an unarmed crowd. The young ones would have tried to escape, but refused to abandon their parents; they knew it would mean the death of the older people, and how was it possible to leave behind the helpless little brothers and sisters without support?'

4.39 p.m.

We drive out of the main square, and through streets that were once at the hub of Jewish life in Wlodawa, down to the River Bug. This is the way that the deportees were brought. They were then driven south along the river bank. Sobibor camp is just under twelve kilometres to the south, and a single station on the railway line.

4.45 p.m.

We reach the River Bug. There are two branches of the river, one, the smaller one, inside Poland, the other marking the border between Poland and Belarus. A bridge leads over the first branch. From its parapet, Jewish gravestones from the cemetery in Wlodawa were thrown down, when the cemetery was being cleared out by the Poles after the war, to make a park. Many of the stones still lie in the mud of the river bank. Leaning over the parapet, one can see them.

Beyond the first branch of the river, on the island between the two branches, is a former Jewish-owned factory. Today most of its windows are bricked up, and it is being used as a store for fodder. We walk past the factory to the Polish border post above the bank of the river. Belarus is on the far bank. From September 1939 to June 1941 this was the border between Nazi Germany and the Soviet Union. From 1945 until 1991 it was the border between Poland and the Soviet Union. Soldiers and border police patrolled the border then. Special permission was needed to get anywhere near it.

Now there is no one in sight, no watchtowers and no guards. The fall of Communism has turned a once highly sensitive border area into nothing more than a pastoral scene. The earlier historical memories are more disturbing. Across this river, on the wooded banks beyond, is the beginning of that vast region in which, starting on 22 June 1941, special SS and police killing squads (Einsatzgruppen) carried out the mass murder of as many as a million Jews east of the River Bug. These Jews were not kept in ghettos or deported to death camps: they were murdered on the spot, or in pits and fields just outside their towns and villages. While the Jews of Wlodawa were being kept in the ghetto here, and throughout the year before they were deported to Sobibor and to their deaths, daily killings were taking place to the east of them, starting with the villages on the far bank of their own river. How placidly it flows today.

As we retrace our steps to the first branch of the river, we come to a Catholic shrine, topped by a crucifix. It has been put up recently by the Wlodawa municipality in memory of those – all of them Jews – who were shot while being driven along the riverbank on foot to the train that was to take them to Sobibor. They were the ones who were too old, too frail or too sick to keep up with the other marchers.

We walk back to the bus. Crossing the first bridge, Jon goes down the steep bank and takes some photographs of the dumped and discarded gravestones.

5.03 p.m.
We leave Wlodawa, and drive westward.

5.15 p.m.
We drive north for one kilometre along an unsurfaced road to what was once a Jewish village, Adampol. All 600 villagers were shot here

in 1942. The Germans took one of the houses in the village, and turned it into a brothel into which they brought Jewish girls from Wlodawa, for the use of German army officers stationed nearby.

We have entered the area where a small group of Jewish partisans – never more than two or three dozen people, not all of them armed – operated in 1942 and 1943. One of their actions was to raid Adampol, and to rescue a number of the girls being held there.

5.30 p.m.

We stop at Lubien, a small village with forests all around it. One of the young Jewish partisans who was later active in this area, Hersh Werner, was living in relative safety here in the early months of 1941. He had been given shelter and work by a local farmer, Stefan, who employed him as a farm labourer and shepherd. Stefan, like almost all the villagers of this region in the inter-war years, and for centuries before that, was a Ukrainian, and a member of the Russian Orthodox Church. He and his fellow-farmers, Werner later wrote, 'were happy that the Germans had conquered Poland, because of the history of Polish repression of the Ukrainian religion, language and culture. Although the Germans were another foreign occupying force, they were viewed in a positive light because they had lifted this repression of the symbols of Ukrainian nationalism.'

Werner later recalled an episode of that summer, which I read out as we stop briefly in the village. It was at the beginning of the summer of 1941. 'German troops started pouring into the area on trucks, motorcycles, tanks, and all kinds of mechanised transports. They were quartered in every house, every barn, and every available shelter. Thousands of them came into the area, and they flooded the surrounding villages. The local people felt something big was going to happen, but did not know what. Lubien was about ten or fifteen miles from the Bug River, which was the Russian–German border. Stefan asked me what I thought was going to happen. He thought that, as a Jew and city dweller, I knew more about current events than he did. I told him I did not know what was brewing, but I was aware of the fact that the Germans and the Russians had signed a non-aggression pact. He told me that with so many Germans around, it was dangerous for me and dangerous for him to have me around the farm.

'One evening, he told me to take the animals early to pasture the next day and also to take an extra blanket. He would then come out to me in the evening and bring the animals back himself. He came when it was getting dark and brought some food for me. He took the animals back to the farm, leaving me alone in the woods. I spread one blanket out near a tree and covered myself with the other blanket. I tried not to fall asleep, as I was afraid of the wild animals in the woods. All I had for protection was a big club-like stick. Early the next morning, Stefan returned with the animals. He blew a previously agreed code whistle and I whistled back. He told me that more Germans were coming into the area, and that the farmers were afraid to go to the fields and leave their households unattended. The farmers knew the Germans would help themselves to anything they wanted, but felt that if the farmers were present in their own homes there might not be as much plundering.

'No one knew what to expect, and Stefan would not let me go back to his farm. I spent four days and nights in the woods, and on the fifth night, just before dawn, I felt the ground shaking. Thousands of artillery guns had opened fire somewhere toward the east, in the vicinity of Wlodawa. Soon afterward, as dawn broke, squadrons of planes began flying overhead. The sound the planes made reminded me of when they had flown over Warsaw and bombed the city. The sound of planes flying overhead lasted for several hours, and I could hear their bombs exploding far away. When the bombardment started, my first thought and perhaps wish was that the Russians were attacking the Germans, or perhaps England, France and America had started fighting them. With renewed fighting, I hoped that Poland would be liberated from German occupation.

'Toward daylight, Stefan showed up with the animals and brought me food. He informed me that the previous evening, just before sunset, all the military units had pulled out from the villages and headed toward the Bug River to invade Russian territory. He told me that it was quiet now in the village, and that if he did not return for me in the evening I should bring the animals back to the farm myself. When I came back in the evening, I saw the farmers standing in the fields, looking eastward where the horizon was red with battle. Everyone was certain that the Russians would be victorious and would soon start chasing the Germans back.'

5.40 p.m.
Having continued westward, we reach the village of Zamolodycze. We are in a remote and rarely visited region. Our driver, who is from Cracow, has never been here before. He is unhappy at the poor state of the roads. The roads that are surfaced are badly potholed. Many are without any tarmac at all.

We stop in the village for a reading. The local farmers in this area were known as Halachis. When you call a Pole a Halachi, Ben points out, 'It means that he is an ignorant peasant.' The village houses are what Caroline calls 'undoubtedly basic'. None of them has running water. Each yard has a well.

This village was the scene of an ugly episode. In a wood near here, the twenty-five members of the Jewish group active in this area were in hiding, women and children as well as men. They lived in dug-outs in the forest. After some months, more than a hundred peasants, local Ukrainians, came to their hide-out and ordered them to leave it. There was a short fight, but the Jews were outnumbered and overwhelmed.

The peasants were armed; the Jews were not. The peasants had lived in their villages with food and freedom to move about; the Jews had been in hiding, hungry and alone, so fearful of being betrayed that, while the peasants had been searching for them, a couple had killed their own child so that its crying would not reveal their hiding place.

'When we were taken out of the hole,' the twenty-four-year-old Hersh Werner later recalled, 'I said, "We must run, or we're done for." The father of the dead child said, "I'm not running." He hadn't got it in him any more.'

The peasants brought the Jews here, to the village of Zamolodycze, and locked them in a barn. Then they took the Jews out one by one. Twenty-one of the Jews were killed. Four managed to escape. These four had then to begin again the search for a hide-out, the search for other Jews, the search for the means of survival. 'You were running from one place to another,' Werner later recalled. 'You had no possessions.'

Eventually this particular group acquired some rifles, and began to ambush German patrols. It also organised, as best it could, the escape of Jews from some of the nearby ghettos. It even succeeded in rescuing several Jewish girls being held by the Gestapo at the farm at Adampol.

On one occasion the group, then twenty-five strong, killed ten German soldiers. As this fight was in progress, one of the German soldiers, and a German woman who was with him, surrendered. Both were shot. 'We had seen such brutality inflicted on the Jews,' Werner later wrote, 'we had no mercy for them. It was the first time that we saw dead Germans in this war, not only dead Jews.'

Revenge was later taken for the killing of Jews in this village. I read Hersh Werner's account of it. 'We decided to go to Zamolodycze,' he recalled, 'to take revenge for the massacre that had taken place there the previous year. Faiga, Zelik's daughter and the only person left from her entire family, and in whose yard all the slaughtered Jews had been buried, led us. It was a Sunday night. We came in, as usual, through the back of the village. From far away we heard the sound of music. As we came closer, Faiga realised that the music was coming from her house. Faiga, who did not have a gun, was carrying an axe she had picked up as we entered the village. She was furious as we came closer to her home, remembering how the villagers had herded her family back to Zamolodycze to be shot.

'We charged into the house. There was partying and drinking going on. I recognised Vasil, the leader of the villagers who had forced the Jews to march to Zamolodycze and had turned them over to the Germans. He ran for the window, but we shot him before he could escape. Faiga recognised one of the men who had dragged her father, Zelik, out of the dug-out in the woods. He was wearing her father's boots. We shot him also, and Moniek took his boots. I recognised Moishe Yohel's boots on another villager and told him to take them off. We shot him too. The others begged for mercy.

'Faiga was enraged, like a wild animal. She knew each of the partygoers by their first names. She ran around her house, breaking everything with her axe and calling out their names as she did so. We were planning to burn down the house, but the people who ran out sounded an alarm, and soon we heard the bells of the church ringing. As we left the house, we saw a mass of villagers coming towards us, and we heard one or two rifle shots. We started shooting back. Chanina fired his flare gun into the air. This lit up the village and scared the villagers, who stopped advancing towards us. Then we retreated into the woods. We were elated that the villagers had seen armed Jews who had come to take revenge. We hoped this would deter them in the future from hunting down and killing Jews in the area.'

6 p.m.

Driving westward from Zamolodycze, we reach Turno, a tiny hamlet four kilometres further west, and stop the bus by the roadside. Across the fields to the south is what used to be the Turno Estate, a small farmstead owned and worked between the wars by a Jew from Warsaw, David Turno. The sun is flooding across the fields, lighting up the marshy ground, and the farms and barns of the hamlet beyond. In the distance is the dark outline of the woods. This too was an area in which the unlucky, but persistent and determined, local Jewish partisan group was active.

I read out an account of an episode here, when, in the autumn of

1943, the young Jews attacked this hamlet, which was then being occupied by the Germans. In what had once been David Turno's barns, the crops had been harvested and were ready to be shipped to Germany. The young partisans managed to reach the barns and set them on fire. They had struck a blow, however small, at the German war economy. It was a moment of triumph for them. Hersh Werner, who set down this story in 1981, recalled: 'As we were pulling out of the burning estate, I noticed a bulky form crawling on all fours, like an animal, and making very strange noises. I showed it to Symcha who was near me, and we both decided that it might be a human being, perhaps a Jew. We both took him by the arms, and dragged him along with us.

'After we covered about five miles from Turno, we sat down to rest and looked at the human mess we were dragging. He was covered with hair like an animal, his clothes were torn, he couldn't stand up on his two feet, and he looked like a skeleton. He could hardly talk, but from his mumblings we learned that this was Yankel, David Turno's relative, and my friend from Warsaw.

'From his mumblings, we understood that he had stayed buried in the barn, in a hole under the feed trough for the cows. No one knew that he was there and he lived there for over a year. He ate the food that was given to the animals and never stood up. The heat from the burning building had forced him out of his hole.

'We walked to our base, and tried to help Yankel. He couldn't hold any food, and the following day he died. We buried him in the woods and I cried over what had happened to my friend.'

6.05 p.m.
We look across the fields to Turno. When I met Hersh Werner in 1981, a few months after reading the above account, I encouraged him to set down his recollections more fully. He did so, but died before they could be published. Entitled *Fighting Back, A Memoir of Jewish Resistance in World War II*, and edited by his son Mark Werner, they were published by Columbia University Press in 1992.

We continue westward, the sun bright across the fields, woods on the horizon.

6.20 p.m.
We reach the village of Uhnin, on the edge of the Makoszka and Ochoza forests. The village lay on the edge of Jewish partisan country. Ben comments: 'It must have used up a lot of German manpower to

control such a vast area as this, as, on its own, a small unit was very vulnerable.'

The forests stretch to the south and west. It was deep inside them, with lakes, swamps and water-filled drainage ditches as protection, that a large group of Jewish partisans formed in 1943. It was joined by the dozen or so survivors of the small partisan group of which Hersh Werner had been a part.

The Jewish partisans who controlled the Parczew forests took whole families into its dark and dense interior. They protected them by digging pits on the higher ground (above the level of the swamp) and covering the pits with branches and earth. In this way, hundreds of women and children were hidden in the depth of the forest, in what was known as the Altana 'family camp'. The Jews knew it also as Tabor (Mount Tabor in northern Palestine, though there were no hills in the forest).

The Jewish partisans, who two years earlier had been very much on their own, were now being helped by Polish resistance fighters of the Communist Armia Ludowa (People's Army), and by Soviet partisans who had been parachuted into the area. For their part, the Germans were helped by Russian soldiers who had been recruited in prisoner-of-war camps to fight alongside the German army. They were commanded by General Vlasov, a Soviet commander who had been captured by the Germans in 1942 and had then gone over to the German side.

At the beginning of 1944 the German army, helped by Vlasov's Russian deserters, was making regular military sweeps to flush out the partisans and destroy the 'family camp'. Hersh Werner was an eye-witness, and a participant, of one such sweep which took place in and around where we are standing. 'From our informers in the Parczew area,' he wrote, 'we learned that the Germans were preparing a major attack in the Makoszka forest. A large concentration of Germans, together with artillery and armoured vehicles, were massing in the villages around Parczew – a sure sign they were about to launch an attack in the forest. We received an order one evening from the Armia Ludowa high command to pull out of the forest as soon as possible. In our area, in addition to our force, there were also an Armia Ludowa group and a Russian partisan unit, each consisting of about eight fighters. The order applied to these two groups as well.

'That same evening, we gathered together the people of the Tabor, who were camped in the nearby woods. We told them that we and the other two partisan units were moving out of the area, and that we expected a major German offensive imminently. We advised them to move immediately to the Ochoza forest to avoid this attack.

'Most of them heeded our advice and started getting ready to go, but some hesitated, especially those who came from Parczew and the surrounding villages. They figured they could find safety in the vastness of the forest, and that the Germans would not find them. However, the great majority of the Tabor group, under the leadership of their elders, left in a hurry that night for the Ochoza forest. We made sure that those who were capable carried guns.

'At dawn, we were attacked. The Germans brought in many troops from the Russian front (which was not far from the forest by this time) for the attack. The Russian army was pressing the Germans back now. The Germans realised that the partisans might hinder their retreat and so decided to try to eliminate this threat.

'They cordoned off our area of the woods with troops and artillery and before dawn opened up a tremendous artillery fire on the forest in our vicinity. We tried to cut through the surrounding ring. The machine-gun and rifle fire was very heavy, and we had to retreat back into the woods to a different area, hoping to be able to find another route of escape.

'The Germans did not advance very far into the forest. They thought we were a very large force from the heavy fire we returned. But they kept the woods sealed. They started out with artillery shelling and then brought in several planes, which circled low over the trees, dropping bombs. The trees caught fire. The planes could not see us under the thick forest foliage, but they dropped their bombs anyway. The shelling and bombing continued for the entire day. We knew the woods very well and tried to cut through the German ring several times, but we were blocked at every turn.

'We were a combined force of almost five hundred partisans. By this time, our group consisted of about three hundred fighters. The Russian contingent of about eighty men was part of the Voroshilov battalion, the rest of which was stationed on the eastern side of the River Bug. They had very good heavy machine guns. The Polish Armia Ludowa group, also about eighty men, were mostly new recruits, but very brave men.

'We tried to disengage ourselves from the German cordon, moving to a different part of the woods. We hoped that toward evening the Germans would pull out, because they had never before fought with us at night. Toward evening we moved in the direction of the village of Uhnin, hoping to break out there. Uhnin was at the edge of the Makoszka forest, from which we could follow small patches of woods that would lead us all the way south to the Ochoza forest.

'We probed the ring in the Uhnin area, and the encircling forces started shooting at us. We answered them with our fire. Then we heard them ordering us, in Russian, to surrender. This order was transmitted over a loudspeaker. The speaker said: "We are Russians. Our leader is General Vlasov. We have it good with the Germans. Surrender and come with us and be part of us. We don't want the Jews, but you Russians are our brothers."

'This part of the enemy ring was manned by soldiers referred as the "Vlasovis". They were former Russian prisoners-of-war, willing to fight on the Germans' side. They did not have a reputation for being good fighting men. Our group became enraged at confronting these turncoats, especially our Russian partisans, who immediately fixed bayonets on their rifles. We threw ourselves at the Vlasovis, tossing grenades and spraying sub-machine-gun fire.

'It was getting dark, and we knew this was our chance to break through. With shouts of "Traitors of the Motherland" coming from our Russians, we rushed straight at them. In a few short emotional minutes we overran their position in fierce hand-to-hand combat. The Vlasovis were massacred, many on the points of the bayonets used by our Russians, who seemed more concerned with pursuing and killing every one of the hated Vlasovis than with leaving the encircled area. It was dark by the time we mopped up the Vlasovis and, having suffered few casualties, we were in a hurry to get as far away as possible. The few Tabor people who had not escaped the previous night followed us. We walked the entire night, finally reaching the Ochoza forest where we rejoined the bulk of the Tabor people.'

6.25 p.m.
We drive away from Uhnin towards the Makoszka forest, north-west to the village of Stepkow, then south to Plebania Wola and the hamlet of Makoszka.

6.32 p.m.
We enter the Makoszka forest. The road runs southward.

6.35 p.m.
We stop the minibus and walk into the forest. The woods are dense, tall trees and thick undergrowth, but in every clearing the floor of the forest is carpeted with patches of blueberries.

6.40 p.m.
After five minutes walking into the woods, one is already in dense undergrowth. 'Here the Germans were not masters,' says Ben, 'you couldn't bring any heavy weapons here.'

6.45 p.m.
Return to the road.

6.50 p.m.
We drive on southward. The extent of the forest on the ground seems so much greater than on the map. It is dense on either side of the road.

6.55 p.m.
We reach the hamlet of Ochoza, now a children's holiday camp. Beyond it, leaving the forest behind us, we cross the Ochoza swamp, but the road is too rough for the bus to pass, and we have to turn round, and return through the forest to Makoszka.

7.05 p.m.
We reach Stepkow, where we entered the forest about forty minutes ago, and turn westward, towards the town of Parczew.

7.08 p.m.
We reach Parczew, and park in a garage forecourt. I give a brief survey of the history of the town from its Jewish perspective. Jews were living here before 1541. The influence of Hassidism was strong. At the time of the outbreak of war in 1939, 50 per cent of the townspeople were Jewish, some five thousand. On 20 November 1939 as many as a hundred Jews were murdered in the town. A ghetto was then established, not only for the Jews of Parczew, but for Jews from all the surrounding towns and villages.

Among the Jews who were brought to the Parczew ghetto were those of Kock, a predominantly Hassidic town twenty-five kilometres to the east, famous for its dynasty of Hassidic rabbis. They shared the fate of the Jews of Parczew, most of whom were deported to Treblinka in August 1942 and murdered there.

I read from Christopher Browning's *Ordinary Men*, about the fate of the Jews of Parczew. In early August 1942, he writes, 'some 300 to 500 Jews in Parczew had been loaded on to horse-drawn wagons and driven five or six kilometres into the woods under police guard. There the Jews had been turned over to a unit of SS men. The policemen left before hearing any shots, and the fate of the Jews remained unknown to them. Rumours of a much larger deportation circulated in Parczew, and many Jews fled to the woods. Most were still in the town, however, when policemen of the First and Second Companies of Reserve Police Battalion 101, along with a unit of Hiwis, descended upon Parczew early on August 19 – just two days after the Lomazy massacre – when 1,700 Jews had been massacred near the town. Trapp – the battalion commander – gave another speech, informing the men that the Jews were to be taken to the train station two or three kilometres out of town. He indicated "indirectly" but without ambiguity that once again the old and frail who could not march were to be shot on the spot.

'Second Company set up the cordon, and First Company carried out the search action in the Jewish quarter. By afternoon, a long column of Jews stretched from the marketplace to the train station. About 3,000 of Parczew's Jews were deported that day. Several days later, this time without the help of any Hiwis, the entire operation was repeated, and the remaining 2,000 Jews of Parczew were sent to Treblinka as well.'

The Hiwis (*Hilfswillige*, or volunteers) were Ukrainians, Lithuanians and Latvians whom SS Sturmbannführer Karl Streibel, the commander of the SS training camp at Trawniki, had recruited from among the Soviet soldiers being held by the Germans in prisoner-of-war camps. About three hundred of these Hiwis had participated in the Parczew round-up. Some 4,000 were trained for duty in Operation Reinhard.

After liberation, four Jews were murdered in Parczew by anti-Semitic Poles.

The nineteenth-century synagogue building survives, as a clothing factory. The building which housed the mikveh also survives; today it is a cinema. There is a monument in the former Jewish cemetery to 340 Jewish soldiers who were killed there on 20 February 1940. They had been held in a prisoner-of-war camp in Biala Podlaska, and were being taken southward with some three hundred others to the Lipowa Street camp in Lublin.

7.23 p.m.

Leave Parczew and drive south. We are driving along the road which in September 1939, immediately after the German conquest of Poland, saw a death march of 880 Jewish prisoners-of-war, coming northward from Lublin and Lubartow (towards which we are going). They had been told in Lublin that they were being taken to the Soviet border, which had just been established on the River Bug. More than four hundred and fifty were killed as they were being marched along this road: shot down in cold blood. Most of the others were killed later on during the march. Most of the survivors, held in the camp at Biala Podlaska, were refused all medical attention and died of typhus.

7.41 p.m.
Juliopol. On 18 October 1940 the Germans killed a hundred Jewish prisoners-of-war on the outskirts of this village, while marching them towards Lublin (in the direction we are going).

7.52 p.m.
Reach Lubartow. The Jewish community here dated from the sixteenth century. The synagogue was built in 1819. A part of it survives. Also surviving are thirty old tombstones, the oldest dating from 1848, which were made into a lapidarium (a small pyramid-shaped structure) in 1938 when the cemetery was being cleaned. In 1939 there were 3,500 Jews here. They constituted 45 per cent of the population. After they had been deported to Belzec and Sobibor in October 1942, almost all the Jewish communal buildings were destroyed.

7.57 p.m.
Leave Lubartow.

8.07 p.m.
We pass the village of Niemce Wood. During the war, several hundred Jews were brought out here on foot from Lublin and shot in the nearby woods. Among them were the patients, doctors and nurses from the Jewish hospital on Lubartowska Street which we will visit tomorrow.

8.14 p.m.
We reach the Lublin city limits.

8.16 p.m.
We pass the Lublin Yeshiva, an impressive inter-war building, which we will visit tomorrow, and, next to it, the Jewish hospital. We drive down Lubartowska Street, the main street of the wartime ghetto, to the River Czechowka.

On the eve of war there were 40,000 Jews in Lublin, 40 per cent of the population. Now there are not even a hundred Jews here. Their synagogue is a room in a house near the city centre, on the second floor of No. 10 Lubartowska Street. It is the only surviving pre-war synagogue in Lublin (the entrance is through the gate of No. 8). Andrzej Trzcinski recounts, in his book *A Guide to Jewish Lublin and Surroundings*, an indispensable book for this part of Poland, that this synagogue was established after the First World War. It belonged to the Society of Undertakers. After the war, it was used as a place of worship by those survivors who returned to Lublin. A plaque in its Memorial Chamber recalls that there were always Poles who, at the risk of their own lives, tried to save Jews. The plaque reads: 'Honour to Poles who brought help to the Jews during the years of occupation, 1939–1942.'

We follow a by-pass road to our hotel. It is strange to be in traffic, after so many hours in the remote and empty countryside.

Reach Raclawickie Avenue, the road to our hotel.

8.27 p.m.
We reach the Garrison Hotel (a former army hotel) on Parachute Avenue. Distribution of keys. We will meet in the lobby in half an hour and go to supper in the Old Town.

8.55 p.m.
Reach my room. There is just time for a shower.

9.10 p.m.
We gather in the hotel lobby.

9.25 p.m.
Leave the hotel and walk along Raclawickie Avenue into Lublin. As we walk, Mike gives a survey of the wartime scene. In 1942, at the height of Operation Reinhard, there were SS and Gestapo living in Lublin, many of them with their families. Himmler intended building a new German quarter in Lublin to accommodate 60,000 SS troops and their families.

9.50 p.m.
Walking into Lublin, we pass first, on the left, the army hospital, then the former Communist Party headquarters, the White House, which during the war housed the SS-Mannschaftshaus/Rasse und Siedlungshauptampt: the Lublin headquarters of the Race and Resettlement Office in Berlin.

We reach the corner of Dlugosza Street. Down this street, on the left, are the surviving gates of the Ogrodowa Street Jewish slave labour camp.

Continuing along Raclawickie Avenue, we reach the former Horst-Wessel-Strasse, on our right. At the end of it we can see a building with columns. It is the former Nazi Party headquarters (Haus der NSDAP), now a Polish army officers' club. It was in this building, in November 1944, that the Polish Communist authorities held the first trial of Majdanek guards.

Raclawickie Street leads on to Krakowskie Przedmiescie, the main street in the centre of town. A few moments later, standing at a street corner, we have to wait a moment because of a red light. Then, as I look at the street's name, the penny drops. This is not just any street, but the notorious Lipowa Street of which I have read so much in the history books. A hundred yards down from this corner was the Lipowa Street prisoner-of-war camp, where Jewish soldiers who had been captured while fighting in the Polish army were held from October 1939 until November 1943, when most of them were sent to Majdanek and killed. The gatehouse of the camp is still there. The last barrack inside the camp was pulled down two years ago.

Walking along Krakowskie Przedmiescie, to our left is that part of Lublin that was closed to Poles during the war. This is where Odilo Globocnik had his kingdom, and from where he operated the Operation Reinhard death-camp system. On our left is the Schutzpolizei (Schupo) building. The head of the Schutzpolizei in Lublin was Konrad Rheindorf, born in Birmingham in 1889, the son of a bicycle manufacturer. He first went to Germany from Britain when he was thirty-four. At the end of the war he was captured by the Red Army and sentenced to twelve years in prison. He was amnestied in 1956 because, having been wounded during the battle for Lublin in 1944, he had been in hospital during the final phase of the German occupation, rather than fighting with his police unit.

We cross Chopin Street. At the far end, on the righthand side of the street, is the building that was the main clothing depot of Operation Reinhard. It is now the Catholic University library. We will visit it tomorrow.

We cross Ewangelicka Street. It is quite short, and at the end of it is an imposing pre-First World War building. This was the headquarters of Operation Reinhard. It is now part of the university Medical School.

Continuing along Krakowskie Przedmiescie towards the Old Town, we reach, on the left side of the street, the courthouse. Here are the law courts, with the County Court opposite. It was to this building

35. Lublin: the wartime headquarters of Operation Reinhard, from where the death camps of Belzec, Sobibor and Treblinka were administered, now a medical college (page 284).

36. Lublin: SS-Brigadier Odilo Globocnik's villa (page 285).

37. Lublin: former Gestapo headquarters (page 283).

38. The Lublin Yeshiva, inaugurated in 1930.
Today it is part of the Catholic University of Lublin (pages 288–9).

39. Warsaw: the Osnos house, a pre-war courtyard (pages 300–1).

40. Warsaw: the pre-war school and hospital building in which Warsaw Jews were held (1942–3) before being deported to Treblinka. To the left of the building is the memorial to the murdered deportees (pages 314–5).

41. Treblinka: the memorial stones (page 335).

42. The Piotrkow ghetto: Ben's courtyard. Ben lived with his parents and sisters in the corner rooms immediately under the roof (page 357).

43. Piotrkow: the Hortensja glass factory (pages 362–5).

44. Piotrkow: the glass factory record book, in which Ben, and his friend Krulik (Israel) Wilder, appear, both with the designation 'Zyd' (Jew) in red against their name.

45. Grabow: the synagogue (pages 373–5) and some of the group.

46. Grabow: the rabbi's house.

47. Grabow: the interior of the synagogue, now a storehouse.

48. Chelmno: the road leading from the mill through the wood, along which the deportees were driven, in sealed gas vans, to the camp (pages 375–6).

49. (above left) Konin: a synagogue window. The synagogue, completed in 1844, is now a public library. This window was remodelled in 1878 in Moorish style (page 385).

50. (above right) Konin: decorated pillars in the synagogue.

51. (below left) Konin: the curtain for the Ark.

52. (below right) Konin: the Jewish high school, built in 1918 (pages 385–6).

that Chaim Hirszman came on 19 March 1946 to give his testimony about Belzec. Having given his testimony, he went home (he lived at 9 Gorna Street). He was shot that night in his home by an 'execution squad' of NSZ men (the NSZ was a right-wing, anti-Semitic Polish organisation). They shot him, it seems, not because he was a Jew, but because he was an officer of the Lublin Communist secret police. 'Just another Jew dead,' comments Mike. 'They murdered Jews all the time.'

Chaim Hirszman's wife and children had been murdered in Belzec. After liberation, he married again. His second wife, Pola, to whom – during the year of their marriage – he had spoken so often about his experiences in Belzec, returned to this courthouse on the day after her husband's murder, and gave such testimony as she could from what he had told her. Among the things she remembered was a planned escape. 'The Germans had discovered,' she told the court, 'that one of the prisoners, a Czechoslovak Jew, had been planning to escape. The SS men ordered the prisoners to build a gallows. They gathered all the prisoners and ordered them to participate in the execution. My husband was told to fetch a rope and tie the convict up. My husband managed somehow to get out of this, since there was one Jew there, an expert in tying up. Before he was hanged, the condemned man said: "I am perishing, but Hitler will die and the Germans will lose the war." '

Just beyond the courthouse, on the other side of the street, is a bank; in the war, it was the headquarters of the German civil administration in Lublin.

Continuing along Krakowskie Przedmiescie, on the left hand side is another bank, a large white building. In the war, this was a branch of the Reichsbank. It was here that Globocnik put the money taken from Jews, and from where it was sent back to the Reich – including gold.

A courier, Erich Fettka, came twice a week by train from Berlin. He delivered the Operation Reinhard salaries and new uniforms, and took back the money and the gold. After the war he became a bus driver in Hamburg.

This bank is on the corner of a square, the former Adolf-Hitler-Platz, now Plac Litewski (Lithuania Square). On the south side of the square is the main post office. In the war, this was the place where the fake death certificates issued for the Jewish victims of the T4 euthanasia operation in the Reich were posted to their relatives after the writers had been murdered. The postal cancellation that the stamps on these cards were given was 'Chelm II'. The return address was Post Office Box 822, Lublin.

On the far side of the square is the Europa Hotel, with a bookshop and a milk bar at the street level. In the war, this was the headquarters of the Goebbels Propaganda Department for the region. A Nazi radio station operated from here.

We are approaching the Old Town. On the left is Swietoduska Wodopojna Street, in which a doorman for the Schutzpolizei, Krause, lived. After the war he became a doorman for the Polish Secret Police – in the same building on Chopin Street that he earlier served for the Germans.

We reach the Old Town Hall. There are fine churches in every direction. Facing the Old Town Hall is a medieval gate, the Brama Krakowska (Cracow Gate), one of the glories of medieval Lublin. This was the main gate into the ghetto, where 40,000 Jews were incarcerated in 1942, and from which 1,500 a day were sent to Belzec. Five hundred years earlier it was the gate into medieval Lublin. Jews were living there even then.

Just inside the Cracow Gate are several buildings which have a Jewish resonance. In the nineteenth century, at No. 10 Bramowa Street was the Jewish outpatients clinic. At No. 8 in the Market Square (Rynek) was the Lublin Jewish community headquarters, and the Jewish library. At No. 10 there lived, in 1835, the Polish-Jewish violinist and composer Henryk Wieniawski: a plaque records his brilliance, though not the fact that he was a Jew.

No. 11 Grodzka Street was a Jewish orphanage from 1862 until 1942. A plaque records: 'On 24 March 1942, the Nazis murdered all the orphans of that house.' The SS took all 108 of the orphans away by truck to a nearby village, Majdan Tatarksi, and shot them.

We have seen so much during an hour's walk on the way to dinner. How full each street and each building is of historical associations, but what grim associations they are. The 1944 edition of Baedeker's *Generalgouvernement* guide book was able to describe Lublin as 'Judenfrei', and to invite German tourists to sample the city's hotels, theatres, restaurants and cafés – centred around the 'attractive' Adolf-Hitler-Platz.

10.25 p.m.

We reach the Golden Donkey restaurant in the heart of the Old Town. We are warned by a local resident, 'Lublin is not safe at night; there are drunks; and there is the Ukrainian mafia in Lubartowska Street. The economic situation in Belarus and the Ukraine is tragic. Ukrainians and Belarussians come in search of work, wheeling and dealing in the market place, buying and selling.'

We talk during dinner about how the Jews were singled out as victims, not only by the perpetrators, but by so many collaborators as well. Jon says, 'Why do they hate us Jews *so much?*' I tell him of the British civil servant who protested that he was not anti-Semitic, having, as he put it (in the summer of 1939), 'nothing but a vague instinct of dislike for anything with a Jewish label'. We discuss whether this attitude (the 'vague instinct of dislike') leads on automatically to worse, or whether it is a buffer and a safety valve.

Midnight

It is pouring with rain. Herut, Angela, Paul and I take a taxi back to the hotel. I spend ten minutes reading about Lublin's Jews (for tomorrow) before bed.

DAY 10

LUBLIN – WARSAW

War and pre-war

7.10 a.m.
Look through the materials for today.

7.30 a.m.
Breakfast with the group. Sobibor has made a strong impact on everyone.

8.45 a.m.
We leave the hotel, with Mike at our side. The driver takes us through Lublin and out to the east, across the River Bystrzyca and along Fabryczna Street. We go under the railway bridge which carried so many of the deportation trains to Belzec. Just to the left, as we go under the bridge, is a small cream-coloured building. This was the villa of Christian Wirth, the former commandant of Belzec, who moved to Lublin when he was appointed Inspector of the Operation Reinhard death camps. Just beyond Wirth's villa are three large hangars, where the clothing of the victims of Operation Reinhard was stored, before being taken by train to the Reich.

We drive for a few hundred yards along the main road until, on the right, stretching below us, are the huts of Majdanek.

9.03 a.m.
We reach the entrance to Majdanek and drive to the museum administration building. There is a big workshop here, set up in order to maintain the surviving camp buildings. It is paid for by the Polish Ministry of Justice. The administration is alarmed because, in two years' time, all funds will be cut off, in order to switch the resources to the Auschwitz Museum, where the large expansion is planned.

9.10 a.m.

We begin our walk towards the camp. On the left is the area used by the Soviet secret police after the war, as a transit camp for Poles being sent to Siberia – tyranny did not end with the defeat of Nazism.

We pass the SS women's quarters. Beyond them is the white villa in which the camp doctor lived. We reach the wartime entrance to the inner camp. There is a map of the site. In front of us is the small square in which deportees were forced to undress, and to the right, the first gas chambers, a wooden structure with a tall brick chimney.

We walk up a slight incline. On the right are many wooden storehouses. Even today, now as part of the camp museum, these still hold some of the belongings of the victims, including shoes, as well as their hair. When the Red Army reached the camp in the summer of 1944, these vast storehouses were still here, their contents awaiting shipment to Germany.

We reach the brick foundations of the SS garage. A gassing van was parked here. Black crows caw in the tall trees.

The barracks area was divided up into 'Fields' (in German, Felder). There were five identical Fields, each with two rows of huts on either side of a large open space. Around each Field was a high fence. In 1944 there were plans to extend the camp by building even more Fields. We enter Field III, the only Field still with huts remaining from the war years. The lines of wooden huts (known as Blocks) are on both sides of a large open space. Two months ago they put up two new huts, to fill in the empty spaces – an example of zealous restoration, to say the least. Two men, one on a ladder, are creosoting Block 12.

We enter Block 14, which is laid out with large wooden bunk beds in several tiers. Each tier housed several dozen prisoners. A terrible sense of claustrophobia, of being penned up, of being treated like cattle, worse than cattle, something 'inhuman' as Paul expresses it, survives, even without people or danger.

We reach Block 19. Those too weak to work were brought here. They were kept without water or food for two or three days – until they died. A cart, pulled by Jewish Sonderkommando members, would come each day and take out the dead bodies and drag the cart up the hill to the crematorium.

In winter the area between the Blocks would be frozen mud. The temperature could fall to minus twenty degrees centigrade, and even minus thirty. In that temperature, roll calls would be held. These roll calls could last for thirteen or fourteen hours. If a prisoner had escaped, then roll call would continue until the prisoner was caught. Hundreds would die of exposure.

The camp commandant, Koch, prided himself on being a cultured man. He encouraged the prisoners to do sculpture. The work he judged best was a column with an ornamental top showing three eagles which was put up in the centre of Field III. Under it, as a memorial, the prisoners secretly placed some ashes of those burned in the crematorium.

Just to the left of the monument is a warehouse that was used to store more shoes of the victims.

We walk up the hill past the entrances to Field IV and Field V – now quite empty – and reach the gas chamber and crematorium. The crematorium chimney is visible from all over the camp, and indeed from the main road, which during the war took all German military and civilian traffic from Lublin to Zamosc (Himmlerstadt) and Lvov (Lemberg), and on to Kiev and the Eastern Front.

As we draw near to the gas chamber, and the large monument containing human ash from the crematorium that has been built next to it, we see on the left the empty land which was to have formed the basis of a massive extension of Majdanek. The plans for the extension show that it was intended that Majdanek, when completed, would be even larger than Auschwitz.

The Field nearest the gas chamber is Field V, where most of the Jewish women and children were held.

As we walk through the camp, there is a constant loud cawing by large black crows. They are at their most numerous, and loudest, here in Field V, and in the big trees by the SS garage.

On 3 November 1943, a gate was made in the top perimeter fence of Field V, and through this gate as many as 4,000 Jews from the huts here in Majdanek – and another 14,000 from the labour camps in Lublin itself, including from the Lipowa Street prisoner-of-war camp – were forced in batches. Naked, whipped without mercy, savaged by dogs, they were pushed forward to the deep ditches that had been dug behind the crematorium, only twenty-five yards from the Field itself. Loud music boomed out from two loudspeaker trucks. Once at the edge of the ditches the Jews were machine-gunned. One of the Germans from Reserve Police Battalion 101 later recalled (as published in Christopher Browning's book about the battalion, *Ordinary Men*): 'I definitely remember that the naked Jews were driven directly into the graves and forced to lie down quite precisely on top of those who had been shot before them. The shooter then fired off a burst at these prone victims.'

An estimated 18,400 Jews were killed in Majdanek that day, almost as many as the number of British soldiers killed on the first day of the Battle of the Somme in 1916.

This was the action the Germans called the 'Erntefest' (the 'Harvest Festival'). From the houses to the south, just beyond the camp's perimeter fence, Poles were seen leaning out of their windows and sitting on rooftops watching the executions.

That same day at least 6,000 Jews were murdered in the slave labour camp at Trawniki, and on the following day 14,000 were murdered at Poniatowa camp. The Jews had been brought to Trawniki and Poniatowa from Warsaw, following the crushing of the Warsaw ghetto revolt.

10.05 a.m.

We are looking into the pits where the 'Harvest Festival' victims were killed. The grass around the pits has been mown. The hay, like the hay we saw being cut at Plaszow, is used by local farmers. Twenty yards away is the crematorium chimney, the gas chambers and the crematorium. The furnaces and chimney are original. The gas chambers were completely reconstructed after the war, from the original German plans (to ensure 'authenticity').

I went inside this building in 1980, and do not feel able to do so again. Others of the group go in.

Everything is so close: the Fields with their wooden huts, the crematorium with its tall, square chimney, the pits of the 'Harvest Festival' massacre; and all are within sight of the main road, along which cars and trucks, now as during the war, hurry towards their destinations. One of the places through which this road passes is Belzec. The German army used this road to take troops and supplies all the way to Kiev and the Ukrainian Front. In 1942 and 1943 the triumphant conquerors were moving south along this road; in 1944 a defeated army was moving north along it. There was also regular German and Polish civilian traffic, serving the towns and villages of the Lublin region. It is not easy to accept the idea of the daily traffic passing by, whilst the daily destruction and killing was so close.

Lublin itself is so near. When, in the days after the massacre, the bodies were burned, this was something that could not be hidden from the busy city. One SS man recalled: 'In Lublin itself it stank terribly for days. It was the typical smell of burned bodies. Anyone could imagine that a great number of Jews were burned in the camp at Majdanek.'

What a terrible place this camp is. We wander about, some staying near the pits, others going down the road alongside the Fields. Mike tells us: 'Some days, nobody comes here. Some days, coachloads come. Every October, a group of Jewish students, the "March of the Living", comes here. They gather from all over the world, visit Majdanek and Auschwitz, and then go on to Israel. It has become an annual pilgrimage.'

In Lublin, Mike tells us, there is still a 'hatred' of Germans. 'In 1989 a coachload of noisy German tourists came into a restaurant in Lublin. The entire restaurant got up and walked out.'

Between 300,000 and 350,000 people were murdered here in Majdanek over a period of three years. In ten months, at least twice that number were murdered in Belzec. In Belzec the victims were almost all Jews. Here in Majdanek there were many non-Jewish Poles as well, and also Soviet soldiers, prisoners-of-war who were brought here after the battles on the Eastern Front, and prisoners from eleven other countries. Of Majdanek's Russian prisoners-of-war, 99 per cent were murdered, as they were in so many prisoner-of-war camps which the Germans set up all over Poland (this is a story we shall hear again, in Piotrkow).

We walk down the hill to Field I. This is where the Soviet prisoners-of-war were held. One of the more grotesque methods of killing them was to hold a roll call in mid-winter, when the temperature was far below freezing, to hose them down, and to force them to stand in the open until they froze to death.

The fate of Soviet prisoners-of-war has been part of our journey. Only yesterday we were at the Borki execution site. In Zamosc, where we were two days ago, there were ten thousand Soviet prisoners-of-war in the Szwedzka Street camp in 1942. One winter day several thousand more Soviet prisoners-of-war in the Karolowka camp near Zamosc had the hose and cold water torture used against them. German fire trucks sprayed them with water in the evening; they were forced to remain in the open all night; and by morning they were all frozen to death. The German attitude was, 'Why waste bullets?'

We have reached the end of our journey around the camp. It has been hard to do more than to give the briefest outline of what it is we are looking at. Some stand a little way off, in silent thought. Others sit on the grass verge.

As we wait by the entrance to Field I, Paul prays by the pits.

10.42 a.m.

We leave Field I and walk slowly towards the administration building. A group of young Poles pass us, laughing and larking. The young men have shaven heads and are wearing braces. The young girls are in short skirts. One is holding a bouquet of flowers wrapped in silver foil. One of the young men is in battle fatigue trousers with his braces hanging down. One of the girls is wearing black hot pants.

Ben engages the youngsters in conversation. They are local school-children. The boys are studying structural engineering in the local technical school. They are, they say, the true 'skinheads', not the 'hooligans' who give Lublin a bad name. They have come here to visit the Catholic cemetery which has been built on a part of the former camp area. They want to lay the flowers on the grave of one of their gang, who was killed in a gang fight with the 'hooligans'. Their friend was wearing the Polish eagle symbol which is their badge, and which all the young men are wearing on their T-shirts. Their friend was killed by the 'hooligans'. He was twenty-seven years old.

Their motto, they say, is 'Poland for the Poles'. Their friend was killed by 'punks', by 'anarchists'. They themselves are the only true skinheads, and their goals are clear. 'We have problems with Gypsies, Japanese and Roumanians,' they tell us. 'Jews aren't a problem either – there aren't any. The Jewish cemetery in Markuszow was desecrated recently. That wasn't us. That was done by the "anarchists", not by us. We are skinheads.'

Caroline comments: 'We are lucky that there are no Gypsies in our group.'

They become eloquent in their own defence. 'Not every skinhead is a Fascist. We went to Auschwitz to pay our respects to the Poles who were killed there, or rather, we wanted to go – it was billed as a Skinhead Festival – but weren't allowed. But we are Poles. Why should we not be allowed to Auschwitz? Jews are allowed.

'There are a lot of skinheads here in Lublin. We are generally against the foreigners who come to the city. But we aren't against the Jews. There are not so many. We are nationalists. We are real skinheads. It is the pseudo-skinheads who are the Fascists. We are against Hitler. We have not painted up any swastikas on the walls.'

They listen attentively, and bemused, as Ben recites a saying he remembers from his childhood days:

> Who are you?
> I am a little Polish boy
> What is your sign?

Ben pauses. Without hesitation, and with a little grin, one of the girls finishes the refrain for him: 'The White Eagle.' It is an incredible connection across time.

11.15 a.m.
We board the bus and drive out of the camp and along the main road back into Lublin. From the main road the whole camp is laid out in front of us, below us. The crematorium chimney is a dark finger on the horizon.

11.17 a.m.
We pass on the left the original gatehouse that led into the camp from the west. Just beyond it was the commandant's house (from which the gas chamber at the entrance to the camp was visible).

11.30 a.m.
We reach the Hotel Unia, at No. 12 Raclawickie Avenue. Here we will rest, have a drink, and prepare for Mike's walking tour. I buy a detailed street map of Lublin, as well as Andrzej Trzcinski's extremely informative *A Guide to Jewish Lublin and Surroundings*, and his book *The Traces of Monuments of Jewish Culture in the Lublin Region*. The book is good, but it has an odd error: it explains that Jewish boys are circumcised on the first Saturday after their thirteenth birthday. It is in fact on the eighth day after their birth. A curious error, considering that Jews lived in the Lublin district for so many centuries. Caroline raises her eyebrows. It seems that not as much of their culture and ritual seeped through as might have done.

12.12 p.m.
We leave the hotel. Mike's wife Barbara (Basia) sings a Parczew partisan song. Robin records it on his tape recorder:

> In the Parczew forest
> Under the pine trees
> When the trees are blossoming
> A young soldier
> Rests in a grave
> Far from where his family is
> And his native land.

12.15 p.m.

We are on Idziego Radziszewskiego Street. During the period of the German occupation it was Reinhard-Heydrich-Strasse (after his assassination in Prague in 1942). In front of us is the Gestapo headquarters. Because of the small square clock on the top of the façade of the building, anybody in trouble was told, 'You are under the clock.' It is now a Polish army club building.

12.20 p.m.

We reach the former Nazi Party headquarters (Haus der NSDAP), on former Horst-Wessel-Strasse, a short street which we glimpsed last night, a pre-war building with fine columns. It is now a Polish army officers' club. In November 1944 the Polish Communist authorities held the first trial of Majdanek guards here (an earlier war crimes trial had been held by the Russians in Kharkov in 1943).

12.25 p.m.

We walk down Lipowa Street (Linden Strasse during the German occupation), to the Lipowa Street prisoner-of-war camp. This was originally a factory for the making of tar paper for roofing. It was turned into a camp for Jewish soldiers in the Polish army, captured on the battlefields in September 1939. Throughout the period of the camp's existence, Poles were allowed to walk in the street, as well as Germans.

At one point the prisoners here had a plan to break out, and to attack Globocnik's headquarters. Another group wanted to break out and run. Neither plan proved possible. The first commandant, Hermann Dolp, was sent to Belzec in 1940 to command the Jewish slave labour camps there, constructing anti-tank ditches. Later, on 28 October 1942, there was a successful escape from the Lipowa Street camp. It was led by one of the prisoners-of-war, Mietek Gruber. He, and the small group that got away with him, managed to reach the woods near Markuszow, north-west of Lublin, where they took under their protection Jews who had escaped from the village of Markuszow a few months earlier.

The wall at the entrance to the Lipowa Street camp survives. There is no plaque. The gatehouse (to the left of the entrance as we look at it from across the street) also survives. It is an ornate, three-storey pre-First World War building, with an impressive first-floor balcony. It is now a Roman Catholic funeral parlour.

12.30 p.m.

Almost opposite the prisoner-of-war camp is Lublin's main Roman Catholic cemetery. When Globocnik's assistant in Operation Reinhard, Hermann Höfle, was burying his infant twin daughters here (they died of diphtheria in 1943), he suddenly jumped into the grave and said, 'This is God's punishment for what I have done to the Jews.' Höfle killed himself in prison in Vienna in 1962 while awaiting trial for his crimes.

We continue through the streets of wartime German-occupied Lublin. At No. 29 Chopin Street (its name remained the same under the Germans) there is a long, grey, five-storey building which used to house the main depository of the Department for Confiscated Enemy Property. The household goods taken from Jewish homes, and the equipment taken from the Jewish hospital, were brought here to be sorted. The best things would go to the SS, the second-best to the Reich.

Today the building is the library of the Catholic University of Lublin.

Across the street is a building where, its plaque informs us, the Polish secret police operated from 1944 to 1953, and in which many of their victims were tortured.

We walk as far as the Krakowskie Przedmiescie (Krakauer Strasse in the German time) and across it, up Ewangelicka Street, to the Operation Reinhard headquarters, the front of which we saw last night when walking into town. It is an impressive building with a mass of office space behind it. Before the First World War it was a school. Before being handed over to Globocnik for Operation Reinhard at the end of 1941 it was renovated by the SS. Under Globocnik and Operation Reinhard it became the administrative office and administrative centre for the killings at Belzec, Sobibor and Treblinka. Today it is the Collegium Anatomicum medical college. Its postal address is No. 1 Spokojna Street (Quiet Street).

Across the road from the headquarters is No. 2 Spokojna Street. During the war years this was the main SS recreational compound in the city. Inside were located (the buildings are all intact today) a restaurant, two bars, a casino, a brothel and a cinema. It was, says Mike, 'a playground with a big fence around it'. The cinema is now a small self-governing college for mature students.[1]

We cross what was the SS compound and reach Wieniawska Street. During the German occupation it was named Von Mackensen Strasse,

---

[1] Six months after our visit it became a gun dealer's shop.

after one of the leading First World War generals – later one of Hitler's field marshals. A few yards down the hill, to the north, is a three-storey school building set back above the road in spacious grounds. We scramble up the bank and into the grounds. This building was the Operation Reinhard storage depot. Here, the gold teeth taken from the Jewish corpses, and other valuables taken from Jews, or from Jewish homes, were sorted. The man in charge of the work here was SS Major Georg Wippern, a former accountant who worked for the German army and then for the SS accountants' office. After the war he returned to Germany and became a senior customs inspector. He was arrested in 1960, but died before he could be put on trial.

We cross Wieniawska Street and go down a short side street, Boczna Lubomelskiej Street, to Globocnik's villa, a 1930s modern construction, quite elegant. The man who built the villa, shortly before the outbreak of war, was a local Pole; he was turned out by the Nazis to make room for Globocnik and had to live elsewhere. But after the war he returned, and he lives in the villa today. His son has recently built another villa next door.

We go on down Boczna Lubomelskiej Street to the large building at the end, in which Globocnik's special SS bodyguard regiment, Police Regiment 125, lived. They guarded Globocnik wherever he went, and also guarded Himmler when he came to the region. A full-sized swimming pool was built for the regiment in the basement. We also look at No. 3 Boczna Lubomelskiej Street, the villa in which the three heads of the 'Ghetto Clearance' Commando lived: Michalsen, Lerch and Claasen. Their task, once the Jews of Lublin had been deported, was to turn everything that the Jews had possessed into utility for the Reich.

1.30 p.m.
We return to Wieniawska Street. One whole block, Nos. 8–10, a five-storey pre-war residential building, arranged around an inner courtyard, was Globocnik's headquarters (as opposed to the Operation Reinhard office). He worked here in his capacity as SS and Police Leader of the Lublin District. On the ground floor today are a tourist office, a hairdresser, a 'baby centre', a butcher's shop and the Yuma coffee bar.

We cross the road and reach a small villa, No. 5 Wieniawska Street, in which Christian Wirth lived when he first came from Belzec to Lublin, for six months in 1942, before moving out to the more spacious villa on the road to Majdanek. It is now a photographic studio.

A drunk comes up and makes himself disagreeable. I remember last night's warning by a local in Lublin.

1.45 p.m.
We return on foot to the Hotel Unia.

2 p.m.
We board the minibus and set off out of Lublin. We pass the site of the Ogrodowa Street slave labour camp, and the sports stadium built there for the German army by the Jewish slave labourers. It is still a sports stadium.

To the west of the stadium was Roza Luxemburg Street. It is now named after the Father Jerzy Popieluszko, the Catholic priest murdered by the Communist secret police in October 1984.

2.03 p.m.
We drive along Tysiaclecia Avenue, along the River Czechowka, and look up at the city. An elegant palace on the slope – now the Lublin Ophthalmic Clinic – is where Globocnik interviewed Franz Stangl before appointing him commandant of Sobibor. Stangl recalled the 'view across the valley and the roofs of the little Jewish houses'. We can see those roofs as we drive along, but the Jews who once lived in them are gone, murdered by the likes of Globocnik and Stangl.

Also on the slope above us is the building used during the war by the administration of the Ostbahn (Generaldirektion der Ostbahn – known as 'Gedop' Lublin). From this building the deportation schedules had to be coordinated with military and civilian rail traffic. Baedeker's 1943 *Generalgouvernement* guide book gives full details of rail journeys available to travellers from Germany: Belzec appears in it as a railway station on the Lublin–Lvov line, though without any facilities (Auschwitz had a recommended hotel).

2.10 p.m.
Our bus takes the main highway that runs below the old castle wall. A main road and wide grass verges are now all that lie below the bastion. Four hundred years ago this area was the flourishing Jewish quarter of Podzamcze (Beneath the Castle). Right up against the outer bastion of the castle is the memorial plaque on the site of Lublin's oldest, medieval synagogue.

The first documented presence of Jews in Lublin dates from 1316. There is speculation, however, that Jews came, perhaps as traders, as early as the ninth century, when a trading settlement existed here. A large horde of silver coins of that period, minted in Muslim lands, and discovered during excavations in Lublin, point to a possible Jewish trading connection.

The Jewish quarter of which the ruins of the synagogue were a part, here below the castle wall, dates from the early sixteenth century. In 1507 the Polish records mention Aaron, 'medical doctor and rector of the Jewish school in Lublin'. In 1518 a Yeshiva was established here. A Polish royal decree later granted it the same rights as other schools of higher education in Poland. Its first rector (a title granted by the Polish king) was Szlomo ben Jechiel Luria, Lublin's most distinguished Jewish sage.

In 1552 a Jewish doctor of medicine, Jehuda Aaron, became the Chief Rabbi of the towns of Lublin, Belzyce and Chelm. We have already visited the two other towns under his religious jurisdiction, Belzec, the site of the death camp, and Chelm, the city of fools.

The synagogue on the road beneath the castle walls was built in 1567. Between 1581 and 1764 the supreme body of Polish and Lithuanian Jewry, the Council of the Four Lands, met regularly in the city (and also in Jaroslaw, which we visited when we drove from Cracow to Zamosc). Many of the Council's chairmen were Jews from Lublin.

In 1602 there were hundreds of Jewish houses in this area. Trade, commerce and learning led to a continual expansion of the Jewish town. Then troubles began: in 1648 the Jewish quarter was crowded with refugees from the Chmielnicki massacres in the east, many of whom died here of hunger. And worse was to come when, in 1655, Russian troops entered Lublin and set fire to the Jewish quarter. Two hundred houses were burned down, and as many as two thousand Jews were killed.

2.15 p.m.
We reach the Old Jewish Cemetery. A plaque above the entrance states (in Hebrew): 'Jewish Cemetery in Lublin, founded in the sixteenth century.' A Polish-language plaque adds: 'Closed for burials, the area is protected as a historic site.'

The cemetery gate is locked. The key is in the custody of a Lublin Jew, Honigman. He arrives and asks for payment to open the gate. I remember the inside from my visit in 1980, hilly, overgrown, with some isolated but impressive gravestones of the great rabbis of old. Several old tombstones have survived here, despite the ravages of time and war. The oldest, dated 1541, is the grave of a leading sixteenth-century Talmudist, Jaakov Kopelman ha-Levi, of whom the inscription on his headstone declares that he was 'expert in the wisdom contained in all the books'.

The tombstone of Szlomo ben Jechiel Luria – known by the Hebrew acronym of his name as the Maharshal – has also survived, albeit partially destroyed. It was once a place of pilgrimage for devout Polish Jews, like the grave of the Remu in Cracow. The Maharshal died in 1573. 'Here reposes the potentate of potentates,' declares the inscription, 'the king and teacher of all the sages.'

During the Second World War, the Germans brought many Jews here to the cemetery, and executed them.

2.37 p.m.

We drive up Lubartowska Street, the centre of pre-war Jewish life in Lublin, to an imposing pre-war building at the corner of Unicka Street. This was the great Lublin Yeshiva, the School of the Sages of Lublin (in Hebrew, Yeshivat Chochmei Lublin), established nineteen years before the outbreak of war in 1939. It is now the Medical Academy of the Catholic University of Lublin. Inside is a small reading room for Jewish visitors who come here.

As we stand in the grounds, looking up at the façade, with eight columns supporting the portico, I speak of the history of this remarkable building. The idea for a new and special Yeshiva here in Lublin was put forward in 1923 by Rabbi Meir Szapira, a leading Polish rabbinical authority and member of the Polish Parliament (the Sejm). He broached the scheme that year at a congress of Orthodox Jewish leaders in Vienna. His aim was to use the traditions of the sixteenth-century Lublin Yeshiva, and the Council of the Four Lands, in tune with the Jewish religious needs of the twentieth century. Money was raised from all over the world. Ben recalls how, before the war, his father gave money towards the building of this Yeshiva. It was intended to be a world centre of Jewish religious learning.

The land for the Yeshiva, which is set in wooded grounds, was given by a local Jew, Samuel Eichenbaum. The cornerstone was laid in May 1924. Thereafter, for five years, Rabbi Szapira travelled the Jewish world, including the United States, raising funds. Inauguration day was 24 June 1930. The main hall, with its balcony, was both a lecture room and the synagogue. It is now a film and lecture theatre. There was another hall that boasted a large-scale model of the Temple of Jerusalem. There was a library which, when the Yeshiva opened, already had 13,000 volumes. There was a dining room and kitchen, a bakery, a laundry, and student accommodation.

Rabbi Szapira died, at the young age of forty-seven, four months before the first graduates received their diplomas in February 1934. Having just accepted a position as rabbi of Lodz, he was preparing to go to Palestine, in order to set up a branch of the Lublin Yeshiva in Tel Aviv. A colourful personality, he was well known for the songs and melodies that he composed whilst dancing with his pupils. When he realised that he was dying he asked his students to dance and sing around his bed; while they were doing so, he breathed his last. His tombstone, in the new cemetery just to the north of here, survives to this day. But his remains, as he had wished, were eventually taken to Jerusalem and reburied there, in 1958.

Rabbi Szapira was succeeded as rector by Rabbi Arie Tzwi Fromer, who directed the work of the Yeshiva until July 1940, when the Germans closed it down. At that time the library had 22,000 books and 10,000 periodicals; all of them were confiscated. The equipment and fittings of the Yeshiva were taken out, to become part of the enormous mass of stolen property that was acquired by the Germans from the homes, shops and offices of the Jews of Lublin, and housed in the building we saw this morning.

2.45 p.m.

We walk a few yards down Lubartowska Street to the Jewish hospital, a handsome building built in Tsarist times, set back in a garden. It is no longer Jewish, but still a hospital.

Built in 1886, it had fifty-six beds. Under successive chief doctors it expanded; by 1930 it had a hundred beds. It was well known in Lublin, and beyond, for the quality of its medicine and its medical care. During the German occupation it continued to function, serving the Jews of the ghetto. Then, on 27 March 1942, at the time of the deportations from Lublin to Belzec, the most severely ill patients were taken to the Jewish cemetery and shot there. The other patients, as well as the doctors and nurses, were taken out of the city to the Niemce woods, and shot there.

3.05 p.m.

We continue down Lubartowska Street to Czwartek Street. A wall plaque in Polish and Yiddish marks the pre-war I. L. Peretz school building. It was intended to be the most modern school of its time. The opening was set for 3 September 1939. Invitations were sent out and a programme prepared. But two days before the ceremony was due to take place the German army invaded Poland, and, on September 2, Lublin was bombed. An era of hope, and many generations of pupils, would come to nothing.

After the war, those Lublin Jews who had survived gathered here, in this building, to make contact with their fellow-survivors, and create what they could of a communal self-help system.

Today the building, like almost all the pre-war Jewish communal buildings, houses a local Polish institution, in this case, the Institute of Labour Medicine and Rural Hygiene.

3.18 p.m.
We return to Unicka Street, where our minibus is waiting. Running north is Walecznych Street. Along it, on the right side, the wall of the new Jewish cemetery is visible. It was established in 1829, when this area was outside the city. The grave of Rabbi Meir Szapira is here, intact (many others were vandalised during and since the war). Today, the cemetery is maintained by the Sara and Manfred Frenkel Foundation of Antwerp. A monument for those Lublin Jews who were murdered here in the war (including the severely ill patients from the Jewish hospital a few hundred yards down the hill) was unveiled on 7 September 1947 by Lublin Jews who had survived the war. A second monument was unveiled on 9 November 1987.

3.20 p.m.
We rejoin the bus and return down Lubartowska Street.

3.25 p.m.
Mike and his wife leave us, near their home on the northern outskirts of Lublin.

3.27 p.m.
We reach the Lublin-Warsaw highway. A sign says that it is 157 kilometres to the capital.

3.55 p.m.
Markuszow. It was here, on 7 May 1942, that the Jewish Council warned all the Jews of the ghetto of an impending German 'action', and advised the community 'that every Jew who is able to save himself should do so'. Two days later, as the Germans were about to arrive to deport the community to Sobibor, four young Jews organised a mass

escape to the nearby woods. The names of the four were Shlomo Goldwasser, Mordechai Kirshenbaum, and the brothers Yeruham and Yaakov Gothelf. For five months the escapees hid in the nearby wood. In October, they were joined by a group of Jewish prisoners-of-war, led by Mietek Gruber, who had escaped from the Lipowa Street camp in Lublin. But then a massive German military operation, using tanks and aircraft, tracked them down – men, women and children – and all were killed.

The wood is clearly visible to the east.

There was a small slave labour camp in Markuszow. Of its 150 inmates – Jews, Poles and Czechs – forty-nine were shot.

As our minibus hurries along the highway, we talk of what we have seen: four terrible death camps in four days, Auschwitz, Belzec, Sobibor and Majdanek.

4.20 p.m.

Kurow. Another small town, all of whose Jews, more than a thousand, were deported, first to nearby Ryki, and then to Treblinka. In the local Catholic cemetery is a memorial to 700 non-Jewish inhabitants of Kurow who were murdered by the Nazis.

4.27 p.m.

Ryki. In 1941 Jews were brought to the ghetto established here from the nearby towns of Kurow, Pulawy, Garwolin and Zelechow. At the beginning of 1942 there arrived 2,500 Jews from Slovakia whom the independent Slovak government of Monsignor Tiso was glad to get rid of. On 7 May 1942 almost everyone in the ghetto was taken to Sobibor and killed. During the 'liquidation' of the ghetto in October 1942 the remaining Jews were taken to Treblinka and killed. A few able-bodied men were sent to slave labour camps.

The synagogue building remains, as in so many Polish towns. But there are no Jews to pray in it. One of the few survivors from Ryki, Shloime Judensznajder (now Solly Irving) lives in London. He was brought to England immediately after the war with the group of teenage survivors about whom I am writing a book.[2] I read out his recollections of his home town. 'I remember, as a very young lad,' he wrote to me, 'my father took me to see his Rabbi. Whilst at the station he bought me golden-coloured cherries and ever since I have felt a

---

[2] The book, *The Boys, Triumph over Adversity*, was published in Britain in October 1996, and in the United States in March 1997.

compulsion to buy golden cherries whenever I see them.

'Another pleasant memory I have is when my family moved into a brick house which seemed like a palace and was decorated, both inside and out, very colourfully in order to receive the Hassidic Rabbi who came to stay for several days and to bless our house. As in all towns, the Jewish population were of mixed professions. My father, together with his brother, were in the grain business. I remember accompanying my father once to the farmers where he used to buy grain. This was ground into flour in our mills. The majority of the non-Jewish population were farmers. My mother made wigs for the poor brides in our town.'

Of his immediate family – his parents and his four sisters – Solly Irving is the only survivor. As we drive on, we discuss the crucial importance of survivor testimony, not necessarily to establish facts, but to recapture the atmosphere of a vanished world.

4.47 p.m.

To the left of the road is a memorial to Colonel Berek Joselewicz, a Jew and a Polish patriot, who was killed in battle with the Austrians in 1809. In the Polish insurrection of 1794 he had commanded a detachment of Jewish volunteers. He was the first Jew to reach the rank of colonel in the Polish army. 'When I was a boy,' says Ben, 'the school I attended in Piotrkow was named after him. He was a hero to the boys and girls of the school. We revelled in his military prowess. But in his day, his military and secular activities led to him being excommunicated by the Jewish rabbinical authorities in Warsaw.'

4.50 p.m.

Along the grass verge at the side of the road, a horse and cart are going in our direction ... and another ... and another.

4.57 p.m.

Garwolin. Some Jews from this town made their way in September 1939 to the Russian border, and found safety across it. One of them was a young woman (Esther) who married one of Ben's cousins when she was in Russia.

From 1942 to 1944 there was a slave labour camp here, which held 4,000 Jewish prisoners. Among the Jews in the first deportation from Paris to Auschwitz was a Jew from Garwolin.

5 p.m.
We cross the River Wilga.

5.05 p.m.
There is a turning to Parysow. This is where Alec Ward, a friend of mine in Britain, was born. We stop just beyond the crossroads, having spotted a restaurant. No one has eaten since breakfast, and there have been understandable mutterings of dissatisfaction. The driver turns back to the crossroads, and we leave the minibus for the restaurant, the Ostoja (Resting Place).

As we wait to be served, I read from Alec Ward's childhood recollection of Parysow. 'On Friday afternoon,' he wrote, 'the Jewish town crier proclaimed the coming of the Sabbath and announced it was time to go to the synagogue. On Saturday afternoon the whole Jewish community seemed to walk in the streets. On Purim people were criss-crossing the streets with presents consisting of freshly baked cakes and biscuits. On Yom Kippur, in the ladies' part of the synagogue, one could hear a great amount of crying. On Simchat Torah there was great rejoicing by the whole community, and on Passover we wore our new clothes of which we were so proud.'

5.15 p.m.
In the Ostoja restaurant Caroline reflects on Lublin: 'An utterly unattractive town.' The drab emptiness of the former Jewish quarter was depressing. It was hard to populate it, in the imagination, with the sort of life that Alec Ward recalled in his home town, the vibrant life of Polish Jewry down the ages – until this age.

6.05 p.m.
We leave the restaurant and continue driving towards Warsaw.

6.25 p.m.
To our left, between us and the River Vistula, is the town of Otwock. Here Jews came every summer to live amid pastoral scenery. It was a place of holidays and relaxation.

It was from Otwock, in April 1942, that 160 young people were sent to a remote forest area near the River Bug, and made to prepare the site of a camp that was to become another Sobibor and Belzec. The name of the nearest village and its railway halt was Treblinka. After three weeks of hard labour, only thirty-eight of these youngsters from Otwock were still alive. An equal number of German Jews, who had originally been deported to Warsaw, and whom the Warsaw ghetto historian Emanuel Ringelblum called 'the cream of the young people', were also sent to help prepare the new camp. Almost all of them also died while working.

6.40 p.m.
We reach the main Warsaw–Brest–Litovsk road – the road to Minsk and Moscow – and turn westward.

7 p.m.
Wawer. A suburb of Warsaw. Here, on 27 December 1939, as a reprisal for two German policemen who were shot in a local tavern, the Germans executed 114 residents. Among those shot were at least eight Jews.

7.15 p.m.
We cross the River Vistula and enter Warsaw. I give a brief summary of the Jewish history before the Holocaust. Warsaw's Jewish community dated back to the fifteenth century. In the 1931 census there were 352,697 Jews living here, almost a third of the total population. Then, it was the second-largest Jewish community in the world. The largest was in New York.

7.25 p.m.
We reach our hotel, the Hotel Harctur, in Niemcewicza Street. It is a former students' hostel. Distribution of keys (this duty always falls to me, as the 'tour leader'). We will meet in the lobby in an hour.

8.40 p.m.
We leave the hotel and walk into Warsaw. As it is Friday night, and the Sabbath has begun, Paul and Caroline will not ride; we walk with them. Various people break off into different groups, depending on their pace. We agree to meet at the monument in Castle Square, at the entrance to the Old Town.

9.05 p.m.
We reach the Jewish Theatre. In 1968 I went to a performance of a Yiddish comedy here.

9.16 p.m.
The Unknown Soldier memorial. This now has (as in 1980 it emphatically did not have) the battle honours and sacrifices which the Communist regime refused to recognise, among them the Battle of Alamein, the Warsaw Ghetto revolt (Getto Warszawskie), the Polish uprising, and the Katyn massacre (the Soviet murder of thousands of Polish officers, prisoners-of-war, many of them Jews).

9.30 p.m.
Castle Square.

9.35 p.m.
We find a restaurant in the Old Town square, and settle down to our evening meal. Ben sits at the head of the table. A portrait of Napoleon looks down on him. Like Napoleon, he is small in stature, and like Napoleon, he is a sturdy and determined leader.

10.35 p.m.
Paul arrives, having been to synagogue. He reports that a group of Israeli girls were singing Sabbath songs.

10.40 p.m.
The borscht arrives.

There is some discussion about the rebuilding and repairing of the barracks at Majdanek. Ros and Jon are particularly upset by it.

The starkness of Belzec and Sobibor was overwhelming. Majdanek, despite the rebuilding, had a sinister air about it.

12.30 a.m.
We leave the restaurant, and walk back through part of the former ghetto area (Twarda Street) to our hotel.

A light drizzle accompanies us as we walk through the night. Angela reflects on how close the villages and towns were to most of the camp sites we have seen. Auschwitz-Birkenau was adjacent to a large town and on a main railway line (Vienna–Cracow). Belzec camp was close to a large village and also on a main railway line (Warsaw–Lvov). Majdanek was on the outskirts of a large town, its killing field and crematorium chimney visible from the nearest houses. The Lipowa Street prisoner-of-war camp was in the very centre of a large town, on a street that Poles were allowed to walk on as well as Germans. Only Sobibor camp was truly remote. Its railway line was built specially to service the camp. Only after the war did it become a regular passenger line (a train drew in just after we arrived). Treblinka, which we will see in two days' time, was also built in a remote area.

1.30 a.m.
We reach the hotel, and go straight to bed, more than eighteen hours after waking up in Lublin.

DAY 11

WARSAW

The largest Jewish population after New York – no more

7.25 a.m.
Wake up.

7.35 a.m.
Sort through my notes for today, and begin work on the readings.

8.30 a.m.
My friend Jan Hoser arrives for breakfast. He will stay with us all day. I first met him in 1957, when I was travelling through Poland on a student exchange. We have remained good friends ever since, and meet each time I come back to Warsaw.

9.15 a.m.
At each town in which we have stopped, I have distributed maps and town plans. I do so again as we gather in the lobby.

9.30 a.m.
We leave the hotel. It is raining, and the streets are awash with puddles. We make our way along Twarda Street to the centre of town. Our journey takes us to the Old Town through a wealth of historical points.

Our first stop is a courtyard behind No. 62 Zlota Street. Here are the remains of the original ghetto wall, erected on 15 November 1940. The area of the ghetto was later restricted, so that this part of the wall lay outside the ghetto after 20 November 1941; hence it survived the destruction of almost every stone of the ghetto in 1943.

The portion of the wall that has survived here is two storeys high. A plaque on the wall reproduces a map of the ghetto and tells its story.

Nearby, where the surviving wall ends, stones have been laid in the pavement where it used to run, with the words: 'Tu byl mur getta' (Here was the wall of the ghetto).

Today, television aerials rise above the top of the wall.

We walk to Sienna Street, to the former Jewish children's hospital at No. 60, a handsome building in classical style. It was opened on 28 June 1878. As the funding came from a wealthy Warsaw Jew, Mejer Berson, and his daughter Paulina Bauman, it was known for many years as Berson's and Bauman's Hospital. Jewish children with infectious diseases were admitted here free of charge. The hospital also had an ambulatory section that treated children of all denominations. Janusz Korczak, the Jewish educator and orphanage director who went to Treblinka with his orphans, worked here for many years.

In 1923 the hospital was closed down through lack of funds, but was reopened a few years later. After November 1941 it was inside the boundary of the ghetto. On 10 August 1942 all the children, doctors and nurses were ordered out and taken to a building at the corner of Leszno and Zelazna Streets, then to a building by the railway sidings in Stawki Street (itself a former hospital) where they were held until being deported to Treblinka, and their deaths.

Since 1952, this building at No. 60 Sienna Street has been an isolation hospital, also for children.

We walk eastward along Twarda Street to Grzybowski Place. Two surviving pre-war buildings remain on the eastern side of the Place, dating from 1880 to 1890. They still have the battered appearance of buildings that have been much shelled and damaged, but never blown up, and have somehow held themselves together. One of them, No. 9 Prozna Street, belonged to Zalman Nozyk, the founder of the Nozyk Synagogue. In typical Warsaw-Jewish fashion, the ground floors of both these houses were shops: one shop here was an ironware shop, the other sold sewing-machine belts.

Grzybowski Place was once one of the busiest Jewish squares in the city. Here, on 15 October 1904, there was a mass demonstration of Jewish workers, protesting against the pogrom in Bialystok in which as many as a hundred Jews were killed. It was a demonstration which in many ways presaged the Russian Revolution of 1905.

As we stand in the rain, I read the account of Jewish life here, as recalled by Isaac Bashevis Singer in his novel *The Family Moskat*: 'The carriage turned into Grzybow Place and abruptly everything changed. The sidewalks were crowded with gaberdined Jews wearing small cloth caps, and bewigged women with shawls over their heads. Even the smells were different now. There was a whiff of the market place in the air – spoiled fruits, lemons, and a mixture of something sweetish and tarry, which could not be given a name and which impinged on the senses only when one returned to the scene after a longish absence.

'The street was a bedlam of sound and activity. Street peddlers called out their wares in ear-piercing chants – potato cakes, hot chick peas, apples, pears, Hungarian plums, black and white grapes, watermelon whole and in sections. Although the evening was warm, the merchants wore outer coats, with large leather money pouches hanging from the belts. Women hucksters sat on boxes, benches and doorsills. The stalls were lighted with lanterns, some with flickering candles stuck on the edges of wooden crates. Customers lifted and pinched the fruits or took little exploratory nibbles, smacking their lips to savour the taste. The stall-keepers weighed purchases on tin scales.

'"Gold, gold, gold!" a beshawled woman shouted from beside a crate of squashed oranges.

'"Sugar-sweet, sugar-sweet!" sang out a plump girl guarding a basket of mouldy plums.

'"Wine, wine, wine!" shrieked a red-faced, red-headed peddler, displaying a basket of spoiled grapes. "Nab 'em, grab 'em! Nuzzle 'em, guzzle 'em! Try 'em, buy 'em!"

'In the middle of the street, truckmen guided overloaded wagons. The heavy, low-slung horses stamped their iron-shod hoofs on the cobbles, sending out sparks. A porter wearing a hat with a brass badge carried an enormous basket of coal strapped to his shoulders with thick rope. A janitor in an oil-cloth cap and blue apron was sweeping a square of pavement with a long broom. Youngsters, their little lovelocks flapping under octagonal caps, were pouring out of the doors of the Hebrew schools, their patched pants peeping out from between the skirts of their long coats. A boy with a cap pulled low over his eyes was selling New Year calendars, shouting at the top of his voice. A ragged youth with a pair of frightened eyes and dishevelled earlocks stood near a box of prayer shawls, phylacteries, prayerbooks, tin Chanukah candle-sticks, and amulets for pregnant women. A dwarf with an over-sized head wandered about with a bundle of leather whips, fanning the straps back and forth, demonstrating how to whip stubborn children. On a stall lit by a carbide lamp lay piles of Yiddish newspapers, cheap novelettes, and books on palmistry and phrenology. Reb Meshulam glanced out of the window of the carriage and observed: "The Land of Israel, eh?"

'"Why do they go around in such rags?" Adele asked, grimacing.

' "That's the custom here," Reb Meshulam answered with a show of impatience ...'

What a contrast Singer's description is with the empty, grey, almost silent Grzybowski Place today. We walk across it, to the western side. After the war, a Jewish theatre was built on the site of the destroyed houses here. It is a centre of Jewish communal life today, for the two or three thousand Jews who live in Warsaw. We are invited in, to see the impressive interior.

There is an exhibition inside of photographs of pre-war Warsaw Jewry. One of the posters for it faces the street. It shows a young couple sitting together at a table (he with glasses) and the caption: 'I ciagle widze ich twarze.' (I keep seeing their faces.)

We walk on a few yards to the Nozyk Synagogue. Its address is No. 6 Twarda Street. A plaque tells the passer-by that it was founded in 1900, by Zalman ben Menasze Nozyk, who died in 1903 (and whose house we have just seen), and his wife Rywka bat Mosze, who died in 1914. In his will, Zalman Nozyk left funds for the upkeep of the synagogue, stating that it should at all times bear his name and that of his wife.

The synagogue building survived the war, being taken over by the Germans and used as a stables, and a store for food. It was much damaged during the Warsaw uprising of August 1944, but was still recognisably a synagogue. It was partly restored in 1945 to serve the religious needs of the few survivors who returned to Warsaw. Detailed restoration began in 1977, and on 19 April 1983, the fiftieth anniversary of the Warsaw ghetto revolt, the first service was held in the restored building. Jews from all over the world participated. Ben was among them. 'It was a very moving occasion,' he recalls. 'Jews and Catholics, rabbis and the Archbishop of Warsaw, sat next to each other, an event that had rarely occurred before.'

Today there are services in the Nozyk Synagogue every Friday night and on Saturday. Indeed, even as we look at the outside of the building, Paul is inside it, praying.

We walk along Twarda Street, crossing the wide ONZ Rondo (United Nations Roundabout) to the older buildings on the far (western) side, to No. 28 Twarda Street. This is known as the Osnos House. It was bought in 1912 by a Jewish merchant, Leo Osnos, who renovated it, and joined it on to the house at No. 1 Ciepla Street. We walk into the courtyard, the walls of which soar above us for five storeys, windows facing windows across the yard. It was here, Jan Jagielski and Robert Pasieczny record in their book *A*

Guide to Jewish Warsaw (my essential companion today), that were to be found 'Grubsztajn's slaughter house, the Lepman and Rep meat shop, Widerszpal's foodstore, Merder's dairy products shop, the bakery of Fresz, Lustman's soap factory, Geller's barbershop, Borensztajn's laundry, Fetman's wine store'.

Ben comments: 'Imagine the smells, not all of them perfumes, in this narrow alley, the incessant coming and going of customers, and the ubiquitous noise and hustle and bustle that were so characteristic of the time.'

When the ghetto was established, No. 28 Twarda Street was at its very edge, bordering a thin finger taken out of the ghetto area by the Germans in order to enable production and distribution of beer to continue at the Haberbusch and Schiele brewery.

Leaving the Osnos House, we pass in the street a small van bearing the company name 'Alamein Security'. Twenty years ago Alamein, in the North African desert, where the Polish army fought in 1942, was a 'non-place' to the Communist regime, which did not recognise the activities of any Polish soldiers outside the Soviet orbit. Now Alamein is inscribed on the battle honours of the Unknown Soldier's memorial here in Warsaw, and on this car.

We walk on to I. L. Peretz's house (we were in his birthplace, Zamosc, two days ago) at what is now No. 1 Perec Street (it was formerly Cegalna Street). One of the most influential Yiddish writers, he was employed from 1866 by the Warsaw Jewish community. His grave can be seen to this day in the Warsaw Jewish cemetery (which we will try to visit tomorrow morning on our way out of the city). His is plot 44, row 1.

We walk on to Chlodna Street. The house at No. 20 is where Adam Czerniakow lived. When, on 22 July 1942, as Chairman of the Jewish Council, he was ordered by the Germans to prepare daily lists of Jews for deportation, he at first complied. I read from his diary, where he describes how the Germans had assured him that 'only' 20,000 Jews in all would be deported, mostly recent arrivals in the ghetto from Germany and Czechoslovakia. Then the Germans increased their demand to 6,000, and then to 7,000 a day. 'When I asked for the number of days per week in which the operation would be carried out,' Czerniakow wrote in his diary on 23 July 1942, 'the number was seven days a week.' Later that day he wrote again: 'It is three o'clock. So far, four thousand are ready to go. The orders are that there must be nine thousand by four o'clock.' And a little later he added: 'They demand of me to kill the children of my nation with my own hands.

There is nothing left for me but to die.' Czerniakow killed himself rather than comply.

We move on to No. 8 Chlodna Street. This was the headquarters of the Warsaw Yiddish daily newspaper, *Haynt*. Near here was the house, destroyed in the war, where a Polish doctor, Professor Raszeja, was killed by the Germans after he had secretly and illegally entered the ghetto on 22 July 1942 to give medical help to a sick Jewish child.

From Chlodna Street we come, still in driving rain, to the site of the bridge that linked the two parts of the ghetto, crossing, in those days, a busy, tram-filled street. The tramlines have been preserved as a memorial. On either side, where modern blocks of flats rise twelve storeys, was once the ghetto, levelled to the ground by the Nazis after the ghetto uprising. All that survives is the church that lay in the centre of the avenue (Elektoralna Street).

From there, we walk along Zelazna Street, to No. 103. At the time of the ghetto, this was the headquarters of the Befehlstelle, the German SS police unit which organised the deportations from Warsaw to Treblinka. A plaque on the building records that thousands of Jews were shot, and many tortured to death, in the cellar.

As the rain continues, it is hard to read aloud to the group, or even to keep them together. It is also very cold. We go down Ogrodowa Street to No. 9. This was the house in which Jozef Lewartowski lived; a member of the Central Committee of the Communist Party of Poland, and a Jew, he was active within the ghetto in urging preparations for resistance, but was caught by the Gestapo in September 1942, and killed.

We walk on to Marchlewskiego Street, cross the street, and continue to a cinema on the south side of Solidarity Avenue, at No. 115. In the ghetto period the address was No. 35 Leszno Street, a place of entertainment and concert hall, the Femina musical theatre: before the war, and now again, the Femina cinema. In the ghetto period, operettas and plays were performed. The ghetto's Jewish Symphony Orchestra also gave concerts here, conducted by Szymon Pulman. 'Everyone in the dark auditorium sat still, profoundly moved,' recalled Janina Bauman of one such concert. 'Then an eighteen-year-old girl sang *Ave Maria* by Schubert. She had a strong, clear voice that seemed to burst through the walls of the hall and rise high above our world with all its daily troubles. The audience cried, and I cried myself.'

In his diary, Adam Czerniakow recorded on 5 May 1942: 'It is Jewish Child's Day. I saw a performance in Femina played by children from schools financed by the Jewish Council.'

In 1987, as a memorial to those who had performed here forty-five years earlier, or had attended concerts here – on the eve of their deportation to death – a late-night concert was performed by the Israel Philharmonic Orchestra, with the violinist Itzhak Perlman.

12.30 p.m.
We walk down Solidarity Avenue (formerly Leszno Street), passing the remnant of a brick wall, standing by itself in the middle of the pavement, planted around with white flowers. A plaque records that this was the wall against which thirty Poles were executed on 26 October 1942. Jan points out that there were many such public executions of Poles at that time, to impress on the population the reality of German power.

12.32 p.m.
We pass the Church of the Virgin Mary on Solidarity Street. During the war, the priest of this church, Seweryn Poplawski, smuggled Jewish children from the Ghetto to safety through the church basement.

The whole north side of this street was within the ghetto. After the ghetto was destroyed, it was reduced, like the rest of the ghetto, to deep rubble. When the war ended, it proved impossible to clear away such a vast amount of rubble – the destroyed brick- and stonework of hundreds of thousands of buildings. The new apartment blocks that were built on the site were therefore erected on a foundation of compacted rubble, its base three feet above the former ground level. As a result, they are higher than the rest of Warsaw, and here, in Solidarity Street, one can see the 'embankment' of rubble (now a grassy verge) on which the whole area stands. It takes eight steps to get to the new ground level.

12.38 p.m.
In pouring rain, we reach Tlomackie Street and the site of the Great Synagogue. Nothing remains of it. It was completed in 1878 and could accommodate 3,000 worshippers in the main body of the synagogue. It also had rooms for the community's religious archives, a library and a religious school. Central heating was installed, with the very latest in radiators spreading heat throughout the building. 'Large and pleasant basements,' one contemporary wrote, 'stretching under the synagogue, are to be rented to private individuals – the community will raise revenue that way.'

The Great Synagogue was blown up by the Germans on 16 May

1943. It was said at the time that a curse had been put on the site. While construction work was taking place in the 1970s and 1980s great difficulties were experienced and many mishaps occurred. Today there is a high-rise building on the site.

12.42 p.m.

We reach Nos. 3–5 Tlomackie Street, the building that faced the Great Synagogue. Before the war it housed both the Main Judaic Library and the Institute of Judaic Studies. The building survived the Second World War almost intact. Construction began in 1928 and the building was formally opened on 1 April 1936. This was one of thousands of buildings throughout Poland which typified the creative energy – cultural, literary, historical, scientific – of Polish Jewry before the war. Some of its rooms were used by the library, and others by the Institute of Judaic Studies, which had been established in Warsaw in 1928. Its task was educating rabbis and secondary-school teachers in Jewish history. Among those who lectured here were the historians and teachers whom I consider somehow to be my predecessors: Dr Majer Balaban, Professor Moses Schorr and Dr Ignacy Schipper. Each of them perished in the war.

There were 30,000 volumes in the library when war broke out. They were taken away by the Germans within three months of the occupation of Warsaw.

With the establishment of the ghetto in November 1941, the work of the charitable organisation Jewish Social Self-Help was organised from here. At its centre was Dr Emanuel Ringelblum, one of the finest of the Jewish historians in inter-war Poland. He made an enormous effort to collect diaries and archival material of the German occupation, not only from the Jews of Warsaw, but from all over Poland. This archive was hidden in milk churns and buried; much of it was recovered after the war. It is kept in this building, which, since May 1947, has been the Jewish Historical Institute. It was from here, fifteen years ago, that I obtained the full text of the notes made by Yakov Grojanowski, immediately after his escape from the death camp at Chelmno in January 1942. We plan to be at Chelmno the day after tomorrow.

12.45 p.m.

It is still pouring with rain. We walk towards the Old Town, reaching the eastern edge of the ghetto and walking towards Dluga Street. There are many sites in this area from the period of the Polish uprising of 1944. All around us were the strongpoints of Polish resistance during the 1944 uprising. 'Here,' says Jan, 'was the fiercest fighting. Every brick was defended.'

The uprising of 1944 had broken out just to the west of the ghetto ruins. To attack the fighters on the edge of the Old Town, the Germans had to work their way forward over the rubble of the ghetto. Jan speaks bitterly of how, as the Germans advanced, they killed all the wounded soldiers and civilians whom they found in the many makeshift casualty stations. He was a young boy, and has many memories of the savagery of those times. His mother, a Polish patriot, was deported to Auschwitz.

12.48 p.m.
We pass a plaque to a group of Polish scouts murdered on 6 March 1943, just before the ghetto uprising. Warsaw is a city of wall plaques and memorials. It is often forgotten that as well as the 3,000,000 Polish Jews who were murdered by the Nazis, 3,000,000 Polish non-Jews were also killed. Walking through Warsaw with Jan, especially here at the edge of the ghetto, one has a sense of these Polish victims of German barbarity. Jews and Poles, having lived side by side for so many years, so many centuries, not always in harmony, were suddenly both under attack. But the Poles did not always feel a sense of identification strong enough to join forces with the Jews, or even to give them arms and ammunition when they resisted the German deportation 'actions'.

German reprisals against Poles, as we discussed at Wawer yesterday evening, were savage.

12.50 p.m.
Another memorial plaque. This one is at the site of a redoubt held by the Polish insurgents along the eastern edge of the former ghetto area, and destroyed by the German Air Force on 31 August 1944.

The redoubt borders on what used to be Nalewki Street. In 1940 it lay just outside the ghetto wall, although, before the Second World War (indeed, before both world wars), it was one of the centres of Jewish Warsaw, a place of intense street trading, with innumerable clothes shops – underwear was a speciality – and factories and workshops. There were three hotels on the street (the Wenecki, the Handlowy and the Londynski), and several dozen sweet shops, cafés and tea houses. It was also a street noted for the bustle of pedlars and negotiators of all sorts, crooks and prostitutes among them. There was a saying: 'Everything was here – and a little bit more.'

A new street now stands on what was once Nalewki Street. In honour of the ghetto uprising it has been given the name Bohaterow Getta (Ghetto Fighters).

I tell the group about a discussion I had twenty years ago with Professor J. L. Talmon – an outstanding scholar, and the author of a three-volume study of totalitarianism – who lived in Warsaw before the war, and who later taught, and died, in Jerusalem. He was greatly concerned that the focus on the Holocaust in Jewish teaching, important though that clearly was, was already, two decades ago, beginning to overshadow the story of the creativity, life, zeal, energy, struggle and achievement of Polish Jewry before the Holocaust. He so wanted the story of inter-war Warsaw-Jewish life not only to be researched and told, but to become an integral part of Jewish teaching and knowledge.

1.05 p.m.
We reach the monument to the Polish uprising of August 1944. It is on the spot of one of the sewer entrances into which the insurgents tried to make their escape. When it was unveiled, it caused great controversy. Because of its heavy style, it is known to the Poles as 'The Wehrmacht monument'. Jan recalls 'an unbelievable quarrel about it: how to change it, how to remove it, even how to destroy it'.

1.30 p.m.
We find a restaurant in the Old Town where we can all sit at a large round table. Yesterday's journey is very much on everyone's mind. We discuss the large concrete monument at Majdanek. I felt it was too bulky, too heavy. Ros found it very powerful. Jon feels it makes an impact – the weight of memory. Those who drive by on the road, even if they do not enter the camp, will see it and ask what it is.

Ros and Jon discuss whether the impact is more or less when one visits a second time. Jon has been to Birkenau four times now, and feels the impact less. I say that I have found the impact greater, through the added knowledge of details, of documents, of individual stories and of memoirs. When I first visited Birkenau, in 1957, I knew so little; even in 1980 there were still areas of the story that I did not know.

Jan tells us about the Polish skinhead movement (some of whose representatives we met yesterday morning at Majdanek). The now ageing head of the skinhead movement in Poland, Benek Tejkowski, was once – thirty years ago – a student leader active in the Communist

Party in Cracow. Later, he studied engineering with Jan. Then they had studied sociology together. After that they broke off all contact. 'He is dangerous, because some people believe in him,' Jan says. 'He attacks anything that he can call quasi-Jewish or quasi-Liberal.' Today, he is banned from appearing on television. 'He is outlawed, but still he has got some understanding with skinheads.'

2.25 p.m.
Angela shows me a fax she has received from her father. It turns out that her mother's mother, who is now over seventy, recalls that her grandparents lived in the town of Belchatow. Their names were Joseph Hanich and Fradel Klug. They lived opposite the chemist shop. During the German occupation, they were shot dead in the street.

This fax reached Angela last night. 'Suddenly the horrors of the Holocaust moved one step closer,' she said. 'What else had I not been told? How many of my family were gassed? It took some time for it to sink in.'

Angela hopes to make an extra journey to Belchatow. We will be spending tomorrow night near there.

2.30 p.m.
We cross the Old Town Square to the museum.

3.30 p.m.
A walk with Jan, Robin, Herut, Ben and Paul through the Old Town. Paul spent the morning in synagogue. Others of the group have been tempted by the prospect of watching the England–Spain European Cup football quarter-final to stay in the centre of town.

3.45 p.m.
We pass some graffiti: a Star of David hanging from a gallows. It is next to an advertisement for a new Bryan Adams rock album. A few doors on is a Jewish restaurant, Pod Samsonem (Samson's Place), which opened in 1958, the year before my own first visit to Warsaw. There are seats outside, but as it is raining we hurry by.

3.50 p.m.
We reach the old Mint. Here, during the Polish uprising in August 1944 – in which more than a thousand Jews also participated – survivors of the ghetto uprising sixteen months earlier – the insurgents tried to block the German route to the Vistula. They also hoped to

impede German rail traffic on the line just to the north, the very line that had been the main deportation line to Treblinka two years before.

The siege of the Mint lasted a month. Two thousand Poles were killed here. Some managed to break out down to the river.

4.08 p.m.

Walking along Konwiktorska Street, we reach the corner of Bonifraterska. Facing us is Muranowska Avenue, which was inside the ghetto. The ghetto wall ran along the middle of Bonifraterska Street. In the middle of Muranowska Avenue is a monument to Soviet aggression. It commemorates a black day for Poland, 17 September 1939, and was unveiled on 17 September 1995, the fifty-sixth anniversary of the Nazi–Soviet partition of Poland, and of the first deportation of Poles to Soviet slave labour camps. The monument, which honours more than a million dead, is a railway wagon with more than a hundred crosses rising from it like people crowded together, and a Jewish gravestone with a Star of David, and a dozen clutching hands.

There were two main deportation phases of Poles by the Soviets. The first was in the early months of 1941, when as many as a million Poles in the Russian-annexed area of eastern Poland were deported to Soviet Siberia and Central Asia. The second was in 1944, after the entry of Soviet forces into Poland as liberators, when members of the Polish resistance forces loyal to the Polish government-in-exile in London, the Armia Krajowa, were arrested and deported to the Soviet Union. There were also mass killings of Armia Krajowa members in the area of Vilna (which had been incorporated into the Soviet Union).

The Katyn massacre is also commemorated here: the murder of tens of thousand of Polish officers who had been captured by the Russians, or overrun by them in eastern Poland in September 1939, held in three prisoner-of-war camps, one of which was at Katyn, near Smolensk, and then murdered eight months later. Throughout the Communist era, the Soviet Union strenuously denied that it had been responsible for the massacre, and blamed the Germans. Only in 1989 was Katyn admitted – by a Joint Polish–Soviet Historical Commission set up by Mikhail Gorbachev – as a Soviet crime. The names of the three mass murder sites are now inscribed on the Polish Unknown Soldier's memorial.

Katyn is also one of the names written at this monument, on a series of metal railway sleepers, each of which has on it the name of a place in which Poles were killed by Russians, including the Lubyanka prison in Moscow.

I speak briefly of the Jews who were also killed at Katyn. They, too, were Polish officers, most of them captains in the army medical service. Some of them were army surgeons of the highest calibre, leading members of the Polish medical profession between the wars. While serving in the Polish army, they were captured with the units in which they served, and taken from their prisoner-of-war camps to be killed – at Starobielsk and Ostashkov as well as Katyn – alongside their fellow-Polish officers. Stalin had wanted the Polish intelligentsia to be wiped out. He made no distinction between non-Jew and Jew.

A list of the Jewish officers murdered at Katyn, Starobielsk and Ostashkov – 427 in all – has been published by Louis Falstein in 1963, and, incorporating former Soviet archives, by Benjamin Meirtchak in 1996. Those murdered include pharmacologists, oculists, dermatologists, laryngologists, obstetricians, psychiatrists – and medical students. I read out the names of some of the murdered men: Maurycy Epstein, an orthopaedic surgeon from Cracow, who was fifty-seven when he was killed; Albert Goldberg, a veterinarian from Warsaw; Jozef Rubisch, a dental surgeon from Rzeszow; Samuel Rozen, a surgeon from Lublin; Aleksander Oberlender, a dermatologist from Tarnow; and Jozef Mozes Szulman, a general practitioner from Tomaszow Lubelski – all towns that we have visited or driven through. We speak, as we often do, of the importance of names, and of the need to record them. But in most cases so little is known beyond the name; so little of the careers and characters and potential of those who were destroyed.

4.25 p.m.
As we walk through what was once the northern section of the ghetto, Ben comments: 'In 1955, as the massive, twenty-year task of rebuilding Warsaw reached the ghetto area, the Poles wanted to leave the ruins of the ghetto intact, as a lasting memorial of man's inhumanity to man. It was a fine ideal, but unfortunately impractical. The Poles needed to rebuild their capital, almost all of which lay in ruins. So they began to build over the whole area. There are almost no old buildings left of a world that is itself no longer. What we see today – block after block of identical, dull apartment buildings – obliterates the memory of a vibrant life. Only the street names give an inkling of the past.'

4.30 p.m.
In 1988 several of the streets leading to the Umschlagplatz were designated Trakt Pamieci (Memory Lane). Along them have been set

low stone (or basalt) blocks giving details of someone who was deported to Treblinka.

We reach the Korczak stone. I read out Janusz Korczak's ten numbered notes from his diary, dated 4 August 1942, written in the orphanage in the ghetto where, with his adult helpers, among them his close friend Esterka – who with his encouragement had escaped from the ghetto but been caught – he struggled to maintain such health and morale as was possible amid so much suffering and starvation:

1

I have watered the flowers, the poor orphanage plants, the plants of the Jewish orphanage. The parched soil breathed with relief.

A guard watched me as I worked. Does that peaceful work of mine at six o'clock in the morning annoy him or move him?

He stands looking on, his legs wide apart.

2

All the efforts to get Esterka released have come to nothing. I was not quite sure whether in the event of success I should be doing her a favour or harm her.

'Where did she get caught?' somebody asks.

Perhaps it is not she but we who have got caught (having stayed).

3

I have written to the police to send Adzio away: he's mentally under-developed and maliciously undisciplined. We cannot afford to expose the house to the danger of his outbursts. (Collective responsibility.)

4

For Dzielna Street – a ton of coal, for the present to Rózia Abramowicz. Someone asks whether the coal will be safe there.

In reply – a smile.

5

A cloudy morning. Five thirty.

Seemingly an ordinary beginning of a day. I say to Hanna:

'Good morning!'

In response, a look of surprise.

I plead:

'Smile.'

They are ill, pale, lung-sick smiles.

6

You drank, and plenty, gentlemen officers, you relished your drinking –
here's to the blood you've shed – and dancing you jingled your medals to
cheer the infamy which you were too blind to see, or rather pretended not
to see.

7

My share in the Japanese war. Defeat – disaster.
In the European war – defeat – disaster.
In the World War ...
I don't know how and what a soldier of a victorious army feels.

8

The publications to which I contributed were usually closed down,
suspended, went bankrupt.
My publisher, ruined, committed suicide.
And all this not because I'm a Jew but because I was born in the East.
It might be a sad consolation that the haughty West also is not well off.
It might be but is not. I never wish anyone ill. I cannot. I don't know
how it's done.

9

'Our Father who art in heaven ...'
This prayer was carved out of hunger and misery.
Our daily bread.
Bread.
Why, what I'm experiencing did happen. It happened.
They sold their belongings – for a litre of lamp oil, a kilogram of groats,
a glass of vodka.
When a young Pole kindly asked me at the police station how I managed
to run the blockade, I asked him whether he could not possibly do
'something' for Esterka.
'You know very well I can't.'
I said hastily:
'Thanks for the kind word.'
This expression of gratitude is the bloodless child of poverty and degra-
dation.

10

I am watering the flowers. My bald head in the window. What a splendid
target.
He has a rifle. Why is he standing and looking on calmly?
He had no orders to shoot.

And perhaps he was a village teacher in civilian life, or a notary, a street sweeper in Leipzig, a waiter in Cologne?

What would he do if I nodded to him? Waved my hand in a friendly gesture?

He may have arrived only yesterday, from far away.

Korczak, the great educator, was deported with his children. I shall be reading some more of his diary tomorrow, when we visit the site of his pre-war orphanage.

4.41 p.m.
We reach the stone memorial to Yitzhak Katzenelson – who was murdered, not at Treblinka but at Auschwitz. Before the war, he had translated the lyrics of Heinrich Heine into Hebrew. He was best known in Poland for his light verses, songs and poems for children: songs that reflected youthful pleasures and the joys of life. During the deportations that took place here, where we are standing, by Katzenelson's own memorial stone, he witnessed the bravery of an elderly Jew, 'the grey-headed Zuckerman'.

Katzenelson later recorded: 'At the shrill sickening commands of the SS, "Herunter!" – "Come down" – all men and women had to descend into the yard of the factory. Amongst those that went down into the yard was the wife of the manager, Krieger. She was a young woman in her ninth month of pregnancy. The vile SS man pushed her over to the side where the queue condemned to go to Treblinka was standing. Thereupon the grey-headed Zuckerman approached the SS man and said, "This woman is an outstanding worker, she is an artist at her job." The SS man stared at the young woman and her abdomen. He then seized hold of his whip and set about Zuckerman with murderous fury. He hit him on the head with the lead-weighted end until the blood poured from him. "What! You want to save a pregnant woman?"'

The pregnant woman was taken away. So too, in that round-up, was Katzenelson's sister-in-law Dora and her sister, Fania. Their mother, Esther Dombrowska, a leading philanthropist in pre-war Lodz, was shot dead in the street by a Ukrainian. 'The Ukrainians and the Germans are good companions,' Katzenelson wrote bitterly a year later. 'May the very memory of these two nations be blotted from the world.'

Katzenelson wrote these words in July 1943, a year after the start of the Warsaw deportations. He himself was taken, together with several hundred Warsaw Jews, to Vittel, in France, not far from the Swiss border, with a view to being allowed to go on to Central America, for which they held valid documents: Central American passports that had been issued to them in Warsaw – Katzenelson and his son held passports issued by the Honduras government. Those who were interned in Vittel were told by the Germans that this camp was a staging post to freedom. While there, Katzenelson wrote an epic poem, *The Song of the Murdered Jewish People*. It included the stanzas:

> I had a dream,
> A dream so terrible:
> My people were no more,
> No more!
>
> I wake up with a cry.
> What I dreamed was true:
> It had happened indeed,
> It had happened to me.

The Nazis did not allow the hopes of those at Vittel to be realised. On 18 April 1944 almost all the Jews there were taken to Drancy, in Paris, and two days later were deported to Auschwitz, where Katzenelson and his eighteen-year-old son Zvi were killed. His wife, and his two younger sons, had been deported from Warsaw to Treblinka during 1942.

Katzenelson's diary, written on the eve of his deportation from Vittel, is a testament to his Warsaw friends who were deported to Treblinka between July and September 1942. Among them was the fifty-seven-year-old writer and dramatist, Shlomo Gilbert. 'You,' he wrote to Gilbert, 'who are so inured to sickness, so scorched in God's own fire. Oh, where are you, and your gentle daughter, who though frail like you, was always alive to the word of God! Just like you!'

Shlomo Gilbert and his daughter were among the 265,000 Warsaw Jews who were gassed at Treblinka. They were not relatives of mine, but being my namesakes, I have always been affected by their story. How could it be otherwise?

4.43 p.m.

A few yards to the east of the Katzenelson stone are Nos. 5–7 Stawki Street. This was the headquarters of the SS Command that supervised the deportations from the Umschlagplatz across the road. While I photograph the building the police are photographing an accident in the road in front of the building. A car and a motorcyclist have collided, nothing too serious.

We cross the road to Nos. 6–8 Stawki Street. Before the war this large, five-storey, somewhat austere building served both as a school and a hospital. Today it is used by various educational establishments, including the Economic High School No. 1, the Centre for Basic Education, and the Organisation of Economic Schools.

The Gestapo kept deportees here after they had been rounded up, and before they were sent to the trains. The railway tracks came right up to the rear of the building. There is a plaque on the building about an episode during the Warsaw uprising. On 1 August 1944 fifty Jews who were working here as part of a slave labour detail were released by a Polish insurgent, Stanislaw Sosabowski. He was a relative of the paratroop commander who was the head of the Independent Polish Parachute Brigade, based in Britain, and who was killed at Arnhem. Thus three wars overlap: Hitler's war against the Jews, Poland's war against the German occupation (and for Polish independence), and the Allied war against the German military machine.

4.55 p.m.

I read the account of the Jew and the tank, an episode of the 1944 uprising. It was recorded by a Pole, Second-Lieutenant Tadeusz Zuchowicz, who had taken part in the liberation of the slave labour camp near here, in which Jews brought from Birkenau were being used by the Germans to sort through the rubble of the ghetto in search of valuables.

Three German Panther tanks approached Zuchowicz's unit. One of them was hit by mortar fire and its crew killed. The other two tanks then retreated up the street, firing their machine guns. The third tank was immobilised and abandoned. Then, as Zuchowicz recalled: 'The commander of the sector shouted: "Who will succeed in entering the immobilised tank and turn the gun and hit the two retreating tanks?" One of the Jews jumped up like a cat and darted in the direction of the "Panther" which was no longer a danger for us. Already he was at the entrance to the turret. We watched holding our breath as he slowly turned the cannon. The two retreating tanks were already two to three hundred metres away.

'Suddenly the air shook with a loud noise and a streak of fire shot out of the barrel of the gun. As we looked on, the tank turned into a burning heap of metal. The second tank escaped. Our victorious Jew emerged with a glowing face while his lips were set in a stern rebellious expression. The commander of the sector, the major, ran towards him and kissed both of his cheeks and pinned the cross of "Virtuti Militari" on the chest of the Jew. We all clapped for him and blessed him.'

5 p.m.

We pause at the corner of Stawki and Dzika Streets. Where once the cries of pain and agony were heard, and the shouts of guards and the barking of guard dogs savagely poised to bite, now a leafy prospect invites a leisurely stroll.

We walk along the street in front of the school and hospital building. At the far (western) end is the Umschlagplatz monument. It has not been here long. In 1980 there was nothing. Those who put up the monument had wanted to carve on it all the names of the Jews deported through here to their deaths, but the number was too large to make it feasible. The Vietnam memorial in Washington has 55,000 names on it. This one would have needed at least 300,000 names. There were also no lists of the deportees, so that thousands, perhaps tens of thousands, of names were not known. It was therefore decided to put up a list of all the Polish-Jewish first names. It is very striking, very effective, even in the unfamiliar Polish spellings (Becalel for Bezalel, Mosze for Moshe, Szoszana for Shoshana).

There is also an inscription in Polish, carved, like the names, on marble. It reads (translated by Ben): 'Along this path of suffering and death more than 300,000 Jews were driven in 1942–1943 from the Warsaw ghetto to the gas chambers of the Nazi extermination camps.'

The tree behind the monument was planted as a symbol of continuity and hope. At least it is not intended that the whole terrible episode should be forgotten. I have always remembered a remark by my Polish-Jewish friend, Stefan Marody (who alas is not in Warsaw this week), when we first met here in the city in 1959: that the atrocities committed by the Mongol conqueror, Genghis Khan, culminating in his erection of a pyramid of the skulls of his victims, had been given, after 700 years, a different focus. The title of a thesis written recently was: 'The administrative work and organisational accomplishments of Genghis Khan'. Perhaps the Central Asian tyrant was indeed a good administrator.[1]

---

[1] After I had typed out this diary entry, I looked up Genghis Khan in the *Chambers Dictionary of World History* (Chambers Harrap, Edinburgh, 1993), where to my amazement I found the sentence: 'Genghis was not only a warrior and conqueror, but a skilful administrator and ruler.' The Polish thesis writer was almost forty years before his time.

Here at the Umschlagplatz, and in the rounding up of Jews in the Warsaw ghetto, the Germans were unable to make use of the Polish police. They considered the Polish police to be too 'soft' and did not trust them to carry out the ruthless orders. They therefore brought in, for this special task, uneducated Lithuanian and Latvian peasants, recruited or conscripted into a uniformed formation known as the Shaulis. One reason why the Shaulis could be effective, Jan points out, was that they did not speak Polish and therefore had no point of contact with the local Polish or Jewish population. 'They did not understand a single word of Polish. Perhaps they didn't understand what was going on altogether.'[1]

The Shaulis wore a yellowish-green type of uniform.

Robin: 'They looked like clowns from a circus.'

Jan: 'For Poles they were exotic. They had been through such bad experiences between 1939 and 1941 during the Soviet occupation of the Baltic States that they were pro-German.'

5.10 p.m.

My first reading is from the recollections of a young Hassidic boy from Lodz, Pinhas Gutter, who had been incarcerated in the Warsaw ghetto. 'Three or four weeks after the uprising had been crushed,' he recalled, 'we were given away by a Jewish informer, threatened that if we did not evacuate the bunker immediately gas would be pumped in. We crept out to face the Germans who stood waiting for us, armed to the teeth, and shouting "Hände hoch! Nicht schiessen!" ("Hands up! Do not shoot!")

'As we emerged, every person was patted down for arms that might be hidden under clothes. It was the end of the day. The sun was going down as we were marched to the Umschlagplatz through the streets of the Warsaw ghetto. Fires burned on both sides of the long column of Jews, a parodic image of the Hebrews leaving Egypt, marching through the divided waters on their way to liberation.

'When we arrived at the Umschlagplatz we were immediately set upon by auxiliary SS of all different nationalities, Ukrainian, Polish and others. We were chased up a stairwell and squashed into rooms packed so tightly there was hardly space to sit. My parents managed to get a small corner where the four of us could huddle. Water was

---

[1] In 1956, some of the Soviet (mostly Mongol) troops who were sent to Budapest to crush the Hungarian uprising believed that they were in Egypt, fighting the Anglo-French invaders and defending the Suez Canal.

being sold by the bottle, but only for gold and diamonds. After several days we were loaded on to cattle trucks and taken to Majdanek.'

I read next from an account of a brave act of rescue from the Umschlagplatz, when an eye-witness, David Wdowinski, recalled how the Secretary of the Jewish Council, Nahum Remba, and his wife, 'used emergency ambulances and drove to the Umschlagplatz to rescue as many children as they could'. Even though Remba and his wife had a certain immunity, they 'took their lives in their hands in this courageous act. In this way, they saved hundreds of Jewish children.'

5.20 p.m.

We walk from the Umschlagplatz back across Stawki Street and into the former ghetto, down Karmelicka Street. It was on 22 July 1942 that the first round-ups took place in these streets – the search throughout the ghetto for Jews to be deported.

I read the recollections of a survivor, Adolf Berman: 'On that very day, the first victims were the Jewish children, and I shall never forget the harrowing scenes and the blood-curdling incidents when the SS men most cruelly attacked children – children roaming in the streets; took them by force to carts, and I remember, fully, those children were defending themselves. Even today the cries and shrieking of those children are clear in my mind. "Mama, Mama," this is what we heard. "Save us, mothers."'

My second reading is from another eye-witness, Alexander Donat: 'I saw a young mother run downstairs into the street to get milk for her baby. Her husband who worked at the Ostbahn, had as usual left earlier that morning. She had not bothered to dress, but was in bathrobe and slippers. An empty milk bottle in hand, she was headed for a shop where she knew, they sold milk under the counter. She walked into Operation Reinhard. The executioners demanded her Ausweis. "Upstairs ... Ostbahn ... work certificate. I'll bring it right away."

'"We've heard that one before. Have you got an Ausweis with you, or haven't you?"'

She was dragged protesting to the wagon, scarcely able to realise what was happening. "But my baby is all alone. Milk ..." she protested. "My Ausweis is upstairs."

'Then, for the first time, she really looked at the men who were holding her and she saw where she was being dragged: to the gaping entrance at the back of a high-boarded wagon with victims already jammed into it. With all her young mother's strength she wrenched herself free, and then two, and four policemen fell on her, hitting her, smashing her to the ground, picking her up again, and tossing her into the wagon like a sack.

'I can still hear her screaming in a half-crazed voice somewhere between a sob of utter human despair and the howl of an animal.'

At the corner of what is now a modern suburban intersection, I read from Vladka Meed's account of what she saw there in September 1942: 'On Gesia-Zamenhof, I suddenly caught sight of an old woman walking all alone. How had she got there? Probably she'd been left alone in the house, and was now seeking a hiding place. I anxiously watched her halting steps. She was conspicuous in the deserted street. Two German automobiles happened to pass by; a young German jumped out and called to the old woman. She was evidently deaf; the German easily caught up with her, pulled out his revolver and fired twice. She toppled, bleeding profusely. The German calmly returned to his car and drove away. The incident had passed like a flash. We were not permitted by the Ukrainians to approach the dead woman, we passed by the corpse with lowered heads.'

When we reach the corner of Karmelicka and Mila Streets, I read another extract from Vladka Meed's recollections: 'Several vans went by, loaded with Jews, sitting and standing, hugging sacks that contained whatever pitiful belongings they had managed to gather at the last moment. Some stared straight ahead vacantly, others mourned and wailed, wringing their hands and entreating the Jewish police who rode with them. Women tore their hair or clung to their children, who sat bewildered among the scattered bundles, gazing at the adults in silent fear. Running behind the last van, a lone woman, arms out-stretched, screamed: "My child! Give back my child!" In reply, a small voice called from the van: "Mama! Mama!"

'The people in the street watched as though hypnotised. Panting now with exhaustion, the mother continued to run after the van. One of the guards whispered something to the driver, who urged his horses into a gallop. The cries of the pursuing mother became more desperate as the horses pulled away. The procession turned into Karmelicka Street. The cries of the deportees faded and became inaudible, only the cry of the agonised mother still pierced the air: "My child! Give back my child!"'

We turn into Mila Street. At No. 18 is a stone monument above the bunker where Mordechai Anielewicz and his fellow-ghetto fighters had their headquarters. Like everything else in the ghetto, No. 18 was blown up and levelled to the ground in the months after the uprising.

The Poles, who from 'Aryan' Warsaw could see the ghetto burning, and hear the shooting and the explosions as the battle raged, recognised the bravery of the ghetto fighters. Anielewicz was awarded the Cross of Grünewald, Third Class.

5.40 p.m.

I read from Mordechai Anielewicz's last letter, written to his friend Yitzhak Zuckerman, who was then on the 'Aryan' side of the city, seeking arms and ammunition. 'Keep well,' Anielewicz wrote. 'Perhaps we'll still see each other. What's most important; the dream of my life has become a reality. I have lived to see Jewish defence in the ghetto in all its greatness and splendour.'

5.50 p.m.

We take a taxi from Mila Street back to the Old Town. A short break for tea and cakes.

Those who had preferred to watch the England–Spain football quarter-final want to go to the Umschlagplatz. They will miss extra time and the penalties.

6.20 p.m.

I set off again, with Angela, Ros, Petra, Caroline and Jon. As Caroline does not want to ride on Sabbath, we walk. I cannot walk at quite the same pace this time.

At the entrance to the Old Town, I say goodbye to Jan. He has been with us for more than nine hours. He has given us a clear perspective of the Polish uprising, and the extent of Polish suffering. The proximity of the places, and the plaques, of the Jewish and Polish stories, reminds us that two peoples were victims, and two peoples suffered, on the same soil, in the same town, in the same streets, and at the same street corners.

6.45 p.m.

We reach Muranowska Street, where it joins Stawki Street, and cross to the Polish monument to the victims of Soviet deportations. Retracing my steps, we look at the memorial stones to Korczak and Katzenelson, the SS headquarters, the deportation building, and the monument at the Umschlagplatz. As we are looking at the monument, each deep in our own thoughts, three young Polish men walk towards us along the street. They make a lunge at Caroline and then continue on their way.

8.05 p.m.

In the former ghetto area, we stop at the same corner to read from Vladka Meed's recollections. We also stop at No. 18 Mila Street. Just beyond Mila Street is the large monument to the ghetto uprising. This is where the ghetto memorial ceremonies are held every year, on the anniversary in April.

8.15 p.m.

We take a taxi to the Old Town. It is nearly dark, and the Sabbath is coming to a cold, wet end.

8.30 p.m.

A restaurant in the Old Town. Despite all we have seen today, there is a jolly atmosphere, almost festive. The group is together after a gruelling experience. It is the end of our eleventh day together. Today is Herut's birthday. I explain this to the head waiter and at the end of dinner he brings in a cake with candles aflame and we all sing 'Happy Birthday' in English, Hebrew and – with help from Ben and Kathy – in Polish.

Over a final glass of wine we discuss the different ways in which aspects of what we have seen have affected us, and will do so once we have returned home. Jon says that for weeks after his first visit to Poland he could not stop talking about it.

12.20 a.m.

We leave the restaurant and return to the hotel. I go with Herut, Ben, and a Polish friend of Ben's who joined us for dinner, and who has a car. It is too late, and too wet, to walk.

Today I have seen the Umschlagplatz monument and the surrounding buildings twice. The first time it was in the rain, the second time it was dry. The second walk over the same ground, so soon after the first, gave me a strange feeling of unexpected familiarity, and contact with the past; but so painful. The same reading, three hours later, is no less painful.

Despite seeing the same things twice within three hours, they in no way lose their poignancy. On the second journey, the Vladka Meed extract about the woman failing to catch up with her child was hard for all of us to listen to, but proved too much for Caroline. There always seems to be some moment, different for each of us, when a place or a story becomes suddenly unbearable.

Often I find the readings very difficult. On three occasions today – and two at Sobibor two days ago, and one at Majdanek yesterday – I was not able to read out a piece I had chosen; on reading it through first, it seemed too painful, too direct, too raw. I always apologised for not being able to do so.

The hardest thing to read about, or to think about, is the children. The hospital here in Warsaw, the hospital we saw yesterday in Lublin; in both, it was the murder of the children that is the stuff of nightmares.

12.50 a.m.

We reach the hotel. It is raining hard again. It is seventeen and a half hours since we set off into Warsaw. We have not seen everything, or even a portion of everything, but we have seen a lot. Among the places I wanted to visit, had it not been so wet and so cold, was the Pawiak prison (on Pawia and Dzielna Streets). Thousands of Poles were tortured and murdered there. Jews also suffered massively in Pawiak. Emanuel Ringelblum was imprisoned there after his underground hiding place in the 'Aryan' side of Warsaw had been betrayed, and all thirty-seven people in hiding with him, including his wife Jehudith and his son Uriah, were seized, tortured and shot. One of those whose story I had hoped to tell was Pawel (Pinkas) Finder, born in Bielsko-Biala – which we went through on day six – a member of the Polish Communist underground, who was murdered by the Gestapo in Pawiak on 26 July 1944.

I hope that what we have seen today will encourage members of the group to return, and spend three or four days exploring the Jewish aspects of the city's story.

1.15 a.m.
Bed.

DAY 12

WARSAW – PIOTRKOW

An orphanage, a death camp and a ghetto – and stones

6.30 a.m.
On waking I sort through my materials for today.

7.15 a.m.
Breakfast with the group.

8.05 a.m.
We rejoin our minibus and drive away from the hotel. It is raining again.

8.15 a.m.
Reach Janusz Korczak's pre-war orphanage at No. 8 Jaktorowska Street (formerly No. 92 Krochmalna Street). The building was erected in 1912. There is a memorial plaque just inside the gate to Piotr Zalewski, a Polish Christian who worked here in the orphanage, and who was shot by the Nazis in 1944. It is now Children's Home No. 2, named after Korczak.

Inside the centre of the front courtyard is a bust of Korczak. At the back of the bust are carvings of children. On the wall of the building is a plaque to Stefania Wilczynska, one of Korczak's helpers, who had worked here with him, and lived here, since 1912, and was devoted to him. In September 1942 she insisted on accompanying the children to the Umschlagplatz, and beyond, as did Korczak himself.

When the ghetto was established, this building was outside it. Korczak, his staff and his orphans were moved to a location inside the ghetto (it does not survive).

Here, where the children once played, I read an account of the deportation of the children and their guardians. It was recorded by

Adolf Berman nineteen years after the event: 'I'll never forget the way
the Germans were shouting at them – "Alle herunter!" "All come
down!" And his only concern, the only concern of Korczak, was that
the children had not had time to dress properly, they were barefooted.
Stefania Wilczynska told the children that they were going on a trip,
that this was a little outing, that at last they were going to see woods
and fields and the flowers they had been yearning for and which they'd
never seen in their lives; and one could see a smile flickering on the
pale lips of those children. After a few hours they were put into the
death carriages and this was the last journey of the great educator.'

It is raining hard. The rain falls heavily from the trees in the
orphanage forecourt. The gate of the main building is open. Inside, in
the hall, are examples of children's patchwork. It is clearly still a
children's home. But there is absolutely no one about.

We go up the steps into the main 'Aula' (the main hall). Again, the
door is open, although there is no one there. On the walls are the pre-
war mouldings of various animals. One of the mouldings shows a
young child surrounded by chicks, which she is feeding. Another shows
an elephant and Winnie the Pooh. I read extracts from Korczak's diary:

It's so soft and warm in my bed. It'll be very hard to get up. But today is
Saturday, and on Saturdays I weigh the children in the morning before
breakfast. Probably for the first time I am not interested in the results for
the week. They ought to have put on a bit of weight. (I don't know why
raw carrot was given for supper yesterday.)

Now that every day brings so many strange and sinister experiences and
sensations I have completely ceased to dream.
The law of equilibrium.
The day of torments, the night soothes. A gratifying day, a tormented
night.
I could write a monograph on the featherbed.
The peasant and the featherbed.
The proletarian and the featherbed.

It's been a long time since I have blessed the world. I tried to tonight. It
didn't work.
I don't even know what went wrong. The purifying respirations worked
more or less. But the fingers remained feeble, no energy flowing through
them.
Do I believe in the effects? I do believe, but not in my India! Holy India!

The look of this district is changing from day to day.
1. A prison

2. A plague-stricken area
3. A mating ground
4. A lunatic asylum
5. A casino. Monaco. The stake – your head.

What matters is that all this did happen.

The destitute beggars suspended between prison and hospital. The slave work: not only the effort of the muscles but the honour and virtue of the girl.

Debased faith, family, motherhood.

The marketing of all spiritual commodities. A stock exchange quoting the weight of conscience. An unsteady market – like onions and life today.

The children are living in constant uncertainty, in fear. 'A Jew will take you away.' 'I'll give you away to a wicked old man.' 'You'll be put in a bag.'

Bereavement.

Old age. Its degradation and moral decrepitude.

(Once upon a time one earned one's old age, it was good to work for it. The same with health. Now the vital forces and the years of life may be purchased. A scoundrel has a good chance of achieving grey hair.)

8.25 a.m.

We drive on, to the Jewish cemetery at No. 40 Okopowa Street. It is closed, but, as we drive past, I say a few words about it. It was established in 1799, nearly two hundred years ago. About 150,000 Jews are buried here; as many as 100,000 tombstones survived the war years. It is one of the few Jewish cemeteries in Poland where burials still take place.

Among the Jews buried here are many distinguished nineteenth-century rabbis and teachers, including Rav Chaim of Volozhin (1749–1821), the founder of the Volozhin Yeshiva, devoted to the study of the Torah; and Rav Joseph Baer Soloveichik (1820–92), who became joint head of the Volozhin Yeshiva at the age of twenty-nine. Among the great Warsaw-Jewish figures of the early twentieth century buried here is Esther Kaminski (1870–1925), an actress who played in the United States, London and Paris before the First World War.

One section of graves is that of Jewish officers and men who were killed while fighting in the Polish army during the German siege of Warsaw in 1939. Also buried here are two of those whose birthplaces we saw in Zamosc: I. L. Peretz and Ludwig Zamenhof. One of the most poignant graves is that of Adam Czerniakow, who committed suicide rather than assist the Nazis in deporting Jews to Treblinka. A substantial book, even a multi-volume work, could be written on the personalities whose stones and monuments are here: most of them facing in the direction of Jerusalem.

I read from Vladka Meed's account of her return to this cemetery in 1945, immediately after liberation: 'Wherever I turned, there was nothing but overturned tombstones, desecrated graves and scattered skulls – skulls, their dark sockets burning deep into me, their shattered jaws demanding, "Why? Why has this befallen us?"

'Although I knew that these atrocities were the handiwork of the so-called "dentists" – Polish ghouls who searched the mouths of the Jewish corpses to extract their gold-capped teeth, I nevertheless felt strangely guilty and ashamed. Yes, Jews were persecuted even in their graves.

'Deliberately, in order not to trample the skulls and not to slip into an open grave, we made our way through this place of rest to the spot where my father's bones had lain. Though the location was well known to me, I could not find his grave. The spot was desolate, destroyed, the soil pitted and strewn with broken skulls and markers.

'We stood there forlorn. Around our feet lay skull after skull. Was not one of them my own father? How would I ever recognise it?

'Nothing. Nothing was left me of my past, of my life in the ghetto – not even the grave of my father.'

8.40 a.m.
Driving out of Warsaw, we pass the back of the Umschlagplatz. From the bus window we can see the north side of the school-hospital building where many of the deportees were held.

8.42 a.m.
We cross the Vistula. From the bridge, looking back at the riverbank, we can see one of the areas of the fiercest fighting during the 1944 uprising.

9.04 a.m.
There is a heavy, misty drizzle. We are (for a few minutes) on a road running along the railway line. The railway goes straight as an arrow from Warsaw to Malkinia Junction, from where a branch line led off to Treblinka.

9.07 a.m.
We leave the Warsaw city limits.

9.25 a.m.
Radzymin. Just south of here, in 1920, the Polish army halted the advance of the Red Army, and frustrated the Bolshevik ambition of raising the Red Flag in Warsaw and Berlin. It was to take twenty-five years before that ambition was realised.

There was a Jewish community here before the war. When, in 1940, the ghetto was established, 2,500 Jews were incarcerated there. During a typhoid epidemic, 700 died. The Jews of the Radzymin ghetto were put to work road-building and ditching: we are on the main road from Warsaw to Leningrad, along which vast quantities of German arms and men passed, in the vain effort to overrun the besieged Soviet city. This was also one of the main roads to the Eastern Front; and to the cities of Kovno, Vilna and Riga, all of which, by 1942, were important German garrisons.

Occasionally a postcard from a Jew in German-occupied Poland reached the West. But any messages other than purely personal ones had to be skilfully disguised. On 23 July 1942 one such postcard was sent from a Jew in Radzymin to his brother in Brooklyn. Referring to three Jewish Holy Days – the solemn fast day of Yom Kippur, the festival of Purim when Jewish children dress up in colourful costumes, and the festival of Tabernacles, or Sukkot, during which Jews build a booth of trellis and greenery, the message read: 'We are eating as on Yom Kippur, clothed as at Purim, and dwelling as at Sukkot.'

The Radzymin ghetto was emptied on 3 October 1942, when all its Jews were deported by rail to Treblinka, where they were killed.

9.30 a.m.
The bus driver drives into a lay-by. He says he has no instructions to go to Treblinka. He turns off the engine. He is disputing with Ben that he has no instructions. We show him the plan that we had sent to his employers. He refuses to start up again for another ten minutes, until Ben remonstrates vigorously with him, and we are on our way again.

9.55 a.m.
Wyszkow. We cross the River Bug. It was here, in September 1939, on this bridge, that some Jews were moving eastward into the Soviet Union (the bridge was, briefly, the border) to escape from German rule. At the same time, others were moving westward to escape from

Communist rule and return to their homes in western Poland. Many years ago I met a woman who had been crossing this bridge from west to east when she met her father, who was crossing from east to west. They continued on their respective ways. She survived the war, her father did not. 'Neither of us could have foretold then what would happen,' she said.

The first killing of Jews took place here on 11 September 1939, when sixty-five were killed. It was typical of the spasmodic, deliberate killings of Jews during those early days of the war.

As we drive over the bridge, we look south, to a wooded area, where, in 1942, Polish peasants provided Jewish partisans with food and clothing, an unusual support for the Jews; but not for long. Within a year the local Poles turned against the Jews, denying them the help without which they could not survive. I read a short passage from Dr Shmuel Krakowski's book on Jewish armed resistance in Poland, *The War of the Doomed*, of how the local Armia Krajowa Polish resistance organisations 'began provoking the Jewish partisans and inciting the village population against them'. The Armia Krajowa did not want a rival partisan force operating in its area: a force that was connected to their Polish resistance rivals, the Communist-controlled Armia Ludowa. 'It is likely,' adds Krakowski, 'that anti-Semitic tendencies were also at work.'

In July 1943 one squad of Jewish partisans in the woods near here, commanded by Mordechai Growas, one of the combat group commanders in the Warsaw ghetto uprising, was attacked by far stronger Armia Krajowa forces, and all the Jews were killed.

In his published lists of Polish-Jewish soldiers killed in the Second World War, Benjamin Meirtchak names several who fell in action in a Jewish partisan unit in the Wyszkow forest in the summer of 1943. Among them were three twenty-two-year-olds, each of them survivors of the Warsaw ghetto uprising: Szlomo Alterman, Chaim Arbuz and Rachel Kirszenbaum. Also killed in battle here was Zalcman Fridrich, one of the few escapees from Treblinka, a man in his thirties. We discuss the problem of preserving names, even of those about whom so little else is known. At least their names should be remembered.

10 a.m.

We are driving through a dense wood, the Puszcza Biala. By 1943, Polish partisans were active in these woods, on both sides of the road, trying to interfere with German military traffic. Several of the group express surprise that the Germans could hold down and control such a vast area, and do so for four years; we have driven through so many forests and wide empty spaces.

10.27 a.m.

Ostrow Mazowiecka. The Nazi–Soviet demarcation line ran eleven kilometres to the east of the town. On September 8, shortly after the arrival of the German army, thirty Jews were executed here. Three days later, 600 Jews were taken outside the town and shot. There is a marker at the roadside to commemorate the second execution: a rare Polish roadside recognition of a site of Jewish executions. Then, all 7,000 Jewish inhabitants were driven across the border into Soviet-occupied Poland.

Just to the north of here, at Komorowo, the Germans set up Stalag 333, one of the largest of the prisoner-of-war camps for captured Soviet soldiers. The bodies of the murdered soldiers were exhumed after the war: a total of 41,592 were counted. At another prisoner-of-war camp, at Guty, sixty kilometres to the north, a further 24,000 bodies were exhumed. In Ostrow Mazowiecka itself, at Stalag 324, as many as 13,000 captive Russians, brought here in July 1941, were murdered in the winter of 1942.

10.30 a.m.

We turn off the main Warsaw–Bialystok road and drive south-east. A road sign indicates that it is twenty-two kilometres to Treblinka.

10.42 a.m.

We reach Malkinia Junction. This is the main Warsaw–Bialystok–Grodno–Vilna railway line, the line along which most of the Warsaw Jews were brought to Treblinka. It is also the line, perversely, along which the Jews of several towns to the east of here, among them Grodno, Lomza, Zambrow and Volkovysk, were brought in the other direction, to Auschwitz.

To reach Treblinka, a branch line ran (and still runs) south, across the River Bug. Considerable preparatory work had to be done here at Malkinia Junction to make the spur line ready, and to improve the connection. Several hundred Jews who had been brought from Warsaw to a slave labour camp across the Bug, at the gravel pits of Treblinka village, were brought here to Malkinia to drain the marshes along the river, to level the ground, and to strengthen the railway embankment.

10.58 a.m.

We reach the River Bug. The railway and the road go over the same single-track bridge, the railway line running in the road. The bridge is so narrow that we have to wait for some oncoming cars to cross first. When I came here in 1959 there was no road bridge at all, and I had to call a peasant from the other side of the river to bring a small boat and row me across. As the boat was full of timber, he had to unload it first. From the other side, he took me on to Treblinka by horse and cart.

11.03 a.m.

We reach Treblinka village. It was here that the slave labour camp was set up to prepare the death camp and the engine sheds, and to level the ground for the railway sidings. The slave labourers were guarded, and tormented, by twenty SS men and a hundred Ukrainians. The commandant was Captain Theo von Eupen. A Polish railway worker here, Franciszek Zabecki, later recalled that the commandant was 'a sadist who ill-treated Poles and Jews working there, particularly the Jews, taking shots at them as if they were partridges'.

At Treblinka station, stretching south, is the base of the specially prepared railway sidings: a long, raised bed of what were once three or four parallel railway lines, on which three or four long trains could be kept at any one time, awaiting the shunting of groups of carriages into the camp, or awaiting the return of the carriages, empty, to the next deportation task.

By the station platform, I read various extracts. The first trains to arrive here reached the station on 23 July 1942, from Warsaw. Among those brought here that day were the children who had been rounded up in the streets. The Polish railway worker, Franciszek Zabecki, later recalled how the first train to arrive that morning 'made its presence known from a long way off, not only by the rumble of the wheels on the bridge over the River Bug, but by the frequent shots from the rifles and automatic weapons of the train guards'. His account continued:

'The train was made up of sixty covered wagons, crammed with people. There were old people, young people, men, women, children and infants in quilts. The doors of the wagons were bolted, the air gaps had a grating of barbed wire. Several SS men, with automatic weapons ready to shoot, stood on the foot-boards of the wagons on both sides of the trains and even lay on the roofs.

'It was a hot day; people in the wagons were fainting. The SS guards with rolled-up sleeves looked like butchers, who after murdering their victims washed their blood-stained hands and got ready for more killing. Without a word, we understood the tragedy, since "settling" people coming to work would not have required such a strict guard, whereas these people were being transported like dangerous criminals.

'After the transport arrived, some fiendish spirit got into the SS men; they drew their pistols, put them away, and took them out again, as if they wanted to shoot and kill straight away; they approached the wagons, silencing those who were shrieking and wailing, and again they swore and screamed.

'Shouting "Tempo, schnell," "At the double, quickly," to the German railwaymen who had come from Sokolow Podlaski, they went off to the camp, to take over their victims there "properly". On the wagons we could see chalk marks giving the number of people in the wagon, viz.: 120, 150, 180, 200 people. We worked out later that the total number of people in the train must have been about eight to ten thousand.

'The "settlers" were strangely huddled together in the wagons. All of them had to stand, without sufficient air and without access to toilet facilities. It was like travelling in hot ovens. The high temperature, lack of air, and the hot weather created conditions that not even healthy, young, strong organisms could stand. Moans, shouts, weeping, calls for water or for a doctor issued from the wagons. And protests: "How can people be treated so inhumanly?" "When will they let us leave the wagons altogether?"

'Through some air gaps terrified people looked out, asking hopefully: "How far is it to the agricultural estates where we're going to work?"

'Twenty wagons were uncoupled from the train, and a shunting engine began to push them along the spur-line into the camp. A short while later, it returned empty. This procedure was repeated twice more, until all sixty wagons had been shunted into the camp, and out again. Empty, they were returned to Warsaw for more "settlers".'

As each train was uncoupled from its engine, and twenty coaches at a time were shunted into the camp, Zabecki witnessed many harrowing scenes. We stand by the railway line and I continue to read from his recollections: 'I saw a policeman catch two young Jewish boys. He did not shut them in a wagon, since he was afraid to open the door in case others escaped. I was on the platform, letting a military transport through. I asked him to let them go. The assassin did not even budge. He ordered the bigger boy to sit down on the ground and take the smaller one on his knee, then he shot them both with one bullet. Turning to me, he said "You're lucky, that was the last bullet."

Round the huge stomach of the murderer there was a belt with a clasp, on which I could see the inscription "Got mit uns", "God is with us"'.

The second incident took place after a train, arriving late in the evening, had been kept overnight at Treblinka station. On the following morning a Ukrainian guard 'promised a Jewess that he would let her and her child go if she put a large bribe in his hand. The Jewess passed the Ukrainian the money and her four-year-old child through the air gap, and afterwards, with the Ukrainian's help, she also got out of the wagon through the air gap. The Jewess walked away from the train, holding her child by the hand; as soon as she walked down the railway embankment the Ukrainian shot her. The mother rolled down into a field, pulling the child after her. The child clutched the mother's neck. Jews looking out of the wagons called out and yelled, and the child turned back up the embankment again and under the wagons to the other side of the train. Another Ukrainian killed the child with one blow of a rifle butt on its head.'

I read aloud a third incident witnessed by Zabecki, which also took place at Treblinka station: 'One mother threw a small child wrapped up in a pillow from the wagon, shouting: "Take it, that's some money to look after it." In no time an SS man ran up, unwrapped the pillow, seized the child by its feet and smashed its head against a wheel of the wagon. This took place in full view of the mother, who was howling with pain.'

A fourth incident which Zabecki later recalled involved a German railwayman, Willi Klinzmann, from Wuppertal (through which we passed on our first day). He was one of the two German railwaymen who supervised the shunting work at the station. Zabecki saw a pregnant Jewess who had managed to break away from the train seek sanctuary in Klinzmann's quarters. But the Germans were without charity: Klinzmann and an SS man who was with him killed her. They kicked her to death.'

Zabecki added: 'I had to go into the office and pass close to the murderers, since the departure of a train to Wolka Okraglik station had to be attended to. My entrance made the criminals stop. In their frenzy they had forgotten where they were, and somebody plucked up courage to break in and stop them in their "duty" of liquidating "an enemy of Hitlerism". They reached for their pistols. Willi, drunk, mumbled "Fahrdienstleiter" (Traffic supervisor). I closed the door behind me. The butchers renewed the kicking. The Jewess was no longer groaning. She was no longer alive.'

11.25 a.m.

As I finish reading, a car draws up and a man gets out. He is an American, Robert Berg. He was born on 15 November 1929 in a small village, Abramow, a hundred kilometres south of here. We passed near it yesterday. 'I am one of only three survivors from Abramow,' he says. Almost all the Jews of Abramow, including all his family (their surname was Rosenberg), were deported to Treblinka. He was taken with a small number of able-bodied youngsters (he was then only twelve) to work at the slave labour camp at Deblin, one of the main German airfields in Poland. He was one of seventy or eighty children there. As the Russians approached Deblin in 1944 he was sent first to a slave labour camp in Czestochowa and then to Buchenwald. He was liberated by the Americans in Mauthausen at the end of the war.

He went back to Abramow last year. 'In the Jewish cemetery, all the stones are gone. I wanted a monument done. I went to the priest. I talked to him and I pleaded my case.' He has come back this year to see what progress has been made.

11.32 a.m.

We drive south, towards the camp, through the village of Poniatowa.

11.40 a.m.

We drive off the main road and along a narrow road that goes through dense woods into the camp. There is a car park and a small (and dilapidated) visitors centre. This is my third visit. I was here in 1959, and again in 1981, both times with Polish friends. Now I walk into the camp area with Ben, whose grandfather, Michael Klein, was brought here from Piotrkow in October 1942, and murdered. He was seventy-two years old.

We will be in Piotrkow this evening. But it, and everywhere else, seem a million miles away just now. Treblinka, like Belzec and Sobibor, is an isolated world of its own, with its own catalogue of horrors. Here at Treblinka, the commandant, SS Captain Franz Stangl, used diesel engines to pump carbon monoxide through pipes into the gas chambers. By October 1942 he had ten such gas chambers working, and boasted that it was possible to kill between 12,000 and 15,000 people a day.

Samuel Willenberg, from Czestochowa, who escaped from Treblinka during the uprising and break-out of slave labourers on 2 August 1943, later recounted an episode at a roll call, when Stangl introduced new regulations for the Jewish slave labourers in the camp: 'Possession of money, jewellery or gold? Death by shooting. Possession of food originating outside the camp? Death by shooting. Damaging belongings of the murdered which had been prepared for transport? Death by shooting. Failure to carry out the camp commander's orders adequately? Fifty lashes. Any violation involving foremen? Fifty lashes. Failure to obey the block overseer's orders? Twenty-five lashes.'

Among the tasks that Samuel Willenberg and his fellow slave labourers had to carry out was cutting the hair of the hundreds of thousands of women brought to Treblinka. This was done minutes before they were sent to the gas chambers. Willenberg recalled a transport that had just arrived from Warsaw: 'The women moved towards us and sat on the stools. Some brought their children along. They looked at us in fright as we, the prisoners, began to cut their hair – black, light brown, or totally white. The touch of the scissors caused a glimmer of hope to flicker in their eyes. We knew they imagined that this haircut was a prelude to disinfection; if they were being disinfected, they were to be left alive. They did not know that the Germans needed their hair to make mattresses for submarine crews, since hair repels moisture. After the haircutting the SS man opened a door and ordered the women out – onto Death Avenue, the one-way road to the gas chambers.

'Hundreds of women passed my way that day. Among them was a very lovely one about twenty years old; though our acquaintance lasted only a few minutes, I have not forgotten her. Her name was Ruth Dorfmann, she said, and she had just matriculated. She was well aware of what awaited her, and kept it no secret from me. Her beautiful eyes displayed neither fear nor agony of any kind, only pain and boundless sadness. "How long will I have to suffer?" she asked. "Only a few moments," I answered. A heavy stone seemed to roll off her heart; tears welled up in our eyes. Franz Suchomil of the SS, the man in charge of sorting gold and dispatching transports to the gas chambers (he was sentenced to six years' imprisonment in 1965) passed by. We fell silent until he was gone; I continued cutting her long, silken hair. When I had finished. Ruth stood up from the stool and gave me one long, last look, as if saying goodbye to me and to a cruel, merciless world, and set out slowly on her final walk. A few minutes later I heard the racket of the motor which produced the gas and imagined Ruth in the mass of naked bodies, her soul departed.'

Since my first visit to Treblinka, various monuments have been built. The one at the entrance to the camp is surrounded by woods – 'in the middle of nowhere,' comments Paul. It reads (its top line covered in moss): 'There was here a Nazi extermination camp between July 1942 and August 1943. More than 800,000 Jews from Poland, USRR, Jougoslavia, Czechoslovakia, Bulgaria, Austria, France, Belgium, Germany and Greece, were murdered. On 2 August 1943 the prisoners organised an armed revolt which was crushed in blood by the Nazi hangmen. In a penitentiary labour camp at a distance of two kilometres from here the Nazis murdered an estimated number of ten thousand Poles between 1941 and 1944.'

As we walk into the camp, through the drizzle, there is another new monument (new since my 1959 visit, that is) of concrete sleepers. These sleepers represent the railway line running into the camp, and continue until they reach a reconstructed platform, the 'ramp' to which all the deportees were brought. Standing stones represent the boundary of the camp, running through the wood and along the railway: the railway sleepers cross through them at the point where the railway entered the camp.

The station no longer survives. It was not in fact a station at all, but a building designed to look like one. It was used as a storehouse for the belongings taken from those who arrived immediately after they were ordered out of the trains. We walk away from the rail spur, up a slight slope, across what the German and Ukrainian guards called mockingly 'Station Square'. Beyond it was 'Reception Square', and just beyond that were the barracks in which the men undressed, and the women undressed and then were shaven.

Nothing survives of the camp buildings. When the killings ended here in the autumn of 1943, the bodies of all the victims were dug up and burned on orders from Berlin, the camp buildings were destroyed, and the ground levelled and planted with trees.

As we walk from the rail spur into the main area of the camp, there are a number of large stones set alongside the path, on which are inscribed the names of the countries whose Jews were brought here from far away. These include the Greek provinces of Macedonia and Thrace, from which 13,000 Jews were brought here and killed. Their stone is inscribed 'Bulgaria', which had occupied both those regions in the war. Bulgarian Jews themselves, however, were protected from deportation by the King and Parliament; indeed, when the war ended there were more Jews in Bulgaria than when the war had begun. There is a memorial stone for Greece (Grecja). Among the Greek Jews who were brought here and killed were more than 43,000 from Salonica. The Germans searched the most remote regions of Greece for Jews to deport. Among those brought here were the three Jews who lived on the Aegean island of Samothrace.

There is a large monument on the site of the gas chambers, a stone on which is inscribed in Polish, Yiddish, French, German and English: 'Never again.' All around are hundreds of stones, large and small, set out in what had been the main area of the camp, each one representing a Polish-Jewish community that was destroyed here.

We walk among the memorial stones. Robert Berg is there. I ask if he has found the memorial stone to his town. He says it was too small to have a special stone. There are many stones here that have no names on them. There were, he says, some 1,200 Jews and 1,200 Poles in his little town. The Jews were tailors, shoemakers, butchers. Some owned a grocery store. 'There were no Germans in our town during the war. It was too remote. Occasionally they would come in to raid, to kill, to plunder. Then came the deportation. My two brothers and my sister were killed.'

As we speak of the enormous numbers of communities that were deported here, of the daily rail traffic that came here, Robert Berg comments bitterly on 'the genius to figure all these things out – all the planning'.

Of the memorial stones to the 800,000 Jews who were murdered here, only one is for an individual. But it is not just for one individual. It is dedicated to Janusz Korczak and 'the children'.

Wandering about the many stones, some of them large and rounded, some small and sharp, Ben and I find the Piotrkow stone. Unlike most of the stones, it has eleven memorial candles at its base. More than 22,000 Jews were brought here from Piotrkow and murdered within seven days. The spirit among the surviving 'Piotrkowers' is strong. 'They keep coming to Treblinka,' Ben comments.

We stand for a few minutes at the stone. Then Ben asks me to go with him out of the camp. He is trembling. As we walk away, back past the larger stones and the railway memorial, and out through the woods, through a dull, relentless, penetrating drizzle, he says to me: 'I have an eerie feeling, how lucky I was to escape it, how easily I could have been one of those here. It is a frightening thought. It was just a matter of sheer chance. So many of my friends are here – so many neighbours – it really frightens me. People who could have lived so long, yet lived such a short life. They could have accomplished so much, but were cut down before they had time to mature. Those who are here, I knew so many of them. They were such lovely people – lovely, decent people, happy people, leading ordinary lives, looking forward to their future, to love and friendship. It is a terrible, terrible feeling.'

We trudge through the woods along a wet path. Ben was so close to so many, knew so many, who were murdered here. Had there been no war, had he grown up with them into adulthood, he would still perhaps have been a Piotrkower, living in his home town until his dying day.

As Ben and I walk away from the camp, I reflect that several of my own great-uncles and great-aunts were murdered here, and many of my cousins. They lived in Czestochowa, and were deported from Czestochowa to Treblinka. I cannot take it in. The persistent drizzle and the squelchy ground underfoot are a distraction. I feel a pain in my chest. A cuckoo is calling loudly through the woods. The cuckoo's call is incessant, loud and ghostly. Then it stops. A life cut short? But then it starts again.

I look for somewhere to sit down. A thought begins to obsess me. I am nearly sixty. There would be many thousands who would be nearly sixty today had they not been murdered here. In the safety of Canada, I was not quite six at the time of the Czestochowa deportations. My contemporaries, those almost six-year-olds who were brought here and killed, would today be parents and grandparents. They would have created so much.

Ben and I reach the visitors centre. Other members of the group are arriving. Ben comments in a whisper: 'One year and one month – 850,000 people, just like this – up the chimney.' Two kilometres from here, he adds, 10,000 Poles were murdered between 1940 and 1944 in a slave labour camp set up in a local quarry. Ben is always concerned that the Polish suffering should not be forgotten.

Suzanne and Kathy have been talking to the man in charge of the camp. He says that a project to build a substantial memorial has been dropped. There is a general feeling among the group that it would be wrong to have more buildings and more memorials. The small visitors centre, with its kiosk window, and a few books on display, could no doubt be improved.

Standing in the drizzle at the entrance to Treblinka, I do not feel like reading, but the group want me to read something. We gather by the edge of the wood, facing the visitors centre, and I find a passage to read. It relates to the German use of deliberate, calculated deception. The theme of deception is one that we have often discussed in class: the German skill in weaving a web of plausible lies and false hopes around the unthinkable reality. The reading illustrates this.

At the end of 1942 special signboards were put up at Treblinka station. Each of the station buildings was given a spurious name:

'Restaurant', 'Ticket Office', 'Telegraph' and 'Telephone'. The main store, containing the clothing of the victims, was covered with train schedules announcing the departure and arrival of trains to and from Grodno, Suwalki, Vienna and Berlin. 'When persons descended from the trains,' a survivor of Treblinka, Samuel Rajzman later recalled, 'they really had the impression that they were at a very good station from where they could go to Suwalki, Vienna, Grodno and other cities.' Rajzman also recalled 'huge signposts' with the inscription 'To Bialystok and Baranowicze', a station clock, and an 'enormous arrow' on which was printed: 'Change for Eastbound Trains'.

As 1943 began, a new German deception was sprung on the surviving inhabitants of the Polish ghettos. Jews were to be sent, it was said, not to 'work in the East', but to a neutral country, as part of a special exchange programme. Germans overseas would return to Germany. Jews from German-occupied Europe would be sent to Palestine.

At Opoczno, all Jews with 'relatives in Palestine' were asked to register. Many came out of hiding to do so. In all, 500 registered. It was yet another trick. On 6 January 1943, all 500 were deported, sent to Treblinka and gassed. Aaron, a young man of twenty-two who was in this deportation, later recalled the journey. As the train set off, he and the other deportees hoped that they were travelling westward, to a neutral country. Then, the train stopped, and the engine was uncoupled. Soon, it joined up again at the other end of the train. 'Within a few moments the train began to move off,' the young man recalled. 'At first there was a terrifying silence. Everybody waited for a miracle to happen or an abyss to open.' His account continued:

'But the miracle did not happen, and within a few moments we knew definitely that the train had changed its direction and we were travelling eastwards.

'It was as though there was an explosion and a collapse in the carriage. People shrieked to the high heavens. The little children in the carriage could not understand what it all meant, but they also began to cry at the tops of their voices.

'I looked at my own family members and it seemed to me as though they had all grown old in a single moment. My little sister Malkale, who was nine years old, understood what it all meant and was weeping bitterly, "Mother, but I never did anybody any harm." My sister Rochele, who was twelve years old, clung to me and said, "Aaron, I am terribly afraid. Look after me..." and she clung to me with all her strength.

'My sister Bracha, who was pregnant, wept in a loud voice. She was about twenty-eight. "But my baby hasn't even been born yet, and never sinned, why is he doomed?" Her husband stood stroking her hair. Looking at them I could no longer restrain myself, and also began weeping; but did my best to weep silently, so that my voice should not be heard.'

It was now plain that the deportees were being taken to Treblinka. Aaron's account continued: 'I looked round at the people. They were images of dread and horror. Some tore their hair, some flung themselves about in despair, and some cursed with all their strength.

'A woman clutched her baby to her breast with all her force. The child began to make strangled noises, while the woman whispered loving words to it and pressed it to her heart all the more.

'"Look what she's doing, look what she's doing. She's gone mad," came cries from all sides.

'"It's my child, mine, and I want him to die a holy death. Let him die a holy death." And by the time people succeeded in getting the child away, he was choked.

'One Jew near us went mad. Round his neck was a white scarf. He took it off and tried to tie it to one of the iron hooks in the carriage wall in order to hang himself. People tried to stop him. He punched and kicked with tremendous force and cried: "Let me hang myself!" They succeeded in dragging the scarf out of his hands and he collapsed in the corner.'

A group of young men in the sealed carriage made plans to try to break out. But many parents argued against such a plan: 'Mother sat at a loss,' the young man recalled. 'What will happen to us?' his mother asked. 'Don't let us separate. Don't let us separate. Death is lying in wait everywhere. Let us die together, at least.'

After a few hours the train came to a halt. It was in the middle of the night. The doors of the carriages were opened, 'and the chill air burst into the carriage and beat down on the exhausted and fainting travellers'. The young man recalled how: 'Into the carriage climbed a group of Mongols and Ukrainians, sub-machine-guns in their hands. The carriage was crowded from end to end, but still room was made for them. Everybody crowded and crushed together in fear, while they began to rob and pillage the passengers. Ample experience had taught them where such travellers hid their belongings. First they went to the women, tore off whatever clothes they were still wearing, thrust their hands into their bosoms and their private parts, and found money and jewellery. They pulled rings off fingers. Most of the travellers were exhausted and had no spirit of resistance. The few who refused or resisted were beaten with the rifle butts. "Diengi davay!" "Hand over the money," they kept shouting and cursing and abusing. It had been clear enough that we were being taken to slaughter.'

Among those in the carriage was the head of the Jewish Council of Opoczno, a man by the name of Przydlowski. It was clear, he told the deportees, that the end had come. 'Anyone who could run away should do so.' Aaron and some other young men decided they would try to make a run for it. First Aaron said goodbye to his parents. But, he later recalled, 'When I came to my sister Bracha I almost changed my mind and wanted to go back on my resolution. "What has my unborn baby done? Why is he doomed never to see the light of the world?" she went on whispering in a tremulous voice.'

The young men made their plans, and jumped. The guards were shooting. Many were killed. But between bursts Bracha's brother managed to jump unharmed, falling into a ditch filled with snow. There, he sank in the snow out of sight. He was, he later recalled, 'in an alien and hostile world', but he had made his escape, and was to survive the war.'

It is good to end with a story of survival. The atmosphere of the camp here, the memorial stones, and the station, are oppressive.

1.05 p.m.
We drive away, out of the woods. Ben remarks: 'It's really well camouflaged, well out of the way.' The camp is not visible from the railway line; the spur runs quite a distance before it enters the camp.

1.08 p.m.
We drive back through Poniatowa village, which is in fact the nearest village to the camp. Everyone is silent. Everyone's face is sombre and frozen.

1.12 p.m.
Drive past Treblinka station, going north, retracing our steps.

1.18 p.m.
We cross the River Bug, driving north, over the rickety bridge which carries both the road and the railway (at a somewhat drunken tilt) on a single carriageway.

1.20 p.m.
Malkinia Junction. Reflecting on Treblinka, Ben says: 'It frightens me. It's enough to renew my nightmares.'

1.37 p.m.
We reach the main Warsaw–Bialystok highway at Ostrow Mazowiecka, and drive back towards Warsaw.

In the bus there is talk, much muted, of what we have seen at Treblinka. Marie later tells me: 'The monument with all its stones really brought it home to me. All these stones made me realise, for the first time after years of studying the subject, the enormity of Nazi crimes. And because I had been stunned and left speechless about all the places of horror we had visited, Treblinka really made me cry. And I understood that no matter how much I would study the Holocaust I would never be able to understand it fully.'

For Paul, the stones of Treblinka proved particularly difficult. 'I turned round to our little group,' he wrote to me later, 'and asked whether prayer is futile. Prayers seemed like mere words evaporating into the air, insignificant compared to the immense destruction. When I said this, the others replied to me that if I felt like that I should not pray. I think they missed the point. For me, my faith in God was never really in doubt. It was and is my starting point in encountering the world. I am not shy of asking the big questions of Him, yet at the end of the day I do not question the importance of Judaism and the need to pray. Whether seemingly futile or not, I would pray anyway, because my faith demands the belief that the Divine is listening.'

Hugo Gryn expressed this dilemma from the perspective of a survivor of Auschwitz. 'All sorts of things happened to my faith during the Holocaust,' he once wrote, 'and although I could not have articulated it in this way, there is one thing that I understood very precisely: what happened to us was not because of what God did, but what people did after rejecting him. I witnessed the destruction that follows when men try to turn themselves into Gods.'

2.10 p.m.
Wyszkow. We recross the River Bug. Ben, in reflective mood, is thinking of all the divisions which the Second World War accentuated, and comments: 'Having a united Europe with its own currency is going to be good for everybody.'

2.20 p.m.
Niegow. A nun in her habit stands at the bus stop in the drizzle.

2.25 p.m.
Trojany. We stop at a roadside café.

3.15 p.m.
We leave Trojany. We are on our way – though it is still a long way –
to Ben's home town. There is one Jew still in Piotrkow; in the war,
aged seventeen, he was a runner for the Jewish police. Now he tries
to get money out of Piotrkowers by promising to use it for the upkeep
of the cemetery. 'He has gone a little mad,' says Ben. 'One would,
being the last Jew.'

3.28 p.m.
Cegielnia. The Red Army reached here in August 1920. There is a
Polish military cemetery here. In Warsaw, the memorial to the Polish
Unknown Soldier is from the war against the Bolsheviks.

3.41 p.m.
Warsaw city limits.

3.46 p.m.
We cross the Vistula at Marymont, and drive south along the river.

3.50 p.m.
We drive under the railway bridge that takes trains from Warsaw to
the east. On the right we can see the Umschlagplatz building.

4.07 p.m.
We pass Warsaw's Okecie airport, driving west. A sign to Piotrkow
gives the distance as 127 kilometres.

Herut tells me how she got her name. In Hebrew, the word means
Liberty. It was given to her after the German invasion of Russia, as a
manifestation of confidence in Germany's eventual defeat. The German
invasion began on the night of 21–22 July 1941. She was born two
days later. A cousin, Nehemia, had been captured by the Germans in
Greece in April 1941 (a Jew, he was serving in the British army). He
was taken to Germany as a prisoner-of-war. Postcards could be sent
to prisoners-of-war through the Red Cross. One was sent him, announcing the birth of 'Liberty'.

Together with his fellow prisoners-of-war, Herut tells me, 'my cousin spent the years of the war in a slave labour camp in Upper Silesia, working in coal mines, replacing rail tracks and working in the fields. When the Soviet army was approaching, the Germans started the prisoners on a death march which lasted three months. On 29 April 1945 they were liberated by American soldiers. The freed soldiers, many emaciated and too weak to walk, were taken to Newcastle and after a period of recuperation they returned to Palestine. My cousin still keeps on reassuring me that at times of distress, it was my name, Herut, which helped to sustain his hopes for returning home.'

4.45 p.m.
Zawady. We cross the railway line along which the Jews of Opoczno were deported to Treblinka.

4.55 p.m.
Zagorze. Ben becomes animated as we approach the town where he spent his youth in the bosom of his family. 'Then he had all his youth taken from him,' is Robin's comment.

5.05 p.m.
I distribute maps of the Piotrkow ghetto. Usually when doing this I have then said something about the town we will be coming to, but this time, Ben will speak.

5.08 p.m.
Ben speaks. In 1939 there were 55,000 people in Piotrkow, of whom 15,000 were Jews. The Jews of Piotrkow had played an important part in the growth of the town since the sixteenth century. After the various expulsions, they always came back (Ben stresses that Jews have never been expelled from Poland as such, but only from individual towns). In the eighteenth century there was a 'blood libel' in Piotrkow, when Jews were accused of using the blood of a Christian child to make their Passover unleavened bread.

Piotrkow's prosperity began in the second half of the nineteenth century, when it was ruled by Russia. There were three or four large factories. Piotrkow was among the first towns in Russian Poland where the trade union movement was very active. The largest Jewish political party in the town before the Second World War was the Jewish Socialist Workers Party, the Bund. There was a Jewish newspaper and a Jewish publishing house.

During the First World War the Russians were driven out by the Germans. Between the wars, Piotrkow was the fifteenth largest city in independent Poland. After Pilsudski's death in 1935 (when Ben was five and a half years old) there were many anti-Jewish regulations. It was difficult for Jews to get into the university, where a strict numerical barrier was imposed. There was graffiti everywhere in those days, typified by the injunction: 'Jews, go to Palestine!' Jews were made to feel that they were not wanted and that they were not Poles. But many Jews born under Polish rule were very patriotic. They found it hard to accept that they were not wanted. 'In the main, relations between Poles and Jews were good, but started to deteriorate after Pilsudski's death, when right-wing forces emerged and gained in strength. Jews lived all over the town. My family had always enjoyed good relations with Poles. We lived next door to each other.'

Piotrkow was bombed on 2 September 1939. 'There was a great panic.' When the Germans entered Piotrkow they took twenty-eight to thirty Jews and shot them. One of the first Jewish victims was Romek Zaks, a student, and a champion swimmer. 'He and his sister were great sportsmen. She survived and lives in Israel. She is now seventy-three, and still goes skiing on the slopes of Mount Hermon.'

Shortly after the German occupation, the Germans demanded an enormous 'fine' from the Jewish community. They then arrested several leading members of the community, and announced that if the fine was not paid, they would shoot the hostages. 'That,' says Ben, 'was really very frightening'. With great difficulty the money was raised and the fine was paid. The hostages were then released.

'There was one announcement after another, strangling Jewish life. Jews over the age of twelve were ordered to wear armbands. Jews were forbidden to use the park and all public places. Until then, I always used to play in the park.'

5.15 p.m.
The driver pulls in to a lay-by. He has been driving for four hours or so without stopping, and must, he says, understandably, have a ten-minute break. Ben urges him to continue – 'we're nearly there' – but the driver waits for ten minutes before driving on. Ben, meanwhile, continues with the story of Piotrkow during the war.

'In October 1939, we were ordered out of our homes, and forced to move into the ghetto. It was the first ghetto that the Germans set up in Poland (it was formally opened – or rather, closed – on October 28). Certain streets, where many Jews already lived, were designated a ghetto. Between five and six thousand people lived there before the war; now 28,000 were forced to live there. There were some Poles living there too; they had to move out. It was in the main a poor area. Many houses had no electricity or inside toilets. There was no running water in the houses; it had to be brought in from the nearby wells.'

In addition to the 15,000 Jews of Piotrkow, Jews from all over western Poland (the areas that were being annexed by Germany) were being expelled. 'An ancient community from Gniezno – the town that had been the first Polish capital, in 996 AD – were sent to Piotrkow. There were about 1,500 of them. They were very Germanised. In mid-December they were put on horses and carts and all the way in the bitter cold they were sent to Piotrkow. When they arrived in the ghetto there wasn't any room for them. They were mostly accommodated in two buildings, the Maccabi sports house and the synagogue. Jewish prisoners-of-war were also quartered in the synagogue. From December 1939 to October 1942 it served as a transit place for people who had been expelled or driven out from other places. For anyone who went in there, it was like obtaining a death certificate. We had soup kitchens to help them, but imagine, five hundred people at any one time in the synagogue, some in bunks, some on the ground. There were no toilet facilities there. It was the first place where epidemics started.'

Ben speaks of the daily life of the ghetto. 'Young people suffered. From fifteen onwards, they could not walk in the streets for fear of being taken for forced labour. In mid-1940 between two hundred and two hundred and fifty were rounded up and taken to build fortifications on the River Bug. One has to give credit to a very courageous and very resourceful man, who was originally from Lodz, who took it upon himself to try to get these young men back. He was taken and beaten up, and one of his lungs collapsed – later, when he was sent to Buchenwald, he didn't survive. But he brought the young men back from the River Bug. He became really their hero. His name was Gomberg. He was a tall man, a good-looking man. He became one of the top officers of the Jewish ghetto police. He was trusted more than the other police.

'There was no real rule that anyone who went out of the ghetto would be shot. Some would be shot, some would be beaten. One SS man taught his dog to go for men's testicles. Our nights weren't safe either. The police would knock on the doors at night to round up young people to be taken away for forced labour. We lived on the third floor, and they were not looking for boys as young as I was. As I was not yet twelve years old, I didn't even wear an armband. However, my father had to use his acrobatic skills to make his way up to the roof, where he used to hide during such round-ups.

'One day I went to visit a friend, and saw an SS officer with his dog. He thought I was a Pole. I was so terrified, I was frozen to the ground. He called me over. I came over, taking small steps, keeping a watch on the dog. He asked me what I was doing in the ghetto. I told him that I was Jewish. He then asked me why I was not wearing an armband. I explained that I was not yet twelve years old. He demanded to see my birth certificate, and I had to go home to fetch it. When I brought it to him I was terrified of what would happen next. He must have been in a happy mood – he laughed, and let me go.

'In 1942 there were rumours of deportation. Some said that the Jews were being sent to "gas chambers". Others accepted the German version, that it was for "resettlement" in areas conquered from the Russians. The Germans made it known that anyone who was gainfully employed would not be deported. There was a rush to get a job. In August, I got a job in the glass factory, thanks to my father. On October 14 the dreaded deportations began. I had my job, and I stayed in the factory while the deportations were taking place.'

5.50 p.m.
We have reached the old Piotrkow–Warsaw road, down which, on 19 and 20 December 1942, more than five hundred Jews were taken from Piotrkow to the Rakow forest, and shot. Among those brought on the second day was Ben's mother and his younger sister. He will tell us the full story later. Sara Helfgott, Ben's mother, was thirty-seven. His sister Lusia was nine. 'Before the war,' Ben tells us, 'young people used to come to the woods and picnic here. This was a hiking place.'

5.55 p.m.
We reach the Piotrkow town limits.

5.58 p.m.
Plac Liteweski (Lithuania Square). The driver puzzles us again by refusing to drive straight on into town (where Ben wants to show us the synagogue) and insists on going straight to the hotel. Ben asks him to drive on. After a heated argument, he agrees.

6 p.m.
We reach the former synagogue, now a public library, but the driver refuses to stop. When Ben expostulates with him, he points to the 'No

Parking' sign in the street. I suggest that he should let us off the bus and drive on. This is ignored. He eventually agrees that, instead of going straight to the hotel, as he was insisting, he will take us to the Jewish cemetery.

6.04 p.m.
We reach the gate of the Jewish cemetery. The street address is No. 93 Spacerowa Street. A woman comes to the gate, she is the caretaker. She says 'Shalom'. She is not Jewish, but she has become used, in the past few years, to Jewish visitors, mostly Piotrkowers from Israel and the United States.

6.05 p.m.
We enter the cemetery. In the area nearest the gate, where there are no tombstones, the caretaker has planted a vegetable patch. Lettuces and onions are poking above the soil.

The cemetery dates back about two hundred years. In the course of clearing the undergrowth, the woman has found some old tombstones, and placed them near the entrance. One of them is just over a hundred years old. It marks the grave of Hava, the daughter of Jakob Yosef, who died in 1874. Her headstone reads:

> A very charitable person,
> she had pity on all,
> the poor and the needy
> and her good deeds
> will be remembered for ever.

At the edge of the cemetery is the mass grave of sixty Jews who were executed here, and a Polish memorial marker. 'Hundreds were shot here during the ghetto period and the deportations,' says Ben.

I read the story of an early episode here. On 18 February 1940 two German sergeants seized two Jewish girls in the town, the eighteen-year-old Miss Nachmanowicz and the seventeen-year-old Miss Satanowska, forced them at gunpoint here to the cemetery, and raped them.

I recount another episode that took place here, among the gravestones where we are standing. It took place on 21 March 1943, the day of the Jewish festival of Purim, when Jews celebrate the defeat of their arch-enemy Haman. That day, Jews who were still living legally in the ghetto (it was five months after the October deportations) were told that there was to be an exchange with German citizens living in the settlement of Sarona, in Palestine. Ten people were needed for this exchange, the Germans declared. All must possess university degrees; that was the only condition for emigration.

The Jews chosen for Palestine were driven out of Piotrkow in Gestapo cars, and then driven round the city a few times, before being taken, as darkness fell, to the Jewish cemetery. A deep pit had been dug. The Gestapo lined up the 'chosen', made derisive speeches amid much drinking and laughter, and then ordered the Jews to undress.

Among the Jews shot that night at the Piotrkow cemetery was Dr Maurycy Brams, a paediatrician and popular figure among the poor Jews of pre-war Piotrkow, murdered with his wife and sixteen-year-old daughter, Hannah – 'Ania'. The teenage girl had managed to run away from the cemetery at the last moment, but the Gestapo chased her among the tombstones until they caught her. Also shot that night was a young lawyer, Simon Stein, killed with his mother, and the psychiatrist Dr Leon Glatter.

Part of the macabre Nazi 'Purim game' was to 'revenge' the ten sons of the Jew-hater Haman. These ten had been hanged in the biblical story. But only eight Jews had been brought from Piotrkow that night, so the Jewish watchman of the cemetery and his wife were included, at the last moment, in the execution.

Ben tells of how, in the winter of 1943, the Gestapo caught a Jewish woman and forced her under torture to give them the names of those who had false Polish passports. Two of them were Ben's uncles: his mother's brother, Jozef Klein, and his father's younger brother, Fishel Helfgott. They were seized, brought here to the cemetery with about fifty others, and shot. A stone in their memory was put up after the war. Jozef Klein was forty-one when he was killed, twenty-five years younger than his nephew Ben is today.

We are standing by another mass grave. This is the grave of the more than five hundred Jews who were shot in the Rakow forest – the road to which we passed twenty minutes ago. Ben tells the story: 'After the deportation of October 1942, when we returned to the small ghetto, people were beginning to return from their hideouts, to a kind of normality. The Germans were well informed. They had their informers. The Germans then used subterfuge. "We need people for work," they said. "You will be safe. But you have to register." People who were not registered were frightened, as it meant that they were illegally in the ghetto. So they came forward. There were a few hundred of them, amongst them my mother and my two sisters, Mala, who was just twelve, and Lusia, who was nine.

'As soon as they were registered, the order went out to round them up. More than five hundred of those who had recently registered were then taken to the synagogue, a tragic place, where thousands had already either died from starvation and epidemics, or had been taken away to certain death. Among those taken to the synagogue were my mother and my sister Lusia.

'On 19 December 1942 a number of SS men went to the synagogue. They asked for fifty young men to volunteer for a special job. Once the job was done, the SS promised, they would be released. The fifty were taken to the Rakow forest. They were ordered to dig five large pits. On completing their work, they were ordered to undress. One of the men shouted out, "Run!" The SS men were taken by surprise. A few of them managed to get away. One or two of those who escaped returned that same evening to the small ghetto and related what had happened.

'When I woke up at eight the following morning I saw my father in tears. He told me how in the early morning those in the synagogue were ordered to walk to the Rakow forest, where they were all shot.

'After the war, when survivors from Piotrkow returned from the camps, they exhumed the bones, which were placed in five large boxes, and buried here in the Jewish cemetery.' Ben points: 'At least I know my mother's and sister's bones are buried here. I don't know where my father's bones are buried.' Ben's father was killed, at the age of thirty-eight, while trying to escape from one of the death marches at the very end of the war.

We are facing the mass grave. Ben stands on the small step at the edge of the grave and says the Kaddish.

6.30 p.m.

We walk through the cemetery. Half the graveyard is empty. In 1943 the Germans began taking the stones away.

We look at the many headstones. One is of the synagogue cantor, Kamenetsky, whom the Jewish community brought here from South America before the war. They were so proud that they could pay him a bigger salary than he was getting across the ocean.

There are a few post-war graves. Of the 22,000 Piotrkow Jews deported to Treblinka, or sent to slave labour camps (like Ben), 200 came back to Piotrkow after the war and lived here. Then, in the early 1950s, most of them went to Israel. The few who remained followed them in 1969, after an upsurge of government-sponsored Polish anti-Semitism.

We come to the grave of Hersz Goldhersz. 'I knew him very well,' says Ben. He was born on 13 December 1922. 'He had a younger brother who was my age; we used to play together. The young boy and his family were all sent to Treblinka. Hersz joined the partisans. He was killed in January 1945 in a skirmish with the Germans, as the Germans were withdrawing, just before the Russians arrived.'

Angela has found the grave of a great-great-great-uncle, Itzhak Mordechai Klug, who died in 1932. His tombstone reads:

> A very decent and honoured man
> he went always on the honest path
> and he was faithful in his business
> all his days
> and strong in his good deeds.

Angela puts a stone on the headstone, the traditional Jewish sign to show that someone had visited the grave. 'It is probably the only stone which has ever been put here, by family,' she reflects. 'I hope this will not, however, be the last.'

As we are about to leave the cemetery, I find three headstones, with names and dates. They read:

> Lajzer Malc
> 21–III–1921
> 9–XI–1945
>
> Sura Uszerowicz
> 1–12–1923
> 9–XI–1945
>
> Ruchla Rolnik
> 28–VI–1885
> 9–XI–1945

I am staggered, and turn to one of my own pages in *The Holocaust, The Jewish Tragedy*. I had not expected to see these three stones here, nor to read these three names. 'In Piotrkow' – thus I had written fifteen years ago (basing myself on a post-war study of Piotrkow, which used the German spellings) – 'a Jewess, Miss Usherowitz, sold her father's apartment to a Pole for six hundred zlotys, the equivalent of about five American dollars. That same day she was murdered, together with a friend, Mrs Rolnik, and a young man, Mr Maltz, with whom she shared her apartment.'

These three were among more than a thousand Jews murdered by the Poles immediately after the war, when they came back to their home towns in search of other survivors, or a safe haven. It had never occurred to me, when I wrote that passage, that I might ever see their graves.

I too, like Angela, place a stone on each grave.

7.20 p.m.
We leave Piotrkow cemetery. I am shivering, not from cold, but from seeing those three gravestones.

7.26 p.m.
We drive back to town, not to the hotel, but, at Ben's urging, to a small car park on the edge of town. From there, we walk down a hill and across the River Strawa, the small stream that goes right around Piotrkow. No doubt in winter it is a torrent. I tease Ben about the smallness of the stream. I am not alone in this. On the eve of Passover 1924, Yosef Berish Rosenblum, known as 'Yerubel', who taught at the Hebrew gymnasium in Piotrkow, and was a witty satirist, penned these lines:

> Do you know the city
> That's at God's mercy,
> Where the River Jordan doesn't flow,
> Nor, either, the Rhine,
> But the genuine
> Strawa itself?

7.30 p.m.
We walk down Wojska Polskiego – Polish Army Street. Before the war it was Pilsudskiego and, under the German occupation, Ostlandstrasse. At No. 33 is the house where, after the war, the Sherit ha'Pleyta (the Remnant of the Survivors) met, in two neglected rooms in the basement, to pray, to eat lunch, to remember their lost ones, and to make their plans to leave Poland forever.

Ben remembers which of his friends lived in which of the houses in the street. Szlamek Winogrodski lived at No. 65. He survived the war and came to Britain with the 732 youngsters about whom I am writing. Today he is Ray Wino.

Several doorways have the cavity in their wooden doorposts in which the mezzuzah was set.

We reach No. 55 Pilsudskiego Street. From here, where the ghetto began, Ben would walk with his fellow-slave labourers to the glass factory each morning, and return each evening. 'One afternoon, two weeks after the deportations, when we passed this doorway on the way out to the glass factory, I pretended to tie up my laces and ran into the entrance here. I waited till the group had disappeared. Then I made my way across to that part of the town where I thought my parents were in hiding with a Polish family. When I met them it was quite a reunion. Later that evening, together with my father, I rejoined my work shift outside the factory and returned with them to the small ghetto.'

7.48 p.m.

We walk up Rwandska Street (Ritterstrasse during the war), which leads to the former ghetto. We are standing opposite the house behind which the ghetto area began. On the other side of this house is the courtyard where Ben and his family lived. As Ben begins to recall the war years here, a drunk comes up and starts pestering us. He seems very hostile and the group are uneasy. We are also very tired. It is almost eleven hours since we left the hotel in Warsaw, and we have only had one small snack since then, quite apart from the harrowing time at Treblinka. Ben does not want to stop now. 'The drunkards are of no consequence,' he says. 'They are completely innocuous. If you push them, they fall over.'

Ben continues talking, but the group are now cold as well as tired, and the appearance of the drunk (who has now gone on into the former ghetto square a few yards further up the street) has unnerved several of us.

Ben speaks of two Jewish families who lived in Piotrkow, who had Egyptian and Turkish citizenship (from before 1914). They were ordered to live just outside the ghetto, here at No. 5. 'On the last day of the deportation the Germans came and took them out and sent them to Treblinka. Poles were standing around here and watching how the Jews were being driven to the selection place. My Jewish friend, the Egyptian citizen, Jerzyk Kam, saw a Pole who was the foreman of the shift where I worked and gave him some food for me. Unfortunately he was deported to Treblinka. Perhaps had his parents not held Egyptian citizenship they may have survived, such were the quirks of fate.'

Ben tells of an occasion when the ghetto was surrounded, and it was dangerous for the Pole who usually helped his father to smuggle flour into the ghetto from the nearby village of Moszczenica to do so. Ben offered to take a message to the Pole. He would, he said, put on his satchel and get over the wall that separated the house where he lived from the outside world, and pretend that he was a Polish schoolboy (which he had been until September 1939). Once on the Polish side of the wall, he said, he would make his way to Moszczenica and warn the Pole not to bring the flour into town. At first his father said, 'You must not do it.' But eventually Ben persuaded his father to agree. 'I said I could do it. I had climbed over the wall before and I could climb over it again.' (Even today, Ben is exceptionally agile, as befits a former British weightlifting champion and Olympic competitor. He is also very persuasive.)

'I went over the wall that was at the back of our courtyard. I came out here, at No. 5. And there in front of me were two guards, and two Ethnic German boys. I walked on. The guards called "Halt" (Stop). I answered, "Schule" (School). The guards looked to the boys for confirmation. To my amazement, the boys said, "Yes." They didn't give me away. I got to Moszczenica just in time. The Pole had already loaded the flour and was ready to set off to Piotrkow. I told him, "The ghetto is surrounded. We have to leave the delivery of the flour for another time." I returned home feeling very proud that I had been able to help out my father from what would have been a very serious situation, and danger. I was the hero of the day.'

8.10 p.m.

It is very cold and very wet. The drunk returns. Robin, with his police experience, advises that we leave and go back to the hotel. He is worried that the drunk may bring reinforcements. Two of the drunk's mates are looking at us from the square. We walk back to Wojska Polskiego Street, and towards the railway bridge. Before the war, says Ben, the bridge marked a sort of undrawn boundary; not many Jews lived beyond it.

8.25 p.m.

We return to the bus, and drive to the hotel. As we drive through deserted streets, Ben comments: 'What a hustling, bustling place it was before the war – and look at it now.'

8.30 p.m.

We reach Roweckiego Street, and our hotel, the Hotel Trybunalski. It is twelve and a half hours since we left Warsaw. I distribute the keys, and, with Ben's help, persuade the hotel to provide supper.

9 p.m.

I leave the hotel with Ben and Paul. We walk down Roweckiego Street to Piotrkow railway station. Darkness has fallen. At one side of the station square is a footbridge over the railway. Across the bridge is Ben's father's flour mill, an imposing building. We look at it for some minutes in silence. In the pre-war years, Ben's father, with his two partners, ran a prosperous business, with many employees, milling and despatching flour all over the region. Ben was then a young lad, six, seven, eight years old, deeply absorbed in his youthful studies. Perhaps one day he would take over the management of this impressive, productive enterprise. Who in 1938 could predict the total collapse of the world of Jewish Piotrkow, of Jewish Poland?

9.20 p.m.

We return to the hotel.

9.40 p.m.

Dinner. Today we began our journey in a pre-war orphanage, wandered through the damp fields of a former death camp, and ended on the edge of what had been a ghetto.

We talk about the impression the different places have made on us, and about the importance of silence after being at the site of a death camp. Someone asks, 'Why was Sobibor so devastating?' Although it is now four days since we were there, the image of the pyramid of human ash remains strong in all our minds, as does the sight of the fields of human ash, where there were so many fragments of bones. It was as if everything had just been dumped there, and left.

DAY 13

PIOTRKOW – KONIN

'The yeast is not there'

6 a.m.

I leave the hotel with Ben, Herut, Suzanne and Kathy. We walk down Sienkiewicza Street, one of the streets in which, before the war, well-off Poles and Jews lived side by side.

We cross Slowackiego Street, one of the main streets of the town. The houses to the left of us were destroyed during the German bombing raid on 2 September 1939.

Reaching Narutowicza Street, we see a plaque on the corner building which records that a meeting of the Polish Communist Party was held here in 1920. On the first floor of the house opposite, Ben tells us, lived a girl who went to the same class as he, and whose mother had converted to Judaism. Both mother and daughter survived the war.

As we look at the first-floor window, a taxi passes. Inside is Angela, on her way to her great-grandparents' town, Belchatow. She is on her own, and I ask Kathy, who speaks Polish, if she would join her. I had hoped to go with her myself, last night, but we ran on too late. I was in Belchatow on my 1980 journey. I tell Ben and the others about a Jew who had been born in Belchatow who appears in the list of just over a thousand Polish-born Jews who were rounded up in France and deported from Paris to Auschwitz on 27 March 1942. Five thousand Jews were deported from Belchatow to Chelmno in August 1942.

It is raining. We walk on to the Halle, the covered market (Hala Targowa). It is a splendid art deco building, the pre-war centre of Piotrkow's trading activity. 'Here was a place of tumult and excitement,' says Ben. The father of Krulik Wilder (a friend of mine from London) used to have a shop here. 'This place is so derelict, it is unbelievable what a bad state it is in,' says Ben indignantly.

Seventy-five per cent of the merchants in the Halle were Jewish. We walk down Piastowska Street. We walk into the courtyard. The building belonged to the Steinberg family. Sevek Steinberg survived the war and came back to Poland immediately afterwards, and got his home back. He died in Lodz twelve years ago.

We go into another courtyard, also owned before the war by a Jewish family. 'These used to be lovely buildings,' says Ben. 'But nothing has been done to them since before the war.'

We go into another yard. 'This was a beautiful house before the war,' Ben laments. 'If I tell you what a lovely house, what a lovely, imposing staircase it had.' The woodwork is broken, the plaster in the stairwell peeling, the floor has broken flagstones. It is as if we are looking at Pompeii rather than Piotrkow. In some ways the catastrophe was the same: a city wiped out. Only the buildings remain, old and weary, as a monument, lived in by Poles who may not even know that Jews lived there before the war.

We reach Aleja 3-Maja. It was on 3 May 1791 that the first Polish constitution was promulgated; the Russians abolished it a year later. It is a fine street running down from a large park. 'It was a beautiful street,' says Ben. 'This was my street and here I ran around.'

We walk up the hill, passing the vinegar factory on the right. It belonged to a Jewish family, Goldfreid.

We cross Aleja 3-Maja to Ben's school, then known as the Berek Joselewicz school, after the Polish-Jewish colonel who was killed fighting for Poland in 1809, one of Ben's schoolboy heroes. In this school, young Jews had received their education for more than fifty years. It is still a school. A plaque on the wall records that during the Russian revolution of 1905 (Piotrkow was then one of the most westerly towns in the Tsarist Empire) there was a strike of young people at the school. Ben remembers the Polish patriotism of his schooldays. 'When I would sing the Polish anthem, I really sang it with great fervour and great excitement.'

He gives us a rendering.

We continue up the hill, to the park. This is where Ben used to play as a boy, until the Germans forbade Jews to go in the park. On the opposite corner is a large hospital, set in its own grounds. This is where Ben's sister Mala was born (she, like Ben, survived the war, and lives in London today).

We return down Aleja 3-Maja. In the rain, the street is grey and drab and empty. Ben populates it with the people of sixty years ago. We pass the former bakery run by Brummer, an Ethnic German. Then Froman's grocery. Next, on the far side of the street, the house (No.

17) where Lajbl Nyss lived. 'He had a stroke two months before the war. He had a young daughter, a year younger than I. Neither of them survived.'

A little below Lajbl Nyss's house is the building that was once the cinema, the Kino Roma. It is a long single-storey building with an ornamental façade. Before the war it was owned by an Italian. Ben was a frequent attender here; it is only a minute's brisk walk from his house. It was here, he recalls, that he saw *The Charge of the Light Brigade* starring Errol Flynn, and the Yiddish film *Yidl mitn fidl* (Yidl with his fiddle) with Molly Picon, the well-known Jewish actress, as one of the stars – she died in the United States only recently. Opposite the cinema is the theatre, Sala Kilinskiego, and next to the theatre, at No. 10, the building in which Cantor Kamenetsky lived, on the second floor.

We cross to the side of the cinema. We have reached No. 9. We enter a courtyard. It is not well tended. It was here that Ben lived as a boy, before the war. He points to a first-floor window with a small balcony. 'That was my room.' A little boy is looking out of the window at us. 'Among my earliest memories,' says Ben, 'is a wedding which took place in our apartment. Here we had all the modern facilities – toilets, bathroom, telephone. It was once a beautiful courtyard. I looked forward to May, to look out at the lilac in blossom.

'On the second floor lived my uncle Marcus, aunt Frania and my cousin Gienek. My uncle and my cousin survived the war, but my aunt died of exhaustion and starvation in Ravensbrück towards the end of the war.'

A lady comes out of the building. She has a daughter who lives in England.

We continue down the street. 'A lot of people I used to know lived here.' Opposite us is the local shtiebl, or prayer hall. Next to it is the house of the family who used to own the electricity company. 'They used to light all the windows in their house. It illuminated the whole street.'

We reach the crossroads of Aleja 3-Maja and Kopernika Street. Ben points out his favourite cake shop – it is still a cake shop – and remembers the blackberry pie. We then cross the stream and begin to climb up again, towards Kosciusko Square: Sachsenplatz in the war. On our right (Ben takes us that way) is a small park. 'Here we used to chase butterflies.' We turn into a narrow street. This is the beginning of the area that was mostly Jewish in the inter-war years – and before then – and was to become the ghetto on 28 October 1939. Ben points out what used to be Kaluszynski's clothing shop.

We walk through the narrow streets, following a wartime map that gives the German names during the ghetto years, and come to the main square. We almost reached this point last night (from the opposite direction) when rain and cold and exhaustion and the drunks made us call a halt.

Ben points out the house where his friend Krulik Wilder used to live. We then cross the square to Ben's house from the ghetto period, No. 4 Plac Trybunalski. We go into the building. A staircase confronts us. 'I was so agile at the time,' says Ben. 'I used to jump from the height of the first floor and land on my feet – like a leopard.'

We go into the courtyard, Ben's ghetto courtyard, and look up at his window on the top floor. Above it is an attic. 'They would come in search of able-bodied men to take them away for hard labour. We would hear the noise as they came closer. My father would then go into the attic and from there on to the roof. I remember so well, the Jews who were caught were assembled in the courtyard. My father was hiding on the roof. Then I heard the sound of singing. It was the Jewish anthem "Hatikvah", The Hope – and now the national anthem of the State of Israel. I jumped out of bed and came to the window. I could see the subdued men singing "Hatikvah". They sang it so softly, so plaintively; this kind of sadness, nostalgia; you could feel their yearning.

'Whenever I am at a Jewish function, and sing "Hatikvah" (as one nearly always does, at the end) I feel a shiver, and remember those bleak nights.'

We leave Ben's courtyard and continue through the ghetto streets. Ben points out the corner where Krulik used to sell armbands and cigarettes. 'Krulik's patch,' he calls it.

'To be a child in the ghetto was not so bad,' Ben comments. And yet, he adds, 'to be a child during the deportations meant, in most cases, the end of one's life.' He and Krulik and a number of others – some of whom later came to England – were lucky to have been given work in the glass factory two months before the deportations. Otherwise they could not have survived.

7.15 a.m.

We reach the edge of the 'small ghetto'. This was formed after the deportation and death of the 22,000 Jews who were in the ghetto in October 1942. It ran along the righthand side of the Alte-Warschauerstrasse – Old Warsaw Street. Before the war, and before the German occupation, it was Judenstrasse. Today it is Grodzka. There were 2,500 people in the small ghetto. It was surrounded by barbed wire.

7.20 a.m.

We go into one of the yards in the small ghetto where Jews were assembled for deportation in December 1942. It was here that Ben's sister Mala persuaded a Gestapo officer to let her return to the ghetto. Ben is inordinately proud of this, and tells us the story on the spot where it took place fifty-four years ago. I read Mala's own account of the episode, which she set down for me three months ago: 'The ghetto was liquidated and only two groups of workers remained. They were to be allocated to the local Hortensja glass factory and the Dietrich and Fischer Bugaj woodwork factory. During this liquidation my cousin Hania and I, as children who were useless for these factories, were lined up outside the barbed wire fence of the ghetto, ready to board the lorries which were to take us to the railway station, for onward transmission to a concentration camp.

'The column was four deep and very long, and we were surrounded by guards with machine guns pointing at us. The woman in front of us, with a baby in her arms, was hit over the head with a rifle. She was in a terrible state, bleeding profusely. I do not know what she had done to warrant this blow. She may just have moved, because her baby was fidgeting. The sight of her in her agony was alone enough to freeze one to the spot. It was certainly very frightening, and we were getting close to boarding the lorry when suddenly I left the line, went up to the SS officer in charge, and asked him if he would allow me to go back inside to my father and brother from whom I had been separated. I must have moved very fast because the guard was obviously not quick enough to shoot. The SS officer looked at me very surprised, probably wondered how I had the courage or the audacity even to speak to him, but smiled and said "Yes".

'He instructed a policeman to take me back, and on the way I said to him, "Just a minute, I have to collect my cousin." My cousin, Hania, was only four years old. He answered that the permission was only for me, and that my cousin would not be allowed to go back with me. I found myself in an impossible situation, my heart was racing and I was terrified at the prospect of leaving Hania or losing the chance of being reunited with my father and brother. I begged and pleaded and said that I could not possibly go back and ask the lieutenant again, and I could not go back into the ghetto without her. He eventually relented.'

Mala and Ben Helfgott, and their father, and Hania, were among less than two thousand survivors of the Piotrkow ghetto. The Piotrkow Jewish community, more than twenty thousand strong on the eve of war, was no more. Mala and Ben, and Hania, were among the fortunate ones. Today Mala and Ben live in London, and Hania in Melbourne.

7.22 a.m.

In the yard where Mala saved herself and her cousin Hania from deportation, an old lady with a broom invites us – with a smile – to live here. She is seventy-eight years old. She says that thirteen people from Israel came here not long ago. They were all former Piotrkowers. She said to them, 'Why don't you take me to Israel? I would like to go.'

She adds: 'They did not take me because I was too young. If I had been older they would have taken me!'

Ben: 'May you live to be a hundred.'

Old lady: 'To 150 – my grandmother lived until 117.'

7.25 a.m.

We have reached the stream again, and cross it. Ben points to a house in which he was telling a friend the terrible news that his father (Ben's) had apparently been arrested. As he was imparting this grave news he looked out of the window and saw his father walking on the other side of the stream. He was back in the ghetto after all. 'I ran over to him; in my haste and joy, I jumped over the stream.'

Ben points across the stream to the southern part of the small ghetto. 'That is the house from which my mother was taken away. People were trying to get out. There were terrible scenes.'

We walk a short way up the hill, to the corner of Alte-War-schauerstrasse and Jerozolimska – Jerusalem Street. From this corner the synagogue is visible. During the period in December 1942, when 523 women and children were imprisoned there, Ben would often come to this corner, as did many others, and watch in case some fortunate person would be released. 'Very often one would see the Ukrainians shooting into the synagogue,' says Ben. 'On one occasion a woman came out from the synagogue and a Ukrainian pulled off her shawl, snatched her baby from her arms, and tossing the baby to the ground, shot it.'

We stand at the corner looking towards the synagogue, and cannot move. It is all so peaceful now.

We walk down Jerozolimska to the synagogue. On our left is Piotrkow Castle.

We reach the corner of Jerozolimska and Wojska Polskiego, and look at the synagogue, now a public library. It is too early for it to have opened. It is a handsome building with crenellations. We walk along Wojska Polskiego in the direction of the hotel. This part of the street was inside the ghetto. It was also one of the main Jewish areas of pre-war Piotrkow. Ben has something to say about almost every house in the street. No. 23 belonged to his cousins' grandparents, the Grynszpans. The building which we go to see in the rear of No. 23 was an elementary school, the Maria Konopnicka School, where mostly Jewish children attended. During the war it was the headquarters of the Piotrkow Jewish Council.

At the front of No. 23, one of the shops was a shoemaker's, where, Ben recounts, 'my mother had our shoes repaired, and often new shoes made. That man worked ten to twelve hours a day. He was an excellent shoemaker. He worked in one room, which served, in addition to his workshop, as a kitchen, lounge and bedroom. Craftsmen worked very hard, but their remuneration was very small. It was enough to support their families for their basic needs, but not for luxuries.'

Next to the shoemaker's shop was that of a man who sold bicycles, Motl Dreikopf. Unlike the shoemaker, he survived the war. By chance, Ben saw him in the street in Tel Aviv a few years ago. '"Motl!" I called out. He was amazed when I went up to him and told him that I used to know his shop in Piotrkow.'

We continue along the street. The ghetto area is to our left. We pass the prison. It is a prison today, and was a prison in Tsarist times a century ago. It was on the edge of the ghetto. It was near here that Ben used to see Russian prisoners-of-war being marched by German soldiers from one end of the town to the other, to their slave labour tasks. 'I used to watch them go by. Each week there were fewer and fewer of them.'

I look in the register of German camps in Poland, one of the reference books I have with me in my knapsack. There were 30,000 Russian prisoners-of-war in the camp just outside Piotrkow, sent each day through the town to their work tasks. By the end of the war, all of them had been killed, or died of hunger and starvation.

We complete our walk. The people in the streets look miserable. The place seems even more miserable. 'Piotrkow is not the same place that it used to be,' says Ben. 'The Jews – the ingredients – have gone. The yeast is not there.'

8 a.m.

We reach the hotel, and join the rest of the group at breakfast. Angela has just come back from Belchatow. She tells me that, thanks to Kathy, who spoke Polish, they had been able to ask various elderly passers-by if they remembered 'a chemist shop with high steps', as recalled by her grandmother. 'By some miracle we found the place my family had lived. I said Kaddish there, and lit a candle in their memory.' Angela also found the house where her grandmother had lived as a little girl. 'It was a town of small, narrow streets, very run down,' she tells us. She is so glad that she went. 'I now know where my relatives lived and what they did.'

Ben speaks of the Jewish Piotrkowers as a group. 'Those who survived were together in Piotrkow for a long time – in the ghetto, in the factories, in the camps. We got to know each other. We lived through shared experiences. After the war, somehow, we always used to get together. We used to contact each other. I used to seek out Piotrkowers as early as the 1950s, when I travelled, representing Britain in international weightlifting competitions. Eventually there was a journal.[1] There were also many people from Piotrkow who had emigrated to Palestine before the war, who served as a link with the past.

'In 1955 I went to Munich to compete in the world weightlifting championships. I was there on the Day of Atonement, and decided to go to the synagogue. As I walked towards it I saw a man walking with a little child. The man was wearing a Homburg hat. I stopped him – without looking – asked him (in German) where the synagogue was. Then I looked at him. "You are Rosenwald," I said, "I was in Bugaj with you." I remembered that he worked in the factory in the garage looking after the two cars of the German boss, Fischer. "How do you know who I am?" he asked. "I used to see you every day," I replied. "Then you are going to break the fast with me," he said, and I did.

'After that, I kept in touch with him. He died of cancer a few years ago. Through him, as of course through others as well, I found out so much about people whom I remembered, and where they were living.

---

[1] And still is. The editor is himself a Piotrkower, Ben Giladi, who lives in Kew Gardens, New York. The first issue was published in 1966, the hundredth issue in 1996.

It greatly increased my knowledge about the pre-war Piotrkow community and its fate.'

8.20 a.m.
Breakfast ends.

8.37 a.m.
We board the bus.

8.44 a.m.
We drive out of the hotel car park, and under the railway bridge, on our way to the glass factory where Ben, and his friend Krulik, and 650 other Piotrkow Jews, worked from 1941 to 1944. They were slave labourers, but the man who was in charge of the factory, and who could have made their life a torment, did not do so. 'His name was Mr Christian,' says Ben. 'He was a good Christian.'

8.46 p.m.
Turning right immediately after the railway bridge, we reach the Hortensja Glass Works. It was built in 1889. Today it has the same name and the same entrance as in 1942. Ben recalls, of the war years here: 'At the gate we were searched. The two people who searched us were Ethnic Germans. They were uncouth and hostile.'

We enter the factory. It is like bedlam: ancient equipment, hot open fires, people milling around stoking the fires and carrying the molten glass. Ben recognises people doing the very things that he had to do.

The workers seem astounded that here is someone who was in this factory, working by the same machines, carrying out the same task, as they are fifty-four years later. For Ben, however, this work saved his life. He was twelve years old when he came here. In the deportations that followed two months after he arrived, he would have been sent to Treblinka and his death, but for his place at the workbench here. 'I came to work here on 12 August 1942. There were two large furnaces. The boys had to take the glass away to the cooling place. They were making bottles, glasses and jars. It was very hot. I did not listen to my mother, who begged me to sleep during the day. My job was to pick up the hot glass on the fork and to take it to the cooling room – ten to fifteen yards away. I had to do it quickly, as the glass would soon burst if left longer than a minute. I had to be quick – up and down, up and down. It was the most monotonous and tedious work I had ever done. Another task was to sit on a piece of concrete and put the wooden mould into water to cool it for a few seconds. This too was very tiring and monotonous.

'On that first night shift, I was getting very sleepy, and quickly tired. Smoke from the wooden mould was affecting my eyes. I was perspiring from the heat that emanated from the furnace. I was being kicked on the head by the glass blowers whenever I wasn't fast enough to place the mould in the right position. It was so hot. I was sweating.

'I got a breathing space when they told me to find out what time it was. I didn't realise that it was a ruse. As soon as I went away they poured molten glass on the concrete, and when I came back and sat down unsuspectingly on the hot concrete, I automatically jumped up. The concrete was too hot for me to sit on. They were enjoying themselves by making me sit down, and every time I jumped up they kicked my head. I was between "the anvil and the hammer".

'That night was probably one of the longest in my life. It was a night of torture. I had looked forward so much to working in the glass factory. I cannot remember now, how I visualised, as a twelve-year-old boy, what my work in the factory would be like, but it was certainly a bitter disappointment.'

The three factories here in Piotrkow, the Hortensja Glass Works, the Kara Glass Works, and the Bugaj wood factory, seem to have been refuges like Schindler's Emalia factory in Cracow, and Madritsch's factory in Tarnow.

A few days after Ben's first night experience here in Hortensja, a man who worked on the same shift approached him and told him that he could fix things up, with the foreman, for a certain sum of money, so that his life at the factory would be easier – by putting him on the reserve. 'You won't be needed so often,' the man said, 'only when there is not a full complement of workers.' Ben recounts what then happened: 'I arranged for my father to meet the foreman. Within a week I was on reserve. From that moment on I worked very little. Three weeks later my father was in the house of one of the Poles who helped him smuggle flour into the ghetto. One of the Polish foremen (we called them Meisters) from the factory turned up. My father asked his name. It was Janota. He wanted the loan of two horses and a cart to take away the produce from his allotment. These Meisters were experienced glass craftsmen. They were given allotments where they grew vegetables and corn. My father asked him: "Are you always in the habit of beating up helpless, innocent, young boys? That boy you beat up three weeks ago was my son."

'The Pole who worked for my father turned round to Janota and said, "I didn't realise you were such a bastard. I'm not letting you have the horses." My father turned round to him and said, "No. Let him have the horses and cart." The next day Janota sent for me. "I met your father yesterday," he said, "He's a nice man." "I know," I said, "a very nice man."

'After that, Janota used to chat to me when he saw me. Then came the October deportations. On the last day of the deportations, the last railway wagon was not full. The glass factory was the nearest place to the railway. The SS came in, and picked up Jews at random. I happened to be working that morning. Someone pushed me into the group of those who were to be taken away. I called out, "I am a Pole." Janota came up and said, "Yes, he is a Pole", and they let me go.

'What would have happened if my father had been a vengeful man? Most likely, I would have been sent to Treblinka. It was because of my father's action that I was saved at that moment. That was to be one of the great lessons of my life. I've always stood up for the underdog, and I've always avoided being vengeful.'

We go into the Hortensja Glass Works' sale room. There are glasses and vases on sale, some of them fine pieces, some very ornate, many coloured Hebron blue. We go into the administration office (on which is a Solidarity sign reminiscent of the heady days of 1981 when this sign was everywhere). They show us a register of all the workers in the factory from 1940 to 1944. I see some familiar names among those marked in red as 'Zyd' (Jew). There (with one 't') is 'Helfgot, Ben'. His date of birth is given, 20 December 1929, and his address, Plac Trybunalski 4. Listed immediately after him in the register is 'Wilder, Izrael', born 3 December 1928, living at Trybunalski 10. These were their addresses in the ghetto.

Another of the youngsters who was saved from deportation was Chaim Fuks (now Harry Fox). He had been deported to the Piotrkow ghetto with his family in November 1939 from nearby Tuszyn. He later recalled his two years in Piotrkow: 'We found a room, and were joined by two other families, all relations. For the first few days there were sixteen of us in one room, but by the end of the week, we had found a room for ourselves. The very first day I was in the Piotrkow Ghetto, I got involved in a street punch-up. I was outnumbered, and Ben Helfgott happened to be there and joined in to even up the fight. We have known each other ever since.

'In the early days my father still worked as a tailor. One of his jobs was turning suits inside out to make them look new again. My mother, ever resourceful, opened a greengrocer shop. There was not much variety in it, but we did not starve. I had my Bar Mitzvah at some stage in the ghetto, but I am confused about this, as my mother was there which means I was only twelve, or that I was born in 1929 – in spite of records found later stating my birth to be 1930.

'As restrictions soon tightened, my father realised the importance of having work, and got a place for my brother John in the Hortensja Glass Works. Some months later my father went to work in the Kara Glass Works. He also got me put on the list as a worker, an action which saved my life.

'In October 1942 all the people of the Piotrkow Ghetto were asked, district by district, over a period of days, to assemble in the main square. Here the women and children were selected to one side, together with all those who did not have a job. Not knowing what was going to happen, as I was young, my father pushed me over to join my mother and sister, but a guard saw my papers saying I was a worker, and sent me back to join my father. My mother and little sister went straight from there to Treblinka and their deaths. My mother was thirty-four and my sister ten.

'The rest of us were taken to our work places, but I was not on the factory list. The managing director of the Hortensja Glass Works lied and said that I was, thus saving my life once more. As my father worked at the Kara factory, we paid a member of the Polish Fire Brigade who were acting as guards, to go and tell my father that I was all right. At night we went back to the ghetto to sleep. Later, when the ghetto was closed, we slept in a camp by the factory. There was one camp for both factories, so he and I were able to be together. We were given no food at work, but we got bread and soup in the camp. My job was to take molten glass over to the machine that made it into bottles.'

9.35 a.m.

We leave the Hortensja Glass Works. A plaque on the outer wall commemorates a left-wing strike that took place here in 1932. Ben says: 'It is worse here now than it was during the war. Now it is so dirty. Then it was so orderly. I will never forget the scene when I first came there at night. It looked so picturesque at night, people blowing glass in all directions, people running with the glass. And then came the anti-climax, when I was so badly treated at work.'[1]

---

[1] Angela later wrote to me: 'After the trip I found out that Dora Klug, a survivor of Bergen-Belsen, also worked in this glass factory.'

9.40 a.m.
We drive out of Piotrkow.

9.43 a.m.
Leave the Piotrkow city limits. Our next stop is to be the marshalling yards at Radogoszcz from which the Jews were deported from Lodz to Chelmno. But the driver is complaining. He does not want to go to Radogoszcz because, he insists, his instructions say Lodz. I point out that Radogoszcz is a part of Lodz, but he is not appeased.

10.02 a.m.
Tuszyn. A one-horse town of one-storey houses. The Fox brothers lived here before the war. John is now in Philadelphia and Harry in London. Three years ago, John, who was born in 1928 (he was then Jona Fuks), set down his recollections of his childhood, of the ten years leading up to the war: 'I was in a class with forty-three children. Three of us were Jewish. When the teacher walked out of the classroom the Poles would throw things at us, curse and spit on us. When the teacher returned she would pretend that nothing had happened. We wouldn't complain because nothing would be done about it, and the other children would beat us up if we squealed on them. Many days I would come home from school with a bloody nose or a swollen lip from getting beaten up in school. Every morning when the school prayer was offered everybody knelt down except the Jewish children. I would not kneel down, of course, and I would get hit from the back and from the front. The teachers would see me getting beaten but they would not interfere.

'These beatings went on in school almost every day. I would come home and cry and complain and say that I didn't want to go to school any more. But my father would insist that I had to go to the Polish school. He would say that if I didn't know how to read and write when I grew up I wouldn't get anywhere in life. He insisted that the only way I would get an education, apart from our religion, was in the Polish schools.

'Throughout the 1920s and the 1930s Jewish youth was changing. We were beginning to move away from the strictly religious point of view and we were becoming more practical. All of the Jews that we knew were involved in discussions, and were listening to speakers and readers, because they were hungry for information and understanding. People knew what was going on in the world even though they were only working people. They made it their business not to be ignorant.

Even though many people were not educated, they were well versed in history. They knew about the rebellions against the Tsar and other important events in history.

'Jews would get together, on Saturday and Sunday or in the evenings, in Zionist clubs, which had speakers nearly every week. We came with our fathers and we listened and when we got home we would ask questions. Everybody was hungry for education. I think that European Jews were the most knowledgeable people on earth, because they wanted to know about the world around them.

'Those early years of my life were good times for me. I knew everybody by their first name and everybody knew me. We had a good feeling toward one another. It was our domain. There was time for everything. Life was good. I felt very comfortable being Jewish in those days. I was very proud of being a Jew. We felt that God was hovering over us and taking care of us, and that he would protect us. I absolutely believed this to be the case. We truly felt that God would protect us, and we did not believe in violence. We were so indoctrinated with our religion and our beliefs that I think that it hurt us when the war came.'

John's brother Harry recalled the arrival of the Germans in Tuszyn in September 1939: 'They rode on motor bikes and gave us sweets. Not long after they told us that as we were Jews, we were not allowed to go to school. At my age, this did not displease me at first. At 2 a.m. on a freezing night, 30 November 1939, the Germans came and screamed at us that we had two hours to leave our home or be shot. They even came inside our house to make quite certain we had understood. Our horse and cart was loaded with my father's tailoring machine and whatever my parents could salvage, and we left our lovely home at 4 a.m.'

The Jews of Tuszyn were driven to Piotrkow (whither we have just come) and incarcerated in the ghetto there, before being deported with the Jews of Piotrkow to Treblinka. Among those deported to their deaths were Chaim and Jona Fuks's mother and sister. Like the two boys, their father was a slave labourer for two years, but he died in Nordhausen in early 1945. The two brothers survived the war.

10.20 a.m.
We reach the southern suburbs of Lodz.

10.45 a.m.

We pass a sign for the Klapsydra bill-board agency. In the pre-war years, the word 'klapsydra' meant a black-bordered notice of a death. Such notices were the common method of announcing that someone had died. During the war, inside the ghetto, a klapsydra was someone who looked as if he was at death's door.

10.55 a.m.

We drive around Lodz. The driver refuses to take us through the town, much to my and everyone else's annoyance. I have been looking forward for many years now to seeing Lodz. He drives around the northern ring road. We thus miss the many surviving buildings of Jewish Lodz, including the Jewish hospitals on Wesola Street and Lagiewnicka Street, the ghetto archive office at No. 4 Plac Koscielny, and the Jewish cemetery, with its 180,000 surviving tombstones.

In the north of the city we leave the bus and, at a point near the Radogoszcz railway sidings from which the deportees were taken from Lodz to Chelmno, I describe how, during the deportations, the Germans lulled the population. To maintain the deception that the deportees were being sent to labour camps, an SS officer visited the Lodz ghetto on 12 April 1942 – ten days after this third major 'resettlement' had ended – to explain the whereabouts of the 44,000 Jews deported from the ghetto since January. All had been sent to Chelmno, and gassed, But the SS officer 'explained' to the representatives of the 115,000 Jews who remained 'that the deportees had all been brought to a camp near Warthbrücken', where a total of 100,000 Jews were already 'located'. The SS man added that some thirty thousand Germans, settlers, he said, from Galicia, had earlier stayed in this camp, and had left behind 'well-equipped barracks and even furniture'. Provisions for the Jews, he assured their worried relatives and friends, 'were excellent, and deportees fit for work were repairing roads or engaged in agriculture'.

Warthbrücken was the German name for Kolo, the town nearest the Chelmno death camp. Workshops were to be set up there 'in the very near future', the SS officer explained. It was an explanation cleverly designed to deceive the ghetto dwellers even more completely. For in the Lodz ghetto, workshops and survival were synonymous, so that the 'large influx of new orders' during April for shoes and knitted goods, as well as for clothing for the German army, gave an even greater sense of security.

To maintain the deception that the camp near Kolo was a work camp, the Germans arranged for postcards to be sent from the deportees to say that they were 'in good health'. One such postcard, sent from a family from Turek who had been deported to Chelmno in January 1942, reached the Lodz ghetto in mid-April 1942. This single card, with its encouraging message, was of sufficient importance to merit a special mention in the Lodz Ghetto Chronicle. No mention was made of the lack of postcards from any of the 44,000 Lodz deportees. At the same time there was ominous news: the arrival in the ghetto of large numbers of sewing machines, in the drawers of which notes and printed matter had been found, from which 'one may conclude that they were sent here from small towns in Kolo and Kutno counties'. But what had happened to their owners? How could so many sewing machines suddenly have become detached from their owners: Jews from at least nine towns in the region – Kolo, Dabie, Izbica Kujawska, Klodawa, Sompolno, Kutno, Krosniewice and Zychlin? In fact, all the owners of these machines had been deported with their families – grandparents, parents, husbands, children, grandchildren – to Chelmno, and gassed there in the four months between mid-December 1941 and mid-April 1942.

I read from two entries in the Lodz Ghetto Chronicle, the first the entry for 6 May 1942: 'Today the third transport of Jews who had been settled here from Germany left the ghetto. The conditions of departure have not changed. Those departing are not permitted to take any packages and, thus, their hand-held baggage has remained at Marysin station.

'During the last resettlement, the local Jews were also at times forbidden to take their packages with them and people's knapsacks were cut off their backs, but, somehow or other, our Jews found a way to cope with that. In response to the order, they would lay down their larger packages and keep the smaller ones, and then, later on, they would put the smaller ones down and pick the larger ones back up. And, if someone were quick-witted enough, he would take advantage of the guard's inattention and save the rest of his baggage as well. This was not a universal phenomenon, but it was, nevertheless, quite commonplace.

'It was a somewhat different story with the well-disciplined German Jews. For them an order issued by a uniformed authority is sacred, and at the first command they all set their baggage down without a thought of trying to retrieve any of it. As consolation they were told that they would receive their baggage on the next train.

'The news of the conditions prevailing at departure is, to a significant degree, causing possessions to continue to be sold. Once again, clothing, linen, shoes, and other odds and ends have been placed on the market and, once again, barter is flourishing in all the gateways on Bazar Square, Wolborska Street, and in the "transports". Whatever people fail to sell in the "city", they either have to throw away on Szklana Street or in Marysin, or, in the extreme, at the train station. Schooled by the experience of recent days, some people have struck on the old idea of putting on a few suits, a few changes of underwear, and, quite frequently, two overcoats. They tie the first coat with a belt from which they hang an extra pair of shoes and other small items.

'And so their faces, cadaverously white or waxy yellow, swollen, and despairing, sway disjointedly on top of disproportionately wide bodies that bend and droop under their own weight. They are possessed by a single thought: to save the little that remains of what they own, even at the expense of the last of their strength. Some people have been overcome by utter helplessness, whereas some still believe in something.

'Fewer and fewer people loaded down with sacks are to be seen, and the later transports are practically without luggage when they come to Marysin. Abandoned umbrellas and canes are strewn over the grounds of the prison. The last and final privilege – to take a "bag and a stick" – has also been retracted from them.'

The next reading is from the entry in the Lodz Ghetto Chronicle for the following day, 7 May 1942: 'A transport of former residents of Hamburg and Düsseldorf left the ghetto today. Possessions, down to the smallest parcels, continue to be taken away. They are only left their bread and, at times, bits of some other food as well.

'The transports are conveyed in the following manner. In the afternoon hours, the deportees make their way to Central Prison or to the small buildings surrounded by barbed wire on Szklana Street. There they remain for the night, and the next day at noon they are assembled into groups and escorted under guard to the camp in Marysin, where they are lodged in the school building on Jonscher Street and in five small buildings on Okopowa Street. They receive food at these assembly points – a ration of bread, ersatz coffee, and soup. Each person is supplied with a loaf of bread for the journey, free of charge. At four o'clock in the morning, special detachments of the Order Service, already expert at performing such onerous tasks, transport the deportees by tram to the Radogoszcz sidetrack station. Half an hour before the train departs – which occurs at 7 o'clock on the dot – secret police

Gestapo officials, accompanied by regular German police, arrive by automobile.

'By then the deportees have been been lined up by the Order Service, in groups of ten in front of the compartment doors, at a distance of two metres from the train. Then they take their places under the eye of the police. It is then that they are ordered to throw away the things they have brought with them. The largest pieces of luggage have already been taken away by the Order Service at the assembly points; those items, and those taken away at the station, are later sent to the office on Rybna Street. Porters carry the sick and the very elderly onto the trains. There are medical stations in operation at the assembly points, and a medical team is on duty at the train station as well. The story circulating through the ghetto concerning the beating of deportees is worth correcting. Such incidents, with minor exceptions, are not taking place. The train is made up of third-class carriages.'

11.05 a.m.
We drive off. A hundred yards from where we had stopped is some large-scale sprayed graffiti, 'Jebac Zydow', 'Fuck Jews'. There are about a hundred Jews in Lodz today. The chairman of the Jewish community is blind.

On the next building someone has drawn the graffiti we have seen so much of on our journey, a gallows with a Star of David hanging from it.

11.16 a.m.
We reach Zgierz, and cross the former Lodz–Chelmno deportation railway line. Shortly after the German army entered Zgierz, on 7 September 1939, seven Jews were picked at random and shot. This was typical of such killings in the first months of the war, when more than 5,000 Jews were executed. In addition to the Jewish victims, a further 11,000 Polish civilians were shot. What was particularly distressing for the Jews was that they, who formed a tenth of the Polish population, constituted a third of those shot. It was an ominous prelude.

11.30 a.m.
Our driver points out an ornate house on the left of the road. 'Gypsy money,' he says. A few yards further on, on the right, an even more amazing edifice, like a mini Taj Mahal. 'More Gypsy money,' he comments. We think of how 'Jewish money' and 'More Jewish

money' might have been a driver's comment sixty years ago.

11.58 a.m.

Ozorkow is on our left (we are driving on the by-pass road; the driver has once more refused to take us into the town). I read from the recollections of Berek Obuchowski (now Bob Roberts) who was twelve years old when war broke out in September 1939. 'Our house was on one floor,' he wrote to me a few months ago, 'with an orchard at the back with apple and pear trees, and gooseberry and redcurrant bushes.'

Perhaps we are looking at Berek's back yard even now. 'At school,' he added, 'I remember one incident when I intervened in a fight between a couple of bullies punching a Jewish boy, and I dragged one of the bullies into the River Bzura and held him there with his feet in the freezing ice. I was quite tough as a youngster, and from that time at school, I was never bullied, although the mother of the non-Jewish boy came the next day and abused me verbally.'

On 21 May 1942 more than two thousand Jews were deported from the Ozorkow ghetto to a 'resettlement camp'. It was in fact Chelmno, to which 500 had been deported from the ghetto two months earlier. All were killed.

I tell the story of how, in a selection of children on the following day, the Secretary of the Ozorkow Jewish Council, Mania Rzepkowicz, refused an offer by the German in charge of the ghetto to exclude her own child from 'resettlement'. She then voluntarily joined the group. Three hundred children were deported that day. No one knew what their destination was. It too was Chelmno. All of them were murdered on arrival.

We are driving towards Chelmno. Along the roadside is a narrow-gauge railway that was used to take Jews from the small towns along this road, and all along its route, to Chelmno.

12.12 p.m.

Leczyca. This was one of the towns where there had been a blood libel three hundred years ago. On 10 April 1942 all 1,700 Jews were deported from the ghetto here to Chelmno. That month, from this whole region, 11,000 Jews were deported to their deaths, some by road and some by rail.

12.15 p.m.

We cross the River Bzura, the scene of fierce Polish military resistance to the Germans in September 1939, and drive west along a country road. As we set off down this road, we cross the narrow-gauge deportation railway.

12.30 p.m.

Grabow. It was in this village that the only known escapee from Chelmno, Yakov Grojanowski, told his story to the rabbi. We leave the bus, and I read Grojanowski's recollection (set down a few days later) of the events of 19 January 1942, as he made his way eastward from Chelmno: 'Now and then I asked passers-by for directions. All the time I was on the alert for gendarmes because I didn't have any documents on me. I finally reached a village seven kilometres away from Grabow. There I arranged with a Polish farmer he would drive me to Grabow for fifteen marks. I put on his fur coat and cap.

'On Monday at two o'clock we arrived at Grabow. The Jews took me for an Ethnic German because I didn't wear a star. I asked for the rabbi. I looked rough; in Chelmno we had had no opportunity to wash and shave.

'I asked where the rabbi lived. "Who are you?" he asked. "Rabbi, I am a Jew from the nether world!" He looked at me as if I was mad. I told him: "Rabbi, don't think I am crazed and have lost my reason. I am a Jew from the nether world. They are killing the whole nation of Israel. I myself have buried a whole town of Jews, my parents, brothers and the entire family. I have remained lonely as a piece of stone."

'I cried during this conversation. The rabbi asked: "Where are they being killed?" I said, "Rabbi, in Chelmno. They are gassed in the forest, and buried in mass graves." His domestic (the rabbi was a widower) brought me a bowl of water for my swollen eyes. I washed my hands. The injury on my right hand began to hurt. When my story made the rounds many Jews came, to whom I told all the details. They all wept.

'We ate bread and butter; I was given tea to drink and said the blessing.'

The rabbi to whom Grojanowski told his story, Jakub Szulman, realised that Grojanowski was telling the truth. 'The place where everyone is being put to death is called Chelmno,' he wrote to relations in Lodz, adding some of the details which he had just heard. 'People are killed in one of two ways,' he reported, 'either by shooting or by poison gas,' and he then listed some of the communities that had been destroyed. 'Do not think that this is a madman's writing,' Rabbi Szulman added, 'it is the cruel and tragic truth (Good God!).'

The rabbi's letter ended: 'O Man, throw off your rags, sprinkle your head with ashes, or run through the streets and dance in madness. I am so wearied by the sufferings of Israel, my pen can write no more. My heart is breaking. But perhaps the Almighty will take pity and save the "last remnants of our People". Help us, O Creator of the World!'

Rabbi Szulman sent his letter to the Lodz ghetto; but it did not arrive there, so it seems, until the summer, and even then, as Lucjan Dobroszycki has written, 'one cannot be sure who in the ghetto had read the letter or even knew of it, much less what influence that letter might have had on the attitudes of ghetto dwellers.'

Yakov Grojanowski left Grabow on 20 January 1942, to take his eye-witness testimony of the daily mass murder at Chelmno – which had already been in operation for six weeks, with the murder of more than fifty thousand Jews – to the Jews of Warsaw. On the day that he set off from Grabow, the conference took place in Wannsee that marked out 11,000,000 more Jews for the same fate.

As we are about to board the bus, I comment that if there was a rabbi in Grabow, there must have been a synagogue. There is an elderly woman who has been watching us from her doorway, and has just turned back to go inside. I ask if she knows where the synagogue is. She says she will take us. As she is hobbling with a stick, we offer to give her a ride there in the bus, but she laughs and says she can get to the synagogue with us on foot – and she hobbles off, leading us to it. The synagogue is scarcely a hundred yards away, in the street next to her house. She says the Germans used it to store corn; that is why it survived. Stored corn requires a well-maintained roof to keep it dry. She herself was not here in the war. She was from the Eastern Galician town of Sambor. In the war she was deported to Germany for forced labour. When the Russians annexed Eastern Galicia in 1945, she came here, to western Poland, as did several million Poles.

She leads us into a large courtyard, at one side of which is a magnificent synagogue. The main part is used for storage, the front part has been converted into a small dwelling. Just beyond the synagogue is the rabbi of Grabow's house. It is strange to feel that it was probably here that Yakov Grojanowski recounted his terrible experiences.

A woman who lives in the rabbi's house (No. 1 Skladowa Street) brings us the key to a side door into the synagogue. We clamber in, and up a storage ladder to the main hall. There are a number of decorations still visible, including, above where the Ark would have been, a coloured Hebrew inscription, from Genesis. The words on the inscription (which I have italicised) are from the verse: 'And Yakov (Jacob) awaked out of his sleep, and he said, Surely the Lord is in this place; and I knew it not. And he was afraid, and said, *how dreadful is this place! This is none other but the house of God, and this is the Gate of Heaven.'*

This is an astounding moment for us all: an unexpected and remarkable sight; a synagogue of lordly proportions, derelict and yet intact, and the scene of a traumatic moment in Jewish history.

1.06 p.m.
We leave Grabow and drive through a pleasant rural landscape, of farms and fields and small woods.

1.22 p.m.
Dabie. A small and attractive village on an escarpment overlooking the River Ner. The 975 Jews of Dabie were among the very first victims at Chelmno, more than a month before Yakov Grojanowski made his escape. On 14 December 1941 they were all driven in trucks to Chelmno, and murdered.

1.27 p.m.
Chelmno. This is the village from which the camp got its name, though the camp itself is just over six kilometres to the north-west. At a later point in the history of the camp, when it was reopened for one month in 1944, the deportees were held here in Chelmno, in the local and somewhat dilapidated castle. But in the 1941 and 1942 period, when most of those murdered at Chelmno were killed, it was in a large brick mill to the north, on the banks of the Ner, that they were held. And it was from the mill that they were driven to the camp in sealed vans, and gassed during the journey. We will start our pilgrimage at the mill.

1.35 p.m.
Powierce. This was the railway halt on the narrow-gauge railway from Kolo, to which most of the deportees were brought. They were ordered out of the trains, and herded down a wide track towards the river.

We turn off the road, and drive down the track, to the hamlet of Zawadki. I describe the mill that lies at the end of the track, just beyond the three or four houses of the hamlet. It was in this mill that the deportees were held – 1,000 of them at any one time – and they were then, in small groups, ordered into the van and driven off.

1.37 p.m.

We reach the hamlet and the site of the mill. The hamlet remains but the mill is gone. Only a few foundations remain, and some overgrown outcrops of brick. When I was here in 1980 it was an imposing, and frightening, building. Now it is gone.

The Gestapo headquarters house is still here. Since 1945 it has been a Polish peasant's family dwelling. The mill is on the bank of the River Warta, which at this point meanders placidly northward, with willows along its banks, and cows grazing in the fields beyond. There is a fisherman on the far bank.

Ben tells us: 'My mother's family, who lived in Zdunska Wola, Sieradz and Lututow, were brought here – uncles, aunts and cousins. All so young!'

I walk a few yards down the track along which the sealed trucks were driven straight through the dark pine woods to the death camp.

1.57 p.m.

We leave Zawadki.

1.59 p.m.

We reach the road, and the site of Powierce railway halt. We drive back south, towards the camp, a distance of about two kilometres. The sealed trucks made a journey of similar distance through the woods from the mill to the camp. As they drove, those inside the van were asphyxiated. When the van reached the camp, the bodies were removed by a small task force of able-bodied Jews, of whom Yakov Grojanowski (the escapee) was one.

2.03 p.m.

We reach the entrance to Chelmno camp. At the side of the road there is a Polish memorial marker, with its distinctive red flame symbol.

Ben says: 'Few visitors come here. They all visit Auschwitz. Few today know who was killed here: from Lodz and the Warthegau, from Germany, from Austria, Czechoslovakia, even from Luxemburg.'

We walk away from the road into a large clearing. The first monument is a Polish one, designed in the shape of a cross. It has nothing to do with the death camp, but with an earlier cruel episode in these woods, the execution of seventy-nine Poles on 5 September 1939. They were brought here from the nearby towns of Dabie, Kolo and Klodawa. The names of nineteen of those murdered are known, and listed on the monument. There were also sixty unknown victims.

Looking at the cruciform design on the monument, Robin comments: 'If Elie Wiesel came here, he would be distressed' (as he was, and as we were, by the crosses in the field beyond Crematorium IV at Auschwitz). There were at least 180,000 Jews murdered here, their bodies dumped out of the gas vans that had been driven on the short journey along the track from the mill at Zawadki. A plaque gives a statistical breakdown of those murdered here:

160,000 Polish Jews
 20,000 German, Austrian, Czechoslovak and Luxemburg Jews
  4,300 Gypsies

The plaque notes that after Heydrich's murder, eighty-two children from Lidice (near Prague) were brought here and gassed. Soviet prisoners-of-war were also gassed here. So, too, were several hundred Poles, uprooted from the Zamosc province to make way for the settlement of Germans.

Ben says to me: 'I've never been to Chelmno before. But I've got an interest here. My mother's immediate family were deported here. We didn't hear from my family after that deportation. One aunt and uncle lived in Sieradz. Another two aunts and uncles lived in Lututow, and another aunt in Zdunska Wola. I had eleven cousins in these three families. With the exception of one, all were sent here. My cousin Katriel Klein, from Zdunska Wola, survived the war; in 1939 he ran away to eastern Poland, and from there was sent to Russia.

'So many cousins and such lovely uncles and aunts – all sent here. We were so close to them. As long as possible, letters, postcards, were coming to us in the Piotrkow ghetto from them, until March 1942, and then it stopped. My mother said, "Something must be wrong. If they are alive they would have made contact with us."

'My cousins were very intelligent. One, Zalek Hildesheim, was an infant prodigy. He was chess champion of the district of Sieradz at the age of eleven, a brilliant mathematician and linguist. He composed songs and was excellent at rowing. Before he was sent to the Lodz ghetto from Sieradz he worked for the German army as an interpreter in both French and English. He was eighteen years old when he lost his life.

'Zalek was not unique. In every extended Jewish family there was, at least, one member whose talents were outstanding. That talent and genius is irreplaceable. Apart from the terrible human tragedy the world will never know what it has lost.'

'My father's immediate family, who lived in Pabianice and Lodz, including my grandparents, Samuel and Rela, also met with their deaths here.'

We walk to the large concrete monument at the centre of the clearing. The inscription on the back of it (away from the road) reads:

> They took us – from old men to sucklings –
> between the towns of Kolo and Dabie,
> they took us to the woods
> and there they gassed and shot and burned us.
> We ask that our future brethren
> should punish our murderers
>
> The witnesses of our suffering
> who live in this area
> once again we plead with them
> To announce our murder to the world.

We walk from the monument to the site of the crematorium. We pass an enormous field in which the ashes of the victims were scattered once it had been decided to dig up all the corpses, and force Jewish slave labourers to burn them. In 1980 when I was here this field was empty. Now there are a number of different monuments. An Israeli flag is flying at the edge of the field of ash. There is a low concrete monument on the site of the crematorium. Near it are plaques for two of the towns whose Jews were murdered here, Zdunska Wola and Lask.

There is one monument erected to a single family, by Hanoch Barak (formerly Kujawski) of Ramat Hasharon in Israel. It is dedicated to his father Nachman, his mother Dwojra, his sister Sura and his brothers Ruven, Michal, Anszel and Icie 'and the rest of the family' murdered here in 1942.

At the north end of the camp, a carved wooden Star of David, painted white, overlooks the pits of human ash.

There is one other town monument, by far the largest and most imposing: concrete panels and a concrete column, with many brass plaques fixed to it. Extraordinary to relate, it is a monument to the 4,953 Jews from Belchatow – the town Angela visited early this morning – who were murdered here. On it are the names of six of her murdered relatives: Moshe, Joseph, Shlama, Chaim, Itz and Issac Klug. Angela comments: 'Seeing these names was the first time I was really able to comprehend how lucky I was to be alive, to be here,' and she adds: 'It is my duty and wish to carry on educating people about the Holocaust. It shall never be forgotten.'

Paul says prayers with Angela. A few others of us join them. But there is a general reluctance to pray to God here, in this place, as there was in all the death camps.

I read a short poem by the Israeli poet Dan Pagis, himself a survivor of concentration camps in the Ukraine, from which he escaped before the end of the war, at the age of fourteen. His poem is about the perpetrators, as described by a victim:

> No no: they definitely were
> human beings: uniforms, boots.
> How to explain? They were created
> in the image.
>
> I was a shade.
> A different creator made me.
>
> And he in his mercy left nothing of me that would die.
> And I fled to him, rose weightless, blue,
> forgiving – I would even say: apologising –
> smoke to omnipotent smoke
> without image or likeness.

As this is the last death camp we will visit, Paul reads the prayer of comfort to be said on leaving a cemetery: 'He maketh death to vanish in life eternal; and The Lord God wipeth away tears from off all faces; and the reproach of His people shall He take away from off all the earth: for The Lord hath spoken it.'

2.55 p.m.
As we walk from the pits to the monument, a drunk approaches. He is one of the workers here who help to maintain the grass verges and the flowerbeds. He tells us he is fifty-eight years old. He has worked here since the war. In a peasant Polish, he tells us again and again, 'I have no money.' Then he becomes lyrical: 'Gentlemen, there are graves here – and here, and here. Graves here – here.'

3 p.m.
Drawing nearer the entrance, we see a large group of tombstones set in a clearing. They are not the graves of those murdered here, but inter-war (and older) tombstones taken from the graveyard at Turek. Ben: 'There's something wrong. These people died before the war.'

It seems that some survivor from Turek had the idea of bringing the tombstones here as a memorial to his town. Jews from Turek were also murdered here in Chelmno. On 7 and 8 December 1941 a total of 1,757 Jews were taken from Turek to the collecting point at Kowale Panskie, and from there, on December 10, deported to Chelmno. They were among the very first Jews to be murdered by gas – six weeks before the Wannsee meeting in Berlin.

Who is to say if these pre-war stones ought to be here? Ought the three or four communities with special monuments to be at one side of the field of ashes, intruding on them? Ought there to be that memorial to a single family? How many more such memorials will be built?

We discuss these questions among ourselves. Jon says: 'The arbitrary communities represented here – it feels wrong. It's one thing to have a memorial to all the communities, like the stones at Treblinka, or the Valley of the Communities at Yad Vashem in Jerusalem, but to leave out the others? It seems wrong. It becomes a hotch-potch. That is part of the power of Treblinka – everybody is remembered – or at Belzec, the one memorial to all those murdered.'

It is the field of ash that acts as the overwhelming monument here; that, and the dense, dark forest on all sides, and the track through the forest – a broad swathe of grass – along which the gas vans came. We are all deeply affected by the mass graves, and also by the curious colour of the grass, a disturbing mixture of pale green and pale russet.

3.15 p.m.

There is a request for me to read. But the impression of the camp, the utter desolation of the field of ash (despite the few monuments), and the isolation of the place itself, have made everyone sombre. I wait a while, and some of us go through the small museum near the road. There is a list of the names of the Czech children from Lidice. There is also a list of the 615 children who were in the deportation from Belchatow; each of them was murdered on arrival with the rest of the deportees. Angela has found the name of two Klug children, her relatives: Ruda Persha Klug and Mojsza Ruwu Klug. It is the first time that she has learned anything at all about her Polish family and their fate.

It makes me momentarily dizzy to think that, today, but for the war, those two children would have been about my age.

We gather by the road. It does not seem right to do the readings in the fields of the camp itself. I read two passages. The first is from Eichmann's visit here. To obtain a first-hand report of the working and effectiveness of the death-camp system, the head of the Gestapo,

Heinrich Müller, sent Eichmann to Chelmno. Nineteen years after his visit, he told the Jerusalem court where he was on trial for his life (he was subsequently executed): 'There was a room – if I remember correctly – perhaps five times as large as this one. Perhaps it was only four times as big as the one I am sitting in now. And Jews were inside. They were to strip and then a truck arrived where the doors open, and the van pulled up at a hut. The naked Jews were to enter. Then the doors were hermetically sealed and the car started.'

Eichmann could not recall how many people were inside the van, explaining to the court (I read out his words, here on the site of the camp itself): 'I couldn't even look at it. All the time I was trying to avert my sight from what was going on. It was quite enough for me what I saw. The screaming and shrieking – I was too excited to have a look at the van. I told Müller that in my report. He didn't derive much profit from my report and afterwards I followed the van. Some of them knew the way, of course. And then I saw the most breathtaking sight I have ever seen in my life.

'The van was making for an open pit. The doors were flung open and corpses were cast out as if they were some animals – some beasts. They were hurled into the ditch. I also saw how the teeth were being extracted. And then I disappeared; I entered my car and I didn't want to look at this heinous act of turpitude. Then I took the car; for hours I was sitting at the side of the driver without exchanging a word with him. Then I knew I was washed up. It was quite enough for me. I only know that I remember a doctor in a white apron – there was a doctor in white uniform. He was looking at them. I couldn't say anything more. I had to leave because it was too much, as much as I could stand.'

According to Eichmann, he had told Müller that the scene at Chelmno was 'horrible, it's an indescribable inferno'.

The second extract which I read is from Yakov Grojanowski (ten years ago, I published the whole of Grojanowski's testimony as a chapter on its own in my book *The Holocaust, The Jewish Tragedy*): 'An SS man ordered us to fall in with our shovels, dressed, despite the frost, only in shoes, underwear, trousers and shirts. Our coats, hats, gloves, etc., had to remain in a pile on the ground. The two civilians took all the shovels and pick-axes down from the lorry. Eight of us who weren't handed any tools had to take down the two corpses.

'Already on our way into the forest we saw about fourteen men, enforced grave-diggers from Klodawa, who had arrived before us and were at work in their shirtsleeves.

'The picture was as follows: twenty-one men in twos, behind them eight men with two corpses, ringed by armed Germans. The people from Klodawa were also guarded by twelve gendarmes.

'All in all we were guarded by thirty gendarmes. As we approached the ditches the men from Klodawa asked us in whispers, "Where are you from?" We answered, "From Izbica." They asked how many of us there were and we replied twenty-nine. This exchange took place while we worked.

'The eight men without tools carried the two corpses to the ditch and threw them in. We didn't have to wait long before the next lorry arrived with fresh victims. It was specially constructed. It looked like a normal large lorry, in grey paint with two hermetically closed rear doors. The inner walls were of steel. There weren't any seats. The floor was covered by a wooden grating, as in public baths, with straw mats on top. Between the driver's cab and the rear part were two peepholes. With a torch one could observe through these peepholes if the victims were already dead.

'Under the wooden grating were two tubes about fifteen centimetres thick which came out of the cab. The tubes had small openings from which gas poured out. The gas generator was in the cab, where the same driver sat all the time. He wore a uniform of the SS death's head units and was about forty years old. There were two such vans.

'When the lorries approached we had to stand at a distance of five metres from the ditch. The leader of the guard detail was a high-ranking SS man, an absolute sadist and murderer.

'He ordered that eight men were to open the doors of the lorry. The smell of gas that met us was overpowering. The victims were Gypsies from Lodz. Strewn about the van were all their belongings: accordions, violins, bedding, watches and other valuables.

'After the doors had been open for five minutes orders were screamed at us, "Here! You Jews! Get in there and turn everything out!" The Jews scurried into the van and dragged the corpses away.

'The work didn't progress quickly enough. The SS leader fetched his whip and screamed, "The devil, I'll give you a hand straight away!" He hit out in all directions on people's heads, ears and so on, till they collapsed. Three of the eight who couldn't get up again were shot on the spot.

'When the others saw this they clambered back on their feet and continued the work with their last reserves of energy. The corpses were thrown one on top of another, like rubbish on a heap. We got hold of them by the feet and the hair. At the edge of the ditch stood two men who threw in the bodies. In the ditch stood an additional two men who packed them in head to feet, facing downwards.

'The orders were issued by an SS man who must have occupied a special rank. If any space was left, a child was pushed in. Everything was done very brutally. From up above the SS man indicated to us with a pine twig how to stack the bodies. He ordered where the head and the feet, where the children and the belongings were to be placed. All this was accompanied by malicious screams, blows and curses. Every batch comprised 180–200 corpses. For every three vanloads twenty men were used to cover up the corpses. At first this had to be done twice, later up to three times, because nine vans arrived (that is nine times sixty corpses).

'At exactly twelve o'clock the SS leader with the whip ordered: "Put your shovels down!" We had to line up in double file to be counted again. Then we had to climb out of the ditch.

'We were surrounded by guards all the time. We even had to excrete on the spot. We went to the spot where our belongings were. We had to sit on them close together. The guards continued to surround us. We were given cold bitter coffee and a frozen piece of bread. That was our lunch. That's how we sat for half an hour. Afterwards we had to line up, were counted and led back to work.'

4 p.m.
We drive away from Chelmno.

4.04 p.m.
We pass Powierce village and the turning to Zawadki.

4.08 p.m.
Reaching the Kolo town limits, we turn west, on to the main Warsaw–Berlin railway. All that remained of the memory of the Kolo synagogue when I was here in 1980 was a large stone on an empty lot, without any inscription.

4.09 p.m.
We cross the River Warta. The camp of Chelmno is to the south, set back from the eastern bank of the river. It was totally hidden from all road and rail – and river – traffic, and from all houses and human habitations. In this respect, it was the most remote of the death camps. All that a fisherman might have seen was the mill at Zawadki and the deportees herded there.

4.14 p.m.

Koscielec. A fine nineteenth-century palace overlooks the road.

4.30 p.m.

Konin city limits. This is our last town. We drive past the tall chimney of the former Spielfogel distillery. In the square facing us is the Ryczke family house. In his book *Konin, A Quest,* Theo Richmond has described each of these buildings, and all the buildings that we are to see here in Konin this afternoon.

The driver begins to make difficulties. He cannot drive us to the main square. There is, he says, no access for buses, only for cars.

4.40 p.m.

The driver finds somewhere in the southern part of the town in which he can park, and we make our way on foot into the centre. It is almost eleven hours since these feet first walked today, through the wet streets of Piotrkow.

Before we set off on foot through Konin (it is fortunately not raining now) I say a few words about the history of the town's Jews. In 1765 there were 133 Jews here. In 1821 Michael Goldwasser was born here in Konin. His grandson, Barry M. Goldwater, a United States Senator was the Republican nominee for President in 1964.

In 1863 a Jew from Konin, Szmo Szlomo, was exiled to Siberia by the Tsarist authorities for taking part in the Polish national insurrection that year. By 1880 there were 3,400 Jews and 2,460 Poles in the town, and another 2,300 Jews in the nearby villages. It was at that time that the Jews were given permission to build a synagogue in Konin (which we will walk to in a few minutes' time), to start a primary school, and to lease land from the municipality.

Our first stop is the former Jewish lending library (of course, almost everything is 'former' here, as everywhere we have been in the past two weeks). It was one of the earliest lending libraries in Poland, and – Theo Richmond told me with pride before we set off – 'one of the finest Jewish lending libraries in all of Poland'. Today it is the office of an insurance company. Shortly after the Germans entered Konin, all the books were taken from the library to the market square and burned, together with all the furniture and fittings from the synagogue. In November 1939, after Konin and the region around it had been annexed to Germany, the Jews of Konin were expelled into German-occupied Poland

We walk along Targowa Street (formerly Zydowska – Jewish Street)

to what was once the centre of Jewish Konin, the Tepper Marek. It is quiet as the grave. We have to use our best imaginings to populate it with merchants and pedlars and shoppers and townsfolk and pious Jews and secular Jews and Jewish children – Ben's age then – and the babble of Yiddish and Polish voices.

5.20 p.m.
We reach Mickiewicza Street (formerly Boznicza Street). Facing us is the synagogue, erected between 1825 and 1844, and embellished in the present Moorish style in 1878. The building is now a library. The synagogue decorations and paintings in the interior have been beautifully, even brilliantly, restored to their former decorative glory. All that is missing – and what a massive 'all' it is – are the worshippers.

The women's gallery has been laid out for a lecture.

Paul says the prayers of the afternoon service.

Next to the library/synagogue is a bakery. It is on the corner of Westerplatte Street (named after a heroic Polish defence against the Germans in September 1939, on the Baltic). It was formerly Ogrodowa Street. This corner building used to be the Jewish community's ritual bath. Behind it, part of the same building, on the Westerplatte Street side, was a Hassidic house of prayer. In the courtyard next to it the Jewish community's hearse was kept. The next house along Westerplatte Street, a single-storey house with a red-tiled roof, belonged to Lola Birnbaum before the war. In 1945 the survivors of the Holocaust who returned to Konin stayed here.

At the end of Westerplatte Street, on the bank of the River Warta, was once the fish market, a centre of Jewish life and bustle, especially on Friday mornings, when every Jewish mother and housewife was about to prepare her Sabbath meal, and make her gefilte fish.

5.45 p.m.
We search for a restaurant, but there is none. In the main square, Plac Wolnosci, there is a plaque to the first two citizens of Konin executed by the Germans, Aleksander Kurowski, a Catholic, and Morche Slodki, a Jew, both shot on 22 September 1939.

Following Theo Richmond's map, we walk downhill, towards the river, and the old wooden bridge. Across the river is modern Konin. We walk one more block on this side of the river, across Wodna Street. A few yards further on, set back in a field, is an imposing structure, the Jewish high school. It was built in 1918. Here modern Hebrew (Ivrit) was one of the languages of instruction – for secular subjects.

One of the headmasters here, for two years (he loathed every minute of it), later emigrated to the United States, where he became a collaborator of Albert Einstein at Princeton University.

I read from the recollections of Arek Hersh, a friend of mine in Britain, who lived for a while in Konin before the war, and recalled how, on their way to school, he and his school pals would encounter one of the town's more unusual characters:

'He was an old man dressed in a fur hat, a Russian-type caftan and high boots with his trousers tucked into them. He had a beard and a large handlebar moustache, and he earned his living by selling edible oils. He owned a horse that he blindfolded with a sack, and which would plod round and round, pulling a wheel which ground the sunflower seeds that produced the oil. We used to watch this process fascinated. The old man used to stop us and talk to us as we passed by his premises. He would ask us to pull his finger, and as we did he would fart. We were absolutely intrigued by this behaviour, but very soon we got used to him and refused to do his bidding. Instead we used to watch other children fall into the trap, and as they did we would fall about with laughter. The old man never seemed to run out of wind and could always oblige.'

We return to town. A man passes us and spits. He calls out, in a tone of contempt: 'Jewish seed.' His spit misses Ben and hits (or only just misses) Robin, an upstanding Anglican. 'It just shows you how ingrained it is,' says Robin.

'There was a follow-up to this episode,' Robin later recalled. 'We had walked on about two hundred yards and saw this individual return with two very large associates. I watched carefully as they strode in our direction. From their body language, the two associates didn't think we were worth bothering with. They stopped, turned and went back.' Ros, watching the three men, felt that they were 'debating what course of action they should take: the square was otherwise deserted and I was overcome with an acute sense of panic. It was as if, for one frozen moment, we had all been transferred back in time when such incidents would often come to a tragic end.'

Our last port of call is to be a surprise for the group (since it may not come off). There is still one Jew living in Konin today, Teresa Blaszczynska. She was born in 1951, the daughter of a Jewish mother and a non-Jewish father. Today she is a practising Catholic. But according to Jewish law, because her mother was Jewish, she too is Jewish. Ironically, under Hitler's laws, with just one Jewish grand-parent, she would also have been Jewish.

I have a letter for her from Theo Richmond. Not knowing if she will be in, I have said nothing about her to the group. Asking them to wait across the street, I knock on her door. No reply. I go to the neighbour, who is in the garden, and who says that she is in. In a few moments she comes to the door. She invites me in, and when I explain about the group, invites them in too.

She gives Ben a hug. He comments: 'First spat on and then hugged.'

Her mother's parents were Sarah and Abraham Rataewski. Her grandfather's monogram, AR, is carved above the lintel of her door. Her mother was his daughter, Nadia. The family were originally from Warsaw.

6.10 p.m.

We walk back through Konin to the minibus. We have not had time to see all the things that Theo Richmond describes, among them the sole Jewish tombstone in the Catholic cemetery, the site of the Jewish cemetery, and – about twenty minutes' drive away – the mass murder site and monument at Biskupie where between eight and twelve thousand Jews were shot. But we have seen much and gained many insights. Perhaps some of the group will return here one day; I hope many of them will feel drawn back to explore at greater length and with more leisure some of the places we have only had time to glance at, or been unable to visit because of the constraints of time, such as the Jewish cemeteries in Lublin, Warsaw and Lodz.

6.25 p.m.

We cross the Warta. In 1943 the river flooded. The Germans used the flood as an excuse to take out all the tombstones from the Jewish cemetery.

6.30 p.m.

We reach the railway station, and check that our train exists. It does.

6.35 p.m.

Hotel Konin. It is in Julian Tuwim Street. Tuwim was one of the most famous poets in pre-war Poland, and a Jew. Every Polish schoolchild knows his poem *Lokomotywa*, about a railway train, written in 1938. In 1959 it was one of the poems through which I tried to learn Polish.

Everywhere we have been, there have been synagogues. Today we have seen three, in Piotrkow, Grabow and Konin. There were probably thirty in all, in the different towns we have driven through today.

We talk about the Gypsies who were murdered in Chelmno. The skinheads to whom we talked at Majdanek had regarded the Gypsies as their No. 1 Enemy, Ben says: 'The Jews in Piotrkow, as elsewhere, were frightened of Gypsies. They feared they would snatch their children. When the Gypsies arrived in town, they would lock their doors.' I remember, in 1980, visiting the synagogue building in Auschwitz town (the town had a sizeable pre-war Jewish population), and finding that Gypsies were living there. They had turned it into quite a comfortable dwelling.

8.30 p.m.

Our minibus driver takes us to Konin station. As we find a place to park in the station forecourt, a skinhead comes up to the bus and raises his hand in the Nazi salute, calls out 'Sieg Heil', and sings a song in favour of Aryans. As we get off the minibus – there are two exits, one at the front and one at the back – he goes from one exit to the other, repeatedly raising his arm in the Hitler salute in the faces of the women as they get off the bus. The driver, who is helping unload the bags from the side of the bus, makes no effort to intervene.

Herut and I are the only ones left on the bus. The skinhead looks as if he is going to get on, but moves away.

The driver drives off, leaving us with the skinhead, who is standing a little way off, shouting abuse. We walk from the car park to the station hall, trailed by the shouting skinhead. He comes in after us. He menaces Petra. He comes up to me and, for a few seconds, I am very scared indeed. We are standing between the ticket desk and the train bulletin board. He wanders from one to the other, lurching and drunk. Then he wanders out of the station, shouting all the time.

Our relief is short-lived. He comes back into the hall, and goes up to individual members of the group, doing the Nazi salute in their faces, and calling out his slogans again and again: 'National Socialism OK', 'Poland – only for the Poles', 'Fuck Europe', 'Fuck the USA', 'Skinheads OK', 'Heil Hitler', 'Heil Poland'. Two Poles come into the station and try to persuade him to leave with them, but they do not try very hard, and seem to find the whole episode rather amusing. He continues going up to one or other of us, and nose to nose doing the Nazi salute and screaming out his slogans, veering away, and then coming back to scream at someone else.

Facing us, the skinhead opens his shirt to show a T-shirt underneath, with the word 'skinhead' on it. Then he comes up to me a second time, leers into my face, then bends down, pulls up his trouser leg and points – there is a black swastika painted, or tattooed, just above his right ankle. Then he suddenly turns away and goes up to Robin, showing him the swastika.

Robin leaves the hall and finds the two friends. In the inimitable tones of a former Detective Inspector (it is Robin's tone, not his words, that undoubtedly impresses them) he persuades these two to come back into the hall and to take the skinhead out. With Robin in close attendance, they push him through the door into the station forecourt. The skinhead stands just outside the glass door, doing the Hitler salute. At one moment, he lurches forward, bumping into the glass, but then moves away. Two policemen appear. They take him behind the station building.

8.50 p.m.

We go into the station waiting room. Everyone is shaken. My great fear was that the skinhead might have had a knife. I could see that Robin was prepared to take physical action if he had laid his hands on anyone. 'He was a nasty individual,' Robin comments. 'He was quite harmless – unless he had a knife on him. That's what I was watching for.'

Jon recalls being in Warsaw in 1993 for the fiftieth anniversary commemoration of the Warsaw ghetto uprising: 'We were confronted by a "Sieg Heil!" as we came out of the hotel.'

9.40 p.m.

We leave the waiting room and go on to the platform. Night has fallen.

9.41 p.m.

The announcer tells us that the Moscow–Brussels and St Petersburg–Aachen express (our train) will be ten minutes late.

9.53 p.m.

The train pulls in. We find our carriage and clamber aboard.

9.55 p.m.

The train pulls out. We are in the couchette carriage of Polish Railways. As the train gathers speed, I stand by the window looking north, waiting for Otoczno station.

10.17 p.m.

We speed through Otoczno. It was here that Arek Hersh was a slave labourer. One of his tasks was to lay track and sleepers on this very railway line. 'This work was terrible, back-breaking for even the fittest of men, and the beatings received were so savage that many actually died from them.' I read from Arek's recollections: 'One afternoon as I was walking towards the wash-house I noticed some strange-looking lorries that had arrived at the camp. These vehicles were all enclosed and were manned by soldiers who had their sleeves rolled up and carried sticks in their hands. These soldiers had SS on their collars, and a skull-and-crossbones insignia on their caps. The lorries were driven to the block that housed the boys and men waiting to go home. They stopped, and the SS men ordered the prisoners out of the barrack and told them to undress, but to leave their underpants on. The prisoners obeyed immediately and the backs of the lorries were then opened up. The SS then proceeded to beat the boys and men on to the lorries.

'The screams and panic which broke out at this treatment were just too terrible. Many were bleeding from the blows that had rained down on them. When everybody was inside the lorries, the doors were closed. Days later I found out from the foreman that as the engine started running it began to pump the exhaust fumes into the back of the lorry. As the vehicle was airtight, this meant that all inside were slowly gassed.

'I don't think I will ever be able to erase from my mind the memory of that terrible day, when I unwittingly witnessed the deaths of my friends. I still shudder when I think that if I hadn't been picked out with those other few boys to work, that too would have been my fate.

'As more and more people were hanged, one of my duties was to help take the corpses down to the little village, which was several kilometres from the camp, where we would help to bury them. I still remember the spot.'

Arek Hersh also recalled the fate of Szymek Hildesheim, whose younger brother was a friend of his from his home town (Sieradz). Szymek Hildesheim was caught in Otoczno trying to persuade someone working in the camp kitchen to let him have a potato: 'Those brutes hanged him and twice the rope snapped, and each time, in a dreadful state of shock, he begged for his life. However those barbarians succeeded the third time. That typified the bestiality of the Germans and their extermination methods in the beginning. I was heartbroken as I watched this terrible scene, and afterwards I helped to bury him.

He was only twenty years of age, a very intelligent person, and one of the nicest young men anybody could wish to know. Here was I, a child of just eleven years, and already I had witnessed some of the most inhuman acts that man had done to man in recent history.'

As I am reading this account, the train crosses the former western (1815–1914) border between Tsarist Poland and Imperial Germany. We are now in that part of Poland that was German until after the Second World War. Ben thinks that the present borders (which are further west, on the Oder) will not last for ever, and that the Germans will eventually regain the lands which they lost in 1945. 'There will be a time when they will come again,' he says. 'But it won't be in our time.' Ben adds: 'Nationalism is a terrible thing.'

10.55 p.m.

The train stops at Poznan. Before 1914 – as Posen – it was the capital of the German province of Posnania. Among the Jews born here was Simon Baruch, a subject of the German Kaiser, who emigrated to the United States in the 1860s to study medicine. His son Bernard became head of the War Industries Board in the First World War, and was responsible for acquiring the raw materials needed by the United States to fight, and to defeat, Germany. In the Second World War, Bernard Baruch played an equally important part in America's war-making capacity.

It was here in Poznan that Himmler spoke to senior SS officers on 4 October 1943. Looking out on the station platform, I read out loud Himmler's reflection that day, and his advice on the killing of Jews: 'I also want to speak to you here, in complete frankness, of a really grave chapter. Amongst ourselves, for once, it shall be said quite openly, but all the same we will never speak about it in public. Just as we did not hesitate on 30 June 1934, to do our duty as we were ordered, and to stand comrades who had erred against the wall and shoot them, and we never spoke about it and we never will speak about it.[1]

'It was a matter of natural tact that is alive in us, thank God, that we never talked about it amongst ourselves, that we never discussed it. Each of us shuddered and yet each of us knew clearly that the next time he would do it again if it were an order, and if it were necessary.

---

[1] Himmler was referring to 'The Night of the Long Knives' – when Hitler ordered the murder of several Nazi Stormtrooper leaders and more than a hundred others whom he wished to see killed, including a former German Chancellor, General Kurt von Schleicher.

I am referring here to the evacuation of the Jews, the extermination of the Jewish people. This is one of the things that is easily said: "The Jewish people are going to be exterminated," that's what every Party member says, "sure, it's in our programme, elimination of the Jews, extermination – it'll be done." And then they all come along, the eighty million worthy Germans, and each one has his one decent Jew. Of course, the others are swine, but this one, he is a first-rate Jew. Of all those who talk like that, not one has seen it happen, not one has had to go through with it. Most of you men know what it is like to see a hundred corpses side by side, or five hundred or a thousand.

'To have stood fast through this and – except for cases of human weakness – to have stayed decent, that has made us hard. This is an unwritten and never-to-be-written page of glory in our history, for we know how difficult it would be for us if today under bombing raids and the hardships and deprivations of war – if we were still to have the Jews in every city as secret saboteurs, agitators, and inciters. If the Jews were still lodged in the body of the German nation, we would probably by now have reached the stage of 1917–18.

'The wealth they possessed we took from them. I gave a strict order, which has been carried out by SS Obergruppenführer Pohl, that this wealth will of course be turned over to the Reich in its entirety. We have taken none of it for ourselves. Individuals who have erred will be punished in accordance with the order given by me at the start, threatening that anyone who takes as much as a single Mark of this money is a dead man. A number of SS men – they are not very many – committed this offence, and they shall die. There will be no mercy. We had the moral right, we had the duty towards our people, to destroy this people that wanted to destroy us. But we do not have the right to enrich ourselves by so much as a fur, as a watch, by one Mark or a cigarette or anything else. We do not want, in the end, because we destroyed a bacillus, to be infected by this bacillus and to die. I will never stand by and watch while even a small rotten spot develops or takes hold. Wherever it may form we will together burn it away. All in all, however, we can say that we have carried out this most difficult of tasks in a spirit of love for our people. And we have suffered no harm to our inner being, our soul, our character.'

11 p.m.
The train draws out of Poznan. I stay awake for one more stop which I have always wanted to see, and while waiting, reflect on the journey: Robin joins me for a drink, and later Ben.

11.50 p.m.
Zbaszyn.

11.55 pm.
Zbaszynek. We are still in western Poland, but from 1918 to 1939 this station was on the German side of the Polish–German border. This was one of the main crossing points, on 28 October 1938, where the Germans drove 15,000 Polish-born Jews out of Germany. From Zbaszynek they were driven at gunpoint across the River Obra into Poland, to the town across the border, Zbaszyn, which we sped through five minutes ago. There, the Poles housed them in disused stables.

One of the deportees, Zyndel Grynszpan, who had been born in Poland in 1886, but had lived in Hanover since 1911, sent a postcard to his son Hirsch, who was in Paris, describing the hardships here. I read it aloud as the train sits in the empty station: 'When we reached the border, we were searched to see if anybody had any money, and anybody who had more than ten marks, the balance was taken from him. This was the German law. Not more than ten marks could be taken out of Germany. The Germans said, "You didn't bring any more into Germany and you can't take any more out."

'The SS were giving us, as it were, protective custody, and we walked two kilometres on foot to the Polish border. They told us to go – the SS men were whipping us, those who lingered they hit, and blood was flowing on the road. They tore away their little baggage from them, they treated us in a most barbaric fashion – this was the first time that I'd ever seen the wild barbarism of the Germans.

'They shouted at us: "Run! Run!" I myself received a blow and I fell in the ditch. My son helped me, and he said: "Run, run, father – otherwise you'll die!" When we got to the open border – we reached what was called the green border, the Polish border – first of all, the women went in.

'Then a Polish general and some officers arrived, and they examined the papers and saw that we were Polish citizens, that we had special passports. It was decided to let us enter Poland.'

Zyndel Grynszpan's son received this account while he was in Paris. He was so indignant that he went to the German Embassy and shot the first German diplomat who agreed to talk to him, the Third Secretary, Ernst vom Rath. While vom Rath lay dying in Paris, a terrible vengeance was planned by the Nazi leaders in Berlin. Vom Rath died on 9 November 1938. That night the Nazis launched the Kristallnacht – the burning of hundreds of synagogues, the murder of more than ninety Jews, and the intensification of anti-Jewish propaganda and hatred. Within a few hours of Winston Churchill protesting against the barbarity of the persecution, Hitler's Minister of Propaganda, Josef Goebbels, declared that there was a 'direct line' from Churchill to vom Rath's assassin.

12.05 a.m.
The train picks up speed, hurtling westward to the River Oder and the Polish–German border.

12.50 a.m.
I am still awake as the train stops at Rzepin, a Polish town fifteen kilometres from the German border (before 1945 it was a small German town, Reppen). A Russian train draws in alongside, going east.

1 a.m.
Polish passport control. It is very quick, unlike the passport control in the Communist days, with the long scrutinies, repeated questionings, and probings under the carriage. Are those severities a thing of the past – for ever?

1.15 a.m.
Kunowice. The Polish border station. Once this town was deep inside Germany, both inter-war and imperial Germany.

1.25 a.m.
The train crosses the River Oder.

It was Stalin who insisted that this be the German–Polish border, pushing Germany further westward than the Western Allies wanted, but enabling him to secure a large swathe of eastern Poland. This area was given to Poland as compensation. The Poles who live here now were mostly brought from those eastern areas in 1945. German towns became Polish towns. German names were changed to Polish names.

1.30 a.m.
Frankfurt-on-Oder. We are back in Germany. It was through this city that 209 Norwegian Jews were brought on their journey to Auschwitz in October 1942. They had left Oslo by ship for Stettin on my sixth birthday. More than nine hundred others managed to avoid deportation by escaping to Sweden, with the help of the Norwegian resistance.

Amid so many stories of murder and destruction, stories of resistance – on whatever scale – are always heartening, as are the individual acts of defiance, and individual acts of courage, that have also played their part in much that we have seen and read in the last two weeks.

DAY 14

MAGDEBURG – LONDON

Echoes of the Holocaust ... wherever we travel

4.15 a.m.
I wake up briefly at Magdeburg.

7 a.m.
Bielefeld. I am woken by the station announcer. 'The Moscow–Brussels express is on platform ...' That is us.

I know many Jews who find it difficult to go to Germany at all. My best friend, Hugo Gryn, a survivor of Auschwitz, and a slave labourer at Lieberose, south of Berlin, and at Sachsenhausen, just north of the city, told me once that he would never spend the night in Germany. Recently he agreed, after much anguished thought, to spend two nights, on a visit (which the camp museum had requested) to Lieberose, where he had been among several thousand Jewish slave labourers forced to build a 'model town' for the SS. He had also visited Sachsenhausen on this journey. In December 1944 he had reached Sachsenhausen with nine hundred survivors of a death march from Lieberose. During the march 2,500 had died of exhaustion, or been shot by the German guards.

Any German guard who was twenty-one at the end of the war would now be over seventy. Many of the guards who tormented Hugo, and the guards on the death marches who murdered all those who were unable to walk further, might well be alive today. But as they grow older, and more and more of them die, there is less and less chance of those whom they tortured meeting them in the street.

9.10 a.m.
Essen. Jews had lived here since the thirteenth century. In 1930 there were 5,000 Jews here, less than one per cent of the population – a

considerable contrast with the far higher Polish percentages. The synagogue, built in 1913, was considered by many to be one of the most beautiful in Germany. When war came, only 1,636 Jews were left in Essen. Most of the others had emigrated. The first deportation took place on 26 November 1941, when 252 Jews were sent to the Lodz ghetto. Most of them were murdered in Chelmno within a few months. Other deportations took place to Izbica Lubelska, and from there to Belzec. In February 1943 a hundred Jews were deported from Essen to Auschwitz in the 'Factory Action' which also saw more than nine thousand Berlin Jews deported. When the war ended, about thirty Jews were still alive in Essen. Their community was re-established. There are less than two hundred Jews in Essen today.

On 5 March 1943, during an intensive British bombing raid on the Krupp munitions works in Essen, the factory that manufactured artillery detonators was destroyed. In order to continue production of this crucial armament – half a million detonators per month – the factory was moved far to the east, out of range of Allied bombers. The site chosen for the new factory was on the approach road to Auschwitz Main Camp, and within sight of Birkenau. This was the Union Factory, in which 1,500 Jewish women worked, and from which explosives were smuggled into Birkenau on the eve of the Sonderkommando revolt.

The Polish conductor of our carriage is reading a book about Romulus and the founding of the Roman Republic.

9.25 a.m.

Duisburg. Jews lived here from the thirteenth century. In 1875, as the community grew, a fine synagogue was built, with a dome that replicated in miniature the dome of the Oranienburgerstrasse synagogue in Berlin. In 1933 the Jewish population was 2,560. By 1939 there were scarcely more than 800. Beginning in 1941 there were several deportations. On 25 June 1942, from this station, 146 Jews were deported to Theresienstadt.

9.40 a.m.

Düsseldorf. Leo Baeck, whose story we have followed in Berlin and Theresienstadt, was a rabbi here from 1912 to 1917.

In November 1941 there was a deportation of 489 Jews from Düsseldorf to Riga, where they were taken (with 10,000 other Jews) to the Rumbuli forest and murdered. In July 1942 there was a deportation of 260 Jews from Düsseldorf to Theresienstadt.

Echoes of the Holocaust are present wherever we travel.

10.06 a.m.
Crossing the Rhine.

10.09 a.m.
Cologne. The train stops for only three minutes. Then we continue westward, on the same route that brought us to Germany two weeks ago.

10.50 a.m.
Aachen (in French, Aix-la-Chapelle). Charlemagne's capital: the cradle of multi-national Europe, and the principal source of Christian Europe. It even has a Polish name: Akwizgran. With the disintegration of Charlemagne's Empire came many centuries of civil chaos and destructive wars. Bismarck's Germany attempted to recreate the Carolingian mastery of Europe, in a moderate form. Hitler's Germany almost succeeded in doing so, in a grotesque form.

The carriages from Moscow and St Petersburg are detached from the train here. We are to continue in our Warsaw–Brussels carriage.

11.15 a.m.
We leave Aachen. Germany will soon be behind us.

1.20 p.m.
Brussels. We have two hours before the Eurostar leaves for Waterloo, time to go into Brussels. I take a taxi with Jon; we have time for hot chocolate and a cake, and a walk through the Grand' Place, before returning to the station.

3.28 p.m.
The Eurostar express pulls out of Brussels.

5.45 p.m. (one hour earlier than European time).
Waterloo. The journey is over. Even in the last hour and a half, as we sped under the Channel and through the fields of Kent, myriad images were already returning to mind; it is the same for everybody. Each of us has dozens of such images: the couple in battledress at Prague station and the skinhead at Konin; the incredibly beautiful synagogue interiors at Lancut and Wlodawa; the unexpected synagogue at Grabow; looking, with Ben, at his home town, his school, his home and his labour camp; the skinheads at Majdanek; people comforting each other at Sobibor.

No doubt the elusive past has been brought very close. As we disperse to our homes, it is like saying goodbye to fellow-adventurers, fellow-searchers after knowledge, and fellow-journeymen.

EPILOGUE

'REMEMBERING THE PAST'

In the weeks and months that followed the journey we were to meet several times as a group, and to reflect, both individually and collectively, on our experiences. After our return, several of the group wrote to me about their reactions and reflections. At the death camps, Robin O'Neil recalled, 'We had tears and moments of individual solitude that could so easily have been misunderstood.' During the readings from the testimonies of survivors and Germans at Belzec, Robin wrote, 'I noticed we were avoiding all eye contact with each other. At Treblinka my thoughts went again to our younger group members. It was not easy for them.'

Jon Boyd was among those who were most deeply affected by the visit to Belzec. His reflections were those of many of the group, perhaps of all of them. 'The camp itself,' he wrote to me, 'was littered with dark red fragments of brick, remnants of the barracks which had stood there before the Nazis had destroyed them in a vain attempt to cover up their crimes. As I stood in that place, I reflected back on the day spent driving there. We had travelled all day, passing through town after town after town. All had housed Jewish communities, a significant proportion of which died on the very spot on which I was now standing. I had seen their homes, eaten in their restaurants and prayed in their synagogues. I had enjoyed their countryside, met their neighbours, and read their history. And now I was standing on their grave, and weeping their tears. When one spends hour upon hour visiting Jewish community upon Jewish community, and ends the day at the site of their mass murder, one becomes deeply conscious of the scale of the Shoah. And that was one road, to one camp, in one country.'

Ros Morris summed up her feelings in a powerful cry, from the depths of feeling, putting in words what many of us could not. 'Nothing prepared me for Birkenau,' she wrote. 'Fifty years on, the trenches dug on either side of the railtrack reek of human excrement and putrid green and bracken water oozes out of cracks in the subsoil. What could it have been like to have been here, for even one day? The enormity of the camp, where the endless line of barracks and searchlights and barbed wire stretch as far as the eye can see, overwhelms me. The debris of the crematoria blown up in one bright spark of resistance speaks mountains where adjectives now fail; a single red carnation is left at the charred roof. One and a half million innocent and defenceless people from all walks of life perished here for no purposeful reason. There was no profit. There was no assembly line. No one could speak of the advantage of these deaths.

'Poland is a land without a soul. There is no spark. Each step is drenched in tears. From Birkenau to Chelmno our feet walked on the ashes of ruined communities; on the brightest of minds and the defeat of ambition. Belzec provided the ashes and bones still visible to the eye and pitifully churned with the foot. At Sobibor we were speechless. One by one the members of the group were touched by the desperate and unseen souls of the dead. Each town, village and empty ghetto where once vibrant communities of Jews jostled with their Polish neighbours was a testament to the Nazi achievement: a ravishment of six million souls.

'It was a sunny day at Birkenau when we visited. The sky was seaside blue and the sun burned our skins. What could it have been like to have been stuffed inside a cattle truck – no ventilation, sanitation, food, water, room to sit, space to stand? No idea of what awaited when the doors finally opened to the bright sun of an azure sky in August or the frozen leaden grey of December? How surreal and how terribly, horribly frightening. An image stays with me of a photograph of Hungarian Jews made to undress at the entrance to the wooded area leading to the gas chambers. Nothing has changed. The Hungarian deportation made its way, naked and defenceless, to death one hundred metres away. The trees stand still, taller and leafier, but the Hungarians have vanished. Once again you read us the harrowing Selection of the 650 boys at Birkenau, of whom only fifty were to remain alive, and again I was appalled and horrified at the base cruelty of the SS. How many times do we ask ourselves, "Did they not [have] children ever?"'

This last question appears in a fragment, damaged by water, of the notes hidden in a metal container in the soil of Birkenau by one of the Sonderkommando, those Jewish prisoners at Birkenau who, as in every other camp, were forced to take the bodies of the murdered ones out of the gas chambers, before themselves being murdered. The selection of the 650 boys took place, as a punishment, after the revolt of the Sonderkommando, in which two of the crematoria were blown up. Of this story, Robin later wrote to me, 'This was awful. This reading shook us all.'

Petra Wöstefeld, the German in our group, had been apprehensive about coming, wondering how she would manage. 'I was very conscious of the fact that I was the only German person on the course, among a majority of Jewish people whom I hardly knew at all,' she wrote to me after our return. Reflecting on the journey, Petra wrote: 'I, for my part, learnt more about the Jewish religion and culture than ever before. On the trip I found out about the others' feelings on the Holocaust. I could also explain my opinions and emotions to them. My initial feeling of apprehension disappeared very quickly. We had a great deal of fun, too, which was immensely important in order to be able to handle our emotions. The ghettos, concentration camps and death camps proved to be a great emotional strain.

'The shock, helplessness and despair that automatically overwhelms one when dealing with the Holocaust was too much to bear at times. I personally was most affected when we visited Sobibor. Somehow it had all become too much for me to handle by that stage. Yet, the support, comfort and sympathy I received from the others was absolutely fantastic. The whole journey brought the subject so much closer to me and helped me in coming to terms with the Holocaust, or at least in the attempt to do so.'

Rachael Fraenkel, who had felt unable to continue the journey beyond Prague, wrote about the day that we spent in Berlin: 'While on the surface it is easy to see these places and treat them like the words in a book – just buildings, just places, just names – underneath was the realisation that it is impossible to have "just history". While the buildings may no longer exist, the people may be dead, the history still lives on and has an impact on people's lives. Seeing the places gives a dimension to the history that can never be gained from the words in a book. Seeing the places, one can almost see the citizens of Berlin in the nineteen thirties and forties, working in, walking into, or just walking past the buildings. Whether or not these people were supporters of the Nazi regime does not matter in this instance. It is the realisation that it was not just a few people who were involved, but a whole society.'

After the group left by train from Prague for Slovakia and Poland, Rachael remained in Prague. The extra day that she spent there introduced her to things that we did not have time to see, showed how each day's itinerary could certainly have added a dimension of thought to what we had done. The 'most painful reminder' of the Holocaust, she wrote, 'was an exhibition in the building of the Prague Burial Society of paintings by children in Terezin. In the majority of cases, the only remnant of the child's life seems to be the paintings they had produced. The mixture of subjects from beautiful countryside scenes to wretched and tormented faces was painful to see. To see such horrific scenes come from the minds of such young people, must surely reflect their mental anguish. All that went through my mind was "so young, so innocent, so dead".'

Rachael also wrote of an experience after we had left Prague: 'The impact of walking into the Pinkas synagogue and seeing bare rooms with every single wall space taken up with the names of Czech Jews who did not survive was phenomenal. Being surrounded by names of people killed because they were Jewish in an old synagogue, the only thing remaining being a Bimah, gave the feeling that the rooms were waiting to be filled by the people whose names were on the wall, rather than those in there reading the names.'

Jon, who returned to Prague a few months after our journey, had a different response to the Pinkas synagogue memorial wall. 'Turning a synagogue into a Holocaust memorial is undoubtedly incredibly powerful, but feels somewhat inappropriate,' he wrote to me after his second journey to Prague that year. 'A synagogue should be a centre of Jewish life not death, and it is unpleasant enough when one is turned into a static museum to be visited in the same way as an art gallery or medieval castle. If a synagogue is going to remember individuals, let it remember those who were associated with it in life, not those who are recalled because of the nature of their death. Holocaust memorials with names are deeply moving and very much part of the Jewish tradition of martyrology. Whether one should overwhelm a synagogue, however, is a different question.'

As our journey had continued, the sense of loss – and of lost communities – intensified. 'As we crossed the endless landscapes,' Angela Jayson later wrote, 'I was saddened remembering that hundreds of thousands of Jews, many of whom died en route or were murdered, were dragged along this and similar routes that we were taking.'

Our own route had taken us, on our sixth day, on the route of one of the main deportation railways, single-track, along which Jews from Hungary, Italy, Croatia, Greece and Slovakia had been deported to Auschwitz. For Caroline Harris, as for others in the group, after visiting Birkenau there was a feeling, she wrote, 'that I would be slightly more prepared for seeing the other camps. I was wrong. The impact of each camp was in no way diminished. This was partly due to the immense differences in their location, size and states of decay.'

Caroline added: 'Being amongst such a small group of people, I felt able to express my emotions and at each camp there was always something which broke through any feeling of numbness I may have had. In combination with the death camps we visited, the lost communities also had a sombring effect. Towns that had been over seventy per cent Jewish looked so non-Jewish that it was almost impossible to visualise their previous bustling Jewish inhabitants. I felt that I was looking for a presence where there only existed an absence. Synagogues that had survived had become museums for an extinct community.

'On reflection, my overwhelming response to the trip is a desire to return to the places we visited and spend more time there as there is so much more to be learned.'

It was only when I came to complete this epilogue that I learned which of my students first had the idea for our journey. It was Herut Hoskin, the grandmother in our group, who had been born in British Mandate Palestine in 1941. She wrote, in her reflections on the journey, and of the places that we intended to visit: 'I have never been to any of these places, but names of towns and villages, some more familiar than others, stir in me feelings of excitement and anticipation. They encapsulate a whole world of Jewish history and Hebrew literature on which I had been brought up. For children growing up in the newly founded State of Israel, the diaspora had mostly negative connotations, but it was nevertheless a fascinating world, a taste of which we sampled in our history and literature lessons – Prague, Cracow, Lublin, Warsaw – centres of thriving Jewish learning and culture.

'Then there are Auschwitz, Majdanek, Treblinka, Sobibor – the final destinations, the end of it all. I thought I would never be able to face the Death Camps, not even as an adult. I had been telling myself that the first year of my MA Holocaust Studies had prepared me for what we were about to witness, but I was anxious in case I found it all too difficult to cope with on an emotional level. I seemed to be swaying between a kind of numbness and a sense of apprehension. My attempts to comfort myself that this was possibly a natural response to the unknown did not seem to ease my apprehension.

'It was one Wednesday in November, during the Holocaust MA seminar, that I brought up the idea of a trip to Poland. I felt at the time, that studying the Shoah from a distance of time and place would be incomplete unless we saw for ourselves where it had all happened. Emotional responses to the atrocities and horror, and empathy with the victims, were not enough in themselves. I felt a need to be connected to the actual places where Jewish communities had once flourished before they were wiped out by violent and senseless means. I was hoping that such a trip would enable me to establish a more concrete link between the past and the present; that it would enhance our studies and would help to create a deeper understanding (if this is at all possible) of the Holocaust.'

Of the morning that we spent in Birkenau, Herut wrote: 'It has often been said that no language has vocabulary adequate to describe Auschwitz, or any other death camp for that matter. We have read about the camps, we have seen films, documentary and fiction. I am standing in Birkenau, this wide, desolate space – a monument to human depravity and misery, and I have no words. It is difficult to describe what I felt. I know that I did not want to talk to anyone, because the experience was very private. There was that uneasy feeling of helplessness, of isolation and anxiety. Like many others, I, also, kept asking myself: "Why? Why? How could the world let it happen? Could it happen again? To me? To my family?"

'I enter one of the barracks, walk around what has remained of the crematoria. I listen to Martin's reading, and this, to some extent, helps to bring the horrific reality of Birkenau to the present. I can confess now to a feeling of guilt I first experienced in Birkenau, and I am not sure how to put it exactly. I felt somewhat ashamed that my emotions at the time, as much as they were perfectly genuine, were not strong, or expressive enough. Elie Wiesel once said that only a person who was "there" had the right to write about the Holocaust. Now I can understand what he meant. And a sad thought crossed my mind later in Belzec, in Sobibor, Majdanek, Treblinka and Chelmno – that these death camps, the ultimate in human suffering, are now graveyards, museums, or monumental parklands. They should be there for posterity, although as monuments they can never measure up to the scale of human misery which prevailed in them over fifty years ago. And then there is this gnawing, worrying thought: what would it be like for visitors, thirty or fifty years from now? With the absence of survivors and eye-witnesses, who will see to it that the Shoah does remain in our collective memory?'

Herut's conclusion is shared, I think, by all of us. And yet, like so much on this journey, it is entirely the conclusion of one individual. We have travelled collectively, and talked and listened collectively, and yet, at the end of each day, and many times during each day, we were on our own, alone with our thoughts and reflections. Herut writes: 'For me, personally, the significance of this trip has been finding a missing link between a Jewish world that no longer exists (although the proof of its existence, whether overt or covert, still lives on everywhere we travelled) and Jewish existence today, fifty-five years after the Holocaust. Moreover, I can see now, more than ever, the importance of keeping the memory of the Shoah alive. I can see the necessity, even obligation, of teaching it to future generations, with strong emphasis on the importance of mutual tolerance and respect among people, whoever they are. Once survivors and eye-witnesses have gone, who will be there to ensure that the memory of what happened is not forgotten?

'And this leads me to another, often talked about issue. I can see the justification in viewing the concept of the Shoah as a unique historical phenomenon. At the same time, however, it is just as important to consider its universal implications. If it happened once, it could easily happen again, anywhere.' Herut adds, echoing the feelings of all of us: 'In remembering the past we also aim at minimising possible catastrophes in the future.'

Our journey will help each of us, in our different ways, to pass on the story of the Holocaust, through teaching, conversation and writing. We ourselves have met on many occasions since the journey, to recall its different moments. It has become an integral part of our understanding of the past. After our return, Angela was told of a remark by a teacher of one of her surviving relatives: 'If all the trees became quill-pens and all the oceans became ink, it would not be enough to write about all the horrors of the Holocaust.' Our journey gave us an insight into some of those horrors, and taught us about some of the perpetrators, about the sufferings and courageous acts of the victims, about the richness of Jewish pre-war history in Europe, and about the pain that can be felt in exploring the past.

MAPS

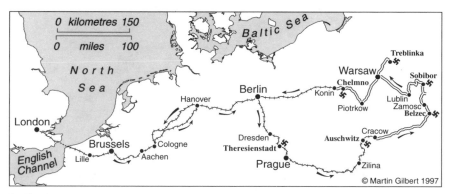

1: The journey

2: The Polish section

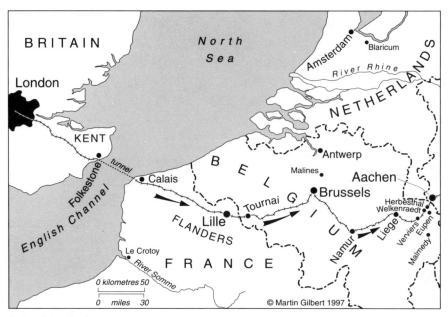

3: London–Aachen

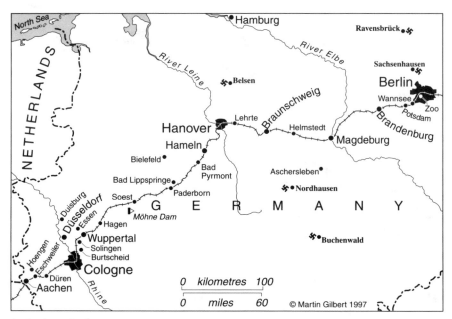

4: Aachen–Berlin

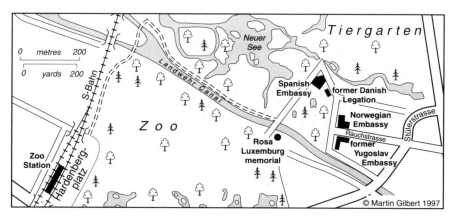

5: Berlin: Zoo–Tiergarten

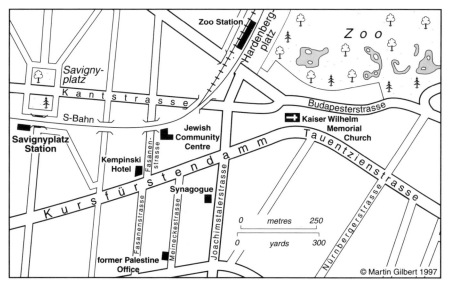

6: Berlin: Kursfürstendamm

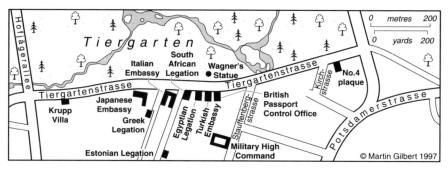

7: Berlin: Tiergartenstrasse

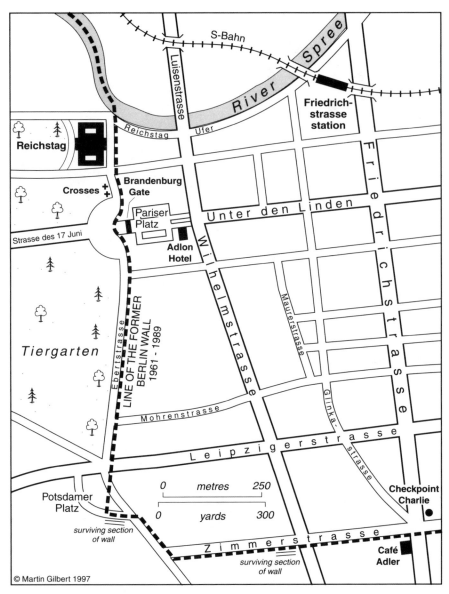

8: Berlin: Reichstag to Checkpoint Charlie

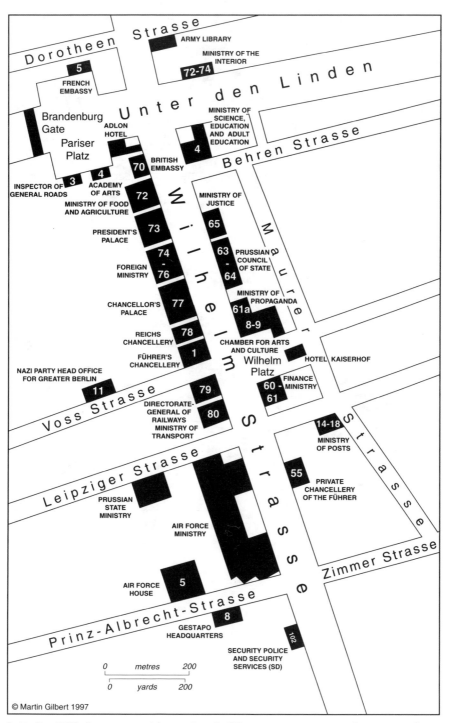

9: Berlin: Wilhelmstrasse, with wartime buildings, street names and street numbers

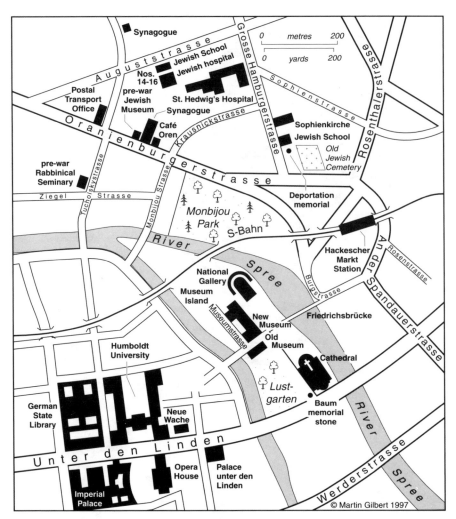

10: Berlin: Unter den Linden–Oranienburgerstrasse

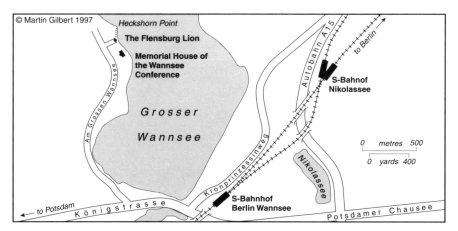

11: Wannsee

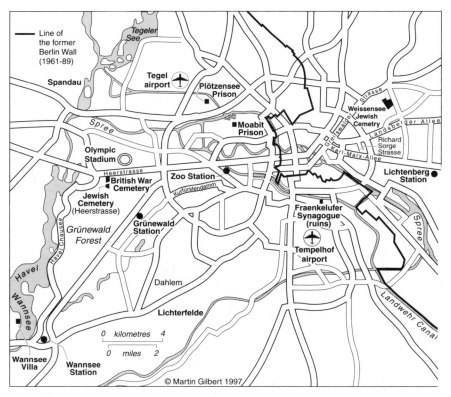

12: Berlin

13: Berlin–Prague

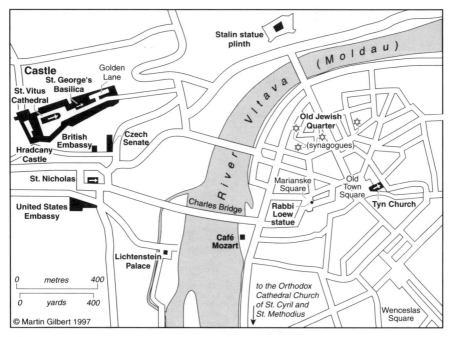

14: Prague: city centre

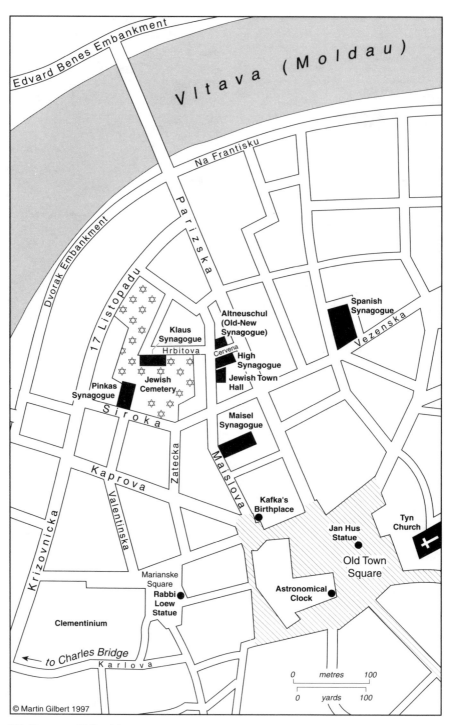

15: Prague: old Jewish quarter

16: Prague–Terezin (Theresienstadt)

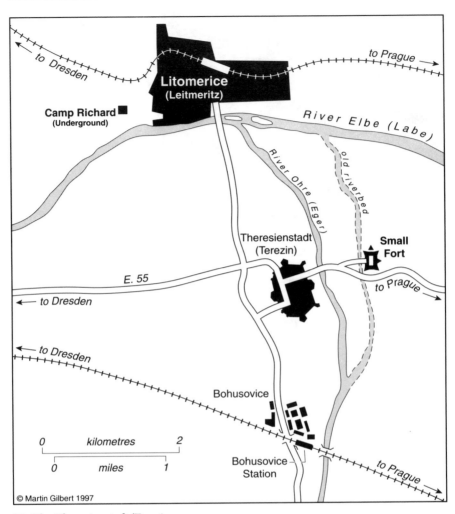

17: The Theresienstadt/Terezin area

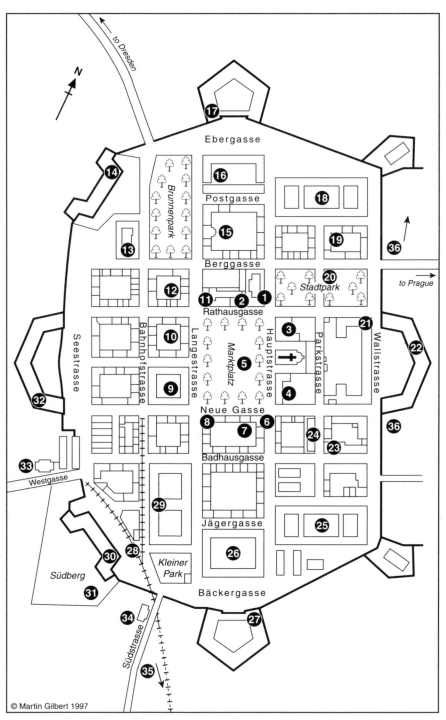

18: The Theresienstadt ghetto

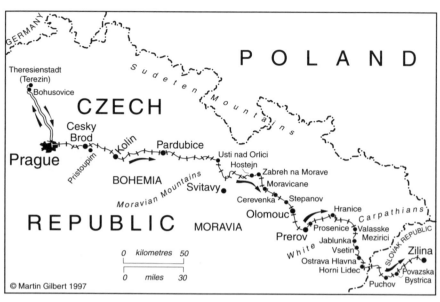

19: Prague–Zilina

20: Zilina and the deportation railways

21: Zilina–Zywiec

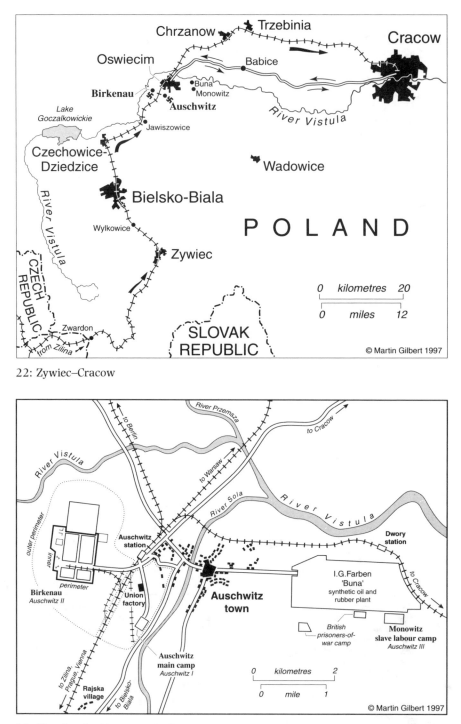

22: Zywiec–Cracow

23: The Auschwitz concentration camp area

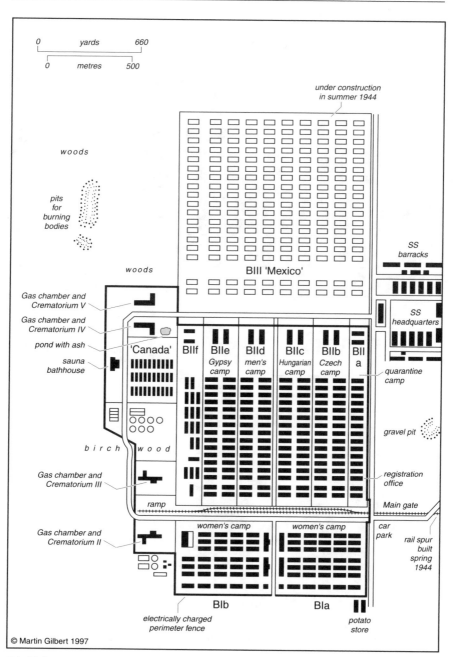

0 yards 660
0 metres 500

woods

pits
for
burning
bodies

woods

BIII 'Mexico'

under construction
in summer 1944

SS
barracks

SS
headquarters

Gas chamber and
Crematorium V

Gas chamber and
Crematorium IV

pond with ash

sauna
bathhouse

'Canada'   BIIf   BIIe   BIId   BIIc   BIIb   BII
                  Gypsy men's Hungarian Czech a
                  camp   camp   camp   camp

quarantine
camp

gravel pit

birch wood

Gas chamber and
Crematorium III

ramp

registration
office

Main gate

Gas chamber and
Crematorium II

women's camp   women's camp

car
park

rail spur
built
spring
1944

BIb   BIa

electrically charged
perimeter fence

potato
store

© Martin Gilbert 1997

24: Birkenau

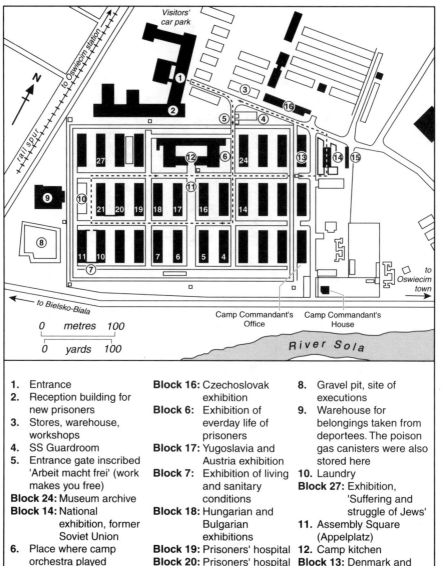

1. Entrance
2. Reception building for new prisoners
3. Stores, warehouse, workshops
4. SS Guardroom
5. Entrance gate inscribed 'Arbeit macht frei' (work makes you free)
Block 24: Museum archive
Block 14: National exhibition, former Soviet Union
6. Place where camp orchestra played
Block 4: Extermination exhibition
Block 5: Exhibition of material evidence of crimes

Block 16: Czechoslovak exhibition
Block 6: Exhibition of everday life of prisoners
Block 17: Yugoslavia and Austria exhibition
Block 7: Exhibition of living and sanitary conditions
Block 18: Hungarian and Bulgarian exhibitions
Block 19: Prisoners' hospital
Block 20: Prisoners' hospital
Block 21: Prisoners' hospital
Block 10: Exhibition of sterilisation experiments
7. Wall of Death, where prisoners were executed by shooting
11. Death block exhibition

8. Gravel pit, site of executions
9. Warehouse for belongings taken from deportees. The poison gas canisters were also stored here
10. Laundry
Block 27: Exhibition, 'Suffering and struggle of Jews'
11. Assembly Square (Appelplatz)
12. Camp kitchen
Block 13: Denmark and Germany exhibitions
13. SS hospital
14. Gas chamber and Crematorium (Crematorium I)
15. Political section (Camp Gestapo)
16. SS garages, stables and stores

□   Watchtowers

© Martin Gilbert 1997

25: Auschwitz Main Camp

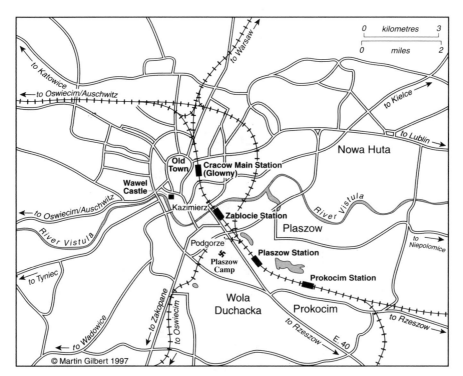

26: The Cracow region

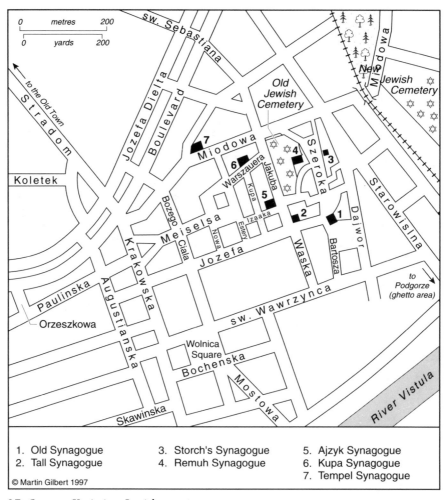

© Martin Gilbert 1997

1. Old Synagogue
2. Tall Synagogue
3. Storch's Synagogue
4. Remuh Synagogue
5. Ajzyk Synagogue
6. Kupa Synagogue
7. Tempel Synagogue

27: Cracow: Kazimierz Jewish quarter

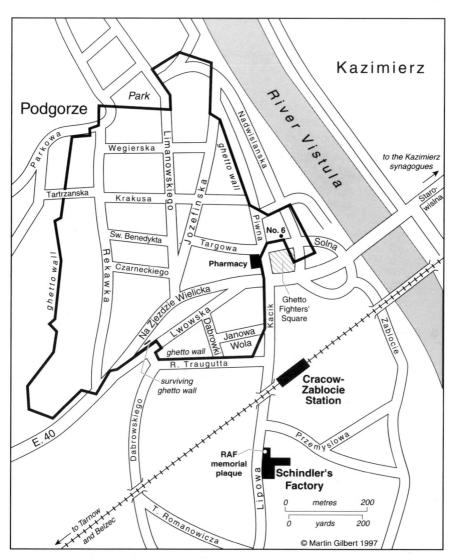

28: Cracow: Podgorze, the wartime ghetto

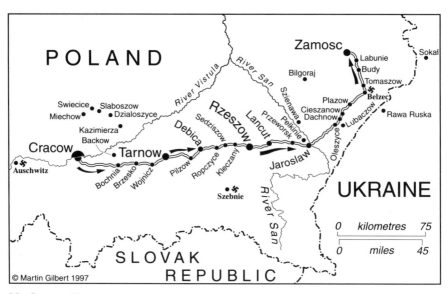

29: Cracow–Zamosc

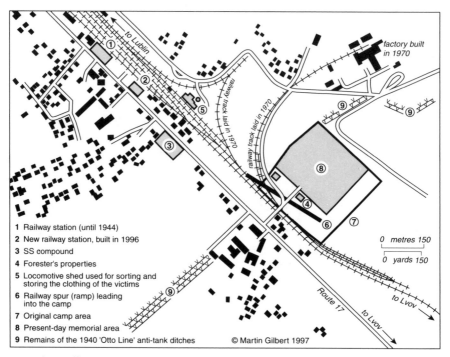

1 Railway station (until 1944)
2 New railway station, built in 1996
3 SS compound
4 Forester's properties
5 Locomotive shed used for sorting and storing the clothing of the victims
6 Railway spur (ramp) leading into the camp
7 Original camp area
8 Present-day memorial area
9 Remains of the 1940 'Otto Line' anti-tank ditches

© Martin Gilbert 1997

30: Belzec village

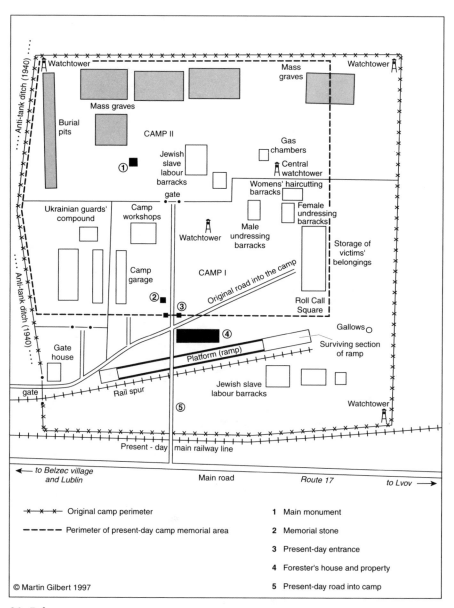

31: Belzec camp

32: Zamosc–Lublin

to Wlodawa

Chelm

Trawniki

to Kiev

to Warsaw

Borki

Rejowiec

Krasnystaw

P O L A N D

Izbica Station Izbica Lubelska

0   kilometres   10

0   miles   6

Zamosc

to Hrubieszow

Szczebrzeszyn

to Belzec and Lvov

to Lvov

© Martin Gilbert 1997

33: Zamosc–Chelm

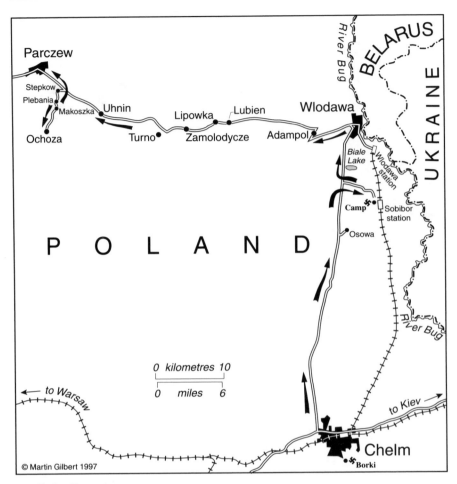

34: Chelm–Parczew

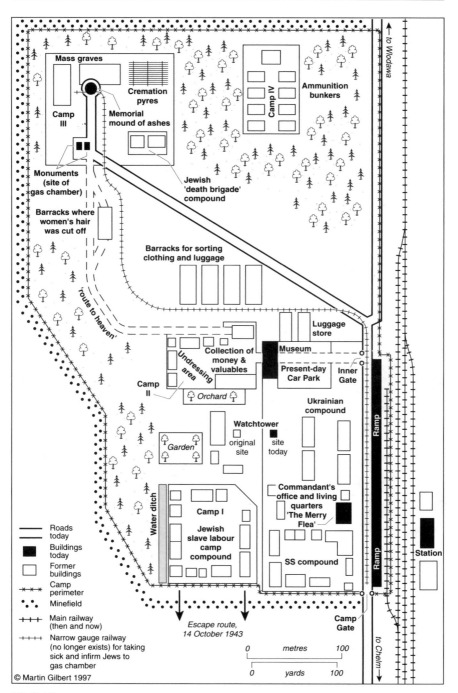

Roads today
Buildings today
Former buildings
Camp perimeter
Minefield
Main railway (then and now)
Narrow gauge railway (no longer exists) for taking sick and infirm Jews to gas chamber

© Martin Gilbert 1997

35: Sobibor

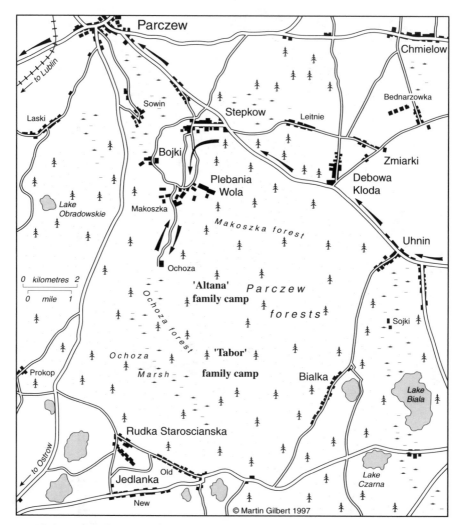

36: The Parczew forest

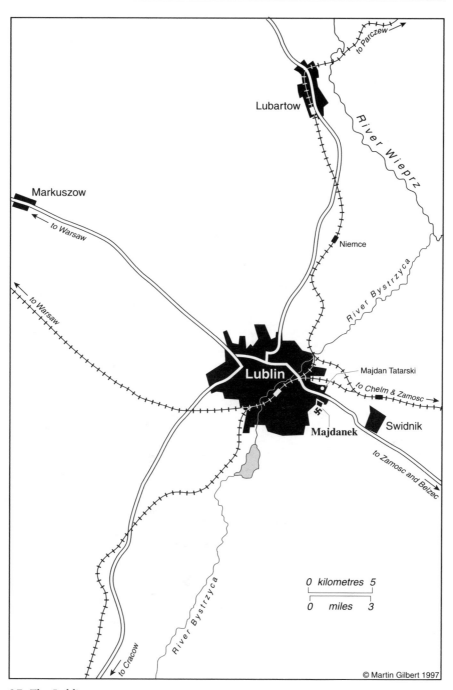

37: The Lublin area

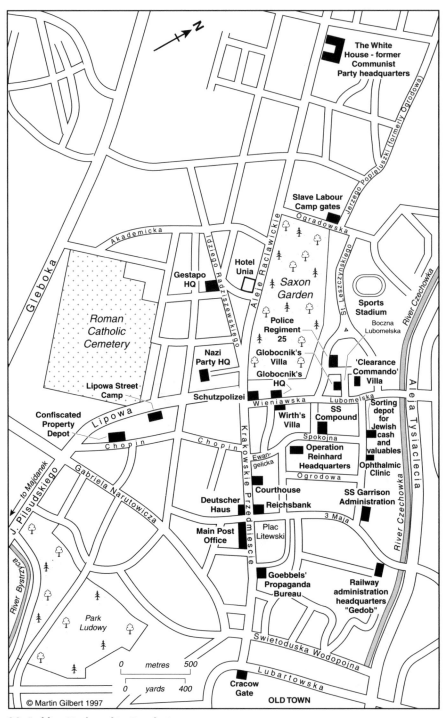

The White House - former Communist Party headquarters

Slave Labour Camp gates

Hotel Unia

Gestapo HQ

Saxon Garden

Sports Stadium

Boczna Lubomelska

Roman Catholic Cemetery

Police Regiment 25

Globocnik's Villa

'Clearance Commando' Villa

Nazi Party HQ

Globocnik's HQ

Lipowa Street Camp

Schutzpolizei

Wirth's Villa

SS Compound

Sorting depot for Jewish cash and valuables

Confiscated Property Depot

Operation Reinhard Headquarters

Ophthalmic Clinic

Courthouse

Deutscher Haus

Reichsbank

SS Garrison Administration

Main Post Office

Plac Litewski

Goebbels' Propaganda Bureau

Railway administration headquarters "Gedob"

Park Ludowy

to Majdanek

0   metres   500

0   yards   400

Cracow Gate

OLD TOWN

© Martin Gilbert 1997

38: Lublin: Krakowskie Przedmiescie

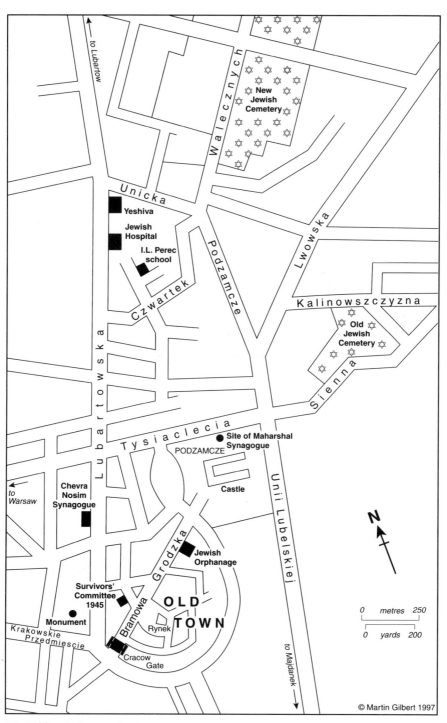

39: Lublin: Lubartowska Street

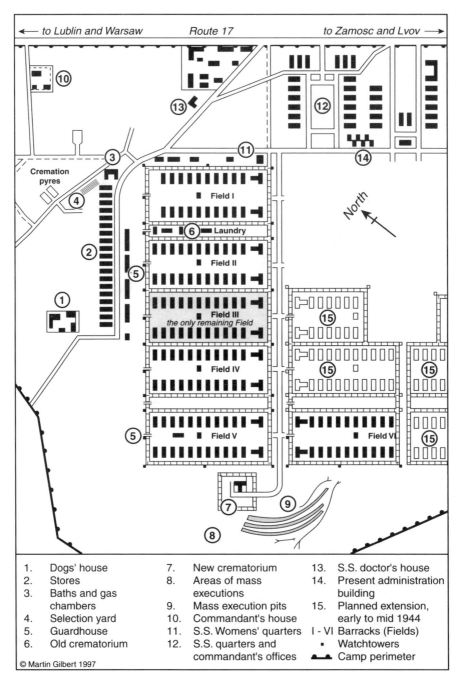

Map legend:

1. Dogs' house	7. New crematorium	13. S.S. doctor's house
2. Stores	8. Areas of mass	14. Present administration
3. Baths and gas	executions	building
chambers	9. Mass execution pits	15. Planned extension,
4. Selection yard	10. Commandant's house	early to mid 1944
5. Guardhouse	11. S.S. Womens' quarters	I - VI Barracks (Fields)
6. Old crematorium	12. S.S. quarters and	▪ Watchtowers
© Martin Gilbert 1997	commandant's offices	▲▲ Camp perimeter

40: Majdanek

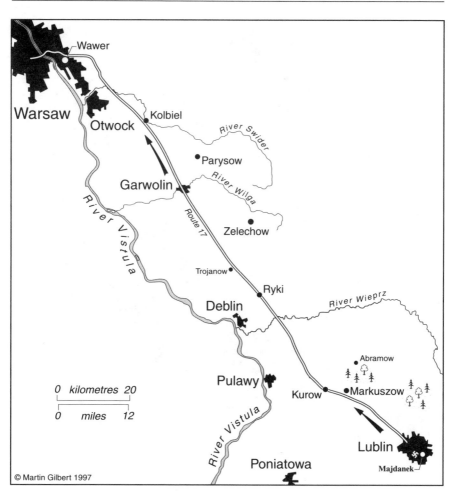

41: Lublin–Warsaw

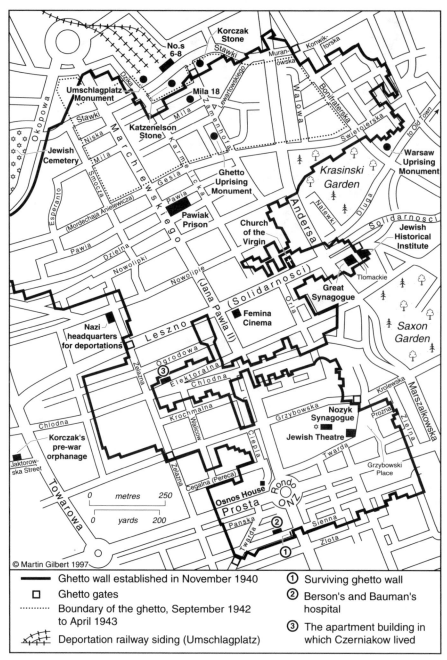

Ghetto wall established in November 1940
☐ Ghetto gates
.... Boundary of the ghetto, September 1942 to April 1943
🚂 Deportation railway siding (Umschlagplatz)

① Surviving ghetto wall
② Berson's and Bauman's hospital
③ The apartment building in which Czerniakow lived

42: The Warsaw ghetto

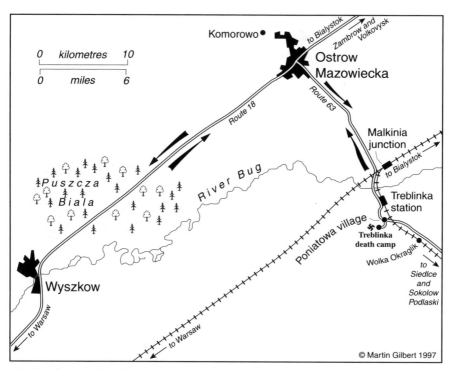

43: Wyszkow–Treblinka

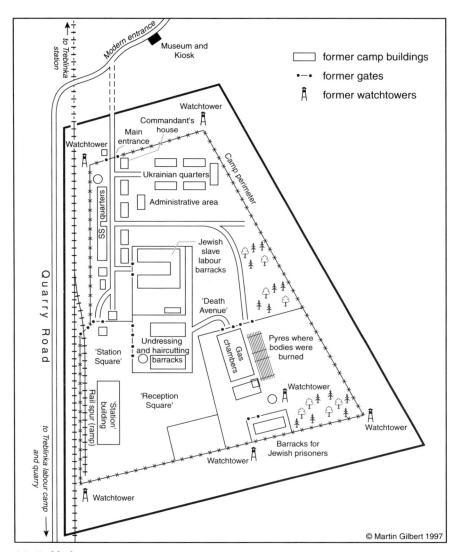

44: Treblinka

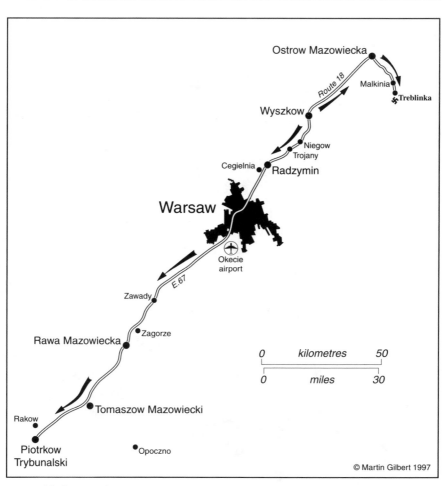

45: Treblinka–Piotrkow

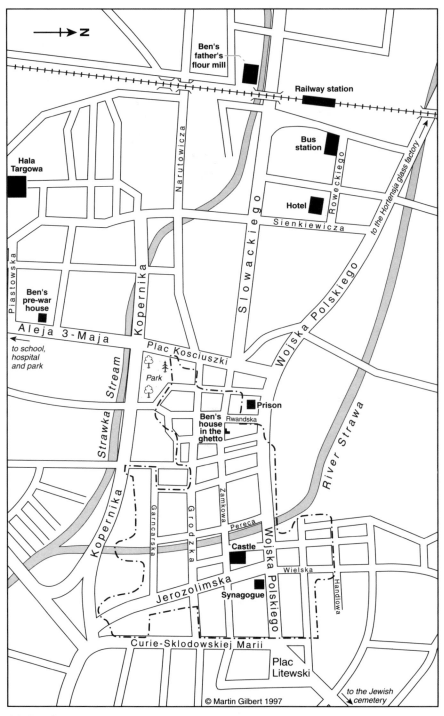

46: Piotrkow town

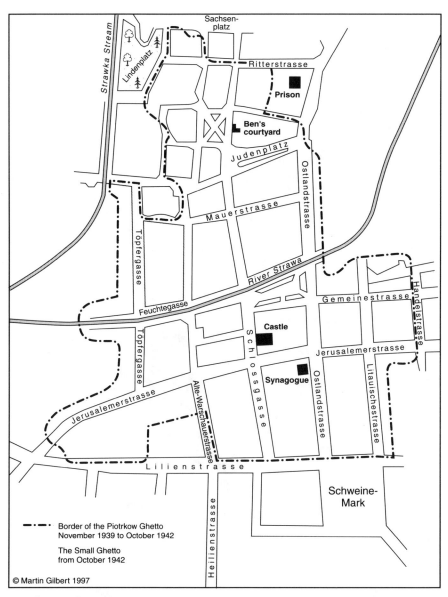

47: The Piotrkow ghetto

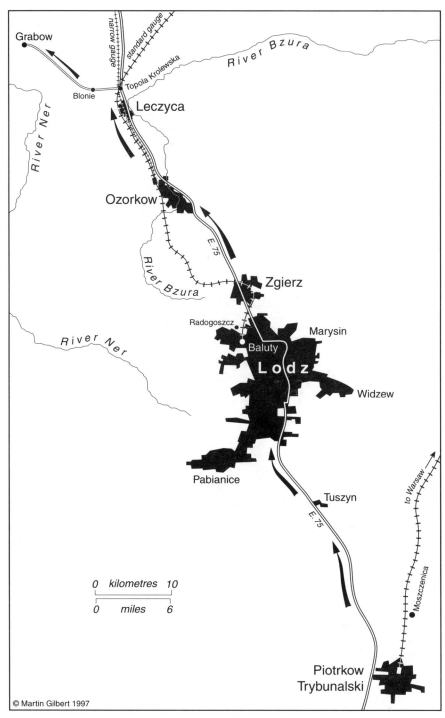

48: Piotrkow–Grabow

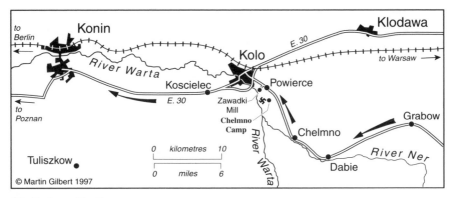

49: Grabow–Konin

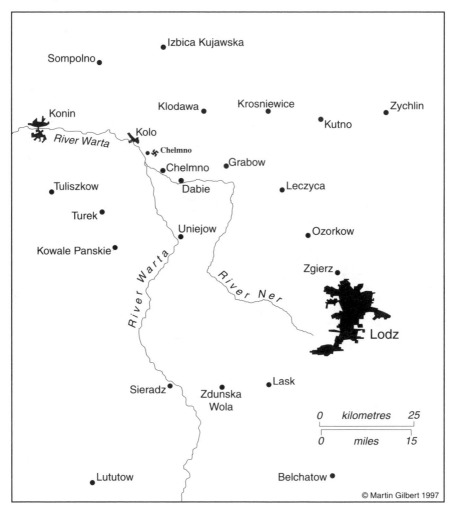

50: Chelmno and the destroyed Jewish communities

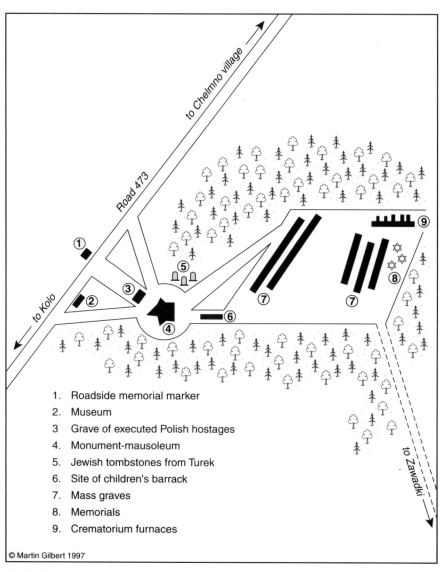

1. Roadside memorial marker
2. Museum
3 Grave of executed Polish hostages
4. Monument-mausoleum
5. Jewish tombstones from Turek
6. Site of children's barrack
7. Mass graves
8. Memorials
9. Crematorium furnaces

© Martin Gilbert 1997

51: Chelmno

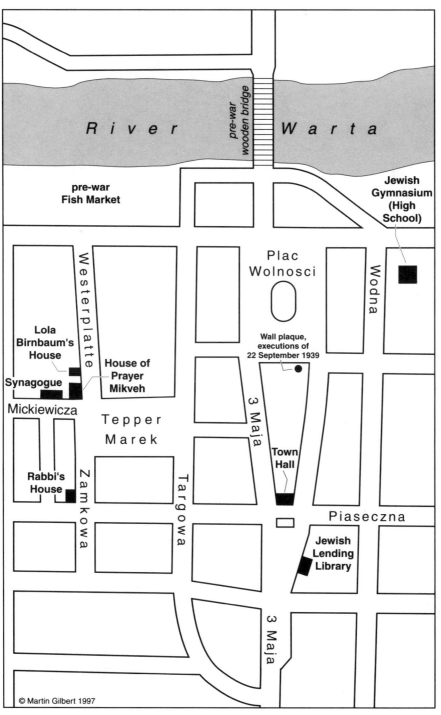

52: Konin

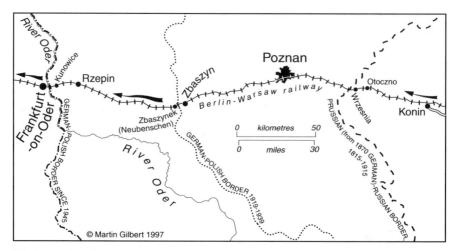

53: Konin–Frankfurt-on-Oder

54: Other towns mentioned in the text

BIBLIOGRAPHY

GUIDE BOOKS

Karl Baedeker, *Austria-Hungary, Handbook for Travellers*, Dulau, London, 1905.

Karl Baedeker, *Berlin and Its Environs, Handbook for Travellers*, T. Fisher Unwin, London, 1912

Karl Baedeker, *Das Generalgouvernement*, Karl Baedeker, Leipzig, 1943.

Birnbaum's 95 Berlin, HarperCollins, London, 1994.

Przemyslaw Burchard, *Pamiatki i Zabytki Kultury Zydowskiej w Polsce* (Memorials and Monuments of Jewish Culture in Poland), Warsaw, 1990.

Ludmila Chladkova, *The Terezin Ghetto*, Nase vojsko Publishing House, Prague, 1991.

Alfred Etzold (and others), *Die jüdischen Friedhöfe in Berlin*, Henschel Verlag, Berlin, 1991.

Jiri Fiedler, *Jewish Sights of Bohemia and Moravia*, Sefer Prague, Prague, 1991.

Peter Fritzsche and Karen Hewitt, *Berlinwalks*, Boxtree, London, 1994.

Ruth Ellen Gruber, *Jewish Heritage Travel, A Guide to East-Central Europe*, John Wiley and Sons, New York, revised edition, 1994.

Jan Jagielski and Robert Pasieczny, *A Guide to Jewish Warsaw*, Jewish Information and Tourist Bureau, Warsaw, 1990.

Sadakat Kadri, *Prague* (Cadogan City Guides), Cadogan Books, London, 1993.

Joram Kagan, *Poland's Jewish Heritage*, Hippocrene Books, New York, 1992.

Renata Piatkowska, *Following the Lost Traces*, Dom Wydawniczy, Warsaw, no date.

Brigitte Röper and others (editors), *Jewish Places in Berlin*, FAB Verlag, Berlin, June 1993 (single sheet map and text).

Ctibor Rybar, *Jewish Prague – Guide to the Monuments*, TV Spektrum and Akropolis Publishers, Prague, 1991.

Scenes of Fighting and Martyrdom Guide, War Years in Poland, 1939–1945, Sport i Turystyka, Warsaw, 1966.

Andrzej Trzcinski, *A Guide to Jewish Lublin and Surroundings*, Jewish Information and Tourist Bureau, Lublin–Warsaw, 1991.

HISTORICAL WORKS AND WORKS OF REFERENCE

Alan Adelson and Robert Lapides (editors), *Lodz Ghetto, Inside a Community under Siege*, Viking Penguin, New York, 1989.

Arieh L. Bauminger, *The Fighters of the Cracow Ghetto*, Keter, Jerusalem, 1986.

Anthony Read and David Fisher, *Berlin, The Biography of a City*, Pimlico, London, 1994.

Jadwiga Bezwinska and Danuta Czech (editors), *Amidst a Nightmare of Crime, Manuscripts of Members of Sonderkommando*, Publications of State Museum at Oswiecim, Oswiecim, 1973.

Jadwiga Bezwinska and Danuta Czech (editors), *KL Auschwitz seen by the SS (Höss, Broad, Kremer)*, Panstwowe Muzeum w Oswiecimiu, Oswiecim, 1978.

Christopher R. Browning, *Ordinary Men, Reserve Police Battalion 101 and the Final Solution in Poland*, HarperCollins, New York, 1992.

Commonwealth War Graves Commission, *Berlin 1939–1945 War Cemetery*, parts 1–3, London, 1966.

Danuta Czech, *Auschwitz Chronicle, 1939–1945*, I. B. Tauris, London, 1990.

Lucjan Dobroszycki (editor), *The Chronicle of the Lodz Ghetto, 1941–1944*, Yale University Press, New Haven and London, 1984.

Dr Willehad P. Eckert and others (editors), *Monumenta Judaica, Katalog, 2000 Jahre Geschichte und Kultur der Juden am Rhein*, Stadt Köln, Cologne, 1963.

Louis Falstein (editor), *The Martyrdom of Jewish Physicians in Poland*, Exposition Press, New York, 1963.

John Freund (editor), *After Those Fifty Years, Memoirs of the Birkenau Boys*, Toronto, 1992.

Ben Giladi, *A Tale of One City, Piotrkow Trybunalski*, Shengold, New York 1991.

Gerald Green, *The Artists of Terezin*, Schocken, New York, 1978.

Serge Klarsfeld (editor), *The Auschwitz Album, Lili Jacob's Album*, The Beate Klarsfeld Foundation, New York, 1980.

Shmuel Krakowski, *The War of the Doomed, Jewish Armed Resistance in Poland, 1942–1944*, Holmes and Meier, New York, 1984.

Marie Rut Krizkova, Kurt Jiri Kotouc and Zdenek Ornest, *We Are Children Just the Same, Vedem, The Secret Magazine by the Boys of Terezin*, Jewish Publication Society, Philadelphia, 1995.

Zdenek Lederer, *Ghetto Theresienstadt*, Edward Goldston and Son, London, 1953.

Callum MacDonald and Jan Kaplan, *Prague in the Shadow of the Swastika, A History of the German Occupation, 1939–1945*, Quartet Books, London, 1995.

Benjamin Meirtchak, *Jewish Military Casualties in the Polish Armies in World War II*, 4 volumes, Association of Jewish War Veterans of Polish Armies in Israel, 4 volumes, Tel Aviv, 1994–6.

Miriam Novitch (editor), *Sobibor, Martyrdom and Revolt, Documents and Testimonies*, Holocaust Library, New York, 1980.

Arnold Paucker, *Jewish Resistance in Germany, The Facts and the Problems*, German Resistance Memorial Centre, Berlin, 1991.

Theo Richmond, *Konin, A Quest*, Jonathan Cape, London, 1995.

Reinhard Rürup (editor), *Topography of Terror, Gestapo, SS and Reichssicherheitshauptamt on the 'Prinz-Albrecht-Terrain', A Documentation*, Willmuth Arenhövel, Berlin, 1989.

Lore Shelley (editor), *The Union Kommando in Auschwitz, The Auschwitz Munition Factory Through the Eyes of Its Former Slave Labourers*, University of America, Latham, Maryland, 1996.

Dr Dezider Toth (editor), *The Tragedy of Slovak Jews*, Datei, Banska Bystrica, 1992.

MEMOIRS

Saul Friedländer, *When Memory Comes*, Farrar, Straus and Giroux, New York, 1979.

Jan Karski, *Story of a Secret State*, Houghton Mifflin, Boston, 1944.

Primo Levi, *If This Is A Man*, The Orion Press, London, 1969.

Rafael F. Scharf, *Poland, What Have I To Do With Thee: Essays Without Prejudice*, Fundacja Judaica, Cracow, 1996.

Rudolf Vrba and Alan Bestic, *I Cannot Forgive*, Sidgwick and Jackson, and Anthony Gibbs and Phillips, London, 1963.

Harold (Hersh) Werner, *Fighting Back, A Memoir of Jewish Resistance in World War II*, Columbia University Press, New York, 1992.

Elie Wiesel, *All Rivers Run to the Sea, Memoirs*, Alfred A. Knopf, New York, 1995.

Samuel Willenberg, *Surviving Treblinka*, Basil Blackwell, Oxford, 1989.

NOVELS, POETRY, FILM

Naomi Gryn (producer), *The Star, The Castle and The Butterfly*, written and presented by Hugo Gryn, See More Productions, London, 1990.

Hilda Schiff (editor), *Holocaust Poetry*, HarperCollins, London, 1995.

Isaac Bashevis Singer, *The Family Moskat*, Martin Secker and Warburg, London, 1966.

Isaac Bashevis Singer, *The Fools of Chelm and Their History*, Farrar Straus and Giroux, New York, 1973.

BOOKS BY THE AUTHOR

Auschwitz and the Allies, Holt, New York; Mandarin, London, 1981.

The Holocaust, The Jewish Tragedy, Holt, New York; Collins Fontana, London, 1986.

Atlas of the Holocaust, revised edition with gazetteer, William Morrow, New York; Routledge, London, 1994.

The Boys, Triumph over Adversity, Weidenfeld and Nicolson, London; Holt, New York, 1996.

INDEX

compiled by the author